SNAKES OF THE WORLD

SNAKES OF THE WORLD

Sterling Publishing Co., Inc.
New York

Library of Congress Cataloging–in–Publication Data
Available

10 9 8 7 6 5 4 3 2 1

Published in 2003 by Sterling Publishing Co., Inc.
387 Park Avenue South
New York, NY 10016

Distributed in Canada by Sterling Publishing
C/o Canadian Manda Group
One Atlantic Avenue, Suite 105
Toronto, Ontario, M6K 3E7 Canada

Distributed in Great Britain by Chrysalis Books
64 Brewery Road,
London, N7 9NT England

Distributed in Australia by Capricorn Link (Australia) Pty Ltd.
P.O. Box 704,
Windsor, NSW 2756 Australia

PROJECT COORDINATOR: Jordi Vigué
SCIENTIST EDITORS–ADVISERS: Manuel Areste, Rafael Cebrián
EDITOR: Gary Haltmann
ILLUSTRATORS: Miquel Ferron, Myriam Ferron, Sergi López,
Eduardo Sáiz Alonso *(pp. 28–29, 30–31. 32–33, 34–35,*
40, 46, 50, 52, 58, 60, 62,103, 107, 111, 187, 190, 217)

PHOTOGRAPHS:
Manel Aresté: *(pp. 101)*, Thomas C. Brennan: *(Pg: 200)*, Brian Bus: *(p: 77)*, Gregor Calvert: *(pp: 42, 74)*, Dennis Desmond: *(p: 132)*,
Jordi Fábregas: *(pp: 24, 69, 70, 159)*, Miguel Ángel Fernández: *(pp: 69, 71, 87, 91, 98, 123, 125, 133, 139, 148, 149, 162, 166,180, 232)*,
John Friemann: *(p: 221)*, Santiago Garcés: *(p: 181)*, Bayram Göçmen: *(p: 44)*, Michael Graf: *(p: 92)*, Chris Harrison: *(p: 95)*,
Alan Hill: *(pp: 9)*, J&R Wildlife Rescue: *(p: 243)*, Nate Kley: *(pp: 43, 48, 167)*, Claudia Krebs: *(p: 151)*, Björn Lardner: *(p: 164)*,
Casey Lazik: *(p: 68)*, Dong Lin: *(pp: 147, 176)*, Andrea Litt: *(p: 183)*, Paolo Mazzei: *(pp: 129, 184, 230)*, Peter Mirstschi: *(pp: 131, 204)*,
Álex Pérez: *(pp: 24, 54, 59, 61, 66, 70, 72, 73, 75, 76, 78, 79, 80, 81, 82, 83, 84, 85, 88, 90, 93, 94, 97, 100, 120, 122, 127, 128, 134, 137, 139, 142,143,*
148, 156, 159, 162, 166, 169, 172, 174, 177, 179, 186, 193, 196, 197, 203, 209, 222, 223, 226, 228, 233, 235, 236, 238, 241, 242, 244),
Björn Rogell: *(p: 170)*, Joe Slowinski: *(p: 45)*, Mardi Snipes: *(pp: 237, 251)*, Tomás Stupp: *(p: 227)*, Hla Tun: *(p:195)*,
Nicole Viloteau: *(pp: 9, 67, 73, 78, 79, 89, 182, 198, 206, 222, 250)*, Laurie Vitt: *(pp: 49, 99, 100, 121, 126 , 135, 136, 138, 140, 141, 154, 155, 156 ,*
158, 161, 175, 202), Harold Voris: *(pp: 109, 213)*, Wolfgang Wüster: *(pp: 3, 5, 37, 51, 55, 110, 121, 126, 144, 150, 152, 153, 157, 158, 163, 167, 168,*
171, 194, 201, 203, 205, 207, 208, 210, 211, 215, 229, 231, 234, 239, 245, 247, 248, 249), Dr. Zoltan Takacs: *(pp: 209, 216, 224, 227, 237)*

PHOTOGRAPHIC DOCUMENTATION: Albert M. Thuile, Joana Burguès
GRAPHIC DESIGN: Paloma Nestares
GRAPHIC ARTIST: María Hernández
IMAGE PROCESSORS: Albert Muñoz, Luis Felipe Gallego
INDEXES AND REFERENCES: Nicole Joncet
TRANSLATION: Lauren Hermele
EDITORIAL COORDINATOR: Miquel Ridola, Jodep Graell

Sterling ISBN 1–4027–0567–0

Whether for religious or cultural reasons, or for naturalist or scientific interests, since distant times, the subject of snakes has rarely stopped materializing in history, beliefs, or in people's daily life. Snakes' shape, characteristics, and people's great ignorance of many of its habits have given rise to an entire series of myths and legends; individuals that are beneficial and, at the same time, man's enemies, have been transformed into a vague paradigm of good and evil and holders of magical and healing powers.

This book is a systematic work on snakes, their families and subfamilies, and their most representative species. In each section, the reader will find the description of their characteristics, habitats, behavior, reproduction, status of the species, etc. A whole range of knowledge is explained so that the reader, whether an expert or a novice on the subject, has precise and specific information.

Aside from the generous quantity of information, a large illustrated section accompanies this work. There are a significant number of realistic illustrations by very experienced illustrators that were created specifically for this publication under the constant assessment and supervision of the collaborating scientists.

Manuel Aresté, curator of the terrarium at the Barcelona Zoo, scientific assessor of the magazine *Reptilia* and collaborator in the reproduction in captivity and reintroduction of species' programs, and Rafael Cebrián, head of the Department of Education of the Iberian Association of Zoos and Aquariums, are constantly researching and in direct contact with snakes; they are the ones who have organized and supervised the contents of this book.

Given the competence of all those who have collaborated in the preparation of this work and its positive outcome, we are confident that this is one of the best publications that could be put into the public's hands in accordance with today's standards. Its interesting contents are enhanced by both an attractive layout and the simple everyday language used to explain them. This is something that will undoubtedly quench scientific curiosity and provide enjoyment to its readers.

JORDI VIGUÉ

REPTILES

Reptiles are a class of vertebrates (animals with a vertebral column, just like fish, amphibians, birds, and mammals) that are characterized by: scale-covered skin, leaving the water to reproduce, and their dependence on atmospheric temperature to regulate body temperature.

CHARACTERISTICS

• Aside from having scales, reptiles' skin is characterized by the periodic renewal of its outer layer through the process of molting.

• The majority of reptiles are oviparous (they lay eggs), although there are some that give birth to live babies. Unlike fish and amphibians, reptiles deposit their eggs on firm land—even those species that spend the majority of their life in water. All reptiles are fertilized internally.

• Because reptiles are animals used to variable temperatures (not cold), they have the advantage that they don't have to eat very frequently to maintain their body temperature. Therefore, they can exploit harsh habitats, such as deserts or those with scarce resources or resources that are irregularly available. Due to this natural advantage, they are the dominant group in deserts. A few reptiles are herbivores and others are omnivores, but the great majority are strictly carnivorous.

Aside from Antarctica, reptiles inhabit all the continents. The majority of them are concentrated around the Equator; from there, a gradual decrease in the number of species can be seen in more northern latitudes. They have a wide variety of forms and sizes and colonize all types of habitats: there are subterranean, terrestrial, arboreal, freshwater, and saltwater species. Almost all of them move on four appendages, although some subterranean lizards and all snakes lack them.

ORIGIN

Reptiles originate from some type of amphibian that managed to become who developed the ability to live on land independent from water, although it is not known which amphibian. The oldest reptile fossil remains known date to the beginning of the Carboniferous period more than 300 million years ago. For a long period of time, that began in the Permian (280 million years ago) and lasted the entire Mesozoic (up to 65 million years ago), reptiles dominated the earth, exploiting and occupying ecological niches that birds and mammals inhabit today.

CLASSIFICATION

Today's reptiles are taxonomically classified in 4 orders:

Chelonia: turtles and sea turtles.

Rhynchocephalia: toads.

Crocodylia: crocodiles and alligators.

Squamata: lizards and snakes.

EVOLUTION OF THE REPTILES

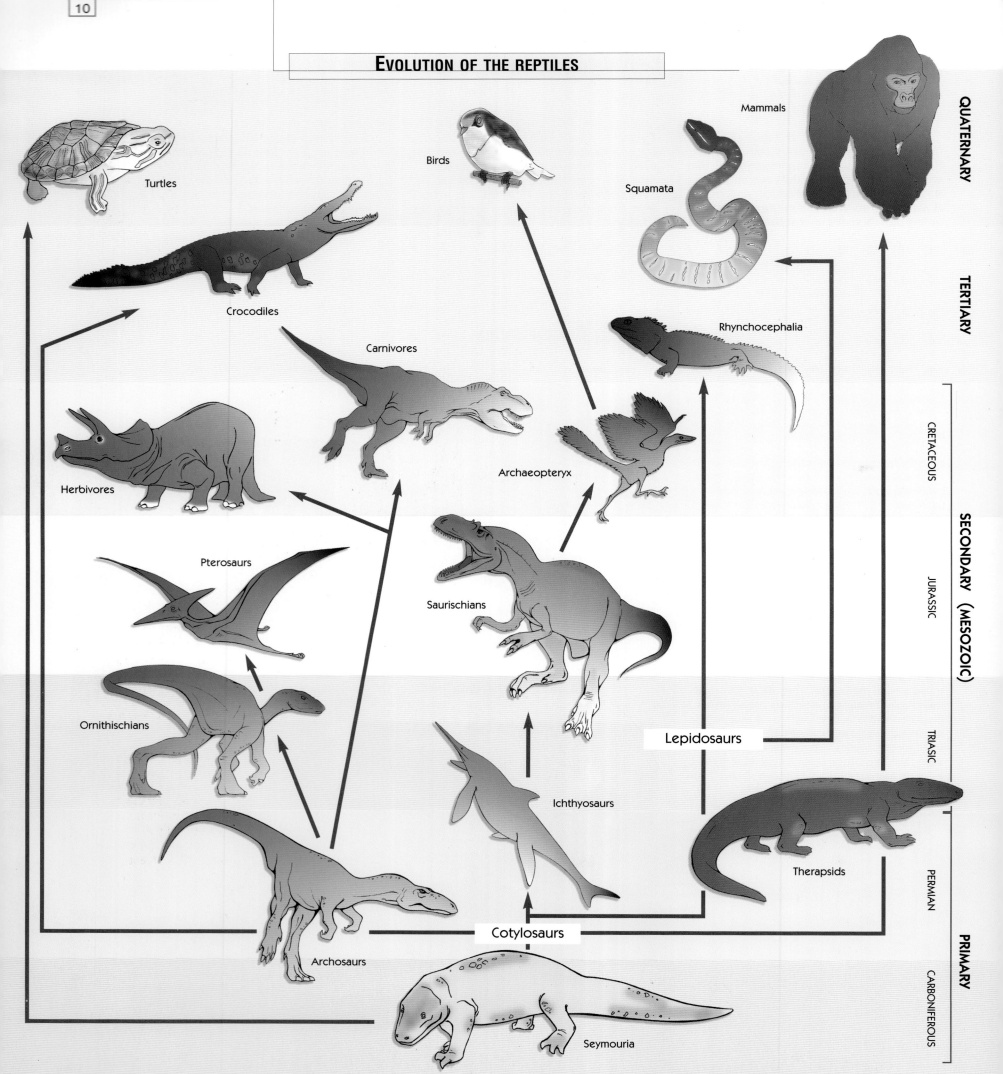

Turtles

Crocodiles

Birds

Mammals

Squamata

Carnivores

Rhynchocephalia

Herbivores

Archaeopteryx

Pterosaurs

Saurischians

Ornithischians

Ichthyosaurs

Lepidosaurs

Therapsids

Archosaurs

Cotylosaurs

Seymouria

QUATERNARY

TERTIARY

CRETACEOUS

SECONDARY (MESOZOIC)

JURASSIC

TRIASSIC

PERMIAN

PRIMARY

CARBONIFEROUS

MYTHS AND LEGENDS

From the dawn of humanity, few animals have been protagonists of so many myths and legends; snakes' iconography and symbolic value echoes in all civilizations on all continents since time immemorial. Although the artistic representation and contents of the mythological narrations naturally vary according to cultural traditions, there are a few common links in all the symbolism regarding snakes.

The concept that could be the most unique and should be stressed the most of all the symbolic tradition surrounding snakes, could be duality; that is, the representation of apparently opposing values. Snakes represent life and death, good and evil, the greatest wisdom and the most primeval desires, masculinity and femininity, healing and poisoning.

They are the symbol of the force of primordial nature, always in contact with the base of fertility. They can rejuvenate and give new life, therefore they represent the reviving force of nature that resurges, unstoppable after death, in a cycle that never ceases.

It is a continuous cycle that has neither a beginning or an end, the unity of two extremes, the representation of the mythical uroborus (the snake that bit its tail in a circle without beginning or end). It represents self-sufficiency in nature, continuous regeneration that encompasses everything–its primordial unity.

It is in western culture, fruit of Judeo-Christian ideas and symbols, where the balance of ambivalence has definitively inclined toward the negative regarding the symbolism of snakes. Snakes were guilty of all Adam and Eve's misfortunes after their from paradise for having eaten the prohibited fruit from the tree of good and evil. Snakes induced the temptation and were cursed by God. From this moment on, snakes started to represent the devil and sin for the Judeo-Christian tradition.

This same idea, repeatedly embedded in the collective subconscious, still marks many people's aversion toward these animals; the horror and

Raphael, *Adam and Eve* (1508–1511), fresco, 120 x 105 cm. Dome of the *stanza della segnatura*, Vatican City. In the Judeo-Christian culture, the image of the snake in paradise as a symbol has constituted one of the important religious topics in order to explain the origin of evil and the suffering of human beings.

In many towns in the Far East, the snake charmers are more than just mere tourist attractions; they have a mysterious, even sacred, significance. A snake moving while listening to the sound of a musical instrument is a reality in which magic, mystery, and the supernatural mix.

disgust that snakes sometimes summon seem like a feeling impossible to repress, like the almost morbid reaction that can often be seen when watching visitors at snake exhibitions. With a mix of terror and fascination they show up to see closely what are, for them, these horrible animals. Isn't it possible that the eternal ambivalence of snakes' symbolism is still demonstrated in this way: terror and fascination? Once again, opposing values complement one another.

Snakes generally lead a very secret life: they can easily appear and disappear, and can go by unnoticed even though they are very close to people. It is difficult to observe the biological behavior and habits of snakes, and the resulting ignorance has fostered. This extreme discetion that makes it the mystery, myth, and legends about ophidians since the beginning of humanity. But what are the actual characteristics of snakes' lives that have influenced these ancestral myths?

Greek sculpture of Asclepius found in 1929 in the Ampurias excavations (Archeology Museum of Barcelona). According to Greek mythology, Asclepius (esculapio to the Romans) was the god of medicine. For this reason, he was represented accompanied by a snake for the magic and healing powers that the snake symbolized.

CONTINUOUS REGENERATION

Snakes are the only vertebrates that completely molt their skin. Periodically, their skin darkens, their eyes become opaque, and the animal stops eating for a time. This apparent aging is followed by complete renewal that the molting and the appearance of a new shinier skin represents. This ability associates these animals with seem to be a magical power of regeneration–the eternal fountain of youth. They are the beings that conquer the decrepitude of old age to start a new life full of strength and vitality.

FERTILITY

Snakes' reproductive behavior fascinated the ancients, who transformed the snake into a powerful symbol of sexuality. Its great capacity for propagation (they are very prolific) and adaptation (they can reproduce by laying eggs and certain species can give birth to live young) explain why they are associated with the old gods of fertility.

In the Judeo-Christian tradition, snakes' great reproductive ability was associated with the sin of lust, and in old engravings, they are shown people tormenting who were predominantly sinners while alive.

They often symbolize masculinity because of their association with phallic forms, and a snake coiled around an egg symbolizes the passions that fuel masculinity and femininity, eroticism, and sexual satisfaction.

WISDOM

Snakes do not have members. This anatomical characteristic, instead of representing a disadvantage, gives them an undeniable advantage of being able to enter holes, to appear or disappear unpredictably, and to reach hidden places that are inaccessible to others. It is not surprising that ancestral wisdom came from the secrets kept in the depths of mother earth's bosom and that snakes were seen as the repository of that secret knowledge.

THE BENEFICIAL SIDE OF SNAKES

Snakes exterminate a large amount of rodents. Since antiquity, rodents have been the main source of plagues that the human race has faced. Also, primitive agrarian societies have often been in direct competition with rats and mice for resources, which were more often than not very scarce. Long periods of hunger and sickness have battered humanity, coinciding with periods of great proliferation of the population. It should therefore not be surprising that in many societies, snakes were sacred animals, worthy of protection and worship, elevated sometimes to the category of a protective deity. Although is also certain that snakes that possess a stronged venom can also kill, maybe these deaths were considered the price that needed to be paid to avoid much greater evils.

SNAKES:
A LOOK AT THE REALITY

Snakes are vertebrates characterized fundamentally by the complete absence of extremities (although the most primitive, like the boidae, still have vestiges of extremities).

SENSE ORGANS

• **Sight.** This sense is not especially well developed in snakes; some of the "blind" varieties distinguish only between light and dark. Nocturnal snakes have a vertical elliptical pupil that better perceives in dim light. The majority of them detect movement better than form, though some diurnal terrestrial and arboreal species have very good vision.

• **Hearing.** This is not their most developed sense either; they do not have external ears, and the only auditory bone is not in contact with a tympanic membrane but, rather with the mandible. In fact, they can hear only low–frequency sounds.

• **Touch, taste, and smell.** All of the senses directly related to the tongue are the most important for snakes. Whether the tongue has direct contact with the surface of an object or just licks the air, it acts as a receptor of chemical signals that are analyzed by the Jacobsen's organ, located on the upper part of the mouth. It allows snakes to follow the smelly trail left by its prey, identify predators, find its kind, and react appropriately during the reproductive period.

Some primitive species have a special sensory system that acts to detect heat; these are called thermoreceptive pits, and are found on the lips (in boas, pythons) or on the front part of the snout (in rattlesnakes). In certain instances they can distinguish a variation of just 32°F.

DIFFERENT TYPES OF PUPILS
Detail of the head. Lateral view.

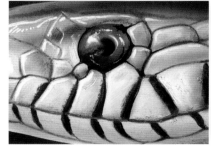

Ptyas mucosus.

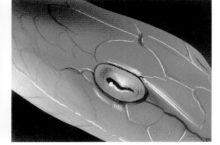

Oxibelis fulgidus.

Genus Typhlops.

Bortrops lateralis.

PHYSICAL CHARACTERISTICS

• They lack eyelids and external ears.

• The majority of their internal organs have adapted to their slender body structure.

• Their body has lengthened owing to the presence of supplementary vertebrae (the majority of snakes have more than 200).

• Their musculature is complex but extraordinarily flexible.

• Many of their organ pairs have been reduced (they may have just one lung, for example), and others have separated to adapt to the little available space (the kidneys, for example, are located one behind the other).

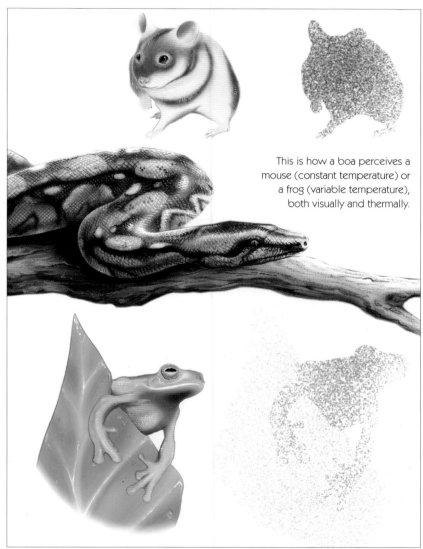

This is how a boa perceives a mouse (constant temperature) or a frog (variable temperature), both visually and thermally.

Nostril

Thermoreceptive pit

RATTLESNAKE
Adult specimen.
Lateral view.

INTERNAL ANATOMY

The extension of the snake's body conditions the structure and disposition of all the animal's internal organs. Therefore, the skeleton of the majority of snakes' skeletons consist only of a small, not very rigid cranium, a vertebral column with numerous vertebrae, and some long flexible ribs.

Their musculature is very complex, made up of numerous individual muscles or muscle groups that act independently of adjacent ones.

Internal organs that are not in pairs, like the liver or the stomach, are narrow and extended, while those that are in pairs in other vertebrae have been reduced in size or have been separated to fit the narrow body as best as possible. In the majority of snakes, the left lung is very reduced or is completely absent; in some species, females have only one oviduct; and in all of them, the kidneys do not lie next to one anothe; rather, the left one is located behind the right.

THE SKIN AND THE MOLTING PROCESS

Snakeskin is impermeable in water, which prevents it from becoming dehydrated in any circumstance, thereby allowing snakes to colonize regions as arid and hot as deserts. Their skin is also very elastic, flexible, and has such an extraordinary capacity for dilation that it allows the snake to swallow prey much larger than its own body.

As in all reptiles, snakeskin is covered with scales. Each of the snake species has a certain number and arrangement of scales, which is an important factor for establishing their taxonomy. The head scales (except on boas, vipers, and a few other species) are large and have characteristic forms, while the back and the flank ones tend to be small and similar among all of them. The back scales are totally smooth on the majority of snakes, but quite a few species have keeled scales (with a keel in the center), and some have granular scales.

COLUBRID
Cephalic scales.
Overhead view.

VIPERIDAE
Cephalic scales.
Overhead view.

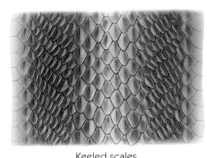

Smooth scales.

Keeled scales.

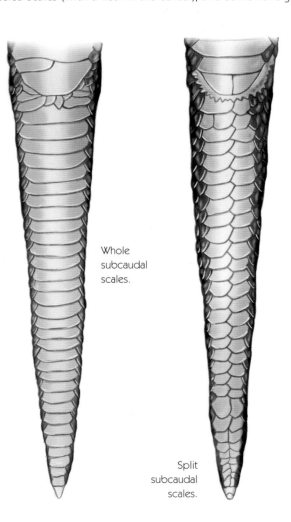

Whole
subcaudal
scales.

Split
subcaudal
scales.

Ventral scales of a
terrestrial snake.

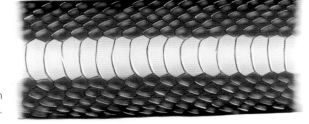

Ventral scales of an
arboreal snake.

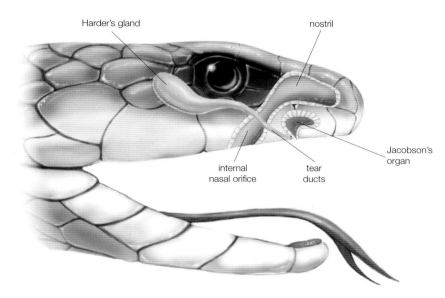

Harder's gland

nostril

internal
nasal orifice

tear
ducts

Jacobson's
organ

ANATOMY OF THE HEAD.
JACOBSON'S ORGAN.

Except on some very primitive or rather very specialized species, the ventral scales are large and arranged in somewhat narrow and elongated plates.

Snake epidermis periodically renews itself in the molting process. Unlike saurians, which molt their skin in small sections in different parts of their body for a certain period, snakes completely renew their skin in just one step; this is why the product of their molting is like a true empty carcass of the entire animal's body.

Molting is preceded by a period of approximately two weeks during which the snake does not eat. The main characteristic that shows that this process has started is that the eye acquires a milky tone and becomes opaque. The frequency of molting varies from species to species, although the majority of them molt one to three times yearly (when in captivity, they tend to molt more often).

THERMAL REGULATION

Snakes are poikilothermal; that is, they do not have a constant body temperature independent of the exterior medium as do mammals. Instead, snakes' body temperature depends on its environment. Also, snakes are thermophile reptiles, and the majority of vital functions must be performed at relatively high temperatures. Extremely hot or cold temperatures should be avoided because they can rapidly cause the animal's death. In fact, each species of snakes has certain minimum and maximum temperatures that could be lethal, as well as critical temperatures above and below which they are incapable of coordinated movement.

Therefore, because they cannot produce their own heat, thermoregulation is achieved by the adaptation of the snake's behavior,–mainly moving from one place to another in search of the most favorable thermic conditions.

In the morning, for example, many snakes heat up from the sun's rays until they reach the adequate temperature for their daily activity, but they take shelter in shady dens (subterranean shelters, rock fissures, tree roots) when the sun is at its hottest. The burrowing species, on the other hand, travel vertically with in the earth following the gradient of the earth's temperature (closer to the surface during the day).

In regions of the earth located at more than 20° in latitude, the winters are too cold for snakes to maintain their normal activity; thus, they take shelter in subterranean refuges and slow down their metabolism through a ritual known as hibernation. In temperate zones, snakes hibernate individually or in small groups, but in the colder regions, they tend to form large groups.

Lateral undulation.

LOCOMOTION

The absence of extremities in no way compromises snakes' ability to move. The majority of snakes are capable of moving on the ground, swimming, and climbing trees or rocks with a fair amount of agility; some species, however, specialize in some of these mediums. For example, few snakes are almost exclusively burrowers.

In general, they do not move by shifting their ribs as is popularly believed, but rather by using the large ventral plates that are directly linked to independent muscle groups. By moving groups of ventral plates, some pushing backwards against the ground and others sliding forwards, they achieve what is called *rectilinear crawling*, which allows them to advance slowly along the

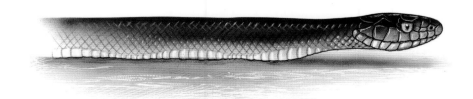

Rectilinear crawling.

ground in a straight line. The quickest locomotion is called *lateral undulation* (serpentine crawling) when the animal's body makes a series of S-curves in which it seems to slide over the surface effortlessly (this is the same type of locomotion used for swimming). To perform this type of locomotion, the back part of each curve of the animal's body is pushed forward using any small irregularities in the terrain to help propel it.

Another form of locomotion, characteristic of desert snakes, is *sidewinding*: the front part of the body makes an arc, the body moves like an spring, and the head forms an angle with respect to the direction of movement. The trail left in the sand in this case is a series of parallel lines.

Sidewinding.

CURRENT TAXONOMIC TABLE

Presently, 2,700 species of snakes have been described that are classified into 13 different families:

Order Squamata
  Suborder Ophidia

    Infraorder escolecofidios scolecophidia
      Family typhlopidae
        Subfamily typhlopinae
        Subfamily anomalepinae
      Family leptotyphlopidae

    Infraorder henophidia
      Family aniliidae
      Family uropeltidae
        Subfamily cylindrophinae
        Subfamily uropeltinae
      Family xenopeltidae
      Family loxocemidae
      Family boidae
        Subfamily pythoninae
        Subfamily boinae
        Subfamily erycinae
        Subfamily bolyerinae
      Family tropidophiidae
      Family acrochordidae

    Infraorder caenophidia
      Family colubridae
        Subfamily colubrinae
        Subfamily natricinae
        Subfamily homalopsinae
        Subfamily dasypeltinae
        Subfamily lycodontinae
        Subfamily calamarinae
        Subfamily xenoderminae
        Subfamily sibynophinae
        Subfamily xenodontinae
        Subfamily dipsadinae
        Subfamily pareinae
        Subfamily elachistodontinae
        Subfamily boiginae
      Family aparallactidae
      Family elapidae
        Subfamily elapinae
        Subfamily hydrophiinae
      Family viperidae
        Subfamily viperinae
        Subfamily crotalinae
        Subfamily azemiopinae

ORIGIN AND EVOLUTION

The first known snake fossils appeared during the cretaceous period, between 135 and 65 million years ago. However, the majority of them are only isolated vertebrates, greatly complicating their evolutionary study. In any case, the accepted hypothesis is that snakes originated from a primitive group of lizards with shrinking extremities, as demonstrated by the fact that both group of reptiles are taxonomically classified in just one order: *Squamata*.

Snake fossil.

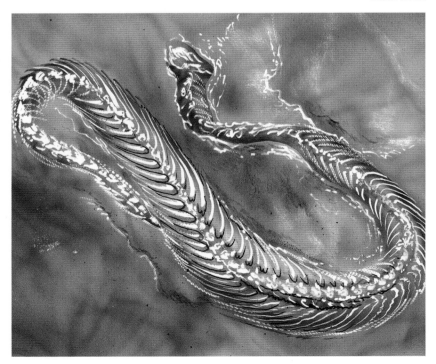

FEEDING

THE MECHANICS OF DIGESTION

Snakes' mandibles are very flexible. Therefore, they can swallow large prey with a greater diameter than their own, starting with the head and taking advantage of the direction of the prey's tegument, hair, feathers, or scales.

The quadrate is a special bone that links the lower mandible to the cranium, acting as a double hinge. The lower mandible can also extend to the sides because a flexible ligament joins the two halves. The sharp curved teeth retain the prey while the mandibles envelop it and the jaw's lateral movements proceed to help swallow it. At the same time, they can move the opening of the trachea to one side in order to continue breathing for the duration of the deglutition. The lack of a sternum also facilitates the ingestion of large prey.

Because they eat such large prey in proportion to their size, they can go for a long time without feeding. They can do so because of the minimal energy they consume for their own corporal processes; they do not need to expend energy to maintain a constant body temperature. Some species, like the European viper, *vipera berus*, in places with extreme climates, may feed only a few times per year.

The digestion of large prey can go on for a long time. While it lasts, the snake remains almost immobile, in a warm, calm place where a higher body temperature will aid digestion. During this process the animal is most vulnerable to predators.

The prey is digested whole; snakes' digestive enzymes are very strong and capable of assimilating even bones and teguments. The egg-eating snakes, *Dasypeltis*, regurgitate the remains of the eggshell once the contents have been emptied into the digestive system.

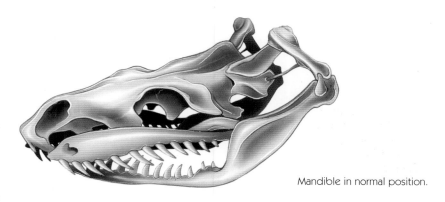

Mandible in normal position.

SNAKE'S CRANEAL SKELETON.

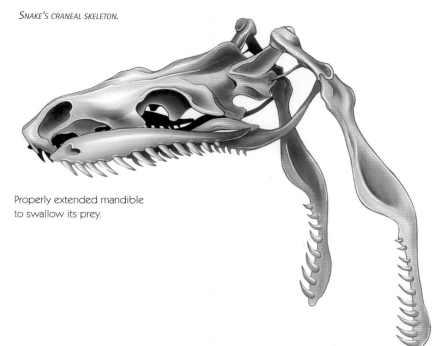

Properly extended mandible to swallow its prey.

THE SEARCH FOR FOOD

Some snakes actively look for prey by patrolling their territory; the *Coluber Constrictor* or the flying Asian culebrids of the *Chrysopelea* genus sometimes tend to do so with the head raised, attentive to any movement. These types of snakes usually have very large eyes and a period of diurnal activity.

Many other species remain still, making the most of their immobility and cryptic coloration, waiting somewhere opportunely for the prey to pass nearby. The prey is then captured either by sight and smell or by thermoreceptive pits, if the species possesses them.

Some species use parts of their body as bait to attract the prey; it is believed that the culebrid of the genus *thelotornis* move their vividly colored tongues like a worm. Other snakes, like the death adders, acanthophis, and some moccasins, *agkistrodon*, shake their tails, which are normally also colorful, to catch the attention of potential prey.

Hydropheinae eating a fish.

SELECTED SNAKE FEEDING HABITS

General species
(Eat a wide range of different species)

- Soft-bodied invertebrates:
  Crowned snake *Tantilla coronata*
  Worm Snake *Typhlops vermicularis*
- Arthropoda:
  Rough Green Snake *Opheodrys aestivus*
- Fish and amphibians:
  Mud Snake *Farancia abacura*
  Viperine Snake *Natrix maura*
- Amphibious reptiles, birds, and mammals:
  American Copperhead *Agkistrodon contortrix*
  Kingsnake *Lampropeltis getulus*
- Birds and mammals:
  Ladder Snake *Elaphe scalaris*
  Indian Python *Python molurus*
- Invertebrates and vertebrates:
  Racer *Coluber constrictor*

Specialist species
(Specialized in feeding on one or a few species)

- Slugs and snails:
  Snail-Eating Snake *Dypsas*
  Slug-Eating Snake *Pareas*
- Earthworm:
  Rough Earth Snakes *Virginia striatula*
  False Coral Snake *Atractus*
- Centipedes:
  Cape Centipede-Eater *Aparallactus capensis*
- Ants and termites (soft parts):
  Flowerpot Snake *Ramphotyphops*
- Crayfish:
  Queen Snake *Regina septemvittata*
- Fish eggs:
  Turtle-Headed Sea Snake *Emydocephalus annulatus*
  Spine-Tailed Sea Snake *Aipysurus eydouxii*
- Freshwater eels:
  Rainbow Snake *Farancia erytrogramma*
- Sea eels:
  Banded Sea Krait *Laticauda colubrina*
- Frogs and toads:
  Common Night Adder *Causus rhombeatus*
  Hognose Snake *Heterodon*
- Lizards:
  Black-Headed Collared Snake *Sibynophis*
- Snakes:
  King Cobra *Ophiophagus hannah*
  Black-Headed Python *Aspidites melanocephalus*
- Snakes (ramphotyphlops):
  Bandy-Bandy *Vermicella annulata*
- Birds' eggs:
  Rhombic Egg-Eating Snake *Dasypeltis scabra*
  Indian Egg-Eating Snake *Elachistodon westermanni*
- Birds:
  Mangrove Snake *Boiga cynodon*
- Mammals:
  Amethystine Python *Morelia amethystina*
  African Burrowing Python *Calabaria reinhardti*

DIFFERENT PHASES OF CAPTURING PREY
COLUBRID CONSTRICTOR

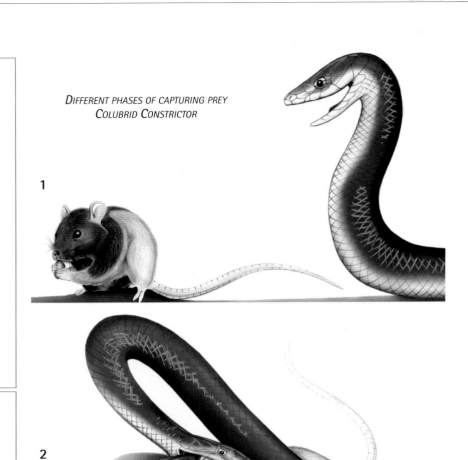

1

2

3

4

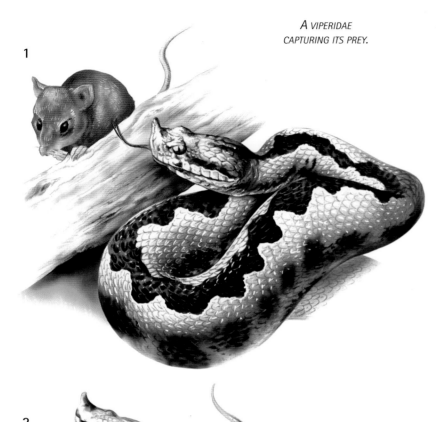

A VIPERIDAE CAPTURING ITS PREY.

1

2

3

WAYS OF CAPTURING PREY

Some snakes, like water snakes of the genus *Natrix*, swallow their prey alive; the prey dies from asphyxiation or from contact with gastric juices.

Other snakes are constrictors; they generally capture the prey with their mandibles, and the surrounding coils cause the prey's asphyxiation. Some constrictor snakes are the *Boidae*, culebrids of the genus *Elaphe*, *Lampropeltis*, etc.

Some species of snakes, poisonous or harmless, capture their prey firmly with their mandibles and do not release their grip (although it can use its coils to help immobilize it, but not to kill it); it does not proceed to swallow the prey until it is dead or very debilitated. Arboreal vipers like the genus *Bothriechis*, often use this technique because they are afraid of losing the prey if they release it; the culebrids of the genus *Coronella* also use this technique.

Other venomous snakes like the vipers of the genus *Viperidae* bite their prey (poisoning it) and then allow the prey to flee and wait until the venom has started to act. Once they sense that the prey could be dead or is very debilitated, the snake proceeds to follow its trail.

PREY SIZE AND TYPES OF FEEDING

The type of prey consumed often depends on the proportionate sizes of the snake and the prey; therefore, adults and young do not tend to eat the same type of prey. Even the males and females in species with a prominent sexual dimorphism (as far as corporal size is concerned) can considerably differ in the type of prey they feed on. The babies of many species of *Viperidae* feed on invertebrates and lizards in their first stages of life and then go on to feed mainly on rodents.

4

VENOM

Although venomous snakes are the best known and most popular, only less than one-fifth of the approximately 2,700 species of snake are venomous. The venomous function of the ophidians may have appeared during the cretaceous and tertiary periods, and probably evolved as a response a parallel evolution to recently appeared mammals. Its origin probably presented itself as a change in the snakes' potent salivary glands.

TYPES OF DENTITION

• **Aglyphous.** Snakes with aglyphous dentition do not have specialized teeth for conducting venom. The majority of aglyphous snakes' teeth do not differ much in size, although some species with a more specialized diet may have differentiation. For example, snakes of the genus *Lycodon*, specialized in trapping lizards, have longer front teeth. This dentition is unique to the more primitive groups of snakes: the *Boidae* and some *Colubridae*.

• **Opisthoglyphous.** In many *Colubridae*, the salivary glands take a special form, also segregating proteins; these are called Duvernoy's glands and may come in contact with a back canaled tooth. The venom is injected when the snake bites and retains its prey to swallow. About one-third of the *Colubridae*, belonging to different subfamilies, have this type of dentition. In general, it is not a very developed inoculation system, and the species that have it do not tend to cause problems for humans; nevertheless, some of them with very active venom and fangs in a fairly frontal position are dangerous to humans. Examples: the boomslang *Dispholidus typus*, bird or twig snakes, *Thelotornis*, or one of the species of the keelback *Rhabdophis*.

• **Proteroglyphous.** In these snakes, deeply canaled fangs located on the front part of the upper maxilla inject the venom quicker. Snakes as poisonous as the mambas, cobras, bungarus, or coral snakes have this system of venom inoculation. Although quicker than the opisthoglyphous snakes, they nonetheless retain their prey for a certain amount of time to inoculate the venom. The spitting cobras that have hollow fangs as a special adaptation (as do the vipers) can project the venom a few yards distant through a small tear-shaped orifice, located in the middle of the tooth.

• **Solenoglyphous.** This is the most evolved system of dentition; the venomous fangs are in the front and are very large; this is why they have a moveable articulation that allows their fangs to remain depressed in the palate sheathed by a protective vein. When the animal wants to bite, it raises its fangs and deeply penetrates them into the victim's body. The fangs are hollow on the inside and have a small hole in their apical zone. The venom is driven under pressure to the point of inoculation, injected like with a hypodermic needle. Therefore, these snakes do not need to retain their prey in order to introduce a sufficient amount of venom. The vipers, rattlesnakes, cottonmouths, and pit vipers all share this sophisticated system of poisoning.

CHARACTERISTICS OF VENOM

Snake venom is a colorless or slightly yellow liquid with 70% of its weight made up of water and most of the rest glycoproteins, comprising by polypeptides and enzymes. The substances that compose it vary in proportion among the different families of ophidians, species, and even among different specimens. They are very complex mixtures that cause a wide range of effects once injected into the victim's body.

DIFFERENT TYPES OF DENTITION AND FANGS

Opistoglyphous
fang section.

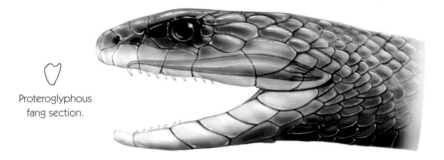

Proteroglyphous
fang section.

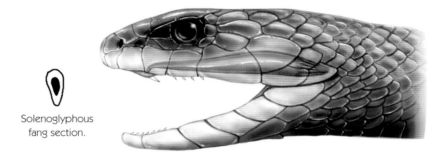

Solenoglyphous
fang section.

Among the most well-known venom polypeptides are the neurotoxins (mainly in the elapidae) that block the transmission of nervous impulses to the muscles, and the cardiotoxins, responsible for cardiovascular depression. Among the enzymes, the following are found: proteases, phospholipases, collagenases, nucleotides, acetylcholinesterase, hyaluronidase, etc.; these affect arterial tension, cytolysis, hemolysis, as well as the breaking up of connective tissue. The glycoproteins (proteins with high molecular weight) are to blame for anaphylactic reactions.

Snake venom has very often been classified into two large groups:
• Neurotoxic (unique to elapidaes and hydropheidae).
• Hemotoxic-cytotoxic (unique to the viperidae).

However, at present, this classification is considered very simplified; some elapidae, like the taipan or the African spitting cobras, have strong cytotoxic as well as neurotoxic effects and vice versa. Some Crotalidae, like *Crotalus durissus* or *Crotalus scutulatus*, have venom that exerts powerful neurotoxic effects on top of hemotoxic or cytotoxic ones.

TOXICITY

When assessing the toxicity of the venom in the victim's body, many factors are involved; some of them may pertain to the victim's physical condition, while others have to do with the snake's characteristics. Here are the most important ones:

• **The snake's age.** This can be a determining factor; although younger animals inoculate with less venom, it can be much more potent.

• **The quantity of venom inoculated.** It can vary, and when inoculated, is not always as effective as it could be; sometimes snakes may bite without introducing venom. A snake may also only manage to bite with one fang. Not all snakes are capable of injecting the same quantityof venom. The species that can inoculate the largest quantity are the Gabon Viper *Bitis gabonica*, the Eastern Diamondback Rattlesnake *Crotalus adamanteus*, and the Bushmaster *Lachesis muta*.

• **The venom's potency.** Differs according to the species and within the same species; each individual can vary, or there can be variation among individuals in different geographic areas. The venom's potency is assessed with what is called LD_{50} Scale, that is, the minimum quantity of venom that could kill 50% of laboratory animals within 24 hours from its injection. LD_{50} is expressed in pounds of the animal's weight. From this information the minimum lethal doses for an adult man that weighs between 132 and 154 pounds is calculated. As a general rule, snakes with a greater potency of venom, like some elapids (sea snakes, Australian elapids, or bungarus), can inoculate with much less, and less potent venom than can other snakes.

TOXICITY OF SELECTED SNAKES

Species	Average inoculated dose, dry weight / mgs	Minimum lethal dose in humans / mgs
Enhydrina schistosa	7–20	1
Notechis ater	30–70	2
Bungarus caeruleus	10–60	5
Echis carinatus	15–40	5
Dendroaspis polylepis	50–100	10
Crotalus scutulatus	30–100	15
Naja naja	150–300	20
Daboia russelli	130–250	30
Bothrops atrox	60–250	60
Bitis gabonica	350–650	60
Bitis arietans	150–250	100
Lachesis muta	280–550	170
Agkistrodon contortrix	40–60	380

IMPORTANCE OF COLORATION FOR SURVIVAL

The wide variety of snakes' colorations and patterns is always closely related to the possibilities of survival of each species in their characteristic environment. Therefore, each snake's color responds to the particular necessities of the habitat in which it lives and the type of life it leads there.

THREE BASIC TYPES OF COLORATION

• **Cryptic or camouflage.** To go as unnoticed as possible, maximizing integration in the surrounding environment. The most common type is when the snake is the same color as the predominating color of its surroundings: the majority of subterranean or terrestrial snakes in open land are uniformly brownish-gray or grayish (*typhlops, leptotyphlops, charina*, some species of the genus *Elaphe*), the arboreal snakes that move among the vegetation are almost completely green (*ahaetulla, dendroaspis, trimeresurus*), and the desert snakes are yellowish, brownish-gray, or reddish, depending on the type of sand (*cerastes, pseudocerastes*).

Cryptic coloration or camouflage in jungle environments.
Trimeresurus albolabris.

• **Disruptive.** Very common, characterized by fairly complex pattern of marks, stripes, and blotches on a general background color. This coloration acts to distort and dissimulate the animal's silhouette over the substrate on which it moves. Characteristic examples of this coloration are found on jungle snakes like the boas (boa, *acrantophis*), the pythons (*python*), or the african vipers (*bitis*).

• **Aposematic.** With contrasting bright and vivid hues, this coloration obtains a result contrary to the previous: to be as visible as possible, generally as a warning of a great potential danger. It tends to consist of a combination of red, yellow, or black bands that are very conspicuous in contrast with the brownish-gray or greenish terrain, or there are patterns blotches, or ocelli, that stand out with loud colors emphasizing the animal's body, head, neck, or tail. This type of coloration appears on a large part of venomous snakes, for example, coral snakes (*micrurus, micruroides*), bungarus (*bungarus*) or some cobras (*naja*), and on some harmless species that perfectly imitate the colors of the venomous snakes as a defensive strategy (*lampropeltis*).

Disruptive coloration on the forest floor.
Deignagkistrodon acutus.

Aposematic coloration.
Micrurus nigrocinctus.

Cryptic or camoflauge coloration in desert environments. *Pseudocerastes persicus.*

Aposematic coloration.
Bungarus fasciatus.

REPRODUCTION

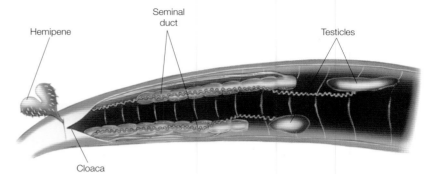

MALE SEXUAL APPARATUS

Hemipene · Seminal duct · Testicles · Cloaca

SEXUAL DIFERENTIATION AND SEX ORGANS

Sexual dimorphism in snakes is generally not very apparent, aside from a few species as in the Madagascan snakes of the genus *Langaha*, which have a prominent nasal appendage that is different depending on the sex.

Generally the females are larger, although there are some exceptions; for example, in some species of the genera *Ptyas, Boiga, Naja, Maticora, Coluber*, etc., the males are larger. Sometimes, there may be a considerable size difference between sexes, like in the anaconda, *Eunectes murinus* in which the females can reach more than 23 feet, while the males are much smaller, measuring only 13 feet.

This difference in size between sexes is also sometimes reflected in a different number of dorsal and subcaudal scales. Another differentiating characteristic is that the males have a relatively longer and wider tail, mainly close to their hemipenes.

Some of the male snakes have much more markedly keeled scales, as in the genera *Natrix* or *Thamnophis*. There are even species like the *Chironius carinatus*, in which the males have keeled scales while the females have smooth ones.

The boidaes, vestigial members in the form of spurs next to the cloaca are more evolved in the males and can be two to three times larger than the females'.

Coloration also may differ according to sex, for example, on the european vipers, vipera aspis and vipera berus, the males have much more contrasting colors and markings.

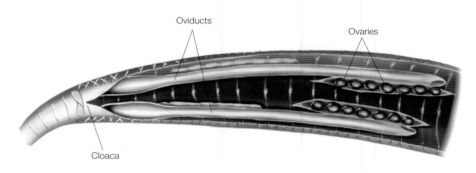

FEMALE SEXUAL APPARATUS

Oviducts · Ovaries · Cloaca

SEXUAL DIMORPHISM IN Langara nasuta.

SEX ORGANS

The ophidian males have two inverted penises, located on both sides of the cloacal opening on the front part of the tail. During copulation, only one of these is used and is evaginated and inverted, using muscular and vascular action, into a shape similar to that of the fingers of a glove.

The form of the penises is very variable, although many have spines, papillae, or fringes used to anchor the penis in the female's cloaca.

The oviducts located on the back part of the abdomen are very elongated and asymmetrical; normally the right oviduct bulges more and extends farthur along the snake's body. The oviducts open behind each side of the cloaca. In ovoviviparous species, the oviduct walls are reinforced to allow for egg retention.

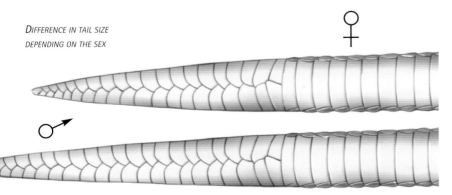

DIFFERENCE IN TAIL SIZE DEPENDING ON THE SEX

NUPTIAL COMBAT, COURTSHIP, AND COPULATION

Although they are generally indifferent to the presence of their kind, during mating season, some species of snake have bright and colorful nuptial combats. Many species of different groups participate in these combats: rattlesnakes, vipers, cottonmouths, mambas, some colubrids, and pythons. Normally they are bloodless ritualized combats that consist of repeated charging with the front part of the body raised followed by an intertwining of the bodies in a fashion similar to that of true copulation.

The weaker specimen retires once exhausted, although it probably could manage to copulate with the females; however, bloody combats have been seen in various species of pythons (*Python reticulatus* and *Chondropython Viridis*), in which the larger male inflicted serious wounds on the entire body of the smaller male. Nevertheless, these observations were made on animals in captivity.

It would be very difficult for an observer who witnessed one of these fights to distinguish a real nuptial fight because some phases of mating and nuptial combat are very similar. Before mating, the male tends to follow the female, sticking out its tongue and rubbing the female's head and body.

DIFFERENT STAGES OF NUPTIAL FIGHTING BETWEEN TWO MALE VIPERS

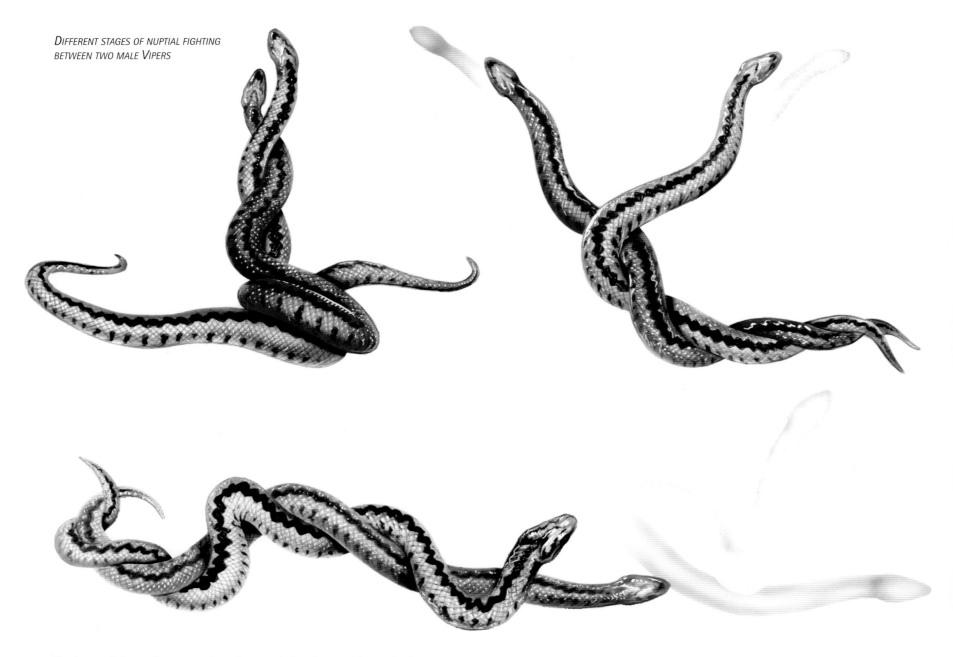

The intertwining tails are another characteristic of courtship; males in some species use their tails to lift the females' tails in order to join their cloacal zones; the boidae use their spurs to stimulate the cloacal zones and lead them to take an appropriate position for penetration. Many male species produce spasmodic movements throughout their entire body during courtship prior to copulation. In some species of the genera *Coluber, Coronella, Elaphe*, and *Lampropeltis*, the male grasps the female by the neck with his mandibles.

COLUBRID COPULATION.

TYPES OF REPRODUCTION

• **Oviparity.** The female lays eggs. When she lays the clutch, the embryo may be in different phases of development; in some species, they may already be very developed, shortening the incubation time.

• **Ovoviviparity.** The eggs remain in the oviducts until the embryo is finished developing; then, already formed, the eggs are expelled. The baby is born enveloped by a transparent membrane that quickly breaks. Ovoviviparity is widespread to a certain degree in almost all of the snake subfamilies; it is the most common in the *Viperidae, Boinae, Elapinae* (*Hydrophinae*), and *Homalopsinae*.

PARENTAL CARE

The vast majority of snakes are limited to laying eggs in an appropriate place or giving birth in the ovoviviparous species. Nonetheless, in some species, the female remains close to the clutch for a few days or coiled up around the eggs to protect them from drying or from possible predators. This latter behavior is common in the *Leptotyphlopidae* and in the *Pythoninae*, as well as in other species such as the mud snake *Farancia*, or in some species of rattlesnakes like the mountain pit viper *Trimeresurus monticola*, or in the Malayan pit viper *Calloselasma rhodostoma*.

In general, there is no real incubation, if incubation is understood as the thermic exchange between the female and the eggs; however, there are species such as the Diamond Python *Morelia spilotes* that sunbathe often so that, once the female's body has absorbed the heat, she can coil up again around the eggs.

There is also the Indian Python, *Python molurus* that has a more complex adaptation: through muscular contractions, it produces body heat to raise the temperature of the clutch. It has been calculated that this system can maintain the temperature of the eggs at 41–44.6°F above average.

The King cobra *Ophiophagus hannah* is distinguished from the rest of the snakes by the complexity of the nest it builds. The female collects a large quantity of vegetation remains and digs a cavity in the center, where she deposits the eggs and covers them with leaves, grass, and earth. The female will remain in the surrounding area defending the eggs from intruders.

COPULATION OF A SAND BOA

Pituophis nelandeuca
Oviparous reproduction. Laying eggs.

Pituophis nelandeuca.
Oviparous reproduction.
Hatching of egg and birth of baby.

Ovoviviparous reproduction.
Birth of a baby.

Elaphe notaeus.
Ovoviviparous reproduction. Babies with their mother.

HABITATS AND ADAPTATIONS

Snakes inhabit all the earth's continents except for Antarctica and they have also colonized both freshwater and saltwater. The only places they are not found are in polar regions and on some islands (Ireland, New Zealand, and some small islands in the Atlantic and the central Pacific).

Therefore, snakes occupy all types of habitats (each one with totally different characteristics and environmental conditions) that they have been able to colonize due to a series of physical, physiological, and behavioral adaptations.

MANGROVE SWAMPS: LAND, FRESHWATER, AND OCEAN ENVIRONMENTS

The mangrove swamps are closed forests formed by different species of mangrove, (trees that grow along the ocean's shore and even in the ocean). These flooded tropical jungles that develop in equatorial regions in the rainy season, and the swamps and marshes found in warm regions, are amphibian environments (where there is a mix of land and water) and are very rich with snakes.

The majority of species have semi-arboreal and semi-aquatic characteristics that are consistent with the mix of the two dominant aspects in these environments: trees and water. The world's largest snakes inhabit the waterlogged South American jungles like the anaconda *Eunectes murinus*, which likes to rest on the thick branches that grow horizontally on the water's surface. It moves along the surface by swimming with great agility like many freshwater aquatic species of the genus *Agkistrodon* that, nonetheless, rarely climbs trees.

On the other hand, among the Asian snakes, there is for example, *Python curtus*, that is much smaller than the anaconda. The *Boiga dendrophila*, a species that possesses extremely powerful venom, is more arboreal than aquatic, but very common in the Asian mangrove swamps.

Other typical inhabitants of the mangrove swamps and flooded Asian jungles, in this case with almost totally aquatic habits, are the file, wart, and elephant trunk snakes of the genus *Acrochordus* (*A. javanicus, A. granulatus, A. arafurae*), that only leave the water occasionally.

In the coastal mangrove swamps of the tropics, a series of sea snakes frequently appear out in the open to reproduce or to simply rest, making rich hunting zones for their predators. Species such as *Laticauda colubrina* or *Hydrophis cyanocinctus* can be seen regularly swimming among the roots of the mangrove trees, and even some of them like *Enhydrina schistosa* swim upriver until reaching a considerable upstream distance.

All these sea snakes, the majority of which can move clumsily on solid land, do not leave the water frequently and have physical characteristics that are perfectly adapted to aquatic life: their body is laterally compressed, especially the back part of the body and tail, they can close their nostrils when submerged, and their lungs can retain a large amount of oxygen, which allows them to stay immersed for long periods of time.

ASIAN MANGROVE

1 *Trimeresurus purpureomaculatus* (Mangrove Viper)
2 *Boiga denchophila* (Mangrove Snake)
3 *Enhydrina schistosa* (Beaked Sea Snake)
4 *Acrochordus javanicus* (Small File Snake)

DESERTS AND ARID ZONES

There is a wide variety of desert zones on all of the earth's continents: there are warm and cold deserts, stony and sandy deserts, some very far from the ocean and others that reach right up to the shore, and some occupy large expanses of terrain while others are fairly small.

Nonetheless, all these arid regions have common characteristics that determine the living conditions of the animals that inhabit them: mainly, the irregular and very low rainfall (generally less than 10 inches of rainfall annually), and the extreme temperature ranges that occur throughout the day (a difference of up to 104°F between daylight and nighttime hours).

Snakes are relatively well represented and well adapted among the vertebrate animals that tolerate these demanding environmental conditions.

Their daily rhythm of activity could possibly be their most important adaptation; they are mainly crepuscular or nocturnal (temperature permitting), avoiding the strongest hours of sunshine by hiding somewhat deep underground or in any shelter.

Some of the characteristics of their metabolism for saving water also favor their survival in arid zones: their urine is not liquid, rather, the uric acid is excreted in crystal form with the feces, the skin lacks sweat glands, they are covered with scales which make them impermeable, and they can go a long time without drinking, obtaining the water they need by metabolizing it directly from their prey's fat.

A large number of desert snakes move on the burning sand by using a special system of locomotion called lateral undulation; this system avoids the most direct body contact with the ground. Many of the species that inhabit stony regions have rough keeled scales that allow them to move with greater agility among the rocks. Some snakes that inhabit sandy deserts are characterized by small horns above the eyes. These act as bait to attract their prey when the animal is buried under the sand, and allows only this part of the body to protrude.

The majority of them have a camouflage coloration composed of either uniform light colors that blend with the terrain, or of blotches, stripes, or patterns that break up the animal's silhouette on the ground.

Many groups of snakes are adapted to arid environments, but especially those of the Viperidae (*Cerastes, Psedocerastes, Vipera, Crotalus*), the Elapidae (*Acanthophis, Naja*), Colubridae (*Philodryas, Alsophis, Chilomeniscus, Salvadora*), and even Boidae (*Eryx, Aspidites*).

North American desert

1 *Lampropeltis getulus californiae* (California King Snake)
2 *Crotalus cerastes* (North African Horned Viper)
3 *Trimorphodon biscutatus* (Lyre Snake)
4 *Crotalus scutalatus* (Mojave Rattlesnake)

JUNGLES AND ARBOREAL LIFE

The tropical jungles are found in a wide band that extends above and below the Equator. They are regions that are characterized for having a fairly constant elevated temperature throughout the entire year (generally close to 82°F), with negligible daily variations and very abundant rainfall (more than 79 inches annually), that is distributed regularly and constantly throughout the year, or rather mainly concentrated in a specific rainy season.

The extraordinary exuberance and richness of the plant cover is a result of the coincidence of these two previously mentioned factors: the trees are large and tall, liana and epiphytal plants are abundant, herbaceous plants are fairly large, and bamboos and other shrub like species grow in an impenetrable underbrush. The fauna that inhabits this environment is also very rich and varied with a biodiversity of species, among the largest that can be found on earth.

Snakes are very well represented in tropical jungles; there are subterranean, terrestrial, and evidently arboreal species. Due to the jungles' elevated and constant temperature, the species of snake that live there do not need to hibernate and they are active during the entire year.

The jungle floor is covered in humus because of the enormous accumulation of plant material that is constantly decomposing; it makes a perfect substrate for burrowing snakes like *Typhlops*, *Leptotyphlops*, *Calabaria*, or *Anomalepis*.

Not very specialized, somewhat slow species live in the underbrush covered and tangled with plant remains. They usually have colorations that perfectly camouflage them, blending the animal in with the leaf, branch, trunk, and root-covered ground; the African vipers of the genus *Bitis* (*B. gabonica*, *B. nasicornis*) are an example. These more terrestrial species are abundant in all jungles; in Asia there are, for example, the *Xenopeltis unicolor*, *Calloselasma rhodostoma*, or *Python reticulatus*, while in South America, among many others, there are the *Anilius scytale*, *Atractus elaps*, *Lachesis muta*, *Clelia clelia*, and *Bothrops atrox*.

However, the most characteristic adaptation of jungle snakes is an arboreal life: they are somewhat light, slender, agile species that often have a prehensile tail and are primarily green–this perfectly blends them in with the surrounding vegetation. Typical examples are *Oxybelis fulgidus* in South America, *Dendroaspis viridis* in Africa, and *Ahaetulla prasina* or *Trimeresurus albolabris* in tropical Asia.

An interesting example of adaptive convergence to the arboreal medium is

found within the Boidae family with two green-colored prehensile-tailed species that are extraordinarily similar: the emerald boa (*Corallus caninus*), that inhabits the South American jungles, and the green tree python (*Chondropython viridis*), that inhabits the jungles in New Guinea and northern Australia.

AFRICAN JUNGLE

1 *Bitis gabonica* (Gabon Viper)
2 *Naja melanoleuca* (Forest Cobra)
3 *Dendroaspis jamesoni* (Jameson's Mamba)
4 *Python regius* (Royal Python)

TEMPERATE MEDITERRANEAN CLIMATES

Temperate Mediterranean climates found in many terrains that extend around the sea located between Europe, Asia, and Africa, are characterized for having mild winters with occasional freezing, and dry hot summers. Typically, it rains irregularly and when it does, it is usually in spring and fall when there may be torrential rains on various occasions. In these Mediterranean regions, snakes are moderately abundant, mainly terrestrial, and possibly aboreal.

One of the snakes' characteristics that live in this habitat is the marked seasonal nature of their behavior; during the cold months of the year they tend to hibernate, withdrawing into shelters that allow them to remain safe from the inclemency of the weather. When the good weather comes in spring, they become very active in order to feed and look for a mate. During summer they move mainly during the early and late hours of the day, the rest of the time taking shelter from the sun's strong rays. When fall comes they increase their daily activity again; they feed constantly in order to face the fairly long period of hibernation.

It should be stressed that this characteristic habitat also exists in certain zones on the planet that are very far from the Mediterranean sea. This type of environment is found in North America, in the region called the Californian chaparral (with species like the *Lampropeltis zonata*), in South America in some coastal regions of Chile, in the southernmost area of Africa (where *Pseudaspis cana* or *Psammophylax rhombeatus* are found), and in the southwestern coastal region of Australia (with snakes such as *Morelia spilota* or *Acanthophis antarcticus*).

The following are representative species of the regions located around the Mediterranean sea: the ladder snake *Elaphe scalaris*, one of the most abundant species in some regions; the Montpellier snake *Malpolon monspessulanus*, an opistoglyphous species that can reach six feet in length; different species of colubrids of the genus *Coluber* (*C. algirus, C. rubriceps, C. hippocrepis*); southern smooth snake *Coronella girondica*; or some vipers such as *Vipera xanthina*, *Vipera aspis*, and *Vipera latastei*.

A series of somewhat aquatic snakes such as the viperine snake *Natrix maura* or the grass snake *Natrix natrix* also inhabit the streams, brooks, and flooded areas that generally appear temporarily in these regions.

Some species such as the Aesculapian snake, *Elaphe longuissima*, are more adapted to life in Mediterranean mountain zones where it is colder and more humid, typical of the holm oak forests of the northeast mountains of the

Iberian Peninsula. The European smooth snake, *Coronella austriaca*, is another example; it is ovoviviparous as an adaptation to a habitat with more severe climatic conditions.

A few are even adapted to colder and harsher climates that almost reach the Arctic Circle, such as the adder *Vipera berus*, that occupies the temperate and cold zones of northern Europe and Asia.

MEDITERRANEAN PASTURE

1 *Vipera latasti* (Lataste's Viper)
2 *Elaphe scalaris* (Ladder Snake)
3 *Malpolon monspessulanus* (Montpellier Snake)
4 *Coronella girondina* (Smooth Snake)

DEFENSIVE BEHAVIOR

As with the great majority of animals, snakes' worst enemy is Man, who directly eliminates them and destroys their natural habitat in many regions of the world. But they also have a large number of natural enemies consisting of birds, mammals, and even other snakes.

HOW TO CONFUSE THE ENEMY

Many birds sporadically include snakes in their diet (storks *ciconia*, herons *ardea*, egrets *egretta*, marabous *leptoptilos*, ravens *corvus*, eagle *aquila*, *terathopius*, kite *milvus*); some of them frequently eat snakes (*sagittarius* serpentarius, *serriema cariama*, road-runner *geococcyx*, bustard *otis*, kookaburras *dacelo*) and there are other species that are authentically ophiphagous, that is specialized in the capture of these reptiles, like the short-toed snake eagle / European snake eagle *circaetus gallicus*, congo serpent eagle *dryotriorchis spectabilis*, or the crested serpent eagle *spilornis cheela*.

Among the mammals that eat snakes, circumstances providing, are foxes *vulpes*, wild cats, *felis*, hedgehogs *erinaceus*, racoon *procyon*, badgers *taxidea*, *meles*, wild boars sus, peccaries *tayassu*, suricates *suricata*, mongoose *herpestes*, *mungos*, and many other species.

Finally, snakes themselves are dangerous to other snakes given that canni-balism is a habitual phenomenon (the largest specimen can perfectly hunt those of a smaller size) and many species regularly hunt other smaller snakes. For example, the King Cobra *Ophiophagus hannah* is a most completely ophiphageous. Many culebrids (*Coronella, Coluber, Eirenne*) capture and consume young snakes of non venomous species, and others eat snakes of the genus *Lampropeltis* or the massurana *clelia clelia* (which also eats venomous snakes).

Snakes can do little about the loss of their habitat caused by Man and the direct persecution people subject them to, but they have developed a series of defense mechanisms to protect themselves from their numerous natural pred-ators that allow them to considerably increase their chances of survival.

The harmless *Lampropeltis mexicana* imitates the coloration of the venomous *Crotalus lepidus* (below).

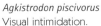

Agkistrodon piscivorus
Visual intimidation.

DEFENSE MECHANISMS

Like the majority of animals, the first method of defense is to try to go by unnoticed by remaining still (often aided by cryptic or disruptive coloration) or escaping quickly until managing to hide in any safe refuge. When these basic systems fail, before defending themselves by biting directly, snakes have a large amount of deterring mechanisms that vary according to species. Among them, the following should be highlighted:

• Intimidation– the game of impressing the enemy. Many species of venomous snakes have vivid colors that clearly warn possible predators of their dangerousness without the animals having to adopt a special posture (the combination of the red, black, and yellow rings of the coral snakes *micrurus* or *micruroides,* for example). But other venomous species with more discreet coloration use intimidating behavior that helps to reinforce the message of dangerousness in the eyes of its enemies: the boomslang inflates its neck to look larger, the puff adder (*bitis arietans*) inflates its entire body to achieve this effect, the cobras (*naja*) raise the front part of their body from the ground and spread their hood, and the cottonmouth (*agkistrodon*) opens its mouth to show the contrasting white color of the interior.

Clelia clelia. Young specimen with aposematic coloration.

Diadophis punctatus. Aposematic coloration on a non venomous snake.

Natrix maura (viperine snake), Imitating a viper's posture.

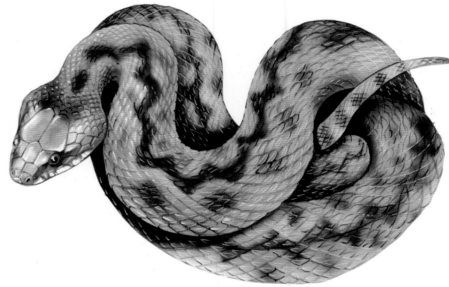

Echis coloratus. Sonorous intimidation.

• Sonorous intimidation. A variant of the previous technique consists of emitting threatening warning sounds: rattlesnakes (*crotalus*) make the tip of their tail vibrate, cobras (*naja*) hiss when raising their body and spreading their hood, and some species (*echis*, for example) may rub the body's scales against each other to produce an audible sound.

• Mimicry. This defensive strategy consists of a completely harmless species having a coloration that perfectly imitates the warning that characterizes determined extremely poisonous species; in doing so, it confuses possible enemies. A paradigm is the species of the genus *Lampropeltis*, whose pattern is very difficult to distinguish from the coral snakes of the genera *Micrurus* or *Micruroides*.

Micrurus (Coral Snake).
Visual and postural intimidation

Crotalus (Rattlesnake).
Sound and postural intimidation.

• **Mimetic behavior.** Harmless snakes sometimes imitate the intimidating behavior of truly dangerous species. Examples of this behavior are the culebrids of the genus *Natrix*, who imitate the hisses and aggressive postures of the vipers of the genus *Viperidae*, or those of the genus *Dasypeltis*, which rub their scales the same way as the poisonous *echis*.

• **Playing dead.** In extreme situations, many snake species (for example in *natrix*, *heterodon*, or *hemachatus*) carry out a true theatric performance that convinces their enemies that they are dead: they twist, turn with their stomach up, remain still, open their mouth, and let their tongue hang out. This behavior may be accompanied by defecation and a smelly secretion from the anal glands, which can also be considered a strategy of smell intimidation.

Naja (Cobra).
Threatening posture.

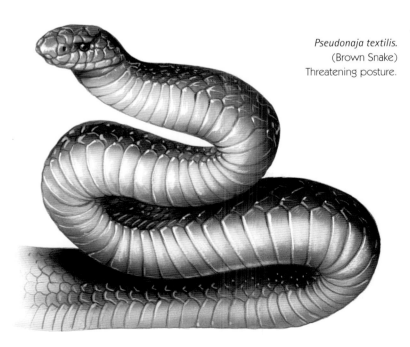

Pseudonaja textilis.
(Brown Snake)
Threatening posture.

Dispholidus tipus.
(Boomslang)
Threatening posture.

FAMILIES / SUBFAMILIES / SPECIES

F. TYPHLOPIDAE

SUBFAMILY TYPHLOPINAE

- *Ramphotyphlops braminus*
  (Flowerpot Snake)
- *Rhinotyphlops schlegelii*
  (Schlegel's Blind Snake)
- *Typhlops vermicularis*
  (Eurasian Worm Snake)
- *Typhlops diardi* (Diard's Worm Snake)

SUBFAMILY ANOMALEPINAE

- *Liotyphlops albirostris*
  (Pink-Headed Blind Snake)

F. LEPTOTYPHLOPIDAE

- *Leptotyphlops dulcis*
  (Texas Blind Snake)
- *Leptotyphlops humilis*
  (Western Blind Snake)

F. ANILIIDAE

- *Anilius scytale*
  (Coral Pipe Snake)

F. UROPELTIDAE

SUBFAMILY CYLINDROPHINAE

- *Cylindrophis rufus*
  (Pipe Snake)
- *Cylindrophis maculatus*
  (Ceylanese Pipe Snake)

SUBFAMILY UROPELTINAE

- *Uropeltis ocellatus*
  (Ocellate Shield-Tail Snake)
- *Uropeltis phillipsi*
  (Phillips's Shield-Tail Snake)
- *Rhinophis trevelyanus*
  (Trevelyan's earth Snake)

F. XENOPELTIDAE

- *Xenopeltis unicolor*
  (Sunbeam Snake)

F. LOXOCEMIDAE

- *Loxocemus bicolor*
  (New World Python, Dwarf Python,
  Mexican Burrowing Python)

F. BOIDAE

SUBFAMILY PYTHONINAE

- *Python sebae* (African Rock Python)
- *Python regius* (Royal Python)
- *Python anchietae*
  (Anchieta's Dwarf Python)
- *Python molurus* (Tiger Python)
- *Python reticulatus* (Reticulated Python)
- *Python curtus* (Blood Python)
- *Calabaria reinhardtii*
  (Calabar Burrowing Python)
- *Liasis amethistinus* (Amethyst Python)
- *Liasis childreni* (Children's Python)
- *Liasis olivaceus* (Olive Python)
- *Morelia spilotes* (Diamond Python)
- *Aspidites melanocephalus*
  (Black-Headed Python)
- *Chondropython viridis* (Green Python)

SUBFAMILY ERYCINAE

- *Eryx conicus* (Indian Sand Boa)
- *Eryx jaculus* (Javelin Sand Boa)
- *Eryx johnii* (Brown Sand Boa)
- *Eryx colubrinus*
  (East African Sand Boa)
- *Charina bottae* (Rubber Boa)
- *Lichanura trivirgata* (Rosy Boa)

SUBFAMILY BOINAE

- *Boa constrictor* (Boa Constrictor)
- *Eunectes notaeus* (Yellow Anaconda)
- *Eunectes murinus* (Common Anaconda)
- *Corallus caninus* (Emerald Tree Boa)
- *Corallus enydris* (Amazon Tree Boa)
- *Epicrates cenchria* (Rainbow Boa)
- *Epicrates strictus* (Haitian Boa)
- *Epicrates inornatus* (Puerto Rican Boa)
- *Epicrates subflavus* (Jamaica Boa)
- *Epicrates angulifer* (Cuban Boa)
- *Sanzinia madagascariensis*
  (Madagascar Tree Boa)
- *Acrantophis dumerili* (Dumeril's Boa)
- *Acrantophis madagascariensis*
  (Malagasy Ground Boa)
- *Candoia carinata* (Pacific Island Boa)
- *Candoia aspera*
  (New Guinea Ground Boa)

SUBFAMILY BOLYERINAE

- *Casarea dussumieri*
  (Round Island Ground Boa)
- *Bolyeria multocarinata*
  (Round Island Burrowing Boa)

F. TROPIDOPHIIDAE

- *Trachyboa boulengeri* (Rough-Scaled Boa)
- *Tropidophis melanurus*
  (Cuban Black-Tailed Dwarf Boa)
- *Ungaliophis continentalis*
  (Banana Boa)

F. COLUBRIDAE

SUBFAMILY COLUBRINAE

- *Arizona elegans* (Glossy Snake)
- *Coluber constrictor* (American Racer)
- *Coluber hippocrepis* (Horseshoe Snake)
- *Coluber viridiflavus* (Western Whip Snake)
- *Coronella austriaca* (Smooth Snake)
- *Coronella girondica*
  (Southern Smooth Snake)
- *Drymarchon corais* (Indigo Snake)
- *Elaphe taeniura* (Beauty Snake)
- *Elaphe guttata* (Corn Snake)
- *Elaphe longissima*
  (Aesculapian Rat Snake)
- *Elaphe mandarina* (Mandarin Rat Snake)
- *Elaphe obsoleta* (Common Rat Snake)
- *Elaphe quatuorlineata* (Four-Lined Snake)
- *Elaphe scalaris* (Ladder Snake)
- *Gonyosoma oxycephala*
  (Red-Tailed Rat Snake)
- *Lampropeltis alterna*
  (Gray Banded Kingsnakes)
- *Lampropeltis calligaster*
  (Prairie Kingsnake)
- *Lampropeltis getula* (Common Kingsnake)
- *Lampropeltis pyromelana*
  (Sonora Mountain Kingsnake)
- *Lampropeltis triangulum* (Milk Snake)
- *Lampropeltis zonata*
  (Mountain Kingsnake)
- *Masticophis flagellum* (Coachwhip)
- *Pituophis melanoleucus* (Bull Snake)
- *Pseudaspis cana* (Mole Snake)
- *Ptyas mucosus* (Dhaman)
- *Spalerosophis diadema*
  (Diadem Snake)
- *Spilotes pullatus*
  (Tropical Rat Snake)

SUBFAMILY LYCODONTINAE

- *Boaedon fuliginosus*
  (Brow House Snake)
- *Farancia abacura*
  (Mud Snakes)
- *Leioheterodon madagascariensis*
  (Malagasy Giant Hognose Snake)
- *Lycodon aulicus*
  (Common Wolf Snake)

SUBFAMILY NATRICINAE

- *Amphiesma stolata*
  (Buffstriped Keelback)
- *Natrix maura* (Viperine Snake)
- *Natrix natrix* (Grass Snake)
- *Natrix tessellata* (Dice Snake)
- *Nerodia fasciata*
  (Southern Water Snake)
- *Nerodia sipedon* (Northern Water Snake)
- *Rhabdophis subminiatus*
  (Red-Necked Keelback)
- *Thamnophis elegans*
  (Western Terrestrial Garter Snake)
- *Thamnophis sauritus*
  (Eastern Ribbon Snake)
- *Thamnophis sirtalis*
  (Common Garter Snake)

SUBFAMILY HOMALOPSINAE

- *Enhydris enhydris*
  (Schneider's Smooth Water Snake)
- *Erpeton tentaculatum*
  (Tentacled Snake)

SUBFAMILY DASYPELTINAE

- *Dasypeltis scabra*
  (African Egg-Eaters Snake)

SUBFAMILY CALAMARINAE

- *Calamaria lumbricoidea*
  (Variable Reed Snake)

SUBFAMILY XENODERMINAE

- *Xenodermus javanicus*
  (Strange-Scaled Snake)

SUBFAMILY DIPSADINAE

- *Dipsas bicolor*
  (Snail-Eating Snake)

SUBFAMILY SIBYNOPHINAE

- *Sibynophis melanocephalus*
  (Malayan Many Toothed Snake)

SUBFAMILY PAREINAE

- *Pareas carinatus*
  (Keeled Slug Snake)

SUBFAMILY XENODONTINAE

- *Heterodon nasicus*
  (Western Hognose Snake)
- *Heterodon platyrhinos*
  (Eastern Hognose Snake)
- *Hydrodynaster gigas*
  (False Water Cobra)
- *Philodryas baroni*
  (Argentine Green Hognose Snake)

SUBFAMILY BOIGINAE

- *Ahaetulla prasina*
  (Oriental Whip Snake)
- *Boiga blandingi*
  (Blanding's Tree Snake)
- *Boiga dendrophila*
  (Mangrove Snake)
- *Clelia clelia* (Mussurana)
- *Chrysopelea ornata* (Golden Tree Snake)
- *Dispholidus tipus* (Boomslang)
- *Erythrolamprus bizonus* (False coral Snake)
- *Macroprotodon cucullatus*
  (False Smooth Snake)
- *Malpolon monspessulanus*
  (Montpellier Snake)
- *Oxybelis fulgidus* (Green Vine Snake)
- *Psammophis sibilans*
  (African Hissing Sand Snake)
- *Tantilla coronata*
  (Southeastern Crower Snake)
- *Telescopus fallax*
  (Mediterranean Cat Snake)
- *Thelotornis capensis* (Savannah Vine Snake)
- *Trimorphodon biscutatus* (Lyre Snake)

SUBFAMILY ELACHISTODONTINAE

- *Elachistodon westermanni*
  (Indian Egg-Eater Snake)

F. APARALLACTIDAE O ATRACTASPIDIDAE

- *Aparallactus capensis*
  (Cape Centipede Eater)
- *Atractaspis bibroni*
  (Bibron's Burrowing Asp)

F. ELAPIDAE

SUBFAMILY ELAPINAE

- *Acanthophis antarcticus*
  (Common death adder)
- *Bungarus caeruleus* (Blue Krait)
- *Bungarus fasciatus* (Banded Krait)
- *Dendroaspis angusticeps*
  (Eastern Green Mamba)
- *Dendroaspis polylepis* (Black Mamba)
- *Dendroaspis viridis*
  (West African Green Mamba)
- *Hemachatus haemachatus*
  (Rinkhals)
- *Micruroides euryxanthus*
  (Western Coral Snake)
- *Micrurus frontalis*
  (Southern Coral Snake)
- *Micrurus fulvius*
  (Eastern Coral Snake)
- *Naja haje*
  (Egyptian Cobra)
- *Naja melanoleuca* (Forest Cobra)
- *Naja mossambica*
  (Mozambique Spitting Cobra)
- *Naja naja* (Indian Cobra, Spectacled Cobra)
- *Naja nigricollis*
  (Black-Necked Spitting Cobra)
- *Notechis scutatus* (Common Tiger Snake)
- *Ophiophagus hannah* (King Cobra)
- *Oxyuranus scutellatus* (Taipan)
- *Pseudonaja textilis*
  (Common Brown Snake)
- *Walterinnesia aegyptia*
  (Black Desert Cobra)

SUBFAMILY HYDROPHIINAE

- *Enhydrina schistosa*
  (Beaked Sea Snake)
- *Hydrophis cyanocinctus*
  (Annulated Sea Snake)
- *Laticauda colubrina*
  (Banded Sea Snake)
- *Pelamis platurus*
  (Pelagic Sea Snake)

F. VIPERIDAE

SUBFAMILY VIPERINAE

- *Atheris squamiger*
  (Green Bush Viper)
- *Bitis arietans* (Puff Adder)
- *Bitis gabonica* (Gabon Viper)
- *Bitis nasicornis* (Rhinoceros Viper)
- *Causus rhombeatus*
  (Rhombic Night Adder)
- *Cerastes cerastes* (Horned Viper)
- *Cerastes vipera* (Common Sand Viper)
- *Daboia lebetina* (Levantine Adder)
- *Daboia russelli* (Russell's Viper)
- *Daboia xanthina* (Ottoman Viper)
- *Echis carinatus* (Saw-Scaled Viper)
- *Vipera ammodytes* (Nose-Horned Viper)
- *Vipera aspis* (Asp Viper)
- *Vipera berus* (Common Viper)

SUBFAMILY AZEMIOPINAE

- *Azemiops feae*
  (Fea's Viper)

SUBFAMILY CROTALINAE

- *Agkistrodon bilineatus* (Mexican Moccasin)
- *Agkistrodon contortrix*
  (Copperhead)
- *Agkistrodon piscivorus* (Water Moccasin)
- *Bothriechis schlegeli*
  (Eyelash-Palm Pit Viper, Oropel)
- *Bothrops asper* (Terciopelo)
- *Calloselasma rhodostoma*
  (Malayan Pit Viper)
- *Crotalus adamanteus*
  (Eastern Dimondback Rattlesnake)
- *Crotalus atrox*
  (Western Diamondback Rattlesnake)
- *Crotalus cerastes* (Sidewinder)
- *Crotalus durissus* (Neotropical Rattlesnake)
- *Crotalus lepidus* (Rock Rattlesnake)
- *Crotalus scutulatus* (Mojave Rattlesnake)
- *Lachesis muta* (Bushmaster)
- *Porthidium nummifer*
  (Jumping-Pit Viper)
- *Trimeresurus purpureomaculatus*
  (Shore Pit Viper)
- *Trimeresurus wagleri* (Temple Pit Viper)

F. Typhlopidae

180 то 200 SPECIES

These snakes are called blind or worm snakes and are widespread, found in almost all regions of the world. They are small burrowing snakes that have both very primitive characteristics and others that indicate a high level of specialization.

Although they live in a similar manner, they do not share the slow and lazy behavior of the saurian lizards; these snakes are quite agile, quick, and both hard to see and capture.

The Typhlopidae's normal habitat is the fairly moist humus of tropical and equatorial zones where the ground is easy to dig to look for food and hide under tree trunks and rocks. They also hide in termite nests where they can easily find food; ants and termites constitute a very significant part of their diet, especially for the small species.

The larger ones include other vertebrates in their diet, but their small mouth, that hardly opens, impedes them from swallowing large prey. Some species seem to just suck the fluids from their prey without swallowing them completely.

When the humidity drops in the dry season these snakes burrow further into the earth. During periods of rain, and at night, they can be found on the surface where they move easily; however, they quickly hide in the ground with even the slightest warning.

GENERAL CHARACTERISTICS

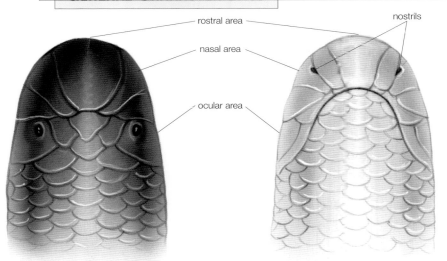

The short head that is not differentiated from the body shows solidly joined bones that form a type of very strong capsule, adapted to the pressure of subterranean life. The upper mandible is mobile with movable teeth, while the lower remains fixed.

The rostral area of the head has enlarged scales. The rostral scales are often larger than the others and are projected forwards, like a wedge; the mouth is small and ventrally located; and the eyes are very small, as would be expected in animals that are very adapted to subterranean life.

Typhlops schlegelii (Schlegel Worm Snake). Adult specimen.

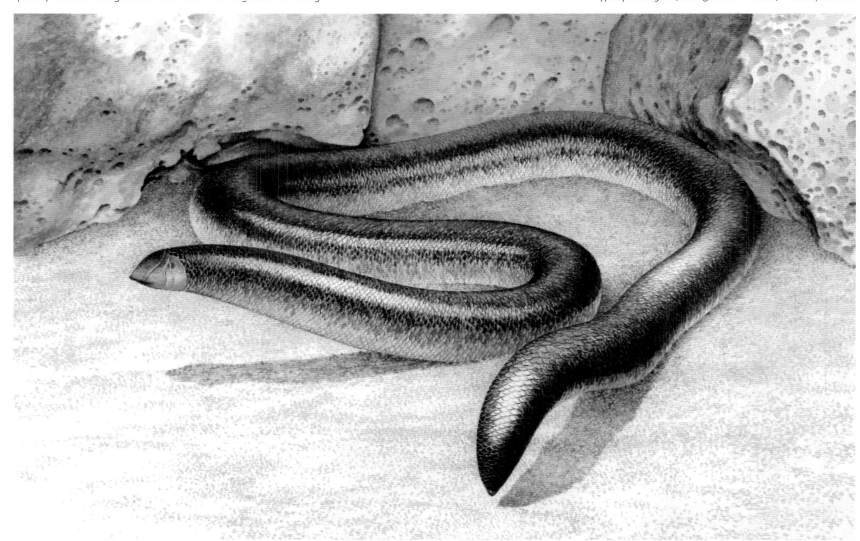

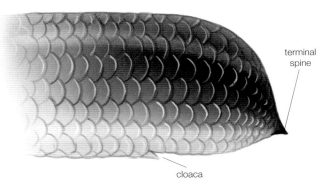

terminal
spine

cloaca

The scales are small, (apart from the cephalic ones) cycloid, smooth, flat, and they are kept extremely clean thanks to the sebaceous glands; this helps the snakes slither with hardly any friction from the subsoil. There is no differentiation between the dorsal and ventral parts of the body. Normally the scales are found in 20 to 40 rows around the body. The hemipenes are extremely long and thin.

RAMPHOTYPHLOPS BRAMINUS
(Flower-pot Snake).
Vestiges of the pelvic girdle.

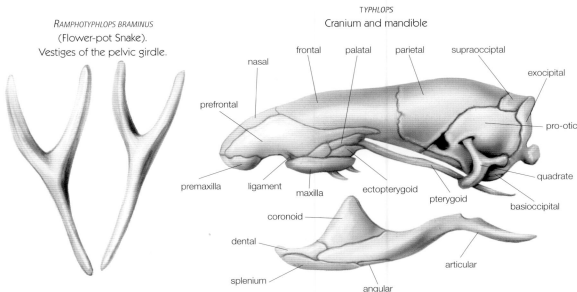

TYPHLOPS
Cranium and mandible

nasal

frontal   palatal   parietal   supraocciptal

exocipital

prefrontal

pro-otic

premaxilla   ligament   maxilla   ectopterygoid   pterygoid   quadrate

coronoid   basioccipital

dental   articular

splenium

angular

SUBFAMILY: **TYPHLOPINAE**

Eurasian Worm Snake

Typhlops vermicularis . Adult specimen in its habitat.

SUBFAMILY: **ANOMALEPINAE**

Liotyphlops beui. Adult specimen in its habitat.

180 SPECIES

• The upper maxilla has movable teeth situated perpendicularly on the axis of the body and is characterized by its ability to move. The lower maxilla lacks teeth and remains fixed without intermandibular articulation. There are vestiges of a reduced pelvis and cartilaginous remains.

• They are pink, yellow, brownish-gray, or black, generally uniform, although the dorsal part is darker than the ventral. Sometimes they have stripes, bands, or blotches that are lighter or darker.

• They have a right oviduct, while the left one has completely disappeared.

• The shedding of the skin does not occur on the entire body at once, rather in large areas.

• They generally lay eggs, although some species (*Typhlops diardi*) are ovoviviparous.

• They reach a length of 6 to 35 inches; the majority oscillate between 8 and 20 inches.

19 SPECIES

• They have teeth on the upper mandible like the Typhlopinae but with only one tooth on each side of the lower mandible.

• The head has scales that are very differentiated and look more like the cephalic plates of the Colubrinae than that of the Typhlopinae.

• The pelvis vestiges are absent.

• The cranial bones are not joined as in the Typhlopinae.

• They are brownish-gray or black, some with a yellow, orangish, or white head or tail.

• The left oviduct may be present, atrophied, or completely absent.

• They live in Central and South America and their type of life is identical to that of the Typhlopinae.

■ Three genera are distinguished:

- *Typhlops*: more than 125 species widely distributed in tropical regions (aside from one, *T. vermicularis* which is in Eurasia).

- *Ramphotyphlops*: 30 species distributed in Australasia and Oceania. Introduced in Africa, America, and other places.

- *Rhinotyphlops*: 25 species distributed in sub-Saharan Africa.

They extend into South America, Central America, sub-Saharan Africa, Greece, Asia Minor, Near East, Southeast Asia, and Australia.

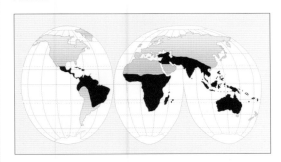

■ According to some authors, three genera are recognized:

- *Anomalepis*: 4 species, distributed in Mexico, Peru, and Ecuador. They have one tooth on each side of the lower mandible.

- *Helminthophis*: 3 species in Central America and in northern South America. Lower mandible without teeth.

- *Liotyphlops*: 12 species from Costa Rica to Paraguay. Lower mandible has only one tooth one each side.

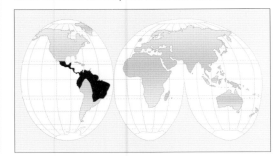

RAMPHOTYPHLOPS BRAMINUS

SUBFAMILY TYPHLOPINAE

(Daudin, 1803)

Flowerpot Snake

Ramphotyphlops braminus (Flowerpot Snake). Adult specimen

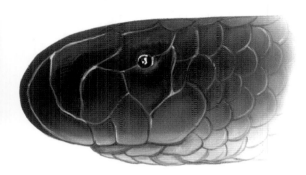

RAMPHOTYPHLOPS BRAMINUS
(Flowerpot Snake).
Detail of the head. Side view.

DESCRIPTION

Like all Typhlopidae, they are vermiform and small in size, only reaching seven inches.

The body is extremely thin and cylindrical, with 20 rows of transversal scales. The number of dorsal scales varies between 300 and 350, and the head is undifferentiated from the body and has diminutive eyes. The tail is very short and ends in a protuberance in the form of a spine.

Its coloration is brownish-gray or blackish-gray, lighter in the ventral region. The mouth, anal region, and end of the tail are cream colored. However, local varieties have lighter colors in some regions.

They can be distinguished from the other very similar species of worm snakes in that the dividing line or suture of the nasal shield touches the preocular shield instead of the second labial shield.

A feature of this species, shared with all worm snakes native to Australasia, is that the males have just one penis.

HABITAT

They live under the earth's surface and are often found under fallen tree trunks, rocks, or vegetation roots, sandy floors, or in the forest's humus.

This snake can sometimes be found moving around on the surface on humid nights or groveling from torrential downpours.

Normally it lives alone although sometimes it can be found in small colonies in places that are especially favorable (under rotten tree trunks for example).

It lives in gardens and often settles in plant stumps that are to be exported; they are widespread thanks to human commerce. This species is so widespread that it is considered to be the snake with the largest distribution area, along with the Elapidae yellow-bellied sea snake *Pelamis platurus*.

BEHAVIOR

• Lives on ants and termites.
• When surprised on the surface it tries to quickly escape under fallen leaves.
• If handled, it tries to use its thin caudal spine, wriggling without stopping in all directions. At the same time it excretes a smelly liquid in its defense.

REPRODUCTION

It is oviparous and lays from two to six minute-sized eggs (.1 to .2 inches), the size of cooked grains of rice.

This species is thought to be able to reproduce parthenogenetically; that is, the females can create new populations by themselves. If this were true, this characteristic would make the colonizing of new territories much easier.

STATUS

It is not internationally protected and appears to have an abundant population.

In India it is commonly called *Sev pamboo*; this name refers to the belief that these snakes enter inside the ears of people who sleep on the floor

DISTRIBUTION

Native of southeast Asia and Australia. Introduced into sub-Saharan Africa, Iran, Arabia, Madagascar, Central America, Hawaii islands, Florida, and points in the United States.

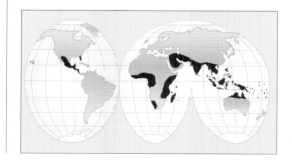

(Bianconi, 1847)

 Schlegel´s Blind Snake

RHINOTYPHLOPS SCHLEGELII
SUBFAMILY TYPHLOPINAE

Phinotyphlops schlegelii
(Schlegel´s Blind Snake).
Adult specimen.

DESCRIPTION

Considered to be one of the biggest Typhlopidae; it reaches 37 inches.

It has 30 to 44 rows of scales around its body.

The number of dorsal scales is very variable, depending on the subspecies, and can exceed 623.

Its snout is rounded off along edges, forming an obtuse angle and a small subterminal mouth.

The snake's coloration is quite variable; in the uniform phase, it varies from brown to black with a yellow stomach; in the blotched phase, it has an irregular series of brown and black blotches on its back, and yellowish-white blotches on its stomach and flanks. There may also be a third stage in which each scale has a black border that forms dark lines when they join during growth.

HABITAT

These snakes are found in termite nests, in humus, or under fallen tree trunks or large rocks. They live in scrubland and grassland regions with a sandy, not very dense floor.

BEHAVIOR

• The numerous specimens are rarely seen because they are almost always underground.

• They can be found on the surface during the rainy season, often groveling in the streets.

• They eat insects, particularly termites and their larvae.

REPRODUCTION

The females lay 12 to 40 eggs, with an already well-developed embryo at the end of spring.

The young are born in five or six weeks.

STATUS

Not endangered.

DISTRIBUTION

From Sudan to northern Angola, South Africa, Zimbabwe, and Mozambique.

■ Four subspecies are identified:

- *R. s. schlegelii:* 36 to 44 rows of scales, in South Africa, Botswana, and Mozambique. They turn up in the uniform and blotched phases.

- *R. s. brevis:* In northeast Africa.

- *R. s. mucruso:* Has 30 to 36 rows of scales. Lives in Kenya, Tanzania, Zimbabwe, Angola, Mozambique, Botswana, and Namibia. Found in blotched and striped phases.

- *R. s. petersii:* Has 34 to 40 rows of scales. Found in Namibia, Angola, and Botswana, only in the blotched phase.

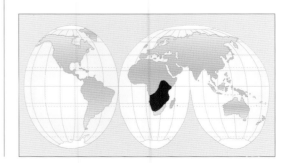

TYPHLOPS VERMICULARIS

SUBFAMILY **TYPHLOPINAE**

📄 Merren, 1820

📄 Eurasian Worm Snake

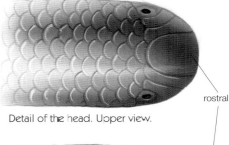

Detail of the head. Upper view.

rostral

Detail of the head. Side view

rostral

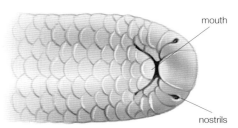

mouth

nostrils

Detail of the head. Ventral view

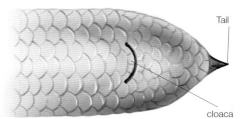

Tail

cloaca

Rear end. Ventral view

Typhlops vermicularis (Eurasian Worm Snake). Adult specimen.

DESCRIPTION

This small snake, whose length oscillates between seven and 12 inches, looks like an earthworm with a slender subcylindrical body, wider closer to the tail.

The rounded head is hardly differentiated from the rest of the body. The eyes are located on the upper part of the head and because they are covered with scales, they look like two minute black points. The mouth is very small and can hardly widen to wolf down the prey.

All the scales are small, round, and smooth, and unlike the majority of snakes, the dorsal and ventral scales are not differentiated. The tail is very short, wide, and has a scale with a spine at its tip.

Generally, the upper parts are brownish-gray, yellowish, gray, pink, purple, and the scales' border darkens towards its caudal part. The stomach is lighter and reveals the internal organs, eggs, and food remains.

HABITAT

Usually found under rocks semi-buried in terrain with herbaceous vegetation as well as along the periphery of fields of cultivation such as vineyards and rice fields, in forest clearings, and areas with scattered trees. They also live in dry areas close to rivers and lakes and even in deltas close to the ocean.

This snake is often found on the surface of recently plowed terrain.

It is a terrestrial and burrowing species that lives in dens similar to that of the earthworm. It is rarely on the surface, and if so, at night or twilight.

An exposure to 10 minutes of sunlight could be fatal to it.

BEHAVIOR

• It lives on small invertebrates, mainly ants and their larvae, termites, spiders, Collembola, myriapods, and other small invertebrates that live on the floor.

• The spine at the tip of the tail acts to help with locomotion; the snake uses its tail like a lever against the ground. It hibernates for two to six months depending on the elevation of its habitat.

• Some authors attribute it with a temporo-mandibular venom gland, although it is naturally a totally inoffensive snake due to its temperament and the very small dimensions of its mouth.

REPRODUCTION

Coupling takes place in the open air in June, normally at night or twilight.

Before coupling, the female attaches herself to the terrain with her caudal spine, then the male coils his body around the female and enters her cloaca.

Between four and six fairly large long eggs with flattened ends are deposited between July and August in subterranean chambers.

The babies measure from 12 to 34 inches.

STATUS

The European laws of animal protection protect this snake.

In many points in its distribution area it is considered to be a venomous species and it is believed that its venom, inoculated by its tail, may be fatal. Therefore, because it is considered harmful, it is killed. It is a so attributed with therapeutic abilities.

DISTRIBUTION

The Balkan Area, Greece, Bulgaria, some Greek islands, Turkey, the Caucasus area, Afganistan, Iran, Iraq, Lebanon, Syria, Israel, Jordan, and northern Egypt.

DESCRIPTION

Can measure up to 169 inches.

The back is black or blackish and the stomach has a uniform black or more diluted gray coloration.

It has 24 to 26 costal rows of scales, rarely 22 or 28.

HABITAT

It lives in the subsoil and is rarely observed on the surface; it is occasionally carried to the surface by strong currents of water after torrential downpours.

BEHAVIOR

• When handled it gives frequent blows in all directions with its tail, trying to administer a blow with its caudal spine.

REPRODUCTION

It is considered a ovoviviparous species and the clutches vary from four to 14.

Females are found pregnant from May to June.

The babies measure between 3.8 to 3.9 inches and are born in September. They reach sexual maturity when they are two years old and already 9 inches long.

STATUS

It is a common species.

 Schlegel, 1839

 Diard's Worm Snake

TYPHLOPS DIARDI

SUBFAMILY **TYPHLOPINAE**

Typhlops diardi (Diard's Worm Snake). Adult specimen. Detail of the head.

DISTRIBUTION

■ Two subspecies have been cited:

- *T. d. diardi:* India (states of Bengal and Assam), Burma, and China.

- *T. d. muelleri:* Indochina, Malay Peninsula, Sumatra, and Borneo.

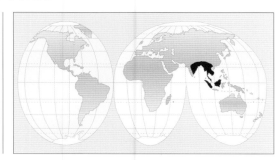

DESCRIPTION

This is a vermiform snake that can reach approximately ten inches.

It is characterized by having one tooth on the lower mandible.

All the body's scales, apart from the cephalic ones, which are the largest, are the same size and are arranged in 22 to 24 rows of scales. The rostral scale is very large; it reaches eye level and is in contact with the frontal scale.

The body is a dark brownish-gray, and the scales' apexes are slightly lighter.

The tail is darker and uniform, while the head is a yellowish-pink.

HABITAT

This is a burrowing snake found on the floor of tropical humid forests.

REPRODUCTION

An oviparous species.

STATUS

The state of its population is unknown.

(Peters, 1860)

Pink-Headed Blind Snake

LIOTYPHLOPS ALBIROSTRIS

SUBFAMILY **ANOMALEPINAE**

DISTRIBUTION

From Costa Rica to Brazil and Paraguay.

Typhlops albirostris (Pink-Headed Blind Snake). Adult specimen.

F. Leptotyphlopidae

+ THAN 80 SPECIES

The Leptotyphlopidae are small (between 4 and 20 inches long) subterranean snakes that are quite similar to the Typhlopidae as a result of adaptive convergence. Although they have different origins, they live in a very similar way.

They are cylindrical, the head is slightly differentiated from the body, and very thin; some species are only .1 inch thick. They have a uniform pinkish, brownish-gray, or creamy coloration, although some species have longitudinal yellow, brownish-gray, or brownish bands. Due to their worm-like appearance, they have been given the name worm snake, just like the Typhlopidae.

They have such primitive characteristics that they seem to fall in between saurians and ophidians. In fact, some authors even consider them apodous lizards and not real snakes.

They live in very varied habitats, from deserts and semi-arid areas to forests and jungles, and their area of distribution covers a good part of America, Africa, Asia, up to the extreme west of India.

Although they spend the majority of their time underground, they tend to come to the surface at night, on rainy days, or on very humid days, and have even been seen climbing trees and bushes.

They are oviparous, laying few but considerable sized eggs in proportion to the adult size. They are totally harmless and mainly live on ants, termites, and their larvae.

■ The family includes only two genera and more than 80 species:

- *Leptotyphlops*: between 80 and 100 species according to different authors (America, Africa, and Asia).

- *Rhinoleptus*: 1 species (Africa).

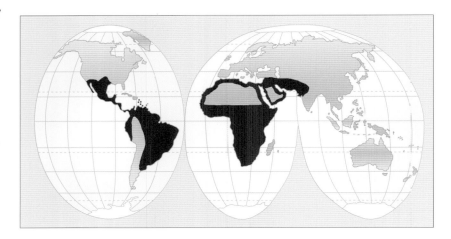

Leptotyphlops humilis (Thread Snake). Adult specimen.

GENERAL CHARACTERISTICS

LEPTOTYPHLOPS MACRORHYNCHUS
Detail of the head.

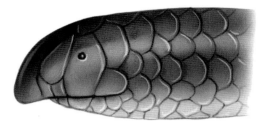

Side view.

Dorsal view.

- The scales on the body are cycloid, overlapping, and the same size in the dorsal and ventral areas. They have a ring-like appearance that makes them look like a worm.
- They have atrophied eyes covered by large irregularly shaped transparent scales.
- The head is covered with large scales, and the rostral scales are the largest; they sometimes even project forwards, covering the mouth.
- The head is hardly differentiated from its body; there is no constriction that could be considered a neck.
- Just like the Typhlopidae, they have just one pair of thymus glands instead of two pairs like the other snakes.
- Reduction, and in some species, complete absence of the left lung.
- Lobular liver.
- Unlike the Typhlopidae, the tail that ends in a conical shape is always longer than it is wide.

LEPTOTYPHLOPS NARIROSTRIS
Detail of the head.

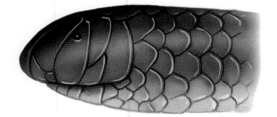

Side view.

Dorsal view.

LEPTOTYPHLOPS
Cranium. Dorsal view.

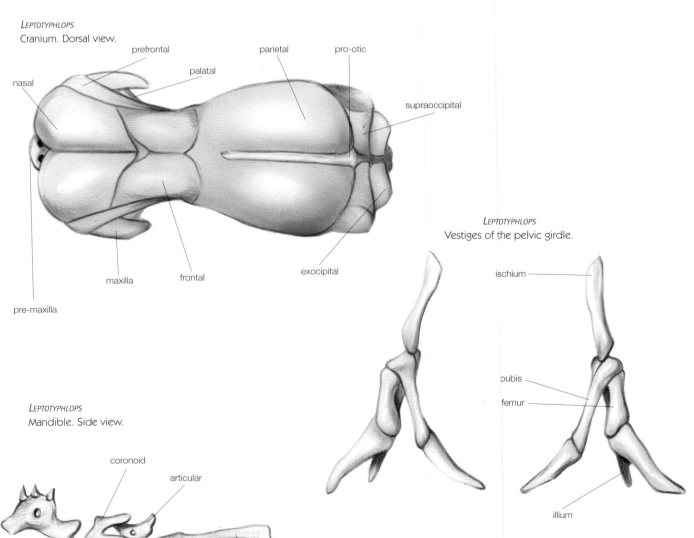

prefrontal
palatal
parietal
pro-otic
nasal
supraoccipital
exocipital
maxilla
frontal
pre-maxilla

- The cranial bones are joined, forming a solid structure, adapted to its subterranean life.
- The maxilla, found securely joined to the cranial cavity, is immobile.
- There is intramandibular articulation.
- The coronoid bone is present in the mandible.
- Reduced dentition: the maxilla lacks teeth and the mandible has only a few small ones.
- Retains vestiges of the pelvic girdle and in some species, even vestiges of femurs, visible on the exterior in the form of small spurs located on both sides of the cloaca.
- The vertebrae are short and compact.

LEPTOTYPHLOPS
Vestiges of the pelvic girdle.

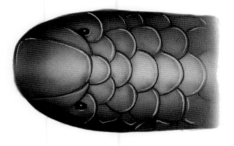

ischium
pubis
femur
illium

LEPTOTYPHLOPS
Mandible. Side view.

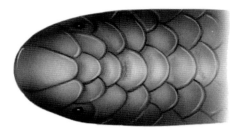

coronoid
articular
quadrate

LEPTOTYPHLOPS DULCIS

FAMILY LEPTOTYPHLOPIDAE

 (Baird and Girard, 1853)

 Texas Blind Snake

Leptotyphlops dulcis
(Texas Blind Snake).
Adult specimen.

DESCRIPTION

It is a small, thin, and cylindrical snake between five and 11 inches long. It is a brownish, reddish, or pinkish color and the head and tail have rounded tips.

There is a small spine at the end of the tail.

There is more than 1 scale on the head between the large scales that cover each eye, and 14 rows of scales around the body, with no elongated ventral scales.

HABITAT

Semi-arid deserts, grasslands, and mountainsides with soft or sandy floors, that facilitate digging, from sea-level to 4,921 feet.

BEHAVIOR

• Burrowing and nocturnal tendencies, this snake only moves on the surface when it gets dark on especially rainy days.

• They are frequently found on humid floors below rocks or fallen tree trunks. Mainly lives on ants, termites, and their larvae.

• In the presence of danger its defense system consists of coiling itself, twisting itself, and, at the same time, emitting its cloacal fluids.

In some zones of its distribution area, it is easy to find among the remains of prey, excrement, and bezoar that accumulate in the nests of the burrowing little owl; this is where they eat the larvae and the chrysalises of parasitic insects of these curious nocturnal predatory little owls with terrestrial habits that nest in subterranean burrows.

REPRODUCTION

Two to seven elongated .6 inch long eggs are laid and deposited on the floor, under rocks or rotten tree trunks, during the months of June and July.

At birth the babies are up to three inches long.

STATUS

Their population is not very well known, although they do not appear to be endangered.

DISTRIBUTION

From the southern area of the United States to central and southern Mexico.

■ Three subspecies are known:

- *L. d. dulcis:* From southern Oklahoma and the center of Texas to the northern Tamaulipas and central Nuevo Leon, Mexico.

- *L. d. dissectus:* From southern Kansas and northern Oklahoma, Texas, New Mexico, and Arizona, to the north of Chihuahua, Mexico.

- *L. d. myopicus:* From central Nuevo Leon to northern Puebla and Veracruz, Mexico.

The species with the most northern distribution of the entire family.

(Baird and Girard, 1853)

 Western Blind Snake

LEPTOTYPHLOPS HUMILIS
FAMILY **LEPTOTYPHLOPIDAE**

Leptotyphlops humilis
(Western Blind Snake). Young specimen.

Leptotyphlops humilis
(Western Blind Snake). Adult specimen.

DESCRIPTION

Small subterranean snake between seven and 16 inches long.

Brownish or pinkish color with a small spine at the tip of its tail.

It only has one scale at the tip of its head, between the large scales that cover each eye, and 14 rows of scales around its body. No elongated ventral scales are present.

HABITAT

Deserts, grasslands, scrublands, and rocky hillsides with sandy floors from sea-level to 4,921 feet.

BEHAVIOR

• Burrowing and subterranean habits, always found in soft terrain.

• When it gets dark on warm and humid nights, they come to the surface in search of the termites and ants they live on; the snakes find them by following their smelly trails. When they devour them, the snakes only suck out the soft contents of their insides.

REPRODUCTION

Two to six elongated and narrow eggs are laid (six inches long) and deposited in the soft ground between the roots or bushes, or under rocks or fallen trees during the months of June, July, and August.

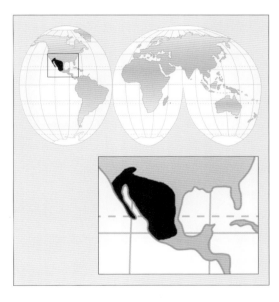

STATUS

Due to their discreet and hidden way of life, this species is not very well known and the current state of its population is also unknown. It does not seem to be endangered, and in some areas is frequently prey to chickens, ducks, and other domestic birds that move freely around farms.

DISTRIBUTION

Southern area of the United States and northeast Mexico.

■ Nine different subspecies have been described:

- *L. h. boettgeri*: Baja California, Mexico.

- *L. h. cahuilae*: Southern California and Arizona (USA) to the center of the Baja California Peninsula, Mexico.

- *L. h. dugesi*: Sonora, Sinaloa, Jalisco, and Colima, Mexico.

- *L. h. humilis:* Southern California, Nevada, and Arizona to the center of the Baja California peninsula, Mexico.

- *L. h. levitoni*: Santa Catalina Island, in the Gulf of California.

- *L. h. lindsayi*: Carmen Island, Gulf of California.

- *L. h. segregus*: Texas, New Mexico, and Arizona to Coahuila, Chihuahua, and Durango, Mexico.

- *L. h. tenuiculus*: San Luis Potosi and Tamaulipas, Mexico.

- *L. h. utahensis*: Southern Utah, Nevada, and the United States.

F. Aniliidae

1 SPECIES

The Aniliidae are primitive snakes with subterranean tendencies and very small but functional eyes covered by a large scale or ocular shield.

Their burrowing capacity is not as developed as in the Typhlopidae and Leptotyphlopidae, and they live only in the soft floor of the jungle -often under wood remains or vegetation. The head is not very differentiated from the body, the tail is short, and the body is almost completely cylindrical and stout. This is why it is called a cylindrical or pipe snake, although its rear area is somewhat dorsiventrally flattened.

■ The family is made up by just one species:

- *Anilius scytale*, lives in the forests and tropical forests of northern South America.

GENERAL CHARACTERISTICS

ANILIUS SCYTALE
(Coral Pipe Snake).
Detail of the head.

Dorsal view.

Side view.

• Small eyes, round pupil, covered with a non-specialized ocular scale.

• Solid cranium (adapted for burrowing) with small teeth in the maxilla, mandible, and palate.

• Small scales on the head, except for the two between the ocular scales.

• Head slightly differentiated from body, with a short tail, and a cylindrical body.

• No marked groove on the chin, unlike the Cylindrophiinae, a subfamily of Uropeltidae that is very similar anatomically.

• There are a few spurs around the cloaca and vestiges of a pelvic girdle, which demonstrates the snake's primitive nature.

• The maxillary bones are barely movable.

• Only the right lung is present.

• Ventral scales are slightly larger than dorsal scales.

• Coronoid bone is present.

Anilius scytale (Coral Pipe Snake). Adult specimen.

 (Linnaeus, 1758)

 Coral Pipe Snake

ANILIUS SCYTALE

FAMILY ANILIIDAE

Anilius scytale
(Coral Pipe Snake).
Adult specimen.

DESCRIPTION

The Coral Pipe Snake is cylindrical with little differentiation between the two conical ends of the body; this is why it is also known by the name of 'two-headed snake' in some places in its area of distribution. It reaches a length of up to two inches.

The coloration of the body is very bright and colorful: bright coral red, with a series of black incomplete rings on the lighter toned ventral part.

In certain populations individual snakes are found with black-bordered red scales, making it appear spotted.

HABITAT

Lives buried in soft floors and in the humus of rainforests and tropical rainforests, both in wet and in slightly dryer ones, almost never far from water.

BEHAVIOR

• With nocturnal and burrowing tendencies, they stay buried during the day under the humid floor of the jungle.
• At night they leave to hunt the prey their prey, almost always small vertebrates like fish,

Amphisbaenia, lizards, and often, small snakes.
• The spectacular coloration of this ophidian represents a typical harmless animal that imitates the appearance of a dangerous species; in this case, the design of the colored rings of the tube snake clearly looks like that of the extremely toxic coral snakes of the *Micrurus* genus. This is why this snake is called the Coral Pipe Snake.
• When it senses danger, it adopts a defensive posture that consists of hiding its head beneath its body and raising the tip of its tail–this even further disconcerts its possible predators.
• In reality, this snake is a totally harmless and a very docile species that, in certain regions, members of some tribes use to adorn themselves; they wear the snake around their neck like a beaded necklace.

REPRODUCTION

Ovoviviparous reproduction.
The females can lay up to 20 live babies, although normally between eight and 15.

STATUS

Unknown.

DISTRIBUTION

Basins in Orinoco and the Amazon up to the high plateau of Mato Grosso.

■ Two different subspecies are known:

- *A. s. scytale*: Southern Venezuela, Amazonian regions of Peru, Ecuador, and Colombia, the Guianas, and northern Brazil.

- *A. s. phelpsorum*: Only located in southeastern Venezuela.

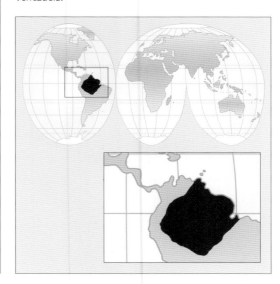

F. Uropeltidae

54 SPECIES

Subterranean burrowing snakes that live in humid and mountainous areas in Asia.

Sometimes they are put together with the Aniliidae in just one family; other authors place the subfamily Cylindrophiinae with the Aniliidae, but recent serological work performed on *Anylius* and *Cylindrophic* show that the latter are closer to the Uropeltidae. They live in humid muddy fields and eat frogs, worms, eels, and small snakes.

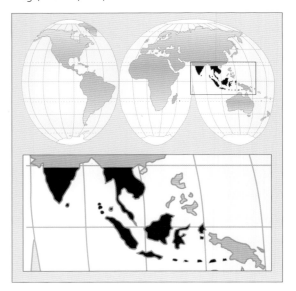

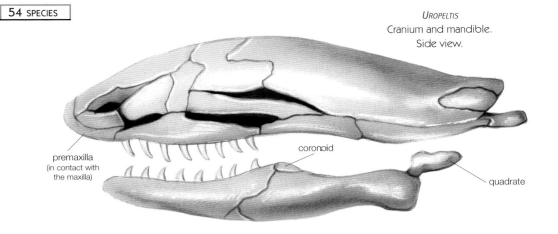

UROPELTIS
Cranium and mandible.
Side view.

premaxilla
(in contact with
the maxilla)

coronoid

quadrate

• The main difference to the Aniliidae is that the Cylindrophiidae have a specialized scale that covers the eyes.

• The scales are flat and slightly larger on the ventral part of the body than the dorsal part.

• The body is short and cylindrical, and the head is indistinguishable from the neck. The tail is very short and ends in an obtuse form, sometimes with a shield.

• The mouth is small and the teeth are numerous and present on both the maxilla and the mandible.

• The upper maxillary bone is joined with the cranial cavity.

• A vestige of three pelvis bones may or may not be present.

• They are ovoviviparous and can give birth to up to 15 already totally formed babies.

• The Family *Uropeltidae* is distributed in India, Sri Lanka, Indonesia, Malaysia, and Southeast Asia.

Cylindrophis rufus (Pipe Snake). Adult specimen.

SUBFAMILY **CYLINDROPHINAE**

Pipe Snake

Cylindrophis rufus
Adult specimen in its habitat.

2 GENERA / 10 SPECIES

• They are small snakes from 20 to 35 inches, predominantly dark colored: brownish or blackish-grays, and the ventral part is brighter and more colorful, made up of white and black stripes.

• There are no teeth on the premaxillary bones and it can move its mandibles like more evolved snakes.

• Its cylindrical body and head, slightly differentiated from the rest of the body, have a somewhat arrow form and are covered with small shields.

• Vestiges of the pelvic girdle and a few small spurs project from each side of the cloaca, similar to the Boidae.

• The right lung is the only working one, and the left lung has disappeared.

• The tail is short and when frightened, it flattens its body, lifts it, and coils itself up, showing the red or orange lower part.

• The scales on the body are wide and smooth, all similar apart from one enlarged ventral row.

• The eyes are small but functional and have an elliptical pupil.

■ There are 10 species that pertain to 2 genera:

- *Anomochilus*: 2 species distributed in Malaysia and Indonesia.

- *Cylindrophis*: 8 species in Sri Lanka, India, Southeast Asia, and the Indo-Australian archipelago.

Local populations call them "two-headed snakes" due to the difficulty in distinguishing between the two end parts of the body.

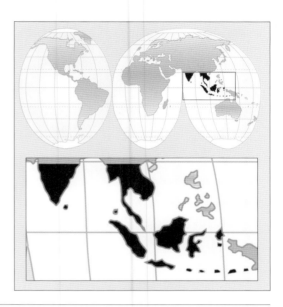

SUBFAMILY **UROPELTINAE**

Phillips's Shield Tail Snake

Uropeltis phillipsi
Adult specimen in its habitat.

8 GENERA / 44 SPECIES

• These snakes have a shield-tail. They are a small size, from .08 to .3 of an inch.

• They have a small head that is not differentiated from the neck, while the tail is short with enlarged terminal scales forming an oval rough spiny shield.

• The snout is pointed and the eyes are very small with a round pupil.

• The cranial bones, just like other primitive snakes, remain joined together.

• The girdles have completely disappeared, and the left lung, although very reduced, is present.

• The maxilla has 6 to 8 teeth, the mandible from 8 to 10, and the palate sometimes from 3 to 4. The teeth are small and uniform.

• It constantly burrows tunnels with its snout, turning it with the neck's powerful musculature and the support that the thick tail provides.

• In spite of its burrowing tendencies, this snake has vivid colors with red and orangish tones, and when they are black, they have a lot of iridescent reflections.

■ Distribution restricted to the southeastern part of the Indian peninsula and Sri Lanka, in mountainous rainforest zones from sea level to 8,202 feet.

- *Brachyophidium*: only one species in southern India.
- *Melanophidium*: 3 species in mountainous zones in southern India.
- *Platyplectrurus*: 2 species in southern India and Sri Lanka.
- *Plecturus*: 4 species in southern India.
- *Pseudotyphlops*: only 1 species in Sri Lanka.
- *Rhinophis*: 10 species in southern India and Sri Lanka.
- *Teretrurus*: only 1 species in southern India.
- *Uropeltis*: close to 22 species in southern India and Sri Lanka.

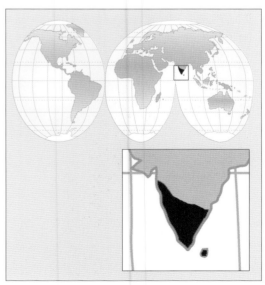

CYLINDROPHIS RUFUS

SUBFAMILY **CYLINDROPHINAE**

 (Laurenti, 1768)

 Pipe Snake

Cylindrophis rufus
Detail of the head.

Cylindrophis rufus
(Pipe Snake).
Defensive behavior.

DESCRIPTION

It has a cylindrical body covered with small, smooth, bright scales. The head, with small eyes, is not differentiated from the body. The tail is short and truncated, similar in form to the head; in fact, it is difficult to distinguish one from the other.

Its length varies from 28 to 35 inches.

The color of the back is a bluish black, iridescent and uniform or with light or orangish transversal bands. The ventral face is white with wide dark transversal bands.

The lower part of the tail is a very vivid red.

HABITAT

Found in soft and moist terrain, rice fields, riverbanks, and open ground in the rainforest.

They hide in holes at the foot of trees or under fallen trees.

It is a good burrower and digs long tunnels of a certain depth.

Sometimes this snake can be found on the surface at night after a strong tropical rain.

BEHAVIOR

• When an aggressor disturbs it, it flattens its body, hides its head, and lifts and folds its tail, imitating the attack of a dangerous snake. At the same time, it shows the strong ventral coloration at the end of its tail. This behavior has two facets: on one hand, it distracts the aggressor from other more vulnerable parts of the body, and on the other, it wants to impress the aggressor with an allegedly aggressive appearance. It mainly lives on small ophidians of the *Typhlops* genus, but also on worms, insects, baby rodents, and fish.

REPRODUCTION

This species is ovoviviparous.

The babies, from two to ten, are born during the rainy season and measure close to eight inches.

STATUS

They are not included on the list of endangered animals and their population is not thought to be in danger.

DISTRIBUTION

Southern China, Burma, Vietnam, Thailand, Cambodia, Malaysia, and Indonesia (Java, Sumatra, Komodo, Borneo, Celebes, etc.).

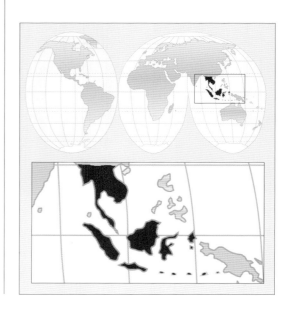

CYLINDROPHIS MACULATUS. Detail of the head.

Upper view.

Side view.

📄 (Linnaeus,1758)

📄 Ceylanese Pipe Snake

CYLINDROPHIS MACULATUS

SUBFAMILY **CYLINDROPHINAE**

Cylindrophis maculatus (Ceylanese Pipe Snake). Adult specimen. Defensive posture.

DESCRIPTION

The snake's body is cylindrical and the head is the same width as the rest of the body. The eyes are small, with elliptical pupils, and open between two scales.

The short tail ends in an obtuse form.

This snake's shape makes it difficult to distinguish the head from the tail.

Although the most common size is six inches, there are specimens that are more than 24 inches long.

The dorsal part is made up of two longitudinal rows of large brownish reddish-gray blotches that are basically regular; the borders of these blotches are black, acting as a background color.

The ventral part is of great contrast; it is made up of bright borders that alternate between white and black.

HABITAT

They live in the rainforest and in humid areas, mainly on the side of the mountains where, during the day they hide under tree trunks, rocks, vegetation, or humus, where they can bury themselves up to a depth of three feet.

They are also found in rice fields and other cultivated land.

BEHAVIOR

• It has nocturnal habits and lives on other terrestrial snakes.

• When bothered it deploys notable behavior that is bright and colorful; it inflates and flattens its body, tries to hide its head among the coils and raise the back part of the body with its folded tail, showing the ventral part of its body that is more colorful and bright.

• The snake acts this way to try to distance a possible enemy from the head, the most vulnerable part of the snake's body, as well as to frighten and disorient its enemy with its display.

• It is normally harmless, although it may sometimes try to bite.

REPRODUCTION

It is ovoviviparous and gives birth to from one to 15 completely formed babies.

STATUS

It is a common species in the humid zones of the island and in its vicinity.

DISTRIBUTION

It is a species endemic to the island of Sri Lanka.

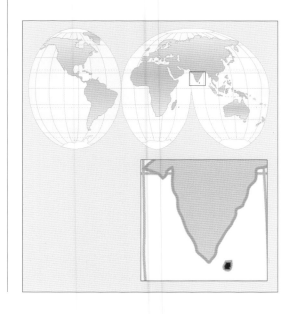

UROPELTIS OCELLATUS

SUBFAMILY **UROPELTINAE**

📄 (Beddome, 1863)

📄 Ocellate Shield-Tail Snake

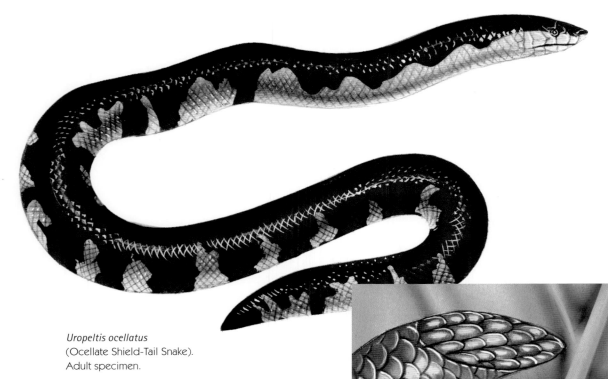

Rhinophis. Detail of the tail.

Cylindrophis. Detail of the tail.

Uropeltis ocellatus
(Ocellate Shield-Tail Snake).
Adult specimen.

Uropeltis. Detail of the tail.

DESCRIPTION

It measures 17 feet and has a compact
constitution.

The females are longer, although their tail is relatively
shorter. The head is thinner than the rest of the body
and pointed at the tip, whereas the neck is indistinguishable from the body. It has small eyes contained in
ocular shields. The tail is short and truncated, characteristically ending in a rough shield with two terminal
spines. It has 17 rows of costal scales and the number
of ventral scales varies between 185 and 234.

The coloration can vary greatly according to its
geographic origin. There is almost no differentiation
between dorsal and ventral scales. The scales are
brownish, olive-greenish, gray, or olive-green on the
borders and lighter in the center. There are large
numbers of irregular bright yellow spots, distributed
along the entire body, that sometimes join, forming
small chains. The stomach is yellow; this extends along
the flanks in borders that alternate with the darker
color of its back.

HABITAT

It lives in moist, not very compact floors of dense
forests in the hills of Nilgiri and Anamalai, in southern
Goa, in southeastern India, between 1,968 and 3,280
feet.

BEHAVIOR

• This snake lives under rocks and tree trunks in the
forest.
• It buries itself with its snout when it senses danger.
• It almost exclusively eats earthworms.
• It is a completely harmless species with a calm
temperament.
• It is thought to use its shield-tail to block the
demand as an aid for digging and defense.
• Actually, when it is bothered, it coils up, hides its
head, and only shows its tail.

REPRODUCTION

It is ovoviviparous.
It gives birth to clutches of three to five babies.
The babies are born at the end of July between four
and five inches long and grow two to three inches
during the first year.

STATUS

This snake does not appear to be endangered and
seems abundant in its area of distribution; more than
100 specimens were found in just one day in Nilgiri.

DISTRIBUTION

Southeastern India, southern Goa, in the Western
Ghats, Nilgiri and Annamalai Hills.

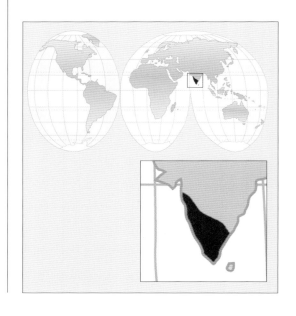

DESCRIPTION

Measures close to ten inches.

The head is pointed and the tail looks very similar on its upper part; this is why it's difficult to differentiate the head and tail at first glance.

Its body is brownish-gray with yellow borders that don't close to form rings, it may also have yellow dots irregularly distributed on the flanks.

HABITAT

Lives on the forest floor, in ground that is not very dense.

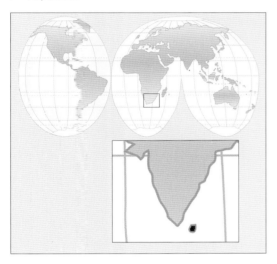

 (Nicholls, 1929)

 Phillips's Shield-Tail Snake

UROPELTIS PHILLIPSI

SUBFAMILY UROPELTINAE

Specimen of *Uropeltis phillipsi*. Its general appearance has a morphology distinct from that of the classic snake; the head is confused with the tail and vice versa.

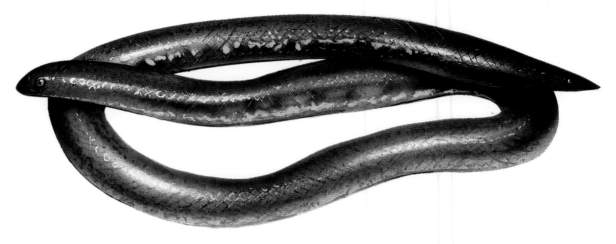

BEHAVIOR

• It is an active burrower that digs tunnels in the forest's loose ground. It is completely harmless and does not try to bite. When handled it tends to defecate, expelling a bad odor as a means of defense. It eats earthworms.

STATUS

It is not common in its area of distribution.

DISTRIBUTION

It is a species endemic to Sri Lanka.

DESCRIPTION

Reaches 12 inches in length.

The pointed snout is projected forwards, and the tail is cylindrical and ends abruptly in a large flat scale with small tubercules, and no terminal spines.

It is a grayish-blue with lighter bands along the flanks. The tail also has a lighter coloration.

HABITAT

It lives in floors that are not dense, in rice fields and in pastures, usually close to sources of water.

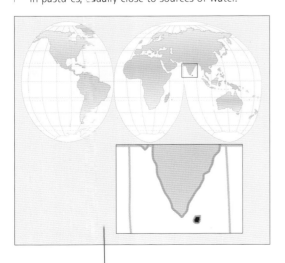

 (Kelaart, 1853)

Trevelyan's Earth Snake

RHINOPHIS TREVELYANUS

SUBFAMILY UROPELTINAE

BEHAVIOR

• It has nocturnal and burrowing tendencies and tends to form small colonies of three to eight individuals. It is harmless and does not try to bite unless handled. When trapped it tends to defecate and expel a foul-smelling liquid. It mainly eats earthworms.

REPRODUCTION

It is ovoviviparous.

STATUS

It is common in its area of distribution.

DISTRIBUTION

Endemic to the island of Sri Lanka.

Rhinophis trevelyanus
(Trevelyan's Earth Snake).
Adult specimen.

F. Xenopeltidae

The Xenopeltidae are snakes with only semi-burrowing tendencies, given that they bury themselves relatively easily, but they move much more often on the floor where they appear agile and fairly quick.

They have primitive features similar to those of the Aniliidae, but also to others who are closer to more modern snakes like the Colubridae. Anatomically, they are also closely related to the Loxocemidae. They are blackish, chestnut, or purplish brownish-gray on the back; the ventral part is lighter. They are known as iridescent snakes, rainbow snakes, or sunbeam snakes due to their iridescent scales (that vary in color according to the light's incidence).

■ It is generally thought that the family is formed by just one species:

- *Xenopeltis unicolor*: Asian distribution, although some authors recognize the existence of a second species, *Xenopeltis hainanensis* (Hu and Djao, 1975), that may be found on the island of Hainan and the provinces of Zhejiang, Guangxi, in southern China.

• Flat head covered with large scales, slightly differentiated from the body.
• Numerous cramped teeth.
• Unlike the Aniliidae, this snake's body is not uniformly cylindrical in its length.
• The tail is short and is a tenth of the total length of the body.
• Wide smooth slightly overlapping dorsal scales.
• Elongated very wide ventral scales in the shape of plates.

• No vestiges of pelvic girdle or spurs.
• Coronoid bone absent.
• Front part of the maxilla has a muscular ligament that allows for certain dilation.
• Presence of left lung that measures about half of the right lung.
• Small eyes with elliptical vertical pupils.
• The maxilla and the mandible have a limited grade of independence.
• Serrated premaxilla and maxilla are in contact.

Xenopeltis unicolor (Sunbeam Snake). Adult specimen.

Dorsal view.

XENOPELTIS UNICOLOR
(Sunbeam Snake).
Detail of the head.

Side view.

XENOPELTIS UNICOLOR
(Sunbeam Snake).
Cranium.

premaxilla

maxilla

Dorsal view.

Reinwardt, 1827

 Sunbeam Snake

XENOPELTIS UNICOLOR

FAMILY **XENOPELTIDAE**

Xenopeltis unicolor
(Sunbeam Snake).
Adult specimen.

DESCRIPTION

Slim snake with flattened head, up to four feet long.

Characterized by its brownish-gray, brownish, or even blackish coloration, but with iridescent metallic tonalities that are very bright and colorful when exposed to daylight.

The ventral area, on the other hand, is a whitish or light grayish color.

HABITAT

Always lives close to water in forests, jungles, and other wooded areas in the fluvial valleys of southeast Asia. They tend to be found in deltas, marshes, and rice fields from the lowlands up to an elevation of 4,265 feet.

BEHAVIOR

• Nocturnal and fairly subterranean; they move easily and frequently on the forest floor where they are usually located under rocks or among other remains of vegetation. They hunt right on the surface and among the fallen leaves, and live on all types of small vertebrates: amphibians, small mammals, birds, lizards, and even other snakes.

• They are completely harmless and if hunted they defend themselves with fast movements and bites, and can even make the tip of their tail vibrate.

REPRODUCTION

It is an oviparous species.

It can lay up to 20 eggs (normally between six and 17), from which small snakes hatch with the same coloration as the adults, but with a white collar around the neck.

STATUS

A species that still appears to be fairly common and abundant in a good part of southeast Asia.

DISTRIBUTION

Indonesia, Malaysia, Singapore, Andaman Islands, Burma, Thailand, Cambodia, Laos, Vietnam, southern China (provinces of Guangdong and Yunnan), and the Philippine Islands.

■ There are no subspecies.

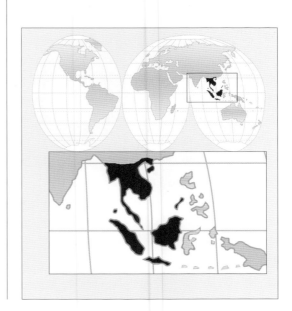

Xenopeltis unicolor
(Sunbeam Snake).
Adult specimen. Detail of the head.

F. Loxocemidae

1 SPECIES

The Loxocemidae snakes have cylindrical bodies, smooth scales, and a wedge-shaped head. These characteristics reveal their burrowing and subterranean tendencies. The coloration is markedly bicolor, with a dark back and a much lighter ventral part.

In spite of the common name they are known by, American Burrowing Pythons, it is likely that they are not authentic pythons, but rather snakes with primitive characteristics (which the existence of vestiges of the pelvic girdle demonstrate), very close to the family Xenopeltidae. In fact, their classification is very controversial; they have also been classified in the family Aniliidae, in the subfamily Pythoninae and Erycinae (within the Family of the Boidae, although anatomically more like the genus *Calabaria* than the genus *Eryx*), and in a subfamily within the Boidae.

■ The family is formed by just one species:

- *Loxocemus bicolor*: inhabits the forests of Central America.

rostral

LOXOCEMUS BICOLOR
(Mexican Burrowing Python).
Detail of the head.

Distribution of scales in the center of the body.

Loxocemus bicolor (Mexican Burrowing Python). Ejemplar adulto.

GENERAL CHARACTERISTICS

- Cylindrical body, lightly compressed laterally.
- Short nonprehensile tail.
- Head slightly differentiated from body.
- Small eyes with elliptical pupils.
- Head scales relatively large, with a very developed rostral, prominent and projected upwards.
- Nasal and anal scales divided.
- Two intranasal scales and two prefrontal scales.
- Body scales smooth, slightly larger than the ventral part.
- From 31 to 35 rows of scales on the middle of the body, and from 23 to 26 rows at the height of the cloaca.
- Large supralabial scales without pits.
- Coronoid bone present on mandible.
- Independent maxilla and premaxilla.
- Left lung reduced.
- Vestiges of pelvic girdle.

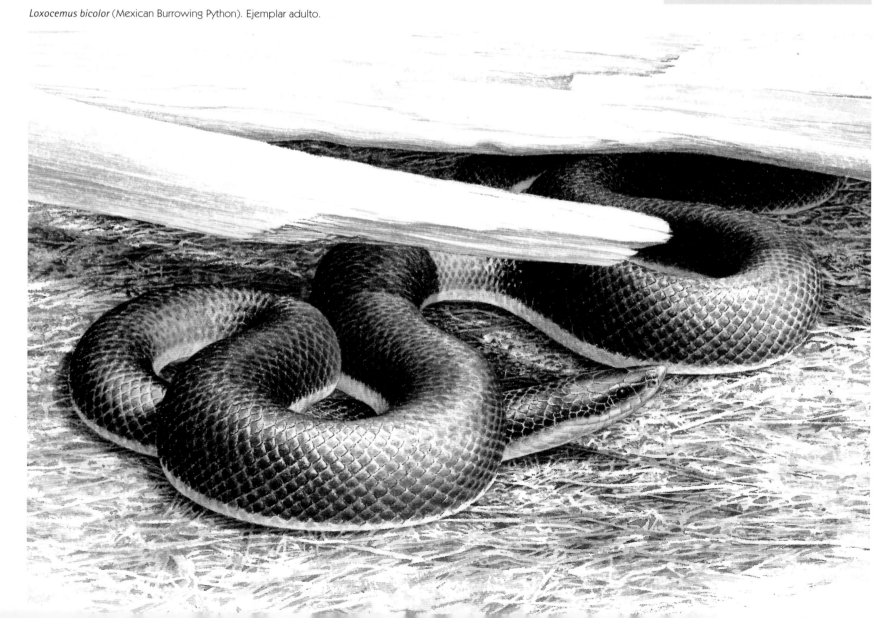

Cope, 1861

New World Python, Dwarf Python, Mexican Burrowing Python

LOXOCEMUS BICOLOR
FAMILY **LOXOCEMIDAE**

Loxocemus bicolor (Mexican Burrowing Python). Adult specimen

DESCRIPTION

Medium snake that does not grow more than five feet long (which is why it is also known by the common name, the *Dwarf Python*).

Its coloration has strong contrasts: the back is a fairly dark iridescent and uniform brownish color, while the ventral zone is almost always a lighter creamy tonality, although snakes with dark stomachs are not rare.

Many specimens have a series of irregular whitish blotches distributed along the entire body.

HABITAT

They live in relatively dry wooded and rocky areas, and in tropical coastal forests that are not too humid.

They always live in zones with soft or sandy floors with a moderate to low elevation (between sea level and 1969 feet).

BEHAVIOR

• This species has nocturnal and burrowing tendencies, and is not usually seen moving on the surface, except when it crosses highways and paths at night or after strong rains.

• It is most frequently found in shrub-like areas and open thorny forests, normally between rocks, in holes in the floor, under the fallen leaves and branches, and in tree trunks.

• Specimens have also been found inside anthills.

• They feed on small mammals, above all, rodents, and on moderate-sized reptiles such as lizards or newborn iguanas.

• They probably also consume birds and their chicks that nest on the floor. In certain coastal areas their predation of iguana eggs and sea turtles has also been confirmed.

• They capture their prey with their mouth and kill it by constriction.

REPRODUCTION

They are oviparous.

STATUS

The current state of its population is unknown, but it seems to be fairly scarce in almost its entire area of distribution, with the exception perhaps of some national parks and other protected zones.

It is classified in Appendix II of the Washington Agreement (CITES), which prohibits its capture, trade, and captivity.

DISTRIBUTION

Northern Pacific coast of Mexico (north of Guerrero and Morelos), Guatemala, Honduras, El Salvador, Nicaragua, and Costa Rica.

■ No subspecies are recognized, although some authors have managed to differentiate two different species (considered by others only as subspecies) according to the existence of the two chromatic phases, light and dark, on the ventral part.

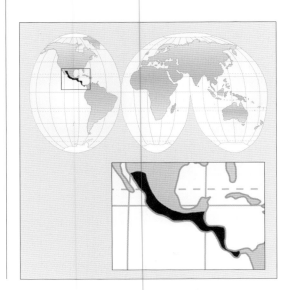

F. Boidae

Boa constrictor (Boa Constrictor). Adult specimen.

36 SPECIES

The Boidae constitute a relatively homogenous group of snakes, generally large or very large in size, found habitually in tropical countries; however, other much smaller burrowing forms are also found in arid regions. The great majority of the large species pertain to this family, which is why, since time immemorial, it has formed a part of the myths from all cultures.

L The Family Boidae is a group of snakes with primitive characteristics, the vestiges of the pelvic girdle stand out among them; its appearance goes back to the Cretaceous period, 65 million years ago. No other group of snakes is as well represented in the fossil record, given that during a good part of the Tertiary period (65 to 23 million years ago) they were the ones who dominated the world of snakes, above all in Europe and North America. Some fossilized species found were true giants; specimens up to 49 feet long have been noted.

Python reticulatus (Reticulated Python). Adult specimen.

GENERAL CHARACTERISTICS

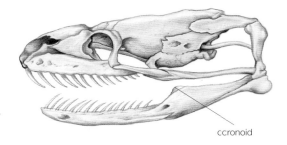

ccronoid

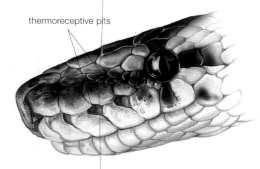

thermoreceptive pits

The head is clearly wider than the neck except in the burrowers.

The mouth is large with teeth that are also large, sharp, and curved back; these are found in the maxilla, pterygoid, and palatine in the boas, and also in the premaxilla in some pythons. The coronoid, the typical form of an extra bone, appears on the lower mandible.

It lacks venomous glands associated with dentition (aglyphous dentition) and captures its prey with the mouth, killing it by constricting its coils. The upper and lower labial scales of many species have a variable number of thermoreceptive pits.

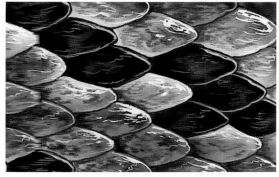

The dorsal scales are typically small and flat. The ventral scales are transversely elongated to form just one row in the animal's entire ventral area, or two in the python's caudal region.

They generally have two lungs unlike 'modern' snakes that only have one functional lung.

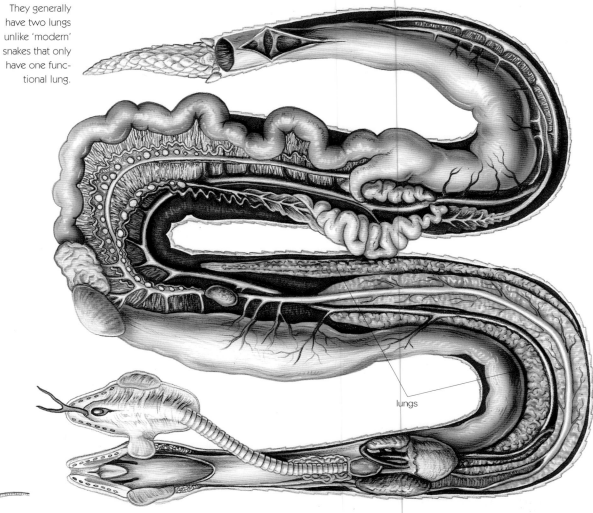

lungs

Many species develop a type of crepuscular or nocturnal life and have a vertical pupil as an adaptation to low intensity light.

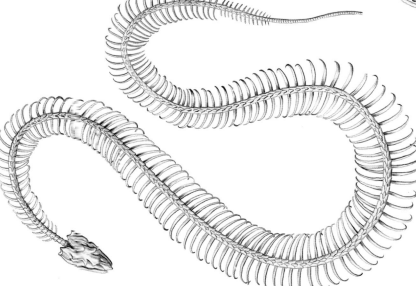

The skeleton has vestiges of the pelvic girdle as well as femur bones that are visible on the exterior in the form of spurs on both sides of the cloaca (they are further developed in the males). Some large species have more vertebrae; the Tiger Python, *Python molorus*, can reach the extraordinary figure of 435 vertebrae.

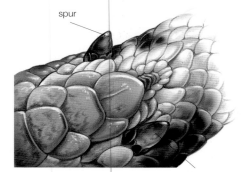

spur

spur

SUBFAMILY: **PYTHONINAE**

Reticulated Python

Python reticulatus. Adult specimen in its habitat.

- The *Python* genus is the most widely distributed; it occupies a good part of Asia and Africa, where the largest species are found.

- The *Morelia* and *Liasis* genera are small- to medium-sized pythons that live in Australia, New Guinea, and the Indonesian region.

- The *Calabaria* is an African burrowing species with subterranean tendencies.

- The *Aspidites* are two medium Australian species that feed on mammals, birds, saurians and, unique among the Boidae, it often captures snakes, both harmless and venomous ones.

- The *Chondropython* of New Guinea is strictly arboreal and extraordinarily similar to the Emerald boa.

6 GENERA / 27 SPECIES

- They are all oviparous, laying a quantity of eggs directly related to the female's size. The female incubates the eggs by coiling up around them.

- They have teeth on the premaxilla.

- They have two rows of scales under their tail.

- They develop an arboreal or rather terrestrial way of life, and are the largest existing snakes.

- The thermoreceptive pits are situated on the labial scales.

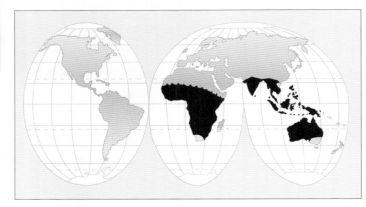

SUBFAMILY: **BOINAE**

Boa Constrictor

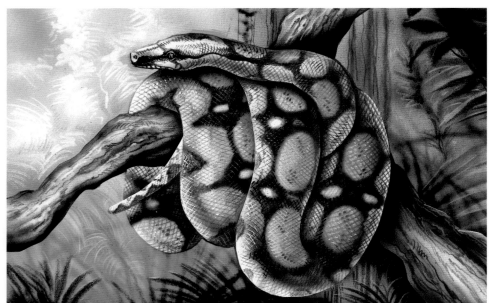

- The *Boa*, *Epicrates*, *Acrantophis*, *Sanzinia*, and *Xenoboa* are medium- to large-sized snakes, basically terrestrial or arboreal, that live in the forests and grasslands.

- The *Eunectes* anacondas are mainly aquatic and one of them, the common anaconda, *Eunectes murinus*, is among the largest snakes.

- The *Corallus* is a snake that is adapted to life in the trees in the rainforest.

- The *Candoia* are small 5 feet long boas that develop a semiterrestrial life and inhabit the forests of some Pacific islands.

Boa constrictor
Adult specimen in its habitat.

8 GENERA / 23 SPECIES

- All are ovoviviparous, that is, they give birth to totally formed babies.

- No teeth on the premaxilla.

- They have just one row of scales under the tail, not two like the pythons.

- They are generally more arboreal than the pythons and, aside from the common anaconda Eunectes murinus, they are smaller in size.

- The thermoreceptive pits are located between the labial scales but not included on them.

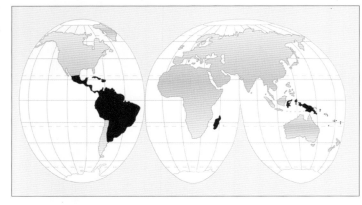

SUBFAMILY: **ERYCINAE**

Sand Snake of Eastern Africa

3 GENERA / 12 SPECIES

• They reproduce ovoviviparously and give birth to totally formed babies.

• They do not have teeth on the premaxilla.

• Short tail, small eyes.

• Head slightly differentiated from cylindrical body.

• Small snakes with burrowing tendencies, generally live in the sand in arid and semi-arid zones.

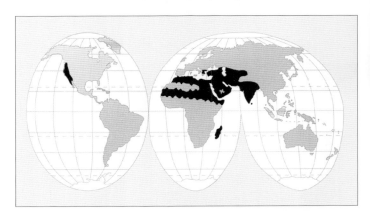

Eryx colubrinus
Adult specimen in its habitat.

- The *Eryx* live in soft sandy floors in Europe, Asia, and northern Africa, where they easily burrow themselves.

- The *Charina* genus also has the ability to burrow, but is capable of climbing trees and swimming with agility as well.

- The *Lichanura* live in eastern North America and are characterized by their lack of large head scales.

SUBFAMILY: **BOLYERINAE**

Round Island Ground Boa

2 GENERA / 2 SPECIES

• Lack pelvic girdle and therefore vestiges of posterior extremities.

• They have certain osteological differences in the vertebrae in respect to the other Boidae.

• The maxilla is divided in two parts, one front and another back.

• It is a subfamily endemic to the Mascarene Islands; that is, they are exclusively found on this small archipelago of the Indian Ocean.

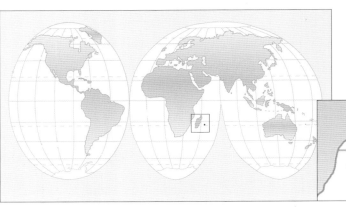

Casarea dussumieri
Adult specimen
in its habitat.

- Only a very small number of *Casarea* survive on tiny Round Island, located 12 miles north of Mauricio Island, where subfossil remains of this species have been found.

-The *Bolyeria* is also found only on Round Island but no species have been found for years in their natural habitat.

PYTHON SEBAE

SUBFAMILY **PYTHONINAE**

 (Gmelin, 1789)

 African Rock Python

Python sebae (African Rock Python).
Adult specimen.
Detail of the head.

Distribution of scales on
the center of the body.

DESCRIPTION

The African Rock Python is the largest African snake. It can grow up to 16 to 20 feet, although the more common size oscillates between ten and 16 feet.

The males are much longer and corpulent. It has a robust constitution with a triangular head smaller than the rest of the body. It has thermoreceptive pits on two of the supralabial scales and four to six on the infralabial scales.

The body scales are small and flat and arranged in 78 to 95 rows. The upper part of the head is dark, blackish, brownish-gray: two light bands start from the snout and go above the eyes. Another yellow band forms an inverted V under the eyes. The back is yellowish, brownish-gray with dark blotches that form a pattern in the form of a staircase. There are two dark bands on the tail, and whether they are continuous or not, they are separated by a light band.

HABITAT

It mainly inhabits open savannahs, particularly rocky zones, where it hides in the holes between the rocks. In other less rocky areas, it also uses the other mammals' burrows.

It likes to live close to rivers where it hides quickly if bothered; it can stay submerged for a long time. It also penetrates the forests and the young specimens are mainly semi-arboreal.

BEHAVIOR

• When born it feeds on rats and when it grows it can feed on large prey such as crocodiles, monkeys, and antelope, constricting them to death. It mainly hunts at twilight.

• During long digestion it is especially vulnerable to predators like licaons and hyenas.

• It can fast for a long time.

• Although it isn't venomous, it is fairly aggressive and, although it would rather escape than attack, when cornered, it can inflict, with its large curved teeth, painful wounds that can become easily infected.

REPRODUCTION

The females lay 20 to 50 eggs, even up to 100 for large females.

The eggs are large and weigh from five to six oz; they are laid three months after copulation.

Once laid, the female coils around the eggs to protect them, although she does not constrict her body (like the Python molorus), to increase the temperature of the nest.

The babies are born 65 to 80 days after and measure two feet.

Sexual maturity is reached between three and five years of age, when they measure between seven and ten feet.

STATUS

The large specimens are found mainly in hunting reserves, in natural parks, and in open terrain; a lack of large prey is a considerable limiting factor. Hunting for human consumption (*bushmeat*) creates a danger for its population, as well as being captured for its excellent quality skin highly suitable for tanning.

It is included in Appendix II of CITES and is protected by law in some countries such as South Africa, where its population is extremely vulnerable.

DISTRIBUTION

Sub-Saharan Africa.

■ Two subspecies are distinguished:

- *P. s. natalensis:* found in the southern part of the continent, starting from southern Kenya, southern Zaire and Zambia.

- *P. s. sebae:* on the rest of the continent they have larger cephalic scales, different coloration, and are larger in size.

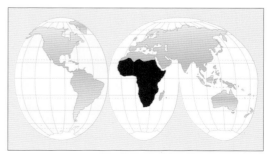

Python regius (Royal Python).
Adult specimen.

(Shaw, 1802)

Royal Python
Ball Python

PYTHON REGIUS

FAMILY **PYTHONINAE**

DESCRIPTION

This snake has a short solid body. It varies from four to five feet in size; the males are shorter and more slender. Some authors, however, cite populations in Ghana with specimens close to seven feet.

On each upper lip there are four, or sometimes five, supralabials containing thermoreceptive pits.

There is a clear band that goes from its black eye to the temples on each side of the head; it separates the nasal orifices.

Large yellowish, light brownish-gray oval blotches or brownish-gray ocelli appear over the dark brownish-gray background. The ventral face is a uniform whitish or yellowish color.

HABITAT

It prefers the shrub-like zones of the savanna with a nearby source of water; it generally shies away from thick-forested zones.

It climbs trees and shrubs in search of food or tranquility.

BEHAVIOR

• The Royal Python hunts lying in wait on a branch on the floor, feeding on small-sized mammals. Each specimen may be specialized in the hunting of a certain species, which is why, once in captivity it may have problems adapting to the food offered. It hunts during the hours of darkness. It has a curious defensive behavior: when it feels threatened, it makes its body into the shape of a ball; this is where its common name *ball python* comes from, hiding its head among its body's coils and remaining completely still. The great development of its musculature makes it difficult to uncoil. Normally it does not display aggressive behavior when handled.

REPRODUCTION

The females lay four to 12 eggs in moist places, such as tree stumps. She coils around the eggs during the period of embryonic maturation that can last from two to three months.

When the young are born they measure on average 18 inches and weigh 2.5 oz.

STATUS

Large numbers of this species are imported to be made into domestic animals; 18,000 specimens alone for the United States in 1984 along with 1,800 specimens for Germany in 1994. Similarly, other countries have also made massive importations. It is not yet known if this species can stand the repercussions of being collected in this fashion.

It appears in Appendix II of CITES. The great majority of imported specimens come from Togo, Ghana, and Benin (where there is a temple dedicated to the worship of this species considered to be a totemic animal).

DISTRIBUTION

Extends from Senegal to the Ivory Coast in Western Africa. It is also found in Sudan and Uganda.

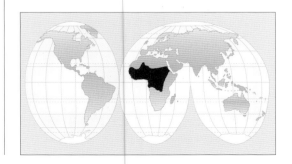

PYTHON ANCHIETAE

SUBFAMILY **PYTHONINAE**

 Bocage,1887

 Anchieta's Dwarf Python

Python anchietae (Anchieta's Dwarf Python) Adult specimen. Detail of head.

Python anchietae (Anchieta's Dwarf Python) Adult specimen with eggs.

DESCRIPTION

The average length of this species is four feet, although some large females can exceed five feet. It has a wide head quite differentiated from the neck, covered in small scales with tubercles.

Each side of the upper lip has five triangular thermoreceptive pits. The scales are small, flat and arranged in 57 to 61 rows. The back has a brown or green background color with a multitude of bands and cream or white blotches bordered in black. The stomach is yellowish with a few brown dots. The young snakes tend to be darker than the adults.

HABITAT

It prefers the stony terrain of rocky outcrops, especially where there are temporary or permanent water sources. It inhabits arid or semi-arid zones characterized by dry, somewhat cold winters and hot summers with precipitation that varies from two inches in some areas of Nambia, up to 24 inches in other areas of Nambia and in the region of Miombo, Angola. It has also been found in mountainous zones in Angola up to an elevation of 6,562 feet, where not much is known about its distribution.

BEHAVIOR

• It has mainly diurnal tendencies, although it also seems to show certain activity at night; it spends a lot of time hidden in the clefts of rocks, which is why it is not often observed. It rarely bites and when it feels threatened, it displays the same behavior as the *Python regius* or the *Calabaria reinhardti*: it coils up in a ball and keeps its head tucked in between the coils. It mainly feeds on terrestrial birds and rodents such as jerboas, terrestrial squirrels, and rats that inhabit the same rocky zones.

REPRODUCTION

The courtship and copulation take place at the beginning of spring (this corresponds to the months of August and September in the southern hemisphere).

The females deposit three to nine eggs in November and December that hatch during the summer rains in January and February.

STATUS

It is a rare species with a very low population density. The zones where it lives are unproductive and very inaccessible. They quite often appear in natural parks and other protected areas, which is why its habitat can be considered safe.

Illegal international trade is dangerous, although it is prohibited in Namibia; due to the high prices charged for this species in the market, there is a fairly significant lucrative traffic. Sometimes the dealers mix it with the somewhat similar *Python regius* specimen from other places in order to evade customs and have it arrive at the sales centers. It is included in Appendix II of CITES.

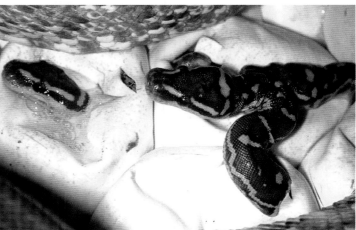

Python anchietae (Anchieta's Dwarf Python) Newborn.

DISTRIBUTION

75 percent of its area of distribution is in Namibia, in the northeastern area of the country, next to the border with Angola, and it is made up by natural parks like the Etosha and the Namib-Naukluft. In Angola, it occupies the southwestern area of the country, from Benguela and Lobito to the Angola border at the Kuneme River.

(Linnaeus,1758)

Tiger Python
Asiatic Rock Python

PYTHON MOLURUS

SUBFAMILY PYTHONINAE

DESCRIPTION

It is a large-sized snake that can grow up to 25 feet. Its body is robust, rounded, and ends with a prehensile tail. The general or background color is a dirty yellowish or grayish tone. It has irregular brown squares with greenish iridescence on the back, from the neck to the tail. On the flanks it has small blotches with some light ocelli in the center. This species is made up by two subspecies with very characteristic features:

- *Python m. molurus*, also called Indian python: characterized by its small size and corpulence (the average maximum size is two inches.).

The head is a characteristic pinkish color, more intense in the young specimens, with a black line from the eye to the neck and a pattern in the form of a Y on the upper part.

- *Python m. bivittatus*: has a similar coloration although it is more contrasted; the background color tends to be more greenish yellow and the irregular dark squares a blacker brown; the red traces on the head also disappear.

The body is generally more solid and larger, growing up to 25 feet. Another very clear distinct characteristic is that the labial scales are separated from the eye by other smaller scales called subocular scales; in the Indian python these are absent.

HABITAT

Normally in the dense jungle but can also be found in open forests, in rocky areas, and along the riverbanks.

BEHAVIOR

• As a curious piece of information about tropical Boidae, it is worth pointing out that the populations in northern India hibernate for a short period.

• They feed on mammals, birds, and reptiles, although they show a special predilection for birds.

• When examining the stomach of some specimens, animals as unusual as sambars, monitor lizards, leopards, and even porcupines were found, among other prey.

REPRODUCTION

Mating takes place during the cold season (December, January, and February). The eggs are laid three or four months later which can consist of almost 100 eggs in the large females.

The female coils up around the eggs and through visible muscular contractions, she is capable of increasing her body temperature to incubate the eggs. In the interior of the nest, the temperature can be two to four degrees above air temperature.

The eggs hatch two months after they are laid.

Python molurus molurus (Asiatic Rock Python). Adult specimen.

Python molurus bivittatus. Adult specimen.

Python molurus molurus
Adult specimen. Detail of the head. Side view.

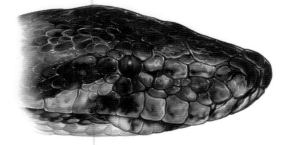

Python molurus bivittatus
Adult specimen. Detail of the head. Side view.

STATUS

Hardly any specimens are free because the beauty of their skin has been highly exploited commercially in the manufacturing of tanned skin, while in other

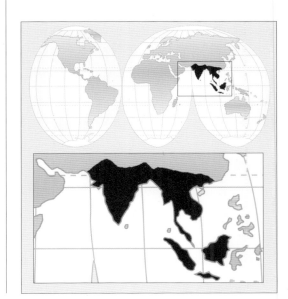

zones, they are hunted for food. The aforementioned, along with the destruction of its habitat, endangers the existence of this subspecies.

P. m. bivittatus is included in Appendix II of CITES, which supposes that a determined number of animals can be traded. This subspecies does not appear to be in such a dangerous situation.

DISTRIBUTION

- *P. m. molurus* inhabits the Indian subcontinent, except to the west of Bengal. It is also found in Sri Lanka, although there, some authors consider it to be a separate species (*P. m. pimbura*). It extends to the north and the west up to Nepal and Pakistan.

- *P. m. bivittatus* inhabits a zone of Indonesia (Borneo, Java, Sumatra, and the Celeb Islands), Burma, Indochina and southern China.

PYTHON RETICULATUS

SUBFAMILY **PYTHONINAE**

 (Schneider, 1801)

Reticulated Python

Python reticulatus (Reticulated Python).
Adult specimen. Detail of the head.

Python reticulatus
(Reticulated Python).
Adult specimen.

DESCRIPTION

Along with the common anaconda, it is the longest snake, and, although it normally does not exceed 20 feet, there are specimens that reach 26 to 30 feet. The males are much smaller than the females and rarely exceed 13 feet.

The body is proportionally thin compared with other large Boidae.

The head is yellowish brownish-gray with a black central line from the snout to the back of the neck and others from the eyes to the mouth's posterior commissure. The eyes are a characteristic orange color with a black pupil. The body's background color can vary from ocher to brick red. The back has lighter rhomboidal patterns, defined by a black line that widens towards the sides around a white or grayish ocellus.

The pattern looks like the mesh of a net, which is where it gets its name.

The ventral face is white or yellowish-white, blotched with brownish-gray or black, with the outer borders also blotched in gray or black. Three or four upper front labials have pits on each side, just like the six or seven back infralabials.

HABITAT

It is found in tropical humid forests.

Frequents marshy areas, small water currents, rivers, and rice fields.

It is often found near towns and cities, where it feeds on rats around the dump.

The chronicles say that it was so abundant in Bangkok for a while that it lived like a semidomestic animal. It is quite arboreal, especially the young individuals, and remains coiled up in the tree branches.

It is an excellent swimmer and can colonize new territories by going deep into the sea.

It was one of the first reptiles to settle on Krakatoa Island after its volcanic explosion in 1883.

BEHAVIOR

• It hunts by lying in wait. The snake remains still waiting for its prey to pass by, then it plunges on its prey with a quick leap. Afterwards, it grabs its prey between its mandibles and forms a few spirals around it, immobilizing it, and beginning to compress it. Depending on its size, it attacks different prey, both birds and mammals. The largest can feed on antelope and pigs and on rare occasions has been cited to have attacked and killed a person, generally children or small field workers.

REPRODUCTION

During rut the males may become immersed in violent fights and inflict serious wounds all over the body.

During courtship the male mounts the female; his spurs tickle around her cloaca until the female accepts the male and he fertilizes her.

After laying the eggs, the female coils in the nest and remains there for the entire duration of the incubation (60 to 80 days).

The quantity of eggs that are laid depends on the size

of the female and can vary from about 20 to almost 100 babies. The newborns already measure 28 inches.

STATUS

Is included in Appendix II of CITES. Its populations are affected by uncontrolled deforestation, and keep withstanding the exploitation of its skin in the international market of leather goods.

DISTRIBUTION

Burma, Thailand, India (Assan, Nicobar Islands), Bangladesh, Malaysia, Indonesia, the Philippines and the Moluccas.

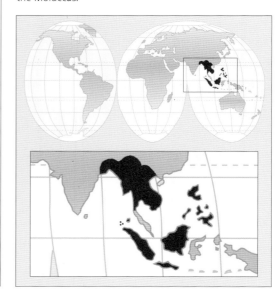

Schlegel,1827

 Blood Python

PYTHON CURTUS
SUBFAMILY PYTHONIAE

Python curtus brongersmai
(Blood Python). Adult specimen.

Python curtus breitensteini
Adult specimen.
Detail of the head.

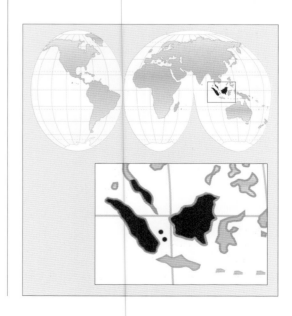

Python curtus (Blood Python).
Adult specimen.

DESCRIPTION

The body is short, solid, and flat with a narrow head in relation to the body, and a short tail. Although it can reach seven feet, it is generally much smaller. The males are smaller and have a more robust and elongated tail.

The coloration is variable and differs considerably in its livery depending on the different subspecies:

Python c. curtus is a golden brown; *Python c. breitensteini* is a brown purple, characterized by a row of granular scales on the lower part of the eye that separates it from the supralabials; *P. c. brongersmai*, called the *Blood Python*, may be a bright and colorful reddish color with alternative cream or gold marks of various sizes and forms.

HABITAT

It prefers very aquatic habitats; it lives close to marshes, rivers, or lakes that are found in the humid jungles.

It stays still for a long time on the forest floor among the fallen leaves; the form of its body and its strongly disruptive coloring make it almost invisible to both its predators and its prey.

BEHAVIOR

• Immobility could be called this species' strategy for survival.

• It is actually able to stay in the same position for days, even weeks; this makes it more likely that its prey will come closer to the snake. Unaware of the snake, it can trap the prey quickly.

• It feeds on birds, small mammals like rats and other rodents, and on bats that it hunts at the entrance to their caves.

• It is possible that the different snakes specialize in the hunting of a certain species; this could explain why the adult individuals that are captured do not easily accept the food that is offered to them. The snake often dies before feeding.

REPRODUCTION

The clutch is sparse and does not seem to exceed 12 or 15 eggs.

The females coil themselves up around the eggs and stay in the nest until the eggs hatch.

At birth, the babies measure from 15 to 18 inches long.

STATUS

Is included in Appendix II of CITES. There are quotas of exportation from Indonesia and Thailand. Its population is decreasing due to the exploitation it has to endure. More than 60,000 animals are collected each year for the marketing of their skin and meat.

DISTRIBUTION

- *Python c. curtus*: inhabits Thailand, Laos, Cambodia, and the Malaysian Peninsula.

- *Python c. breitensteini*: found in Borneo.

- *P. c. brongersmai*: lives on the Malaysian Peninsula and in eastern Sumatra.

CALABARIA REINHARDTII

SUBFAMILY **PYTHONINAE**

 (Schlegel,1851)

 Calabar Burrowing Python

Defensive posture of *Calabaria reinhardtii*.

Calabaria reinhardtii (Calabar Burrowing Python).
Adult specimen. Detail of the head.

DESCRIPTION

Although it can measure up to three feet, 24 inches is a more common length.

Its appearance is very different from common pythons and indicates a special adaptation to subterranean life. It lacks thermoreceptive pits and teeth in the palate and premaxilla. It has a short conical head that is hardly differentiated from the neck, with a widened rostral scale that helps it to bury itself in the subsoil.

The tail is short and ends brusquely in a blunt shape that is not easily distinguishable, at first sight, from the head. The eyes are small and have a vertical elliptical pupil.

The scales are flat, and the ventral scales are very narrow. It is a chocolate brown color with yellowish or reddish blotches that become black on the head and caudal area. The tail also displays some white blotches that have different forms on each individual.

HABITAT

A nocturnal species that inhabits forested regions where it leads a subterranean life, normally hidden in the humus, the rodents' burrows, and the anthills and termite nests.

It can also climb fairly easily.

BEHAVIOR

• When it senses danger and cannot hide quickly, it coils itself up, remaining still, and uses its tail as a false head. This behavior is similar to that of the Royal python, *Python regius*, and the Angolan python, *Python anchietae*. Its hunting technique represents other remarkable behavior. Instead of violently leaping onto its prey, trapping it with its mouth, and then strangling it with its coils like other pythons do, it prefers to asphyxiate its victim by squeezing it against something solid. This is because this species tends to hunt in burrows where there is not sufficient space to coil around the prey; it is therefore much more convenient to crush it against the walls. It feeds on rodents, especially rats, although it prefers to nourish itself on the rats' litter.

REPRODUCTION

It is cited to have clutches of three to five eggs that are large in size compared to the female adults; they measure from three to 4 inches in length.

STATUS

There is no concrete information on the state of its population. Like all Boidae, it appears in Appendix II of CITES.

This snake is very feared by some people in the regions where it lives–people think it is a two-headed snake.

DISTRIBUTION

Western Africa, from Liberia to Cameroon, Gabon, and Zaire. Also on the Island of Fernando Po.

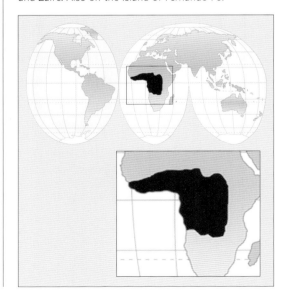

(Schneider,1801)

Amethyst Python, Scrub Python

LIASIS AMETHISTINUS

SUBFAMILY PYTHONINAE

Liasis amethistinus (Amethyst Python).
Adult specimen. Detail of the head.

Liasis amethistinus (Amethyst Python).
Adult specimen.

DESCRIPTION

It is the longest Australian snake. The maximum size it can reach is 26 feet, although the majority of spec - mens are a much smaller 11 feet.

The body is thin and the head large, elongated, with big scales, and easily distinguishable from the rest of the body. A dark line extends from below the eyes to the commissure of the mouth. The lips are a cream or white color.

The coloration of the back varies from yellowish brownish-gray to brownish-gray with abundant and irregular black or dark brownish-gray angular zigzagged bands. The back part of the body and the tail are dark. The scales have an iridescent reflection; this is where the scientific and common name of the species comes from.

The ventral surface is white or cream colored. The specimens that live in open forests are much lighter than the ones that live in the dense jungles. The young specimens are less brightly colored and have fewer markings than the adults. Sometimes this species is classified within the *Python* or *Morelia genera*. The snakes of the Liasis genus along with the *Aspidites* genus are considered the most primitive pythons.

HABITAT

They inhabit rainy jungles where there are monsoons, mangrove swamps and sometimes dryer zones, where sclerophyll forests and savannahs are found. It hides in tree holes, openings in rocks, caves, abandoned buildings, and under thick vegetation.

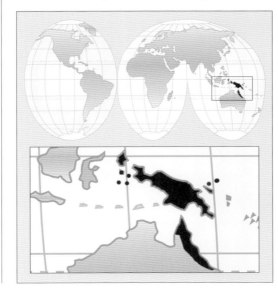

BEHAVIOR

• Although it is normally nocturnal, it can often be seen in the jungle clearings basking in the sun. The large individuals are predominantly terrestrial, while the younger ones like to spend more time hanging from trees or shrubs.

• It feeds on birds and mammals, among which large *wallabies, Macropus agilis*, and *possum* are included.

REPRODUCTION

Clutches of seven to 20 eggs have been found. The newborns measure 24 inches.

STATUS

Included in Appendix II of CITES. Like all Australian fauna, it is subject to being banned from international trade.

DISTRIBUTION

Northeastern Australia in Queensland, from the Cape York Peninsula to Townsville.
It is also found in New Guinea and the Moluccas.

LIASIS CHILDRENI

SUBFAMILY **PYTHONINAE**

Gray, 1842

Children's Python

Liasis childreni
(Children's Python).
Adult specimen.

DESCRIPTION

This small python can reach a size close to five feet, although the most common length is around three feet.

The head is large and well differentiated from the neck, and the body is robust with a prehensile tail. The head is covered with large symmetrical scales. The background color varies with all different tones of brown. The pattern is generally dark; sometimes there may be no pattern but rather numerous relatively small blotches that often look like transversal bands. A dark line generally passes between the eyes, joining the nostril to the temple. The ventral surface is white or cream colored. In the Northern Territory and in western Australia there are populations that lack this species' pattern. Some authors classify this species in a new genus, *Bothrochilus*, which could be distinguished from *Morelia* and *Liasis* (except for *Liasis amethistina*) because of its large cephalic symmetrical scales, not small fragmented ones.

HABITAT

It prefers humid and semi-humid areas in northern Australia where there are rocky zones, rainforests, and savannahs generally close to the water.

BEHAVIOR

• It is a species with nocturnal habits that hides in caves, cracks in rocks, holes in trunks, abandoned burrows, termite nests, and under fallen leaves.
• It eats lizards, birds, and small mammals.
• Some individuals frequent caves and feed on bats.
• Although it is predominantly a terrestrial species, it can climb trees in search of food.

REPRODUCTION

It lays around 15 eggs at a time.
The female coils up on top of the eggs and defends the nest from predators.
The newborns measure ten inches long.

STATUS

It is included in Appendix II of CITES and, like the rest of Australian fauna, there are great restrictions against its trade.

DISTRIBUTION

Northern Australia, from the Kimberley region in Western Australia, through the Northern Territory, to northeastern Queensland.

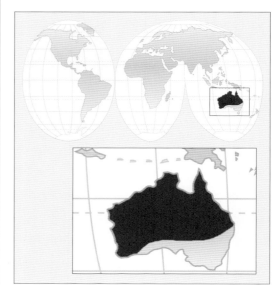

LIASIS OLIVACEUS

SUBFAMILY **PYTHONINAE**

Liasis olivaceus (Olive Python).
Adult specimen.

📄 Gray, 1842

📄 Olive Python

DESCRIPTION

It is a large species in which some individuals may exceed 18 feet. The head is well distinguished from the rest of the neck. The body is robust with lustrous scales and a certain pale reflection.

■ Two subspecies are known:

- *L. o. olivaceus*: a dark olive, yellow olive, or brownish-gray olive color, lighter or faded along the sides. The lips, sides of the throat, neck, and ventral surface are white or cream colored. The most common size is eight feet.

- *L. o. barroni*: is differentiated from the normal form because it has fewer rows of scales; it has 58–63 instead of 61–80, and more ventral scales, 374–411 instead of 355–377. It also reaches a larger size (individuals larger than 21 feet have been cited, although this information has not been verified).

HABITAT

It inhabits arid to humid climates in northern Australia. It prefers rocky landscapes, particularly those that border watercourses.
It hides in rocks' crevices, caves, and abandoned burrows.

BEHAVIOR

• It has nocturnal and terrestrial habits. It feeds on mammals, birds, and reptiles.
• The adults consume large mammals like the *rock wallaby*, capturing it when it goes to drink.

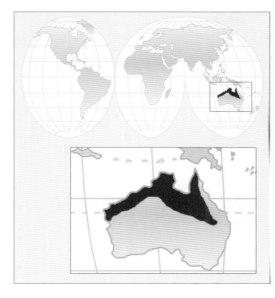

REPRODUCTION

Little is known of its reproductive habits. It has been cited to lay 11 eggs at one time, that hatch after an incubation period of 71 days. The largest newborns measure 15 inches.

STATUS

Like all wild Australian fauna, its trade is very restricted.
It is included in Appendix II of CITES.

DISTRIBUTION

Northern Australia, the region of Pilbara, Western Australia, through the upper part of the Northern Territory, to northeastern Queensland.

The *L. o. barroni* is only found in the region of Pilbara in western Australia and is separated from the other subspecies by the Great Sandy Desert.

MORELIA SPILOTES

SUBFAMILY PYTHONINAE

 (Lacepede,1804)

Diamond and Carpet Python

They coil up around the eggs to help them incubate and protect them from possible enemies.

Newborns measure close to 12 inches and weigh .5 oz.

STATUS

This is the most common Australian python.
It is protected by Australian legislation and included in Appendix II of CITES.

Morelia s. variegata (Carpet python).
Adult specimen.

Morelia s. spilotes (Diamond Python).
Adult specimen. Detail of the head.

DESCRIPTION

It has a large head, quite differentiated from the neck, a robust body, and a prehensile tail. The head is covered with small irregular scales. Its maximum size is 14 feet. It has five thermoreceptive pits on each lower lip.

■ This species is divided into three subspecies, each with very marked characteristics:

- *M. s. spilotes.* Called *Diamond python*, has a background color that varies from gray to black. Many scales are individually blotched with a cream color. Many specimens have scales that are totally blotched, a white or cream color distributed along the body's dorsal and lateral surfaces; these scales appear grouped together and adopt the form of a diamond. The lips are a light cream color or strongly barred in black. The tongue is blue, and the ventral surface is cream colored or yellowish green, blotched with a dark gray.

- *M. s. variegata.* Named *Carpet python*, it has an extremely varied dorsal coloration. It is made up of at least four different varieties, distributed in many other geographic regions. The most common is a background coloration that goes from light to dark brown with irregular wide bands that are lighter in the center, with black borders.

- *M. s. imbricata.* Has a similar coloration, but its dorsal scales overlap a lot and are lanceolated with fewer ventral and subcaudal scales.

HABITAT

It is the most common in coastal wooded zones.
It has nocturnal habits but is sometimes found during the early hours of the day, warming itself in the sun.

It is arboreal and terrestrial, and prefers to hide in holes in tree trunks, cracks in rocks, and in caves.
It is often found in buildings, even in urban zones.

BEHAVIOR

• It kills by constricting its prey, mainly mammals and birds, although sometimes it hunts lizards.

• All the different types have an unpredictable temperament: there are large differences between individuals; while some specimens are pacifist and allow handling, others puff and bite strongly.

REPRODUCTION

During spring, fights have been observed when the males gather in small groups for this purpose. The fights occur during daytime. The males intertwine their bodies, raising their heads up to heights that exceed three feet from the floor, and although these fights are highly ritualized, sometimes the snakes bite hard, which can cause dangerous wounds to their adversary.

The females lay between nine and 52 eggs.

DISTRIBUTION

- *M. s. spilotes*: exclusively inhabits the coastal zone of New South Wales.

- *M. s. imbricata*: found in southwestern Western Australia.

- *M. s. variegata*: from Kimberley in Western Australia, to the northern area of the Northern Territory, a large part of Queensland and New South Wales to some zones in southern Australia.

It is also found in southern New Guinea.

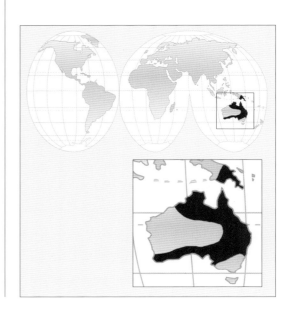

(Krefft, 1864)

Black-Headed Python

ASPIDITES MELANOCEPHALUS

SUBFAMILY PYTHONINAE

Aspidites melanocephalus
(Black Headed-Python).
Adult specimen.

DESCRIPTION

Can reach a maximum size close to ten feet. Its head is lightly pointed and indistinguishable from the neck. The body is robust with a clearly triangular cross-section. It has small eyes with a dark iris and a vertical elliptical pupil. The head scales are enlarged in the form of symmetrical shields. It does not have thermal pits and its tail is not prehensile.

The dorsal coloration varies from light to dark brown with numerous thin and dark transverse bands on the body and tail; in some specimens these may fuse at the vertebral line. The head, neck, and throat are a brightly colored black. The ventral surface is a cream color generally with black blotches. The young individuals, although they are replicas of the adults, have more contrasting colors.

It is distinguished from the *Aspidites ramsayi*, the other species of the genus, because it is smaller and does not have the black hood on the front part.

HABITAT

It can be found in a large variety of habitats, although it prefers the forests and rocky terrain with the humid and subhumid client of northern Australia.

It is not found in very arid terrain.

It is a terrestrial and nocturnal species, although it may sometimes be found active on cool days, above all after rain.

It hides in holes in tree trunks, cracks between rocks, and in burrows of monitor lizards and mammals.

BEHAVIOR

• The front part of the body is a shiny black that allows it to absorb a maximum amount of solar radiation, exposing a minimum part of the body.

• Although it also eats birds and mammals, it is relatively specialized in eating reptiles (this is exceptional for pythons); it even eats venomous snakes of the *Elapidae* family.

• It is normally inoffensive when hounded, but may appear to be a dangerous species when it raises the front part of the body in an S shape, like many other venomous and nonvenomous species, puffing strongly and hitting repeatedly.

REPRODUCTION

It can lay eight to 11 eggs per clutch. The newborns are 20 inches long.

STATUS

Is considered an endangered species. Protected by Australian legislation and appears in Appendix II of CITES.

DISTRIBUTION

Northern Australia, extending towards dryer areas in the interior of the continent.

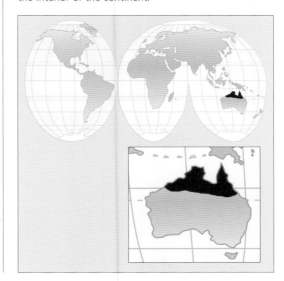

CHONDROPYTHON VIRIDIS

SUBFAMILY PYTHONINAE

 (Shlegel, 1872)

 Green Python

Chondopython viridis (Green Python). Adult specimen.

Chondopython viridis (Green Python).
Adult specimen. Detail of the head.

DESCRIPTION

This beautiful snake can reach six feet; the males,
however, are smaller in size and have a longer
and more robust tail.

It is arboreal, has a prehensile tail and is bright
green.

It has a vertebral line that often discontinues from
white or yellow. Blotches of the same color may appear
distributed throughout the entire body.

Some completely blue (cyanomorph) individuals
were found, although it is much more common to find
only blotches of this color irregularly distributed
throughout the body.

The tip of the tail is very thin and blue. The ventral
part is a cream or bright yellow color.

The young specimens are different colors than
theadults, lemon yellow, bright orange, or brick red.
They have a much more marked and continuous vertebral line. It is not unusual that babies of different
colors appear in the same clutch.

The coloration of the young is maintained for
approximately three years and the transition to green
is slow; it lasts quite a few weeks.

The body has a triangular cross-section, with the
head clearly differentiated from the trunk.

The teeth become large and are extremely curved
back. The thermoreceptive pits found on the supralabial
scales are very characteristic.

The pupils are vertical and the iris brown.

This species is an exceptional example of evolutionary convergence with the Emerald boa, *Corallus
caninus*. Both share almost the same habitat and form
of life–therefore their physical form is very similar.

However there are significant differences between
them: the thermoreceptive pits are much more prominent in the boa, taking up the entire upper mandible,
while in the python, they only occupy the front supralabial scales.

HABITAT

Jungles, monsoonal forests, and bamboo thickets.
They are completely arboreal and, due to their color,
are almost invisible between branches and epiphytal
plants, which allow them to be completely camouflaged
in this medium.

BEHAVIOR

• The posture that they tend to adopt, completely
coiled around a branch with the head resting on the
body, is very characteristic. In this fashion, they can
spend long periods of time practically immobile, drinking
the rainwater that is retained in between their coils. They
feed on rodents, birds, and sporadically on bats which
they tend to surprise with a quick attack. During the
attack, the snake holds onto a branch with its strong
prehensile tail. Captive young snakes have been observed
using their tails as a lure to attract their prey.

REPRODUCTION

The boas give birth to already developed babies
while the Green python lays eggs.

Eleven to 25 eggs are laid per clutch, and the snakes
display the typical protective behavior and incubation
of the python eggs.

The clutches are incubated on the floor.

The Green python is included in Appendix II of CITES.
The number of specimens for exportation is subject
to a fairly restrictive quota.
It is considered vulnerable in New Guinea.

DISTRIBUTION

New Guinea (West Irian and Papua), northern
Australia (Cape York) and some adjacent islands from
the group of Aru, Shouten, and Solomon.

■ No subspecies are known.

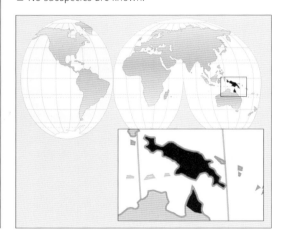

Chondropython viridis (red variety). Young specimen.

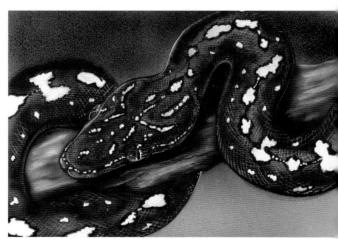

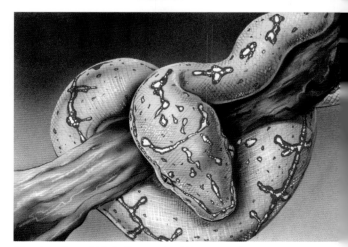

Chondropython viridis (yellow variety). Young specimen.

BOA CONSTRICTOR

SUBFAMILY **BOINAE**

 Linnaeus, 1758

 Boa constrictor

Boa constrictor in it's natural habitat. Adult specimen.

Boa constrictor. Young specimen.

DESCRIPTION

One of the most popular of large snakes; its image is constantly reproduced in movies that take place in the jungles, occasionally inappropriately because the movie takes place far from the American continent which it exclusively inhabits. Its character is also falsified; it is generally a calm animal that would hardly attack a human being and even less likely try to devour it, given that it is not an appropriate size to do so.

It is medium sized although specimens have been found more than 16 feet long; its normal size varies between eight to 13 feet. It stands out due to the morphology of its small triangular head, strongly differentiated from the rest of the body by its neck, which is much thinner than the rest of the animal. It lacks thermoreceptive pits, although some scales are sensitive to thermal variations.

The coloration and pattern of the body are very typical although very variable as would be expected from a species with such a wide distribution.

The background color varies from light gray to a bright cream color; the dorsal patterns are dark brownish gray, but some species' tails are an intense red. The flanks have dark rhomboidal patterns with a light center.

HABITAT

It is a fairly adaptable species and can be found in a wide variety of habitats, mainly in the tropical rainforest, but also in dry semideserts like plains, such as in Peru, and savannah zones with isolated trees such as in Venezuela, or in dry coastal environments, such as some zones in the Caribbean.

It can be found in areas under cultivation.

BEHAVIOR

• When it is young it spends a lot of time in the trees, although, when it is longer, it spends the majority of its time on the floor, hidden in animals' burrows, under large rocks, in tree roots, or trunks. Its coloring allows it to go unnoticed along the forest floor where it surprises its small- and medium-sized vertebrate prey.

Boa constrictor. Adult specimen. Detail of the head

REPRODUCTION

It reaches sexual maturity when it is five or six years old.

During mating, the male's entire body produces rhythmic contractions while it stimulates the female's cloacal zone with continuous rubbing of the spurs.

Copulation takes place with the intertwining of the tails. The boas are ovoviviparous and very prolific (the large females give birth to more than 50 babies that can be up to 20 inches long at birth).

STATUS

It is a species with such a wide distribution that it is difficult to generalize the state of its population. It does not, however, seem to be especially in danger, aside from places where the natural environment has been seriously altered.

The species is included in Appendix II of CITES, except for the subspecies, *Boa constrictor occidentalis* of Argentina, which appears in Appendix I.

DISTRIBUTION

Very wide distribution, from the center of Mexico to northern Argentina. Also in the Lesser Antilles, The Dominican Republic, Trinidad and Tobago, and Saint Lucia.

■ Eight subspecies are distinguished:

B. c. constrictor, B. c. amarali, B. c. imperator, B. c. nebulosa, B. c. occidentalis, B. c. orophias, B. c. melanogaster and *B. c. sabogae.*

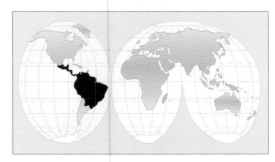

EUNECTES NOTAEUS

SUBFAMILY **BOINAE**

 Cope, 1862

Yellow Anaconda

Yellow Anaconda (*Eunectes notaeus*). Babies on top of their mother.

Yellow Anaconda (*Eunectes notaeus*). Adult specimen.
Detail of the head.

DESCRIPTION

Fairly smaller than the common anaconda, it usually measures between seven and ten feet, and some specimens reach a maximum of 13 feet. The males are, however, much smaller.

Their general coloration is also much lighter than the common anaconda with yellowish, gold, or light greenish tonalities, with two series of dark vertebral blotches along the entire back. The head is elongated, differentiated from the neck, with 13 to 15 supralabial scales that are never in contact with the eyes.

They do not have visible thermoreceptive pits.

HABITAT

They live in streams, brooks, slow moving rivers, wetlands and marshes in the interior of forest regions.

BEHAVIOR

• It has very aquatic habits; it is a good swimmer that does not tend to go far away from the proximity of the water. When alarmed, it submerges itself quickly in the water and remains hidden in the muddy bottom.

• Its diet is varied and includes fish, birds (especially aquatic species), medium mammals like pacas and

Yellow Anaconda (*Eunectes notaeus*).
Adult specimen in water.

agoutis, and reptiles such as young caymans.

• The young individuals, on the other hand, seem to feed exclusively on fish.

• Although it is not a venomous snake, it is one of the most feared species by snake attendants due to its aggressive character.

• Its strong curved teeth are capable of inflicting serious wounds to attendants who try to touch it. At birth, the young are already very aggressive, biting hard and repeatedly at the slightest attempt of trying to get close to them.

REPRODUCTION

They are ovoviviparous; the females give birth to babies that are already perfectly formed with a coloration similar to the adults, but with more intense tonalities. The number of newborns varies from three to 17.

STATUS

Its population does not seem very abundant, although there have not been many recent studies on their current status. The destruction of its habitat and increase in its direct persecution by making access to its surroundings easier, seem to be the main problems it is faced with.

This species is protected by Appendix II of the CITES.

DISTRIBUTION

It is found in southern Brazil, Paraguay, Eastern Bolivia, Uruguay, and northern Argentina.

■ No subspecies are known.

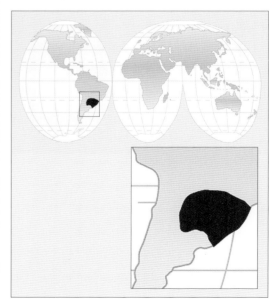

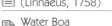 (Linnaeus, 1758)

Water Boa
Common Anaconda

EUNECTES MURINUS

SUBFAMILY **BOINAE**

Eunectes murinus (Common Anaconda's).
Adult specimen close to the water.

Eunectes murinus (Common Anaconda's).
Adult specimen. Detail of the head.

DESCRIPTION

The Common anaconda is considered the largest
snake in the world; it often reaches more then 20 feet
in length and there are individuals that reach up to 26
feet. It is possible that 30 feet long specimens exist.

For a long time, the Zoological Society of New York
has been offering a reward of 5,000 dollars for anyone
who brings a 30 feet long animal to them, but up to
this moment, the reward has never been granted. These
large animals are always females; the males reach
much more discreet sizes. It has a solid and heavy
body; the dorsal coloration tends to be a grayish
or greenish chestnut brown with large black ovoid
blotches that give it a great ability to camouflage
itself in spite of its enormous size.

The ventral part is a yellowish gray with sporadic small
dark blotches. The short tail is significantly prehensile.

HABITAT

They occupy all types of aquatic jungle habitats:
streams, calm rivers, wetlands, and marshes.

They are also found in floodable zones like the Plains
of Venezuela.

BEHAVIOR

• Although it can easily climb trees, it is an
eminently aquatic species. It is an excellent swimmer
and even has its nasal orifices on the upper part of
its snout to make breathing easier while its entire body
is submerged. With a great capacity to stay under
water without breathing, it never goes far away
from water. It remains coiled up along the shores,
as well as up in the trees' branches.

• When it feels threatened, it submerges itself for a
long time. It feeds on all type of animals of a certain
size, preferably mammals and aquatic birds, although it
also consumes fish and even caymans.

• The largest specimens can hunt prey as large as
subadult capybaras or tapirs.

REPRODUCTION

It reproduces ovoviviparously; the female gives birth
to a number of babies that oscillates between four and
40, depending on the size of the mother.

Their coloration is similar to the adults'. The babies'
size at birth can reach 24 to 28 inches.

STATUS

Although its direct capture is a threat to its future,
the massive general destruction of the forest is the
main cause that could endanger these animals.

It is protected by Appendix II of the CITES
agreement.

DISTRIBUTION

Found in Trinidad and in all of tropical South
America east of the Andes, from Venezuela and
Columbia to Bolivia and northern Paraguay.

■ Two subspecies are distinguished:

- *E. murinus murinus*: inhabits the entire Amazonian
basin.
- *E. murinus gigas*: found in Venezuela, Columbia,
Guyanas, and Trinidad.

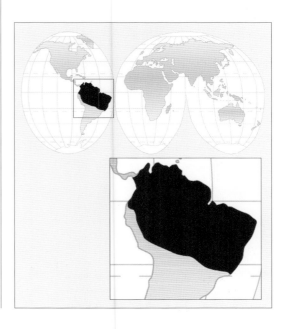

CORALLUS CANINUS

SUBFAMILY BOINAE

 (Linnaeus, 1758)

 Emerald Tree Boa

Corallus caninus (Emerald Tree Boa) Adult specimen.

Corallus caninus
(Emerald Tree Boa).
Detail of the head.

DESCRIPTION

This species is perhaps the most beautiful of all the boas; it has a long head that is well differentiated from the rest of the body, with large eyes and a vertical pupil. The teeth on the top part of the maxilla are very long and wide, a typical adaptation of arboreal snakes that prevents their prey from falling to the floor.

The tail is very strong, short, and prehensile.

The dorsal coloration is a bright emerald green, with irregular white or yellow blotches along the entire vertebral column, sometimes forming a continuous dorsal band; the color of the ventral area varies from a subdued white to a lemon yellow. In reality, its apparently bright and colorful coloration carries out the important function of camouflaging it among the dense foliage of the trees where it lives. As in all the *Corallus* species, the large thermoreceptive pits are very visible, both on the lower and upper labial scales–these help the animal find its prey. The largest specimens of this species hardly exceed seven feet in length.

HABITAT

Preferred environments are the humid jungles and forests of the entire Amazonian basin, especially zones close to the watercourses, lagoons, and marshes.

BEHAVIOR

• It is an arboreal snake with crepuscular and nocturnal habits that almost never goes down to the jungle floor. During the day, it tends to stay at rest in the trees' branches, helped by its strong prehensile tail, and lets its body fall from one side to another, to balance the awkward distribution of weight.

• It feeds itself by preference on birds and small mammals.

• It kills its prey by constriction; the prey is often devoured while the snake suspends itself from a branch by the tail and the back part of the body.

REPRODUCTION

This species is ovoviviparous; the mother gives birth to already developed young.

Their coloration is very different from the adults; they are a terra cotta red, orangish or greenish blue, although they already have the white blotches along their back. The young inhabit thickets where their colors also appear cryptic.

STATUS

There is no recent information about its current status. It does not however seem to be endangered, although its populations are seriously affected, like many others, by the unstoppable deforestation of Amazonian jungle.

It is protected by Appendix II of the CITES agreement.

DISTRIBUTION

It is present in all of Brazil and the adjacent forests of the northern part of South America.

■ There are no subspecies.

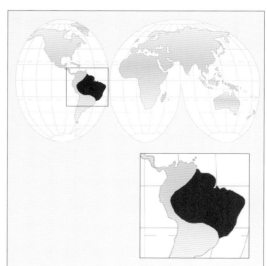

(Linnaeus, 1758)

 Garden Tree Boa
Amazon Tree Boa

CORALLUS ENYDRIS

SUBFAMILY **BOINAE**

Corallus enydris
(Garden Tree Boa).
Adult specimen.
Detail of the head.

DESCRIPTION

This species has a slender and somewhat laterally compressed body that can reach more than seven feet in length. The head, large and well differentiated from the body, has round eyes and a vertical pupil. The thermoreceptive pits are well developed and found between labial scales. The tail is strong, short, and prehensile. The teeth on the front part of the mouth are long, curved, and sharp. With a large chromatic variability, the color of the body may be grayish, brownish, orangish, or yellowish, with a series of dark circular blotches with lighter sunspots on their interior (absent in some specimens). The ventral part tends to be whitish with random gray blotches.

Some authors classify this species as *Boa endyris*, and it may also be found by the name *Boa cooki*.

HABITAT

Found in tropical rainforest regions, it tends to avoid very thick wooded zones; it is habitually found in more open secondary forests, in agricultural areas (especially in banana plantations) and even in sufficiently wooded gardens. It is almost always found in zones close to rivers, streams, marshes, and lacustrine areas.

BEHAVIOR

• Although an eminently arboreal species, it moves on the ground more often than the *Emerald boa*.

• It is a snake of great agility and swiftness when necessary, and it feeds mainly on birds and small mammals, although lizards and different species of amphibians are also included in its diet.

• It often captures its prey by supporting itself from a branch with the help of its powerful prehensile tail.

• It has crepuscular and nocturnal habits.

• Unlike *C. caninus,* that has a docile character, this is a very aggressive snake that defends itself by biting, and can inflict painful wounds with its long sharp teeth.

REPRODUCTION

It is ovoviviparous and the babies are born already developed.

The coloration of the babies is also very variable; in the same litter, specimens can be found with blotched patterns, or with a yellowish, orangish, or uniform red color.

STATUS

It has a very ample geographic distribution, and is a fairly common species in many zones, favored by its suitable ability to adapt to humanized environments.

It is also a boa that is very habitually in captivity; various generations exist that have been born in terrariums all around the world.

It is classified in Appendix II of the Washington Agreement (CITES).

DISTRIBUTION

From Costa Rica and Panama to Bolivia and southern Brazil. It is also on the islands of Trinidad and Tobago, Grenada, Grenadines, St. Vincent, and other small islands close to the continent.

■ Two subspecies are known:

- *C. e. enydris.*: with less than 50 ventral scales and rounded dorsal scales, it inhabits almost all of South America.
- *C. e. cooki*: with more than 50 ventral scales and rhomboidal scales, it is found in Central America, in Caribbean islands, and northern South America.

EPICRATES CENCHRIA

SUBFAMILY **BOINAE**

 (Linnaeus, 1758)

Rainbow Boa

Epicrates cenchria alvarezi. Adult specimen.

Epicrates cenchria maurus Adult specimen. Detail of the head.

Epicrates cenchria cenchria Adult specimen. Detail of the head.

DESCRIPTION

Its large head, obviously differentiated from the body with small eyes and a vertical pupil, characterizes this boa. The upper labial scales have three shallow thermal pits while the lower ones have 11. The body is rather thick and covered with flat scales with characteristic iridescent reflections, especially after molting. These reflections, characteristic of all Boidae, are found more pronounced in this species because of the fact that the microscopic epidemic chains are linked together and reflect the light like a prism.

The ten subspecies have different morphological characteristics (size, color, pattern). In the common subspecies, *E. cenchria cenchria* the upper parts have bright reddish brown coloration with numerous ring-shaped thick blotches with a light center along the vertebral line of the trunk. A longitudinal series of large light colored ocelli with a black edge are found on the flanks. The blotches and ocelli are more pronounced in the young.

The upper parts of the *E. cenchria maurus* are a uniform darkish brownish-gray. The flanks are lighter and have from two to three irregular rows of dark, very diffused brownish-gray blotches. The ventral face is lighter in color and grayish. However, the babies are born with a much brighter coloration.

The E. c. alvarezi is a light chestnut color on the head; a dark chestnut color on the back, and has large lighter ocellar blotches, bordered in black, following the vertebral line. There is a double series alternating with rounded blotches on the flanks. The ventral part is a pearly white, with blurry dark blotches on the tail's third distal.

Some subspecies can reach a length of more than seven feet; others do not exceed 5five feet.

HABITAT

The rainbow boa inhabits wooded zones or savannahs with abundant vegetation. Sometimes it is also found close to or in marshes and fields under cultivation.

It is generally a terrestrial species that only climbs trees when in danger.

It normally lives and hunts on the floor and has crepuscular and nocturnal habits.

BEHAVIOR

• Like the great majority of snakes, the females are larger than the males, and have a relatively shorter and narrower tail, without the bulging produced by the hemipenes.

• They are powerful constrictors and hunt a large variety of small mammals and birds.

• Its labial pits detect differences in temperature and facilitate the capture of homoeothermic animals.

REPRODUCTION

They reproduce ovoviviparously.

Mating takes place in the most hidden zones in the forest and is preceded by nuptial combat between males.

The gestation takes 4.5 to seven months. The number of babies may be between eight and 28, depending mainly on the female's size.

Some males reach sexual maturity when they are two and a half years old, and 31 inches long, while the females mature from four years old and on. The babies of *E. c. maurus* measure from 14 to 16 inches.

STATUS

No concrete information is available about the state of its populations, although, like all Boidae, it is included in Appendix II of CITES to prevent possible trade abuse.

Its populations' main danger, as for many species, is the loss of their habitat due to fires and the uncontrolled cutting of trees.

DISTRIBUTION

Very widespread, covering almost all of South America except Chile and southern Argentina.

■ The ten subspecies according to the CITES are:

E. c. cenchria, E. c. alvarezi, E. c. assisi, E. c. barburi, E. c. crassus , E. c. gaigei, E. c. hygrophilus, E. c. maurus, E. c. polilepis and *E. c. xerophilus.*

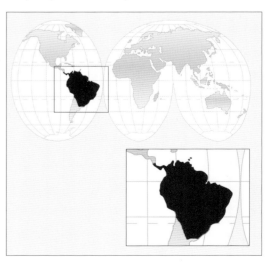

EPICRATES STRIATUS

SUBFAMILY **BOINAE**

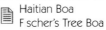
(Fischer, 1856)

Haitian Boa
Fischer's Tree Boa

Epicrates striatus (Haitian Boa).
Adult specimen. Detail of the head

Epicrates striatus (Haitian Boa) Young specimen.

Epicrates striatus (Haitian Boa) Adult specimen.
Detail of the head.

DESCRIPTION

This snake is a considerable size; the adult specimens can measure up to eight feet in length. After the Cuban boa, it is the largest snake native to the Caribbean islands.

It has a white or reddish gray background color with numerous small black blotches along the flanks and a series of dark rectangular marks bordered in black (60 to 122) along the back, which makes it look striated.

It has a large triangular head well differentiated from the body with small eyes and elliptical pupils.

The body scales are small and smooth while the labial scales and those on the front part of the head are considerably larger. The males have between 270 and 299 ventral scales (76 to 102 subcaudal scales), and the females between 266 and 298 (76 to 94 subcaudal scales). The thermoreceptive facial pits are not very pronounced.

It has been classified within the genera *Homatochilus* with the name *Homatochilus striatus*, and also as *Epicrates versicolor*.

HABITAT

It lives in a large variety of habitats; both humid ones as well as dryer ones, from sea level to an elevation of 3,937 feet, but always with a certain cover of vegetation. Therefore it is habitually found in pine plantations, fairly open wooded masses, and mangrove swamps.

BEHAVIOR

• Nocturnal and very arboreal, during daylight it remains resting inside worm-eaten hollow tree trunks, dry stumps, crevices in rocks, birds' nests, or on' horizontal tree branches, sometimes at very considerable heights (large specimens have been found resting at more then 66 feet). It also likes to climb straw roofs. The young snakes eat lizards (they are especially fond of the *Anolis*), while the adults prefer to eat birds and small mammals.

• They have been seen hunting fowl and domestic cats in inhabited zones.

REPRODUCTION

They reproduce ovoviviparously, and give birth to up to 50 live babies per litter after 192 to 224 days of gestation. However, the number of babies tends to be fairly smaller (10 to 30).

STATUS

Many subspecies are in a precarious situation due to the limited area of their habitat, which faces numerous detrimental changes: introduction of foreign animals, increase in human settlements and population, uncontrolled tourist development, etc.

It is not habitually in captivity, although it would adapt well to it; it can be handled without problems.

However, when frightened, it expels a foul liquid from its anal glands.

It has been bred many times.

Like all Boidae, it is classified in Appendix II of the Washington Agreement (CITES).

DISTRIBUTION

The Isla Española, Bahamas, and other small nearby islands.

■ Eight different subspecies have been described:

- *E. s. striatus*: Isla Española, Haiti (Morne l'Hôpital, Jacmel, southern coast of the Tiburón peninsula), the Dominican Republic (Valle de Neiba, Sierra de Baoruco, Oviedo). Also on the small islands of Gonâve and Saona.
- *E. s. ailurus*: Cat Island and Alligator Cay (Bahamas).
- *E. s. exagistus*: Western Tiburón Peninsula and Île-à-Vache, in Haiti.
- *E. s. fosteri*: Bahamas (North Bimini, South Bimini, and East Bimini Islands, as well as on Eastern Cay).
- *E. s. fowleri*: Bahamas (Andros Island and Berry Islands; Chub Cay and Great Harbour Cay).
- *E. s. mccraniei*: Bahamas (Ragged Islands; Margaret Cay and Little Ragged Island).
- *E. s. strigilatus*: Bahamas (New Providence Island, Rose, Eleuthera and Long; also on Exuma Cays; Compass Cay and Great Exuma Cay).
- *E. s. warreni*: Tortuga Island (Haiti).

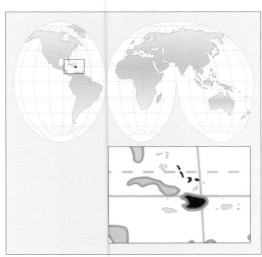

EPICRATES INORNATUS

SUBFAMILY **BOINAE**

 (Reinhardt, 1843)

 Puerto Rican Boa

Epicrates inornatus (Puerto Rican Boa).
Adult specimen.

DESCRIPTION

This medium species reaches six feet in length and is the largest snake on the island of Puerto Rico, where it is also known by the name *Culebron*.

The color of its body is extremely variable; it is generally dark brown or grayish, but it always has a series of large dark angular marks along the back (66 to 73) and small blotches on the flanks that turn into a line along the head. The head is large and well differentiated from the body; some supralabial scales are in contact with the eyes. The color of the stomach is dark, a brownish or grayish color.

The males have between 263 and 273 ventral scales and between 66 and 74 subcaudal scales, and the females have between 258 and 267 ventral scales, and between 68 and 75 subcaudal scales.

It has been classified as *Boa inornatus* and also as *Piesigaster boettgeri*.

HABITAT

Typical inhabitant of characteristic rainforests on the island of Puerto Rico; it can also be found in rocky areas, in caves, and in plantations. It is even capable of adapting to human presence, and it is not unusual to see it in urban and suburban areas.

BEHAVIOR

• Terrestrial, arboreal, with nocturnal habits, it remains hidden during the day. It is not, however, unusual to observe it basking in the sun in sunny areas.
• In the adult state, it feeds mainly on rodents (*Mus, Rattus*), both savage birds and fowl, and bats (*Brachyphylla, Monophyllus*), that the snakes lie in wait for at the entrance of their caves. The young prefer to consume insects, small lizards, and iguanas.

REPRODUCTION

Reproduces ovoviviparously.
The females give birth to between 23 and 32 young after 6 months of gestation.

STATUS

Is a fairly rare species everywhere, although it seems somewhat more abundant in the Mogotes region on the northern coast of the island. Its current scarceness can be attributed to, aside from the destruction of its habitat, the direct pursuit of a part of the population for its oil (a practice that still continues today, even though it is totally illegal; traditionally used for

medical purposes to treat arthritis), and the introduction of foreign animal predators, especially the Indian mongoose *Herpestes auropunctatus*, introduced to the island during the XIX century.

This boa is protected in Appendix I of the Washington agreement (CITES) and classified as a *Minor Risk* by the UICN, but susceptible to soon being placed in the *Vulnerable* category.

The Federal Law of Endangered Species of the United States also protects it.

DISTRIBUTION

It is a species endemic to the island of Puerto Rico.
■ Although up to three different subspecies have been described, they have generally not been recognized as being valid.

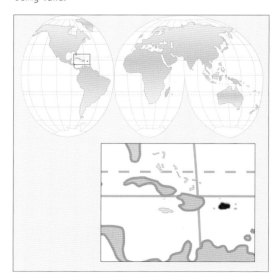

EPICRATES SUBFLAVUS

SUBFAMILY **BOINAE**

 Stejneger, 1901

 Jamaican Boa

Epicrates subflavus (Jamaican Boa).
Adult specimen in its habitat.

Epicrates subflavus (Jamaican Boa).
Adult specimen. Detail of the head.

DESCRIPTION

A medium snake; the largest specimens may exceed 7 feet in length. It is the largest terrestrial predator native to the island of Jamaica. The head is well differentiated from the body and the small eyes have a vertical pupil. The tail is prehensile.

The body is quite flattened dorsally, and is covered with small smooth scales that are much larger on the head and the snout (12 supralabial scales). It has 41 to 47 scales on the middle of the body, 277 to 283 ventral scales, and 78 to 79 subcaudal scales. The back is a yellowish, reddish-brownish, olive green, or silver-gray color. It has dark black random blotches on the front part, and wide dark angular black bands on the middle of the body that join on the back part and the tail, and end up being almost completely black. The head tends to be olive green with two postorbital black borders and the chin a greenish-yellow color. The stomach is an orangish or creamy color with black blotches that are more numerous towards the posterior part, which also ends up being almost completely black.

The young are an earthy or pinkish color with a lightly blotched front part and a back part with fairly marked bands. The entire ventral zone is of a cream color.

HABITAT

It inhabits fairly dense savannah and forest zones of moderate or high humidity, often in places close to rocky outcrops.

BEHAVIOR

• It is a fundamentally terrestrial species in the adult state, but it displays good climbing abilities when young, which is why it can also be considered arboreal.
• It is active at night, and during the day stays hidden in the rocks' cracks, burrows, caves, or even between tree branches. In the early hours of the morning it tends to bask in the sun on top of large rocks.
• Its hunting technique is to lie in wait.
• After capturing the prey in its mouth, it asphyxiates it through constriction.
• It feeds on small vertebrates, mainly on the abundant rodents introduced to the island of Jamaica *Mus*, *Rattus*), but also on bats and birds.
• The young prefer to eat small lizards.

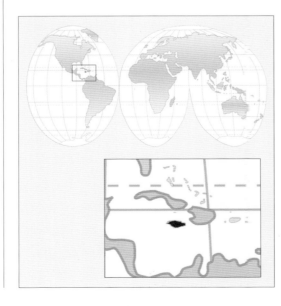

REPRODUCTION

It reproduces ovoviviparously.

The females are larger than the males and give birth between the months of October and December to between 15 and 20 babies, depending on their size (the largest number known is 33).

STATUS

Today, it is an endangered species rarely found in nature. The main causes for this situation are the destruction of the forests on the island for the development of agriculture; predation by introduced animals (both domestic and wild); and the increase of the human population with the added impact to the environment that they represent.

A certain number are maintained in captivity and there are some breeding programs that have been quite successful in the last few years, such as the Reptile Breeding Foundation of Picton, of Canada, or the Jersey Wildlife Preservation Trust of Great Britain.

This species is protected by Appendix I of the Washington agreement (CITES), and classified as *Vulnerable* by the UICN.

DISTRIBUTION

This species is endemic to the island of Jamaica and the miniscule Goat Island.

■ No subspecies have been described.

EPICRATES ANGULIFER

SUBFAMILY **BOINAE**

 Bibron, 1843

Cuban Boa

Epicrates angulifer
(Cuban Boa).
Adult specimen.

This species can adapt itself to human presence and live close to plantations. However, the continuous persecution provoked by a multitude of negative legends about this snake, along with the lack of animal protein that the Cuban population suffers from, make this a hunted snake, which can further jeopardize this species. Environmental education campaigns have tried to make the peasants respect this emblematic species of Cuban fauna.

It is included in Appendix II of CITES and is classified as *Low Risk* by the IUCN's red list, although it is pending on a new rating.

The zoos of the world have an International Studybook for this species to regulate its young in captivity. New international studies are planned to examine the state of its populations.

DESCRIPTION

This is the largest species of the ten that make up the genus *Epicrates*, and distributed in the Caribbean islands and in a large part of South America.

It can reach more than 13 feet in length, although today the specimens found rarely exceed 8 feet.

The males are considerably smaller.

Unlike other species of the genus *Epicrates*, it has a line of subocular scales that separate the eyes from the labial scales. There is a series of 13 to 14 upper labial scales with thermoreceptive pits that are not very deep or absent.

The coloration is very variable, but a golden yellow predominates, speckled with a dark gray.

It has an irregular series of 42 to 65 rhomboidal marks. As in other species of the genus, the metallic iridescent reflections are characteristic; they may shine with different intensity according to the angle they are observed from and the light's incidence.

The ventral part is gray or yellowish. The young individuals have more contrasting colors than the adults.

HABITAT

It inhabits the forests and wooded plains.
The majority of its habitat has been destroyed to create sugarcane fields.

BEHAVIOR

• This species prefers to be on land, although sometimes it is found in the treetops and in the bushes.

• It normally seeks refuge in the rock crevices and between old tree stumps.

• It prefers to feed on rodents, both indigenous ones like the Jutia, and invasive species on the island like common rats. Sometimes it enters caves in search of bats.

• When bothered it may try to bite with fury; if trapped, it expels a smelly whitish liquid substance from the cloaca intended to repulse the attacker.

REPRODUCTION

Like all boas, it gives birth to babies that are already completely formed. It gives birth to 2 to 8 babies, not very many, but of a considerable size.

The young are very aggressive.

STATUS

The loss of its habitat, as well as the peasants' persecution of it, has produced a decrease in its population.

DISTRIBUTION

This species is autochthonous to the Island of Cuba.

It is also found on the Isla de Piños and on Cayo Cantiles.

■ No subspecies are recognized.

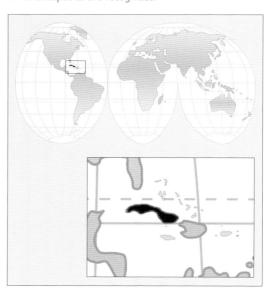

DISTRIBUTION OF THE GENUS EPICRATES

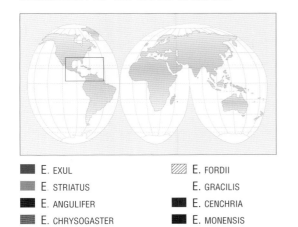

- ◼ E. EXUL
- ◼ E. STRIATUS
- ◼ E. ANGULIFER
- ◼ E. CHRYSOGASTER
- ◼ E. SUBFLAUUS
- ▨ E. FORDII
- E. GRACILIS
- ◼ E. CENCHRIA
- ◼ E. MONENSIS
- ◼ E. INORNATUS

Epicrates cenchria (Rainbow Boa).
Adult specimen in its habitat.

Epicrates cenchria (Rainbow Boa).
Adult specimen eating its prey.

Epicrates cenchria (Rainbow Boa).
Adult specimen.

SANZINIA MADAGASCARIENSIS

SUBFAMILY **BOINAE**

📄 (Dumeril y Bibron, 1844)

📄 Madagascar Tree Boa

Sanzinia madagascariensis (Madagascar Tree Boa) Adult specimen.

Sanzinia madagascariensis
(Madagascar Tree Boa).
Young specimen.

This snake has also been cited in some dryer zones on the eastern coast and in the arid region of Toliara.

BEHAVIOR

• Its diet is mainly based on small and medium mammals, although it does not dismiss other types of vertebrates.

REPRODUCTION

It reproduces ovoviviparously; the females give birth to four to 16 babies that can measure between 17 and 19 inches after six to eight months of gestation.
The newborns are more aggressive than the adults, biting at the slightest stimulus.

STATUS

It seems to be the most abundant species of all the boas of Madagascar and adapts to a certain extent to changes in its medium; this is why it fairly successfully resists the unstoppable degradation of the Malgache forests. In any case, to regulate expected excessive trade for use as a domestic animal, it has been included in Appendix I of CITES.
It is classified as *Vulnerable* on the red list of endangered animals.

DESCRIPTION

It is called mandrita by the Malgachian people.
The taxonomy of this species is currently being debated and some authors call it, perhaps hastily, *Boa manditra*, including it in the same genus as the widespread boa constrictor.
Some differences, like the existence of thermoreceptive pits and a smaller number of chromosomes in the Madagascar Tree Boa (2n=34) and (2n=36) in the boa constrictor, seem to advise prudence and to continue taxonomic study.
The background coloration is variable; in the eastern rainforests it acquires a greenish tonality, while in the dryer forests its coloration is browner. It has two dark longitudinal series that are diamond-shaped with a yellow center on both of the body's flanks.
The coloration of the young is much more bright and colorful, with vivid contrast between the reddish background and the yellow and black blotches distributed along the entire body. There are also local differences in the tonality, according to the geographic location.
The head is relatively small, easily distinguishable from the neck with only one dark line on each side that goes from the eye to the end of the mouth. There are generally 13 pits on the upper labial scales and 12 on the lower labial. The eyes have a vertical pupil and are in contact with the labial scales. This species can reach a size of more than eight feet long.

DISTRIBUTION

It is endemic to the island of Madagascar, where it mainly inhabits the coast of the island. It is not surprising that Boidae are found in Madagascar, even though the natural distribution of this subfamily is commonly found in large parts of the American continent. To understand this phenomenon it is necessary to remember the geological history of the planet. In periods before the Cretaceous, America, Africa, and Madagascar were united in one large continent, Gondwana, where the subfamily Boinae originated. Once the continents separated, the Pythoninae occupied Africa, and the Boidae remained in America and Madagascar.

■ No subspecies are recognized.

HABITAT

Its preferred habitat is in the rainforest, although it is also found in the secondary forest, and in deforested zones; it also frequents the outskirts of some cities, attracted by the large quantity of rodents that proliferate around human centers.

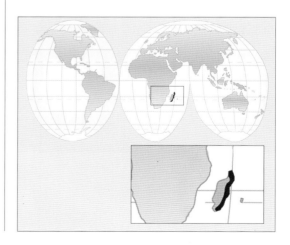

Acrontophis dumerili (Dumeril's Boa).
Adult specimen. Detail of the head.

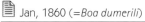 Jan, 1860 (=*Boa dumerili*)

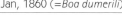 Dumeril's Boa

ACRANTOPHIS DUMERILI

SUBFAMILY **BOINAE**

Acrontophis dumerili (Dumeril's Boa). Adult Specimen.

DESCRIPTION

Dumeril's Boa is one of the species of the genus *Acrantophis* that exists and lives exclusively on the island of Madagascar.

The other species is *A. madagascariensis*. Recently, studies based on phylogenetic analysis (A. Kluge, 1991) have situated these two species within the genus *Boa*.

It is a robust, medium snake that normally measures between five and six feet, although some adults can reach seven feet. The head is large, differentiated from the body, and with a somewhat prominent snout, typical in boas. It has between 17 and 19 supralabial scales, and small eyes with vertical pupils. It has a short, fairly prehensile tail.

The coloration of the back is a pale brownish-gray with two series of dark longitudinal blotches; it also has a few black lines behind the eyes. *A. madagascariensis* is distinguished by its smaller head scales and a larger number of periocular scales; between 11 and 16 (compared with the six to ten of the other species).

It is known by the name *do* by Madagascar's inhabitants.

HABITAT

This species inhabits humid zones close to streams and other small courses of water that run through the rather dry forests of eastern and southern Madagascar.

BEHAVIOR

• It has terrestrial habits and tends to spend the day hidden among the fallen leaves in the forest and is active at twilight and at night.
• It feeds, for the most part, on small mammals.

REPRODUCTION

It is a ovoviviparous species that gives birth to a reduced number of young; normally between two and seven.

The babies are exceptionally large at birth, three to four times larger than those of the *Boa constrictor*. Its reproductive strategy is related to the rare presence of large predators in Madagascar.

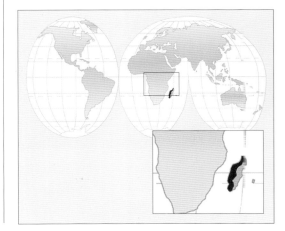

STATUS

The two species of the genus *Acrantophis* are rather scarce in all of their area of distribution.

In some regions Dumeril's Boa is liked by the local population and is even used to combat plagues from rats. However, in other regions it is feared and eliminated as soon as it is found.

Its populations are also detrimentally affected by deforestation and the systematic destruction of its habitat.

It is not frequently in captivity although it has been successfully bred in different zoos such as those in Dallas and Chicago.

It is classified in the CITES agreement in Appendix I, that of Maximum Protection. It is classified as *Vulnerable* in the IUCN's red book of endangered species.

DISTRIBUTION

It is only found in the middle western part of the island of Madagascar, with a greater presence in southern and central regions close to the coast.

It is also found, possibly introduced, on the island of Reunion, one of the Mascarenas Islands, close to Madagascar.

■ There are no subspecies.

ACRANTOPHIS MADAGASCARIENSIS

SUBFAMILY **BOINAE**

(Dumeril & Bibron, 1844)

Madagascar Boa
Malagasy Ground Boa

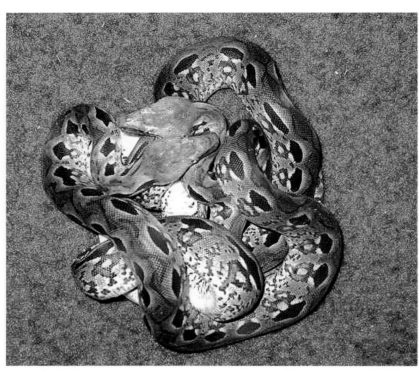

Acrantophis madagascariensis
(Malagasy Ground Boa).
Adult specimen.

DESCRIPTION

It is the largest boa of Madagascar; the largest specimen seen was 11 feet long, with the average size of adults being eight feet.

The Madagascar Boa is a species endemic to Madagascar, just like the only other species of the genus *Acrantophis*, Dumeril's Boa. It has recently been classified in the genus *Boa*, specifically as *Boa madagascariensis*.

It is a voluminous snake, with a solid and cylindrical body, and a head that is well differentiated from the body with a slightly pronounced snout.

The eyes are small with vertical pupils.

The body scales are small and smooth, while the head scales are somewhat larger (unlike *A. dumerili*, whose head scales are very small).

The color of the body is a pale brownish color, with dark lobular blotches distributed longitudinally along the body.

REPRODUCTION

It reproduces viviparously, and gives birth to between two and six young after a gestation period of eight or nine months.

These are extraordinarily large snakes; they measure up to two inches and can weigh up to seven oz. Because Dumeril's Boa is also so large, it seems that its size is an adaptive reaction to the lack of large terrestrial carnivores on the island of Madagascar.

Just like Dumeril's Boa, it is known by the name *do* by the indigenous people, although in some regions it is also known as *ankona*.

Acrantophis madagascariensis
(Malagasy Ground Boa).
Adult specimen.

HABITAT

It inhabits regions of warm humid or subhumid forests, habitually not very far from rivers, streams, and other lacustrine areas.

BEHAVIOR

• This species is typically terrestrial and nocturnal; during the day it remains resting among the floor's vegetation or under the trunks of fallen trees.

• It feeds mainly on micro-mammals and the kills them by constriction.

STATUS

Because it is a large animal with a calm temperament, it is easily found and hunted by the local people. However, the most serious problem that it faces today is the destruction of its habitat.

The forests on the island of Madagascar are disappearing at one of the highest and fastest rates in the world.

It is even more rarely in captivity than *A. dumerili*, and also appears classified by the CITES agreement in Appendix I, and is considered *Vulnerable* by the IUCN.

DISTRIBUTION

It inhabits the northern half of Madagascar, mainly to the extreme west. It is also found on the small very deforested Island of Nosy Be. To the extreme south of this island, it is found in the Integral Nature Reserve of Lokobe, a very well conserved zone of the original tropical humid forest.

■ No subspecies of the Madagascar Boa are recognized.

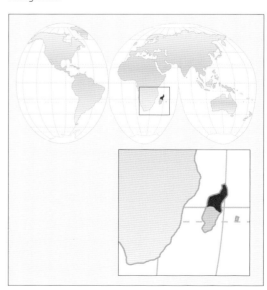

 (Schneider, 1801)

Pacific Island Boa
Solomon's Ground Boa

CANDOIA CARINATA

SUBFAMILY: **BOINAE**

Candoia carinata
(Pacific Island Boa).
Adult specimen.

DESCRIPTION

It is a small species, which only grows up to three feet long, much less than the largest of the boas (*Candoia bibroni*) that inhabit the islands of the Pacific Ocean, and can reach more than five feet in length. The females are larger than the males.

Its body is solid and heavy, somewhat flattened laterally. The flattened head is large and well differentiated from the body. The eyes are small with vertical pupils. The nose is prominent and truncated, and the tail is strong, short, and prehensile. The body scales are keeled and the head scales are small, irregular, and have short tubercles.

The males conserve vestiges of the pelvic girdle in the form of spurs.

The coloration of the back is very variable; it ranges from greenish, brownish, or reddish. The pattern s also very variable; species have been found with smal dark blotches along the body, others are considerably striped, and some have a uniform coloration without blotches or stripes. The ventral part is a whitish or grayish color with or without dark blotches.

HABITAT

Humid forests, marshy areas, and zones close to brooks and streams that traverse the jungle.

BEHAVIOR

• Species are of primarily terrestrial habitats, but also quite often show semi-arboreal tendencies, frequently climbing the shrubs and small trees thanks to the help of their powerful prehensile tail.

• It feeds on small mammals (including bats on some occasions), birds, lizards, and presumably also on amphibians.

• During the day it stays hidden between the rocks or vegetation, and shows activity at twilight and nighttime.

• In spite of the large geographical separation between them, the boas of the genus *Candoia* seem very closely related to the South American and Caribbean boas of the genus *Epicrates*.

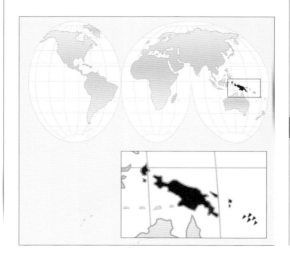

REPRODUCTION

Reproduces ovovivaparously; the females give birth to between ten and 15 babies (sometimes quite a lot more) after a gestation period of up to eight months.

STATUS

In the last few decades, many islands of Melanesia and Polynesia have suffered from a significant diminishing of their natural environment; this has been especially detrimental to the forests and therefore to all the species that inhabit them, such as the Pacific Boa.

Also, this species is a highly valued source of food on some islands, and is therefore frequently hunted by the locals. As a result, its populations are in decline in many places.

It is fairly habitually found in captivity, and has been repeatedly bred in different zoos and in many private international collections.

It is protected by Appendix II of the Washington agreement (CITES).

DISTRIBUTION

New Guinea and other Pacific archipelagoes: Salomon, Palau, Sulawesi, the Moluccas.

■ Although not always accepted, some researchers can distinguish two different subspecies: The Pacific Boa *C. c. carinata*, and the Santa Cruz Boa *C. c. paulsoni*.

CANDOIA ASPERA

SUBFAMILY **BOINAE**

 (Gunther, 1877)

 New Guinea Viper Boa
New Guinea Ground Boa

Candoia aspera (New Guinea Ground Boa). Adult specimen.

DESCRIPTION

It is a relatively small species; the largest specimens only reach three feet.

Its body is thick, strong, lightly compressed, and the head triangular and well differentiated from the body. The flattened large and angular head ends with a straight, somewhat oblique snout. It has small eyes and vertical pupils. The tail is very short, conical, and unlike other species of the *Candoia* genus, is not prehensile. The body scales are keeled and the head is covered with small irregular scales that have many small tubercles or short keels. The males have anal spurs that generally do not appear on the females. The females are double the size of the males.

The background coloration is very variable; a yellowish, reddish, or brownish, with dark vertebral blotches distributed longitudinally along the body. The ventral zone is yellowish with or without dark blotches.

This species has a wide variety of colors and patterns, and it is worth pointing out that the specimens that live in regions where the venomous viper *Acanthophis* is found, share a coloration and behavior that is extraordinarily similar to that of this dangerous species. For this reason (and due to its own appearance) it is also known by the name *viperina of New Guinea*.

HABITAT

Rainforests, marshy forests, and other humid warm areas.

BEHAVIOR

• It has mainly terrestrial habits, but it also has a clear aquatic tendency, which is why it is frequently observed swimming.
• It feeds on frogs, lizards, micro-mammals, and it sometimes also captures small fish.
• It is mainly active at twilight and at nighttime.

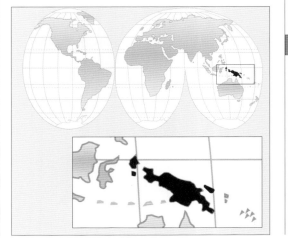

REPRODUCTION

It reproduces ovoviviparously; it tends to have between ten and 15 babies that are born already very active.

Some large females have had up to 30 babies in one clutch.

STATUS

It is considered an irascible and aggressive species, and it is not frequently in captivity, although it has been successfully raised on different occasions.

Its exact status in its natural environment is unknown. It is protected by the Washington agreement (CITES) in Appendix II.

DISTRIBUTION

New Guinea, Archipelago of Bismark, the Islands of Almirantazgo, Indonesia (Muluccas Islands, Waigeu, Batanta, Misool, Salawati).

■ No subspecies are recognized.

This snake shares a good part of its geographic distribution with *Candoia carinata*, the New Guinea Tree Boa, as well as with other various species of pythons of the genera *Morelia* and *Chondropython*. There is, however, no direct competition between them because they exploit different habitats.

📄 (Schneider, 1801)

📄 Rough-Scaled Sand Boa
Indian Sand Boa

ERYX CONICUS
SUBFAMILY ERICINAE

Eryx conicus
(Indian Sand Boa).
Detail of the head.

DESCRIPTION

This snake has a thick and cylindrical body with a very short and extremely round tail. The head is slightly differentiated from the body, and has small eyes with vertical pupils. The snout is in the shape of a wedge, a characteristic that makes it a more efficient burrower.

The body scales appear markedly keeled, with a large central keel, which gives it a rough appearance, unique among Sand Boas.

The ventral scales (168 to 176) and subcaudal scales (17 to 23) are wide and extended. The palatine teeth and the front maxillary teeth are curved and lengthened.

It is a light reddish, or grayish color, and it has conspicuous dark blotches, distributed in a zigzag along the back, with small sunspots on the flanks.

The ventral zone is a whitish coloration.

The females that can reach up to 35 inches, are much larger than the males, which are a little more than 20 inches.

This species is classified in a different genus, *Gongylophis*, within the same family of the Erycinae.

In some works, it can also be found with the scientific name, *Gongylophis conicus*.

HABITAT

Found not only in the sandy desert zones, which is the preferred environment for the majority of the species of the genus *Eryx*, but more commonly in steppe regions, agricultural areas, in dry forests and even in some humid forests close to the coast.

BEHAVIOR

• It is a burrowing snake with crepuscular and nocturnal habits; during the day it remains buried or hidden in holes, under rocks, or in tree trunks.
• It feeds on rodents, small sized lizards and even other Sand Boas.

REPRODUCTION

It reproduces ovoviviparously; it gives birth to between three and 12 considerable sized babies during the months of June and July.

The young look the same as the adults. The females reach sexual maturity after three to four years, while the males reach sexual maturity when they are two years old.

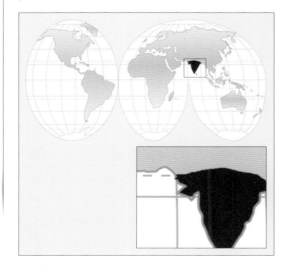

STATUS

It is a fairly common species in many places within its area of distribution and is even used sometimes by Indian snake charmers.

It is frequently in captivity, is easy to feed, and breeding is not very complicated.

It is valued for its pacific docile character; the fact that the adults tolerate handling very well, and rarely bite (only newborns tend to bite and, on occasion, pregnant females).

The Indian Sand Boa is the second most common Sand Boa in captivity in the United States.

This species is protected by the Washington agreement in Appendix II.

DISTRIBUTION

Indian subcontinent.

■ Two subspecies are distinguished:

- *E. c. conicus*: India and Pakistan.
- *E. c. brevis*: Sri Lanka.

ERYX JACULUS

SUBFAMILY **ERICINAE**

 (Linnaeus, 1758)

 Caucasian Sand Boa
European Sand Boa
Javelin Sand Boa

E. jaculus
(Javelin Sand Boa)
Adult specimen.

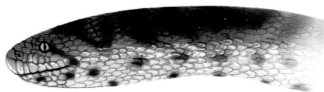

E. jaculus (Javelin Sand Boa).
Adult specimen. Detail of the head.

REPRODUCTION

It mainly reproduces ovoviviparously, although it seems that some populations are oviparous as an adaptation to certain environmental conditions.

Six to 20 already perfectly formed babies are born between the end of July to September, and are five to six inches long.

STATUS

Although it is an innocuous and harmless species, in many places in its area of distribution, it is considered to be a very dangerous animal that bites, and is always killed when found.

In some places it is also captured for dietary reasons. Its global status is, however, unknown due to how inhospitable many areas of its habitat are, and the fact that it has hypogenic and discreet habits.

This species is protected by the Washington agreement (CITES) in Appendix II.

DISTRIBUTION

Southeastern Europe, the Near East, and northern Africa.

■ Three subspecies are distinguished:

- *E. j. jaculus*: Syria, Iraq, Iran, Israel, Jordan, northern Saudi Arabia, and northern Africa from Egypt to Morocco.

- *E. j. familiaris*: Turkey, Georgia, Armenia, Azerbaijan, and northeastern Iran.

- *E. j. turcicus*: Romania, Yugoslavia, Albania, Bulgaria, Greece, Corfu, Cyclades, and western Turkey.

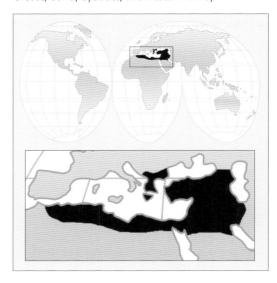

DESCRIPTION

This small burrowing boa has a thick and cylindrical body and only measures between 12 and 31 inches in length, although specimens longer than 20 inches are rare. The females are much longer than the males. The head is small with no neck, and the snout is rounded and lightly depressed downwards. The eyes are minuscule and have vertical pupils. The tail is short (2.4 to 5 inches) and extremely conical.

The body and head scales are small, bright, and somewhat keeled, which makes it look granular. The ventral scales range from 160 to 205 and are very narrow and lengthened. The males conserve vestiges of the pelvic girdle in the form of spurs, located at the sides of the cloaca.

The dorsal coloration is grayish, brownish-gray, yellowish, or reddish, with one or a series of dark blotches that longitudinally traverse the body.

These blotches may be independent or quite united, forming a type of reticulum. The stomach is a whitish or yellowish color.

HABITAT

Preferably in arid and semi-arid zones with soft or sandy floors, although they are also found in alluvial regions, terrain under cultivation, stony sandy shores of rivers, lakes, and hillsides with few trees.

They live from sea level to an elevation of 5,577 feet.

BEHAVIOR

• This species has burrowing tendencies and spends the majority of the day buried in the ground or hidden under rocks or fallen tree trunks.

• It can be out on the surface at twilight, nighttime, or at sunrise.

• It basically feeds on micro-mammals, although other prey such as lizards, terrestrial birds or even some soft-bodied invertebrates like slugs also form a part of their diet.

• The name *Javelin Sand Boa* comes from the way they capture their prey: the attack is quick and sudden, performed with the velocity and precision with which a javelin is thrown.

(Russell, 1801)

 Brown Sand Boa
John's Sand Boa
Indian Sand Boa

ERYX JOHNII

SUBFAMILY ERICINAE

DESCRIPTION

It is the largest of the Sand Boas; adult females are larger than the males, which can reach more than three feet in length.

The body is cylindrical, but fairly slender and not as solid as other species of *Eryx*. The head is slightly differentiated from the body and the tail is short with a rounded tip. The eyes are very small with vertical pupils. The body and the head are covered with small bright scales that are very slightly keeled.

It has between 194 and 209 ventral scales and between 26 and 36 subcaudal scales.

The coloration of the body is a uniform brown with tonalities that vary from reddish to blackish. The young are an orangish color with black transversal bands all along their bodies. As they get older, these bands disappear completely and the body darkens until it acquires its characteristic livery brownish-gray. However, some specimens retain the neonatals' orangish color. The adults of the subspecies *E. j. persicus* also conserve the black bands on the tip of the tail. The ventral zone has a light tonality with random dark blotches.

HABITAT

It mainly lives in arid semi-desert plains where there is an abundance of bushes and dry rocky hills and where the floors are always soft or sandy. It can also be found in areas under cultivation and regions that are somewhat more humid.

BEHAVIOR

• These are snakes with burrowing tendencies, and tend to remain semiburied in the sand, with the body hidden and the head hardly sticking out to lie in wait for the small mammals and lizards it feeds on. As in all *Eryx*, it captures its prey with its mouth and asphyxiates it by constricting the coils of its body before ingesting.

• It is a crepuscular and nocturnal species.

• When it feels like it is being attacked, it shows defensive behavior that consists of hiding its head, lifting the tip of its tail and moving it backwards and forwards to confuse the aggressor. Good proof of the efficiency of this technique is the frequency with which specimens are found in their natural environment with scars on their tails.

REPRODUCTION

They reproduce viviparously and the females give birth to a number of babies that can exceed fifteen.

The males have small spurs around the cloaca that are vestiges of posterior extremities.

STATUS

It is a common species in a good part of its area of distribution, given that it tends to be unperceived due to its discreet subterranean habits.

Eryx johnii (Brown Sand Boa) Adult specimen.

Eryx johnii (Brown Sand Boa)
Adult specimen. Detail of the head.

It is often found, however, in the hands of the snake charmers who often mutilate the tail to make it look even more like the head, and who present it to the public as an extraordinary two-headed snake.

It is becoming more and more popular as a domestic animal due to its beautiful coloration and docile character.

It has successfully been bred in captivity.

This species is protected by Appendix II of the Washington agreement (CITES).

DISTRIBUTION

Arid regions between the Iranian plateau and to the north of the Gulf of Bengal.

■ Two different subspecies are recognized:

- *E. j. johnii*: eastern Pakistan, northern India, and Bangladesh.

- *E. j. persicus*: Iran, Pakistan, and northeastern India.

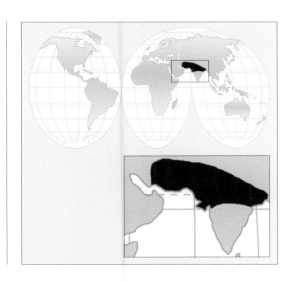

ERYX COLUBRINUS

SUBFAMILY ERICINAE

 (Linnaeus, 1758)

Kenya Sand Boa
Egyptian Sand Boa
East African Sand Boa

E. colubrinus
(East African Sand Boa).
Adult specimen.

DESCRIPTION

A small burrowing snake that does not usually measure more than 26 inches in length.

It has a robust and solid body and the head is hardly differentiated from the body.

The rostral scale is large and prominent, which is why the upper mandible seems longer than the lower one. It has very small eyes with vertical elliptical pupils.

The tail is very short and hardly makes up a tenth of the body's total length.

The scales are small and slightly keeled (the keels are only slightly more visible on the tail), while the head scales look granular.

The background color of the body is whitish, yellowish, orangish, or a creamy color, with dark irregular brownish or reddish blotches along the back. The ventral zone has an even lighter tonality with small sunspots that are not always present.

HABITAT

Semidesert zones, thicketed regions, dry savannahs, and places with rocky outcrops in somewhat more humid environments.

Always in soft or sandy floors.

BEHAVIOR

• Crepuscular and nocturnal.

• During the day it generally stays buried in the floor, although it also tends to seek refuge under rocks, inside small mammals' burrows, or within thick accumulations of vegetation.

• It mainly eats rodents, but can also hunt small reptiles and chicks of birds that lay their eggs on the ground.

• As in all the *Eryx* species, it stays semiburied in the sand when hunting its prey; the upper part of the head hardly juts out, and it lies in wait like this until it suddenly leaps on its prey.

REPRODUCTION

It reproduces ovoviviparously.

The females can have between six and 20 babies that look very much like the adults, but with a paler complexion that becomes darker with age.

STATUS

No information is currently available about the state of its populations in their natural environment, but it is a snake that is fairly often in captivity.

In the United States, it is the most common Sand Boa and the one that has been most successfully bred. Different varieties have even been achieved among which the albinos stand out, especially valued by breeders. It is protected by Appendix II of the Washington agreement (CITES).

DISTRIBUTION

Northern and eastern Africa, and a small population in the extreme south of the Arabian Peninsula.

■ Two subspecies are distinguished:

- *E. c. colubrinus*: Yemen, and northeastern Africa, from Egypt to Air (Nigeria), Ethiopia, and Somalia.

- *E. c. loveridgei*: Southern Somalia, Kenya, and northern Tanzania.

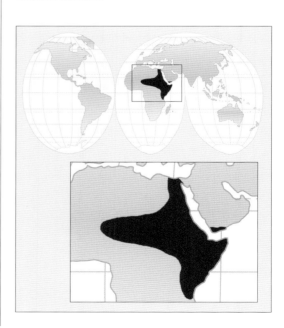

📄 (Blainville, 1835)

📄 Rubber Boa

Charina bottae (Rubber Boa).
Adult specimen.

CHARINA BOTTAE

SUBFAMILY ERICINAE

Charina bottae (Rubber Boa).
Scales in an adult specimen.

DESCRIPTION

A small burrowing snake that measures only between 16 and 33 inches long, has a compact and cylindrical body with a bright and elastic appearance, apparently rubbery, from which it derives its popular name.

It has a slightly prominent conical head and a short blunt tail; it is another species that is called a *two-headed snake* because it is difficult to distinguish the two extremes of its body.

The body scales are small and smooth, while the head scales are considerably large. The eyes are small and have vertical pupils. The back is a uniform olive green, brownish, reddish, or dark brown color while the ventral zone is lighter with diffused dark blotches on the flanks.

The young tend to have a pinkish tonality for a certain time, but they do not take long to acquire the adult color.

The adult males have well developed visible spurs that are smaller on the female and almost always hidden.

HABITAT

It lives on the periphery of marshy forests and especially in the large masses of conifers, although it also lives in extensive open grassy regions (prairies), as well as in scrubland and sandy zones close to the course of water.

BEHAVIOR

• It mainly has burrowing habits and it is a crepuscular and nocturnal species.

• During the day it can be found under rocks, in spaces between tree roots, or among the forest's humus.

• In spite of its primary adaptation to subterranean life, it is a good swimmer and thanks to its prehensile tail, is also capable of climbing bushes and small trees.

• It has a strong resistance to low temperatures, and it is a constricting species that feeds on small rodents, birds, lizards, salamanders, and even small snakes, while the young mainly capture insects.

• It is calm and not very aggressive, and when it is in danger, it displays a defensive behavior that other species of Boidae also display: it coils up forming a compact ball, hides its head in the interior of the coils, and lifts the tail in the direction of its potential enemy.

REPRODUCTION

It reproduces ovoviviparously; it gives birth to between two and eight young, six to eight inches in length, between the months of August and September.

Some specimens have lived more than ten years in captivity.

STATUS

It still seems fairly common in some regions of its area of distribution, but in general, its populations are in decline.

It is protected in Appendix II of the CITES agreement.

DISTRIBUTION

East coast and central North America, from southern Canada to northern California.

■ Three subspecies are distinguished:

- *Ch. b. bottae*: Canada (south of British Columbia) to central California.

- *Ch. b. umbratica*: California (San Bernardino and nearby counties).

- *Ch. b. utahensis*: eastern North America, Rocky Mountains from northeastern to northern California to British Columbia, and in the east to Utah, Nevada, and Wyoming.

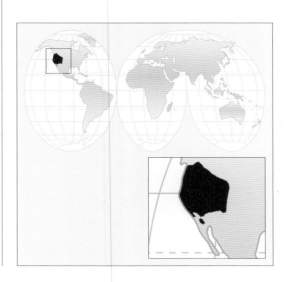

LICHANURA TRIVIRGATA

SUBFAMILY ERICINAE

 Cope, 1861

Rosy Boa

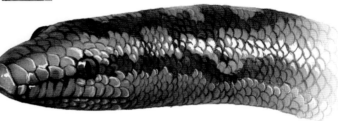

Lichanura trivirgata (Rosy Boa).
Adult specimen.
Details of the head.

DESCRIPTION

Solid, smooth, and bright medium snake; adult specimens rarely exceed 3 feet in length.

The head is narrow, not very differentiated from the body, and the tail is short with a rounded tip.

The color of the body can be gray, brownish, reddish, or pinkish, with somewhat defined dark brown or pink longitudinal bands all along the body.

The exact taxonomy of this snake is also very controversial. According to some authors, this species pertains to the same genus as the Rubber Boa, *Charina bottae*, and is called *Charina trivirgata*, while for others, two different species should be distinguished: the Mexican Rosy Boa, *Lichanura trivirgata*, and the Coastal Rosy Boa, *Lichanura roseofusca*.

HABITAT

Desert, semidesert, rocky areas or scrubland, generally close to places with some degree of humidity such as springs, rivers, and bottoms of rocky canyons.

Due to this tendency, it is usually found in irrigated agricultural zones located in arid regions.

It is found from sea level up to an elevation of 3,937 feet.

BEHAVIOR

• It has terrestrial, almost semiburrowing habits, and tends to spend the daytime hidden in burrows, under large rocks, or simply buried in the sand.

• At the beginning of spring, it tends to appear active in the morning before the temperature rises, but afterwards, it adopts crepuscular and nocturnal habits; it leaves to hunt its prey at sundown. It basically hunts micro-mammals, although it does not hesitate in climbing a low bush to capture small birds, which frequently complement its diet.

• It is a constricting species.

• It is not very aggressive; when it is bothered it coils up in a ball and hides its head inside the coils.

REPRODUCTION

The males have some small spurs on both sides of the caudal scale that they use to stimulate the females during mating.

It is a ovoviviparous species; the females can give birth to three to ten young after 110 and 134 days of gestation.

STATUS

It does not seem to be abundant in any part of its area of distribution, but it is not considered a species in an extremely critical situation either.

It is frequently in captivity, and breeds easily.

Through selective breeding, spectacular varieties in coloration have been achieved.

Some captive specimens have managed to live more than 18 years.

This species is classified in Appendix II of the CITES agreement.

DISTRIBUTION

From southern California to northern Mexico.

■ Three subspecies are distinguished:

- *L. t. trivirgata*: from southern Arizona to Sonora and Baja California (Mexico).

- *L. t. gracia*: southeastern California, southwestern Arizona, and western Sonora.

- *L. t. roseofusca*: southeastern California and northeastern Baja California (Mexico).

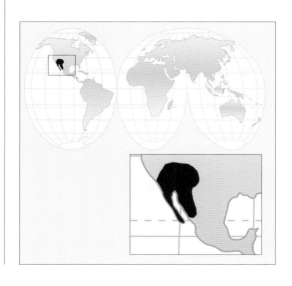

(Schlegel, 1837)

Round Island Ground Boa

CASAREA DUSSUMIERI

SUBFAMILY BOLYERINAE

DESCRIPTION

Relatively small and thin species, does not reach more than four feet in length.

It has a cylindrical body, a thin head that is well differentiated from the body, and small eyes with vertical pupils. The tail is long (a quarter of its total length), prehensile and sharp. Its maxilla are divided into two parts, front and back, a unique characteristic among the Tetrapoda.

The body scales and the back part of the head are small and keeled, with a large central keel. It has between 227 and 235 ventral scales and between 120 and 133 subcaudal scales.

The dorsal color is of a light uniform brown or with two dark longitudinal bands and a lateral series of small almost black blotches. It has two dark lines on each side of the head that crosses the eyes. The stomach is a uniform yellowish color or it has small black blotches. This animal is very similar to a certain species of South American boas of the *Epicarates* genus. Unlike the majority of boas, it does not have anal spurs.

HABITAT

Survives only in the small areas of tropical forests that are conserved on Round Island; today they have practically disappeared.

BEHAVIOR

• This snake has terrestrial and nocturnal habits; it feeds on small mammals, frogs, lizards, and geckos. Thanks to its prehensile tail, it can occasionally climb shrubs and small trees.

• Although during the day it tends to remain hidden in subterranean burrows of considerable humidity or cracks in the rocks, in contrast with the other Round Island Boa, *Bolyeria multocarinata*, it is not a species that burrows very much.

REPRODUCTION

It reproduces oviparously; mating takes place around the month of May.

The clutch oscillates between three and ten eggs that take between 61 and 67 days to hatch.

STATUS

Wiped out on the island of Mauricio, extremely scarce on Round Island, and found in very serious danger of extinction. The main causes of this situation are due to the destruction of the habitat, and mainly, to the introduction of foreign species such as rats, rabbits, cats, and pigs.

However, important efforts have been made, for years already, to try to save this species from extinction. Therefore, Round Island is currently a natural reserve, access to the island is strictly regulated, and

Casarea dussumieri
(Round Island Ground Boa).
Adults specimens.

the populations have been controlled (and in some cases, eliminated) from invading species.

Also, there is a small colony of this species in captivity in the Jersey Wildlife Preservation Trust, an important conservationist institution founded by Gerald Durrell on the Isle of Jersey, in the canal of la Mancha, that is carrying out a successful program of breeding in captivity.

This species is classified in Appendix I of the Washington agreement (CITES), which explains its maximum protection, and it is classified as *Endangered* by the UICN.

DISTRIBUTION

Only on Round Island, close to Mauricio, one of the Mascarenas Islands, an archipelago located in the Indian Ocean.

■ There are no subspecies.

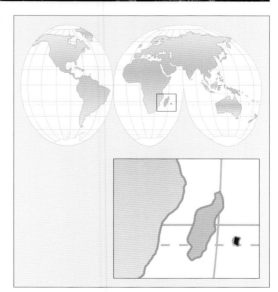

BOLYERIA MULTOCARINATA

SUBFAMILIY BOLYERINAE

 (Boie,1827)

 Round Island Burrowing Boa

Bolyeria multocarinata
(Round Island Burrowing Boa).
Adult specimen.
Detail of head.

DESCRIPTION

Small subterranean boa; the adults do not exceed three feet in length.

As an adaptation to its hypogenic life, its small pointy head is not differentiated from the practically cylindrical body. It has very small eyes with vertical elliptical pupils. The non-prehensile tail is very short and has an extremely rounded tip–a characteristic similar to that observed in the species of the genus Eryx.

The body scales are small, hexagonal, and slightly juxtaposed. The scales on the front part of the head are, on the other hand, considerably large. It has between 192 and 200 ventral scales and 83 to 92 subcaudal scales.

The dorsal coloration is a pale brownish or olive green color with small dark irregular blotches along the body. It has two dark lines on each side of the head behind the eyes. There are vertical stripes on both sides of the tail, and the ventral zone is a yellowish color that is often blotched.

It does not have vestiges of posterior extremities in the form of anal spurs, and it has maxilla formed by two halves, a quality that it shares only with *Casarea dussumieri* within Tetrapoda vertebrae.

HABITAT

Originally lived in the soft floor of the tropical humid forests characteristic of Round Island.

BEHAVIOR

• This species has nocturnal and subterranean habits; it feeds on micro-mammals, and presumably also amphibians and small reptiles (skinks and geckos).

REPRODUCTION

This snake's form of reproduction is unknown.

STATUS

No specimen is known to be in captivity and none have been observed free since 1975, which is why this species is probably already totally extinct.

The same applies as for the *Casarea dussumieri*; as well as the destruction of its habitat, the most significant cause that has led to this irreparable status, has been the introduction of foreign animals by humans (rats, cats, pigs, rabbits, and others).

This species is classified in Appendix I of CITES (Washington Agreement) and as *Extinct* by the UICN.

DISTRIBUTION

Only on Round Island, close to Mauricio (where this species previously lived), one of the Mascarenas Islands, an archipelago located in the Indian Ocean.

■ There are no subspecies.

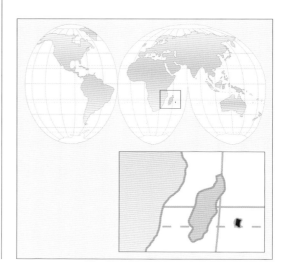

F. Tropidophiidae

21 SPECIES

Are considered in many ways to be an intermediate step between the Boidae and the Colubridae.

They have vestiges of the pelvic girdle, a characteristic unique to the Boidae; however, some species of the genus Tropidurus lack these vestiges.

They are small snakes that do not exceed three feet in length, which is why they are called Dwarf Boas.

They are mainly terrestrial, although they sometimes climb trees and lead a stealthy, mainly nocturnal, life.

Many of them have bright and colorful defensive behavior which sometimes includes expelling blood from the mouth and eyes.

■ Four genera are distinguished:

– *Trachyboa*, with two species that live in Panama, Colombia, and Ecuador.

– *Tropidophis*, with 16 species extended mainly along the length of the Caribbean, although a few species are found in South America.

– *Ungaliophis* has two species that are distributed from southern Mexico to western Colombia.

– *Exiliboa placata*, endemic to the upper zones of Oaxaca (Mexico).

GENERAL CHARACTERISTICS

Their outward appearance is similar to the Boidae and are differentiated from them by the following characteristics.

• They have a lengthened hyoid bone in the throat.

• The left lung has totally disappeared.

• They have large cephalic shields, more similar to modern snakes (Colubridae).

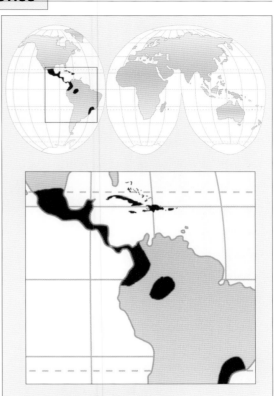

Trachyboa boulengeri (Rough–scaled Boa). Adult specimen in its habitat.

TRACHYBOA BOULENGERI

 Perracca, 1910

 Rough–Scaled Boa

Trachyboa boulengeri
(Rough–scaled Boa).
Adult specimen.

DESCRIPTION

This small, 20-inch snake, has an unusual appearance for a Boidae. Its body is covered with very keeled scales that determined its common name.

The wedge-shaped head is well differentiated from the rest of the body, and it has relatively large and conspicuous eyes with orbital scales in the form of a crest. The rostral scale is absent and it has nine to ten supralabial scales. The tail is short and corpulent, slightly prehensile, and not compressed like the rest of the body.

The body is brown and changes to a reddish color on the stomach. It has two lines of black dots on the flanks. The males have cloacal spurs.

HABITAT

It leads a discreet life, hidden among the humus and the vegetation. It is found in mountain rainforests.

It is a terrestrial, nocturnal, and crepuscular species that is often found close to water.

BEHAVIOR

• When bothered, it displays a bright and colorful defensive behavior: it coils itself up, forming a ball, while at the same time secreting a nauseating liquid from the cloaca; then its eyes turn red, and it expels drops of blood from its mouth from the rupture of a few of the palate's blood vessels. In this manner, it manages to appear dead and even in a state of putrefaction, thereby dissuading its potential predator.

REPRODUCTION

It is a ovoviviparous species.
In captivity, it has fed exclusively on frogs.

STATUS

No information is to be had about the status of its populations.

DISTRIBUTION

Colombia, Ecuador, and Panama.

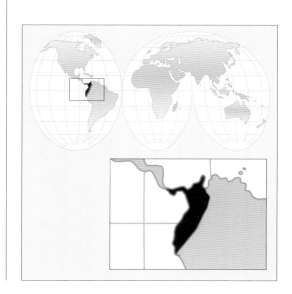

📄 (Schegel,1837)

📄 Cuban Black-Tailed Dwarf Boa

TROPIDOPHIS MELANURUS

Tropidophis melanurus
(Cuban Black-Tailed Dwarf Boa)
Adult specimen.

TROPIDOPHIS MELANURUS
(Cuban Black-Tailed Dwarf Boa)
Adult specimen.
Detail of the head.

Side view.

DESCRIPTION

Medium snake that can reach a length of three feet.

The body appears solid and somewhat compressed; the head is well differentiated from the rest of the body, the tail short and prehensile. The fourth or fifth supralabial is in contact with the eye.

The scales are keeled aside from four or five rows of more exterior scales.

The color is highly variable: it varies from reddish to bluish to light tones without blotches. Two dark longitudinal lines with yellow blotches constitute the most common pattern. It has a black tail.

HABITAT

It is found in very humid and wooded zones, always close to a body of water in places with an abundance of rocks.

Sometimes it can also be found on garden walls.

BEHAVIOR

• It is a crepuscular species that hides during the day under rocks, in very humid areas.
• It is timid, and is rarely seen in the exterior.
• When it feels trapped, it coils itself up, hiding its head in the ball of coils, and emits a smelly substance from its anal gland.
• It is probably capable, just like other species in the family, of reddening its eyes and expelling blood through its mouth due to the rupture of blood vessels when it is very bothered, feigning death and trying to dissuade a potential predator.
• It feeds on small mammals, lizards, and frogs.

REPRODUCTION

It is a ovoviviparous species.
They have been repeatedly raised in captivity.

STATUS

The state of its population is unknown.

DISTRIBUTION

– *T. m. melanurus*, on the Island of Cuba
– *T. m. bucculentus*, Navassa Island
– *T. m. dipsodes*, Island of Cuba.
– *T. m. ericksoni*, Island of Cuba and the Isle of Piños.

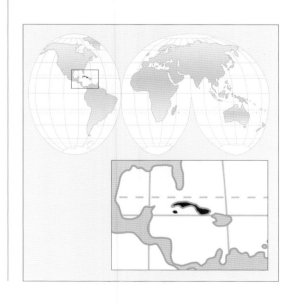

UNGALIOPHIS CONTINENTALIS

 Muller, 1880

📄 Banana Boa

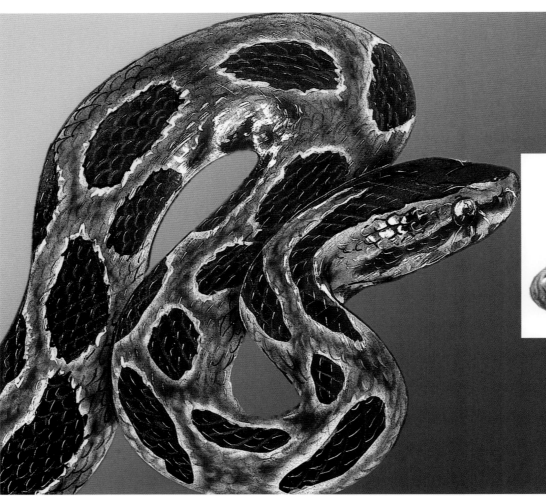

Ungaliophis continentalis
(Banana Boa)
Adult specimen.

UNGALIOPHIS CONTINENTALIS (Banana Boa)
Adult specimen. Detail of the head.

Side view.

The newborns measure an average of six inches. The males reach maturity when they are two years old, and the females when they are three.

STATUS

There is no information about the state of its populations.

To date it has been a rarity in museum collections and in zoos. Until the end of the 1960's, only four specimens had been found. Today, much more is known about this species, and it is bred by individuals and by some zoos.

DISTRIBUTION

From Mexico (Chiapas) to Honduras and Nicaragua.

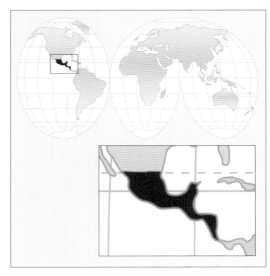

DESCRIPTION

Is a small snake: females reach a length of 22 to 24 inches and males of 18 inches.

Its head is slightly differentiated from the rest of the body and the eyes are quite prominent with gray irises and a rounded pupil.

The coloration of its skin is very characteristic of this species. The background color is brown, bronze, or gray, while the coloration of the stomach can vary from light gray to brown. The upper part of the head has a forked mark that turns into a discontinued double row of oval marks with yellow borders; these are found on the animal's back. Black and orange blotches are visible on the flanks.

Both males and females have small anal spurs that are one inch long.

HABITAT

Found in a wide variety of vegetated zones, from the tropical jungles of the lowlands to pine forests in the mountainous zones.

It hides under tree trunks or bark, although it can also be found between epiphytal vegetation given that it also has certain arboreal tendencies.

BEHAVIOR

• When bothered, it contorts itself and adopts extravagant positions, expelling a smelly liquid from the cloaca.

• On rare occasions it may also bite while trying to coil up around the fingers of the person who is handling it.

• Another defensive strategy that it may adopt when very bothered is to coil itself up, hiding its head between the coils like the *Python regius* or the *Calabaria reinhardtii*.

• It is thought to feed on lizards and frogs.

• The young in captivity have accepted feeding on fish, maybe for their similarity to tadpoles that can be found in the small water receptacles bromeliady and epiphytes plants.

REPRODUCTION

Its reproductive behavior is peculiar; it is the only snake species that, when mating, the male is said to bite the female's tail. In the meantime, it uses its anal spurs to position the body so that it has contact with the female between the cloacae.

The gestation period lasts for five to six months and the female can give birth to an average of three to six young.

F. Acrochordidae

3 SPECIES

The Acrochordidae are snakes with completely aquatic adaptations that are characterized by their wide and depressed head, hardly differentiated from the body, and solid flat body covered with dermal folds. Both the dorsal and ventral scales are small, juxtaposed, and granular.

They are known by the names Wart or Elephant Trunk Snakes due to the presence of skin folds, and as file snakes due to the rough appearance of the granular scales and because of their aquatic and predatory life.

They have both the primitive features characteristic of the Boidae and others that are more evolved and closer to the Colubridae, which is why their exact taxonomic classification is very controversial. Therefore, though they have been classified as a Colubridae subfamily, they are actually considered to constitute their own characteristic family that lies between primitive and colubrid snakes. They appear to be closer to the latter, which is, in reality, due to a phenomenon of adaptive convergence.

■ The family is made up of just one genus, *Acrochordus*, with 3 different species:

– *A. arafurae*, only found on the southern coast of New Guinea and in northern Australia (Queensland and the Northern Territory).

– *A. granulatus* that has sometimes been classified by the name *Chersydrus granulatus*.

– *A. javanicus*, lives in fresh and salt water in southeastern Asia, Indonesia, and northern Australia.

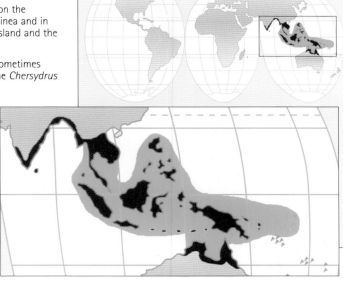

Acrochordus granulatus (Marine File Snake). Adult specimen in its habitat.

ACROCHORDUS
Detail of the mouth.

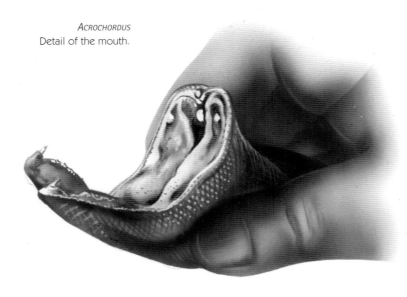

ACROCHORDUS GRANULATUS
(Little File Snake, Marine File Snake).
Cranium.

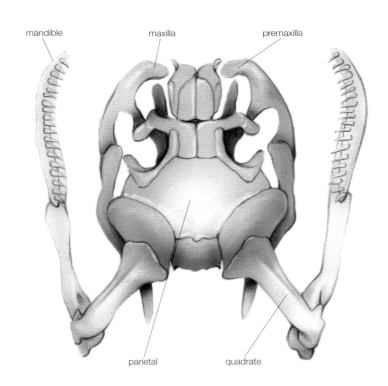

mandible   maxilla   premaxilla

parietal   quadrate

GENERAL CHARACTERISTICS

Characteristics of the family:

- Large, wide, fairly flat head that is posteriorly elongated and slightly differentiated from the body.
- Large wide mouth with movable maxillary bones.
- Small, granular, and juxtaposed scales.
- The head scales are as small and granular as the rest of the body, except for the larger labial scales.
- Free premaxilla without teeth.

- No vestiges of the pelvic girdle or posterior extremities in the form of spurs.
- Coronoid bone absent.
- Valvular nostrils located on the upper part of the snout.
- Small eyes with round pupils, also located very high up.
- Absence of ventral plates.
- One large lung that extends almost along the entire body.
- Prehensile tail that is not laterally flattened.

Acrochordus granulatus (Marine File Snake). Adult specimen.

Acrochordus javanicus (Javan File Snake, Javan Wart Snake, Elephant Trunk Snake).
Detail of the skin.

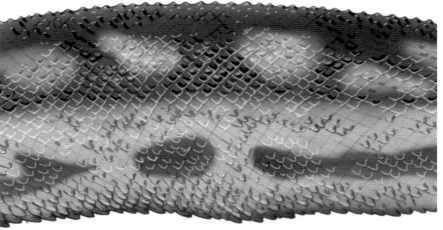

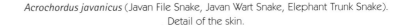

Side view.

(Schneider, 1799)

Little File Snake
Marine File Snake

ACROCHORDUS GRANULATUS

FAMILY **ACROCHORDIDAE**

Acrochordus granulatus
(Little File Snake)
Adult specimen.

DESCRIPTION

Smaller than the Java Shark Snake, it does not usually exceed four feet in length.

It is also distinguished by its less solid body, widened scales on the back, a longitudinal ventral keel, and a characteristic cutaneous fold similar to a suture that extends along the ventral part of the body from the neck to the base of the tail-its function is still discussed.

The skin is not, however, as wrinkled or in such excess as on the *A. javanicus*.

Its sharp tail is slightly compressed.

The body's coloration is dark with a series of alternating white and black bands that are dorsally wide, thinner on the flanks, and can extend along the ventral zone.

HABITAT

It is found in all type of coastal habitats, mainly in estuaries and on seashores, but it is also found in brackish, sometimes shallow calm water. It has been seen moving in the mud at low tide from one pond close to the sea to another.

It tends to frequent mangrove swamps and it lies in wait for its prey between the roots.

BEHAVIOR

• Aquatic, nocturnal, and fish-eating, it feeds mainly on small fish, although it has been seen eating small mollusks and crabs.

• It spends a lot of time submerged in the water, and when it needs to renew its reserve of oxygen, it comes to the surface and remains semi-submerged, only exposing its nostrils.

• It is normally not seen on land, where it moves with difficulty.

• In spite of its disconcerting appearance, it is a completely harmless animal, although, if bothered, it may turn around and even bite.

REPRODUCTION

It is viviparous, and between five to 15 young are born per clutch that measure nine inches in length after six to eight months of embryonic development-one of the longest periods known among snakes. The striped patterns are very marked in the young, and with age, it becomes less contrasted and darker.

The females do not reproduce every year; rather, they reproduce every other year.

STATUS

Although it is totally innocuous and non-venomous, it is often killed because it is confused with sea snakes that are extremely venomous due to their similar coloration and aquatic nature.

It is also hunted because its skin is very valuable, like all the species of the genus *Acrochordus*, and because people eat it for nutrition. For these reasons its current status is not exactly known; it does, however, seem to be declining rapidly.

DISTRIBUTION

Both of India's coasts, Sri Lanka, the coasts of Malaysia and Indonesia, the Philippines (Luzon, Cebu, Bantayan), New Guinea, the Solomon Islands, and the northern coast of Australia.

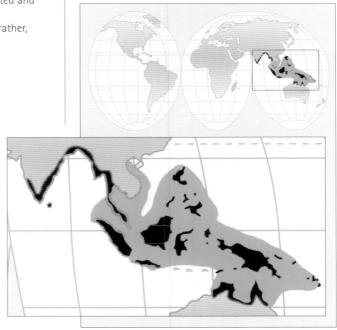

ACROCHORDUS JAVANICUS

FAMILY ACROCHORDIDAE

Hornstedt, 1787

Javan File Snake, Javan Wart Snake
Elephant Trunk Snake

DESCRIPTION

Is the largest representative of the genus given that the adult females are larger than the males (only three to five feet), and can exceed eight feet in length.

With a wide head and a solid body, the nostrils are located on the upper part of the snout and have valves that close to impede water from entering when they submerge themselves.

The absence of ventral plates is another one of its adaptations to aquatic life.

The dorsal coloration is brown, olive green, or a dark gray, with some black marble–like blotches along the sides. The ventral zone is much lighter.

Because there is a lot of skin and it is wrinkled, granular, and has numerous folds, this species is most frequently called Elephant Trunk Snake, singled out from three of the genera *Acrochordus*.

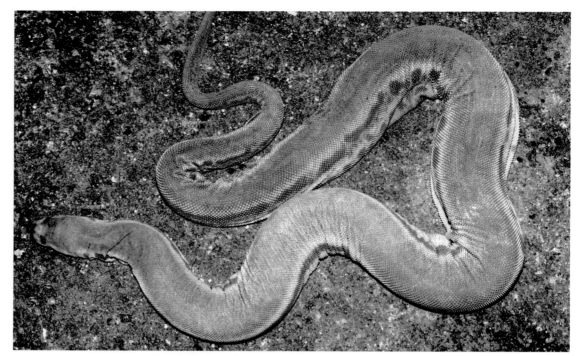

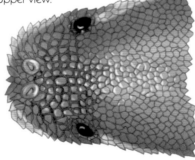

Side view.

Upper view.

Frontal view.

Acrochordus javanicus
(Javan Wart Snake).
Adult specimen.

ACROCHORDUS JAVANICUS
(Javan Wart Snake).
Adult specimen.
Details of the head.

STATUS

Until recently it was considered abundant, but it is excessively pursued for its skin, which is used in leather goods. This skin is highly valued and known by the name of karung. In many areas of its distribution this name is also used to refer to the animal.

It is also valued as food by the local population, who consider it an exquisite delicacy.

The impact of these negative factors is provoking a significant decline of its populations.

DISTRIBUTION

Thailand, Cambodia, Vietnam, southern China, and Indonesia.

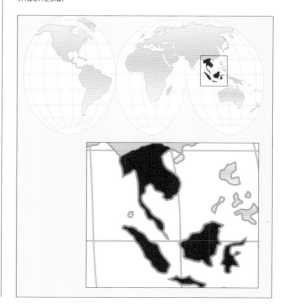

HABITAT

Always found in aquatic environments; mainly frequents fresh water or brackish estuaries, canals, deltas, and low parts of rivers. They move around in salt water very rarely.

Very abundant in deep swamps covered with an abundant amount of submerged vegetation. It can occasionally move along the floor, but not without difficulty.

BEHAVIOR

• It has a completely aquatic life, is an excellent swimmer, and its diet is almost exclusively based on fish, although it also eats amphibians and tadpoles. The perfectly developed dentition adapted for capturing of these slippery creatures is what permits this diet.

• It is capable of staying submerged for quite a while, and when it comes up for air, only the upper part of the head, where its nostrils are located, emerges.

• It spends the day hidden among the bottom vegetation with its prehensile tail often anchoring it to the plants. At sunset it abandons its refuge to patrol its hunting territory.

• It also lies in wait when within the vegetation: taking advantage of its abrasive scales, it wrinkles up its body in successive curves, and when an interesting fish comes by to inspect the snake's strange convoluted skin formed by this position, it suddenly tightens its body and captures its unsuspecting prey in this way.

• It is harmless.

REPRODUCTION

It does not leave the water even to reproduce; it is ovoviviparous and expels its young directly into the water.

It is a very prolific species that gives birth to between 15 and 40 young that measure ten inches in length. The young leave the water more often than the adults.

F. Colubridae
(COLUBRID OR TYPICAL SNAKES)

2,500 SPECIES

This family alone contains two–thirds of today's snakes, and it is extremely difficult and very controversial to classify taxonomically. There is no systematic value placed on the differentiations between opisthoglyphous and aglyphous colubrids or between species that may or may not have parotid or Duvernoy's glands; these characteristics appear independently in the different lineages.

They are called modern snakes along with the Elapidae and the Viperidae, and together represent up to 83% of all snakes. Their light skeletons and quickness and flexibility have turned them into the prototype of all snakes.

These snakes have gone through a great diversification and live in the most varied environments, highly specialized in their adaptations.

Some of them are burrowers and have a reinforced head in order to penetrate the ground, others are arboreal and have an elongated thin body, and others are aquatic with nostrils on the upper part of the snout.

They may be diurnal or nocturnal.

They are generally medium snakes; the extreme sizes range from six inches to 12 feet.

The Colubridae are very rarely found in the sites from the beginning of the Tertiary period in Europe and North America. When they became relatively abundant in the Pliocene and the Pleistocene periods, they were already actual genera, which is why paleontology is not very helpful for this snake's taxonomic classification.

It seems that this group originated in intertropical zones, of which little is known today, and then, more recently, extended to temperate zones.

They are widespread in all temperate, desert, and tropical regions; they are only absent from very cold regions, from some islands and, curiously, from the southern part of Australia, where they have been usurped by the Elapidae.

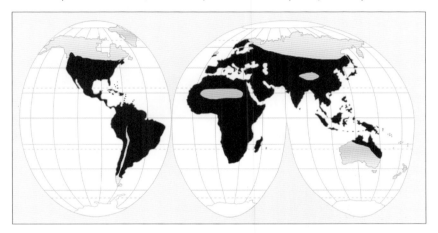

Ahaetulla nasuta. Adult specimen in its habitat.

GENERAL CHARACTERISTICS

COLUBRIDAE
Adult specimen.
Ventral and subcaudal scales.

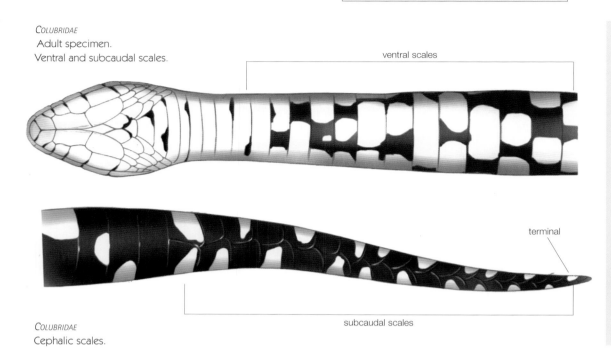

ventral scales

terminal

subcaudal scales

COLUBRIDAE
Cephalic scales.

- Very small dorsal scales that are fairly rhomboidal and overlapping. The ventral scales are transversally larger in just one row.
- The head may or may not be differentiated from the neck, and the eyes are generally large. It is covered with typically arranged large cephalic scales.
- Numerous curved back pointy teeth occupy the length of the maxilla and the dentary bone, and usually the palatine and pterygoid bones. The teeth on the posterior part of the maxilla may have venomous glands (opisthoglyphous), but without very developed or efficient canines.
- The coronoid is absent from the lower mandible.
- The front cranial bones are flexible and moveable within the cranial cavity.
- They do not have a working left lung.
- They do not have vestiges of the pelvic girdle.
- The hemipenes may have spines and a serrated crown.

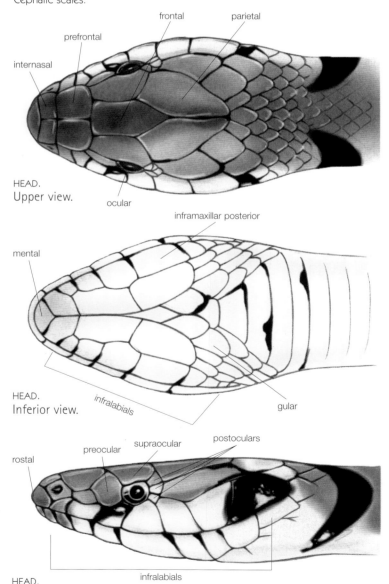

frontal

parietal

prefrontal

internasal

HEAD.
Upper view.

ocular

inframaxillar posterior

mental

HEAD.
Inferior view.

infralabials

gular

rostal

preocular

supraocular

postoculars

HEAD.
Side view.

infralabials

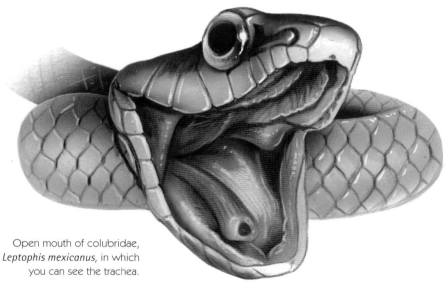

Open mouth of colubridae,
Leptophis mexicanus, in which
you can see the trachea.

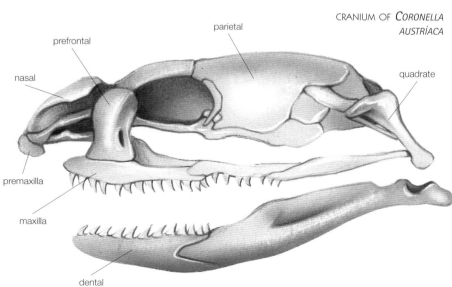

CRANIUM OF *CORONELLA*
AUSTRÍACA

parietal

prefrontal

nasal

quadrate

premaxilla

maxilla

dental

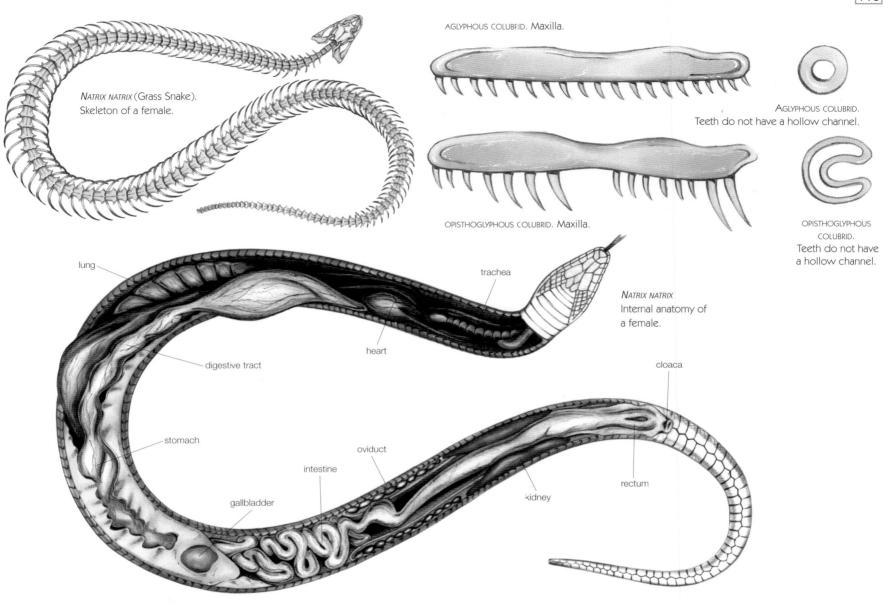

NATRIX NATRIX (Grass Snake).
Skeleton of a female.

AGLYPHOUS COLUBRID. Maxilla.

AGLYPHOUS COLUBRID.
Teeth do not have a hollow channel.

OPISTHOGLYPHOUS COLUBRID. Maxilla.

OPISTHOGLYPHOUS
COLUBRID.
Teeth do not have
a hollow channel.

lung

trachea

NATRIX NATRIX
Internal anatomy of
a female.

heart

cloaca

digestive tract

stomach

oviduct

rectum

intestine

kidney

gallbladder

SUBFAMILY **COLUBRINAE**

Colubrids or Typical Snakes

Elaphe obsoleta
Adult specimen in its habitat.

+ 50 GENERA / +/−900 SPECIES

• A rather slender body.

• The head appears to be covered with large regular symmetrical scales and has large eyes.

• The nostrils are laterally located.

• The ventral scales are wide and the tail long.

• It generally has few teeth on the upper mandible and no venomous fangs

• There are diurnal (*Coluber*), or nocturnal (*Pituophis*), species that inhabit dry zones. Others prefer more humid terrain, generally forests, and are capable of climbing trees and bushes (*Elaphe*), or they are burrowing snakes that inhabit dry zones (*Salvadora*).

• There are no highly specialized aquatic or arboreal species.

■ Comprised of 51 genera:

– In Europe: *Coluber* (also in northern Africa, northern Asia, and North America), *Elaphe* (with a similar distribution except for

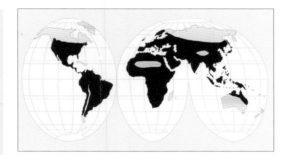

northern Africa), *Coronella* (Europe, northern Africa and western Asia), *Eirinis* (eastern Europe and western Asia).

– In Asia: *Dendrelaphis* (also in Australia), *Stegonotus* (also in Australia), *Eurypholis*, *Gonyophis*, *Gonyosoma*, *Hydrablabes*, *Iguanognatus*, *Liopeltis*, *Ptyas*, *Rhynchophis*, *Zoacys*, *Lytorhynchus*, *Spalerosophis* (also in northern Africa).

– In Africa: *Duberria*, *Gastropyxis*, *Hapsidophrys*, *Meizodon*, *Philothamnus*, *Prosymna*, *Pseudaspis*, *Scaphiophis*, *Thrasops*.

– In North America and/or Central America: *Cemophora*, *Contia*, *Opheodrys*, *Stilosoma*, *Arizona*, *Chilomeniscus*, *Chionactis*, *Drymarchon*, *Drymobius*, *Lampropeltis*, *Masticophis*, *Phyllorhynchus*, *Pituophis*, *Rhinocheilus*, *Salvadora*.

– In the Neotropics: *Chironius*, *Conopsis*, *Dendrophidion*, *Drymoluber*, *Leptodrymus*, *Leptophis*, *Mastigodryas*, *Pseudoficimia*, *Pseustes*, *Simophis*, *Spilotes*.

SUBFAMILY **NATRICINAE**

Water Snakes

38 GENERA / +190 SPECIES

• Its characteristics are poorly defined and are not uniform.

• Colubrids with a head that is very defined from the neck, and a solider body.

• The dorsal scales are usually keeled, perhaps the family's most defined characteristic.

• The dentition is very variable, and while the majority of the species have an aglyphous dentition, there are genera with opisthoglyphous dentition; *Rabdophis, Pseudoxenodon, Macrospithodon, Macrophis, Balanophis*; even some species like *Rhabdophis tigrina* can inflict bites that are dangerous to humans.

• They are fairly aquatic, not very specialized colubrids; in fact the tendency towards an aquatic life varies greatly from one species to the next.

• Its diet normally includes amphibians and fish.

• The majority lay eggs, although some are ovoviviparous.

■ The geographical distribution of the genera is:

– North America: *Carphophis, Diadophis, Nerodia, Seminatrix, Regina, Stoteria, Tropidoclonion, Virginia.*

– North and Central America: *Thamnophis.*

– Central and South America: *Adelophis, Amastridium, Chersodromus, Diaphorolepis, Helicops, Hydromorfus, Hydrops, Paraptychophis, Pliocercus, Pseudoeryx, Ptychophis, Trimetopon.*

– Africa: *Afronatrix, Grayia, Limnophis, Natriciteres, Natrix* (also in Europe).

– Asia: *Atretium, Balanophis, Macropisthodon, Macrophis, Oxyrhabdium, Pararhabdophis, Pseudoxenodon, Rabdophis, Sinonatrix, Xenelaphis, Xenochrophis.*

– Asia and Australia: *Amphiesma.*

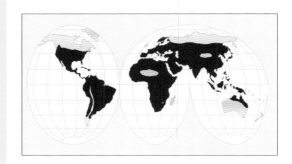

Xenochrophis piscator
Adult specimen in its habitat.

SUBFAMILY **HOMALOPSINAE**

Australasian
Water Snakes

11 GENERA / 35 SPECIES

• Highly specialized aquatic snakes with important adaptations for aquatic life: nostrils located on the back that can be closed when the animal is submerged; it has small eyes pointed upwards.

• Its body is fairly solid; the head is not very differentiated from the neck; and the tail is not laterally flattened.

• They all have venomous fangs on the posterior part of the upper mandible; the venom that is harmless to humans seems to be very active in the fish and crustaceans they feed on.

• They live in rivers, lakes, marshes, and coastal zones with mangrove swamps. A large number can also be found in the rice fields and in their irrigation systems.

• They are ovoviviparous.

• They are found in southeast Asia, the Philippines, Indonesia, and in the coastal region of northern Australia.

■ Some of the genera it covers are:

– *Enhydris*, with 16 species, distributed in this subfamily's entire area of distribution.

– *Homalopsis*, with a widespread very aquatic species.

– *Cerberus* and *Fordonia*, are found in coastal environments and zones with mangrove swamps.

– *Bitia*, a monotypic genus, which inhabits rivers from the south of Burma to the Malayan peninsula and Sumatra.

– *Erpeton*, is also a very aquatic species whose ventral scales have been greatly reduced, which is why it moves along the floor with great difficulty.

– *Myron*, is a monotypic genus found in New Guinea and in northern Australia in coastal zones.

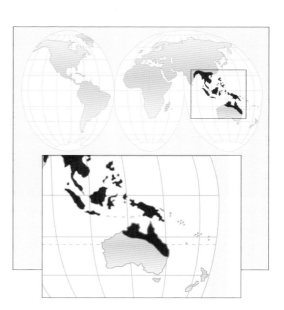

Xerpeton lenticularis
Adult specimen in its habitat.

There are six species, and they are all African:

- *D. atra*: Zaire, Uganda, Kenya and southern Sudan.

- *D. fasciata*: West of Uganda, north of Zaire, Central African Republic, and from southern Chad to Gambia.

- *D. inornata*: South Africa.

- *D. medici*: Somalia, southern Kenya, Tanzania, northern and central Mozambique, and northeastern Zimbabwe.

- *D. palmarun*: Angola, Zaire.

- *D. scabra*: Almost all of sub-Saharan Africa, and some isolated populations in southern Morocco and also in Arabia.

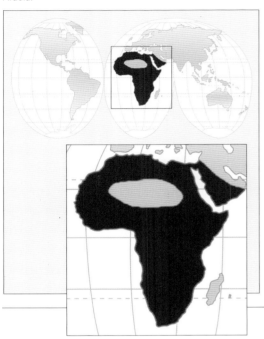

1 GENUS / 6 SPECIES

• They are snakes specialized in eating eggs, which is why they have undergone important adaptations: the maxillary bones are tightly joined together while the mandibles are very loosely joined. The teeth are small and scarce and are found exclusively in the back part of the mouth.

• The skin on both sides of the mouth has a great potential for expansion.

• The cervical vertebrae have hypophysis that extends them to the mouth of the esophagus; they are covered with enamel and look like authentic teeth. When the egg goes through the esophagus, these teeth break it, and its contents are emptied into the digestive track.

• They have a small slightly elongated head that is not differentiated from the neck; the snout is rounded.

• They have very keeled scales, especially on the flanks.

• They are oviparous and can reach 4 inches in length, although they are generally smaller.

SUBFAMILY **DASYPELTINAE**

African Egg-eating Snakes

Dasypeltis inornata
Adult specimen in its habitat.

■ Distribution:

– Asia: *Anoplohydrus, Aspidura, Blythia, Cyclorus, Dinodon, Dryocalamus, Elapoides, Haplocercus, Haplonodon, Lepturophis, Lycodon, Oligodon, Opisthotropis, Oreocalamus, Plagiopholis, Rhabdops, Rhynchocalamus, Tetralepis, Trachischium, Xylophis.*

– In Africa: *Boaedon, Bothrolycus, Bothrophthalmus, Chamaelycus, Compsophis, Crytolycus, Dendrolycus, Dromicodryas, Glypholycus, Gonionotophis, Heteroliodon, Hormonotus, Lamprophis, Lioheteredon, Liopholidophis, Lycodonomorphus, Lycophidium, Meelya, Micropisthodon, Pararhadinaea, Psedoxyrhopus.*

– In South America (neotropics): *Adelphicos, Atractus, Geagras, Geatractus, Geophis, Ninia, Tropidodipsa* (found in Mexico).

– In North America: *Farancia* (the relation with this subfamily is controversial).

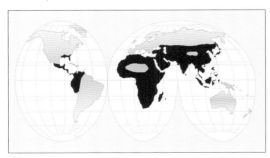

50 GENERA / + 200 SPECIES

• They form a not very homogenous or characteristic group, with fairly primitive features, and can be considered as a transition towards the Colubrinae or Natricinae.

• They are small and medium snakes that lead a fairly discreet terrestrial life. There are even some semi-burrowing species; others live in the trees, in the muddy fields, or in the water.

• The main characteristic of the group, from which comes its name, is the differentiation of the teeth into large fangs that are found grouped on the front and back of the upper maxilla, and in the front part of the lower mandible. They also have a multitude of smaller teeth. Their fangs are not venomous.

• Some species have a large trapezoidal head that is well differentiated from the body.

• There are some terrestrial species such as *Lamprophis, Boaedon, Liohetetodon,* etc.

• Others are burrowers; they have small eyes and a head small and undifferentiated from the body, such as *Lycodon, Aspidura, Atractus,* etc.

• Others such as *Dinodon, Farancia,* etc., live in very humid or aquatic media.

SUBFAMILY **LYCODONTINAE**

Wolf Snakes

Lioheterodon modestus
Adult specimen in its habitat.

SUBFAMILY **CALAMARINAE**

Dwarf Snakes

9 GENERA / **70** SPECIES

• They are small sized burrowing snakes (8 to 30 inches); the head is hardly differentiated from the rest of the vermi-form–like body; and they have smooth scales and a cylindrical body and tail.

• The head is conical and covered with a reduced number of large scales, with the rostral scale often projected forwards like a spade. The cranium is particularly rigid and compact.

• The body is covered with a small number of rows of scales (from 13 to 19).

• The short tail tends to end with a pointed scale that allows the snake to anchor itself in the subterranean tunnels it inhabits.

• They are rarely found on the floor, only sometimes at night or after a strong rain.

• They eat insects and earthworms; some species are specialized for eating ants and termites.

• They lay eggs.

■ Distribution: They inhabit Indochina, the Indo–Australian archipelago, and the Moluccas.

– Five monotypic genera: *Brachyorrhus, Padangia, Pseudorhabdion, Rhabdophidium, Typhlogeophis.*

– Four polytypic genera: *Agrophis, Calamaria, Calamorhabdium, Idiopholis.*

Calamaria lumbricoidea
Adult specimen in its habitat.

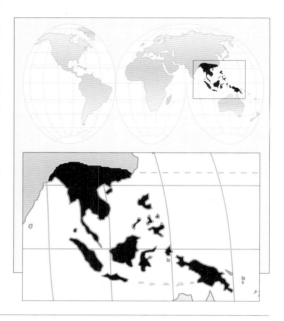

SUBFAMILY **XENODERMINAE**

Odd–scaled Snakes

7 GENERA / **13** SPECIES

• The vertebral apophyses are modified because they are flattened and widened, forming a series of osseous plates; this is a unique characteristic of the group.

• The labial scales also display visible modifications in many genera. They may be covered with small protuberances, like Achalinus, or the rear margins may have very noticeable borders.

• The dorsal scales are generally keeled, and may also be very altered. In Xenodermus, the dorsal scales and flank scales are juxtaposed and alternate between large and small sizes; this is a unique characteristic among the ophidians. Stoliczkaia has widened dorsal scales on the column and Nothopsis has granular and rough scales.

• They are found in humid habitats such as swamps or rainforests.

• They lay eggs.

■ Distribution:

– *Achalinus:* lives under fallen tree stumps or under the surface humus in southern China.

– *Fimbrios* in Indochina and *Stoliczkaia* in India and Borneo; they are poorly known but display some similarities with *Achalinus*. *Nothopsis*, called American Shar< Snake has a surface similar to the Acrochordidae.

– Five Asian genera: *Achalinus, Cercaspis, Fimbrios, Stoliczkaia, Xenodermus.*

– Two genera in the Neotropical region: *Nothopsis, Xenopholis.*

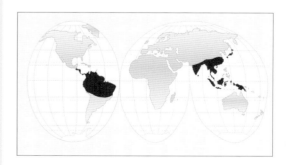

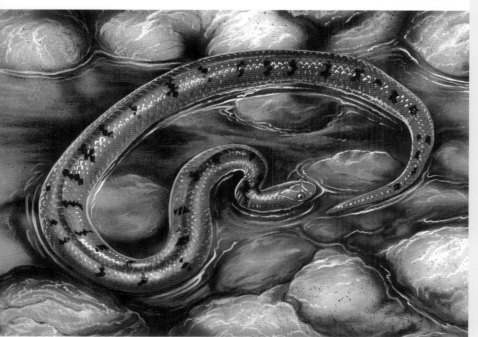

Xenopholis scalaris
Adult specimen in its habitat.

■ The three genera are very geographically separated:

– *Sybinophis*, with seven species, inhabits southeast Asia.

– *Liophidium*, with five, inhabits Madagascar.

– *Scaphiodontophis*, with five, in Central America.

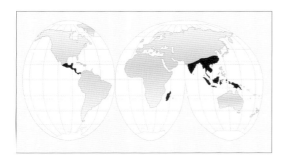

3 GENERA / 17 SPECIES

• Reduced–sized snakes, 12 to 32 inches in length.

• Their solid head is slightly differentiated from the rest of the body.

• Their teeth are very numerous, sharp, and blade–like, both on the mandibles and on the palatine and sphenoid bones, which allows them to powerfully seize large prey.

• The dentary bone is articulated very loosely with the rest of the lower mandible.

• The dorsal scales have somewhat developed tubercles in the cephalic and caudal regions.

• They are terrestrial and nocturnal snakes that feed on lizards and snakes.

• They are oviparous.

SUBFAMILY SIBYNOPHINAE
Many–toothed Snakes

Scaphiodontophis annulatus
Adult specimen in its habitat.

■ Distribution: They are found in the America's.

It covers the genera: *Alsophis, Antillophis, Arrhyton, Conophis, Cyclagas, Darlingtonia, Ditaxodon, Dromicus, Heterodon, Hypsyrhinchus, Ialtris, Leimadophis, Liophis, Lioheterophis, Lygophis, Paraxyrhopus, Philodryas, Platynion, Rhadinaea, Rhadinella, Sordellina, Synophis, Tretanorhinus, Umbrivaga, Uromacer, Uromacerina, Xenodon.*

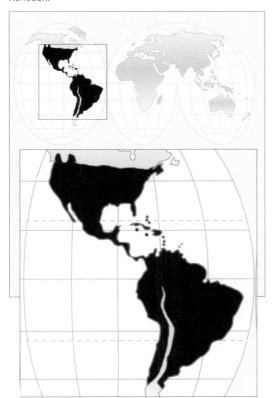

27 GENERA / + 50 SPECIES

• Heavy bodied medium snake with a wide and flattened head.

• Its snout has a sharp border, the rostral scale is pointed and slightly flattened upwards, which is why they are called hognose snakes. This adaptation allows them to burrow with ease.

• The very varied dentition is similar to the Lycodontinae, but there are species that have very advanced venomous fangs on the posterior part of the upper mandible.

• A common characteristic of many members of this group is their spectacular display when bothered; they flatten and inflate their bodies, especially the neck area. They can also raise the front part of their body like cobras, puff strongly, and bite. During the last phase of their defensive behavior they may play dead. This last phase of conduct is easier to observe in Heterodon and Xenodon.

• The majority of species are terrestrial, fairly bound to humid or aquatic environments. Many of them feed on amphibians. There are a few that are arboreal, such as Philodryas and Uromacer.

SUBFAMILY XENODONTINAE
Odd–toothed Snakes

Xenodon simus
Adult specimen in its habitat.

SUBFAMILY **DIPSADINAE**
American Snail–eating Snakes

3 GENERA / 48 SPECIES

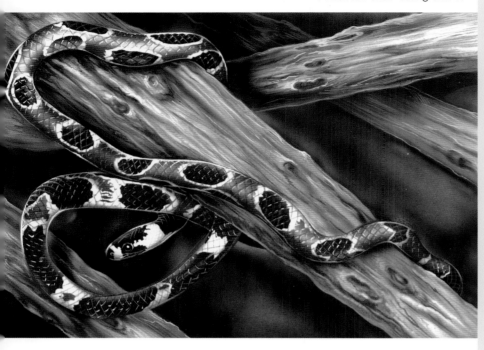

Dipsas colesbyi
Adult specimen in its habitat.

• These are small arboreal and nocturnal snakes (10 to 30 inches). They have a thin, laterally flattened body, a voluminous, almost cube–shaped head that is very differentiated from the body, and a short snout and large eyes.

• The lower mandibles are more rigid than in other colubrids and have, unlike other colubrids, large curved fangs on the front part of the mouth.

• They almost exclusively feed on snails and slugs and are very adapted to this dietary regimen.

• The species of the genus Dipsas, close to 33, are the most specialized in this monophagous dietary regimen. Sibon, with 9 species, has less dietary specialization, but also hunts amphibians and small lizards. Sibynomorphus, with 6 species, is less adapted to an arboreal life.

■ The family Dipsadinae extends to Tropical America.

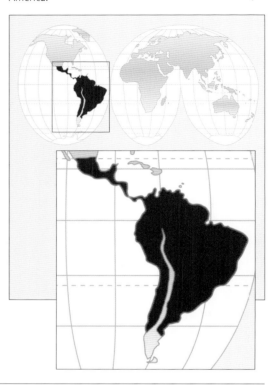

SUBFAMILY **PAREINAE**
Asian Snail–eating Snakes

2 GENERA / 16 SPECIES

Pareas margaritophorus
Adult specimen in its habitat.

• This subfamily has characteristics that are very similar to the Dipsadinae, and, even though they are of different origins, it is believed these two subfamilies have experienced an evolutionary convergence.

• The head is voluminous, markedly differentiated from the rest of the body, with large eyes and vertical pupils.

• The lower mandible is rigid and has large fangs placed in a forward position on the upper mandible.

• Its large scales are fused together on the ventral part of the head.

• These adaptations enormously aid feeding on snails, which are easily extracted from their shells. .

• They are nocturnal and arboreal snakes that reach up to 35 inches.

■ Distribution:
They inhabit southeastern Asia in jungles and mountain forests.

– The genus *Pareas* comprises 15 species.

– *Haplopeltura* is a monospecific genus.

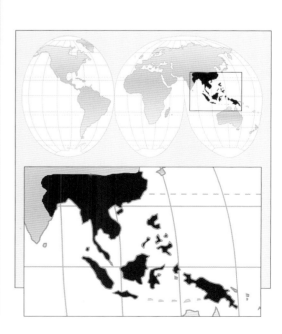

SUBFAMILY **ELASCHISTODONTINAE**

Indian egg–eating Snakes

1 GENUS / 1 SPECIE

• This subfamily is very similar to the African Dasypeltis; the two have undergone an evolutionary convergence even though they do not share a common origin.

• The head is not differentiated from the body. It has experienced a large reduction in teeth, only maintaining those on the posterior part of the upper mandible.

• Some authors cite two small opisthoglyphous fangs on the posterior part of the upper mandible.

• The neck's hypophyses are modified as small teeth that cut the eggs when going through the esophagus.

• Unlike the Dasypeltinae, the dorsal scales are flat and the row of vertebral scales is slightly larger.

■ *Elachistodon westermanni*, is the only species that inhabits India. Very rare.

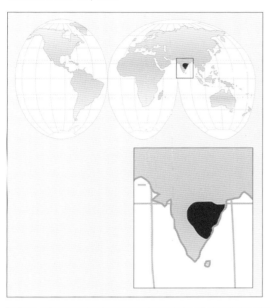

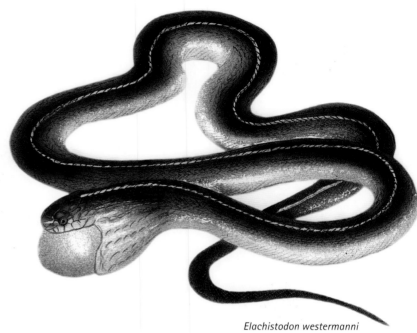

Elachistodon westermanni
Adult specimen in its habitat.

SUBFAMILY **BOIGINAE**

Rear–fanged Snakes

73 GENERA / + 400 SPECIES

• Small to medium snake.

• It has somewhat larger fangs, bound to a venom–secreting gland, approximately posteriorly located on the upper mandible.

• The venom gland's ducts open near the fangs and produce a neurotoxic secretion, but there are no vesicles that store the venom and the teeth do not have venom secreting canals; this is why envenomation is not very efficient.

• The effect of the Boiginae's venom on humans is varied and can be lethal in the Thelotornis and Dispholidus, African colubrids that also have venomous fangs in a very forward position.

• In other species the teeth are in a posterior position on the mandible and only inoculate venom when the snakes have trapped the prey and are preparing to swallow it (Malpolon, Psammphis, etc.).

• Some Boiginae are totally adapted to an arboreal life, which is why they are called Liana snakes such as Ahaetulla, Oxybelis, or 'flying' snakes like Chrysopelea.

• Others such as Malpolon and Psammophis are terrestrial diurnal species.

• Only Hydrodynastes displays a totally amphibian life.

■ Distribution:

– The following genera are in Central and South America: *Apostolepis, Clelia, Drepanoides, Elapomojus, Elapomorphus, Enulius, Erythrolamprus, Excelencophis, Gomesophis, Hydrodynastes, Imantodes, Manolepis, Opisthoplus, Oxybelis, Oxyrhopus, Farapostolepis, Phimophis, Procinura, Pseudoblabes, Pseudoboa, Pseudoleptodeira, Pseudotomodon, Rachidelus, Rhinobothryum, Scolecophis, Sipholophis, Stenorrhina, Symphimus, Simpholis, Tachymeris. Tantillita, Thamnodynastes, Toluca, Tomodon, Tripanurgos.*

– In North America (some extending into Central America): *Coniophanes, Ficimia, Gyalopion, Hypsiglena, Leptodeira, Sonora, Tantilla, Trimorphodon.*

– In Africa and Madagascar: *Alluaudina, Amplorhinus, Chamaertortus, Choristocacalamus, Crotaphopeltis, Dipsadoboa, Dispholidus, Dromophis, Geodysas, Hemirhagerrhis, Hypoptophis, Ithycyphus, Langaha, Lycodryas, Madagascorophis, Mimoophis, Psammophylax, Pythonodipsas, Rhamphiophis, Thelotornis, Xenocalamus.*

– Africa and Asia: *Psammmophis, Boiga* (also in Australia), *Macropotodon, Malpolon* and *Telescopus* (these last three also inhabit Europe).

– Only in Asia: *Ahaetulla, Chrysopelea, Dryophiops, Hologerrhum, Psammodynastes.*

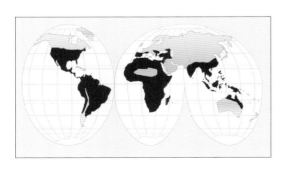

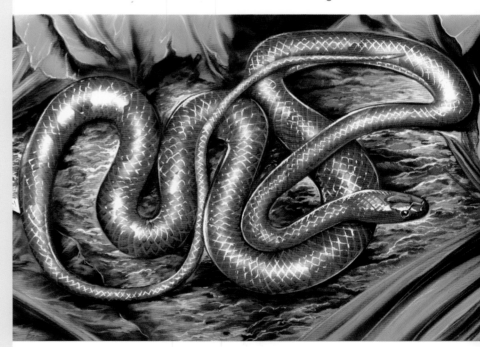

Oxiropus pelotarius
Adult specimen in its habitat.

ARIZONA ELEGANS

SUBFAMILY COLUBRINAE

 Kennicott, 1859

 Glossy Snake

Arizona elegans
(Glossy Snake).
Adult specimen.
Detail of the head.

DESCRIPTION

Can vary in size from 26 to 70 inches.
This snake shares a certain similarity with *Pituophis*, (bull snake) but it has flat keelless scales. The scales are shiny and give the animal a clean appearance.
The snout is somewhat pointed, overhanging the receded lower mandible.
The pupils are slightly elliptical.
It has 25 to 35 rows of scales, two prefrontal scales, and an undivided anal scale.
It has a dark line that follows the angle of the mandible towards the eyes.
The background color of the body is yellowish-beige with a variable number of blotches and fairly light brown dots that tend to vary according to the subspecies. It also has a similar number of smaller blotches on the flanks.
The subspecies located further west are also called faded snakes due to their very light colored livery.
The ventral surface is whitish and lacks marks.
The young individuals look the same as the adults, but the blotches are darker.

HABITAT

Can be found in a wide variety of environments throughout its area of distribution, but seems to prefer dry, open, and sandy zones.
It lives in deserts, prairies, coastal zones with thicket, and plains with artemisia bushes from sea level to an elevation of 558 feet.

BEHAVIOR

• It is an excellent burrower that spends the majority of its time buried in the sandy or soft substrate. It emerges at night or in the early hours of the morning on hot days.
• It is very rarely found on the ground or below rocks in broad daylight.
• Above all, it is specialized in hunting lizards, although sometimes it feeds on small mammals.
• It kills its prey by constriction.
• When handled it may bite.

REPRODUCTION

Mating season is in spring.
Three to 24-egg clutches are laid in summer, with each egg measuring two inches.
The young are born ten to 12 weeks and measure seven to eight inches.

STATUS

It is not considered endangered, although it does seem to be in great decline in a few areas due to the loss of loose substrate in some valleys, necessary for burrowing.

DISTRIBUTION

Southern Mexico, Texas, and eastern Nebraska to central California, southern Utah.

■ Nine subspecies are distinguished although they are not very defined; seven of them are in the United States:

– *A. e. elegans:* Kansas Glossy Snake with 39 to 69 large blotches.

– *A. e. arenicola:* Texas Glossy Snakes, 41 to 58 blotches.

– *A. e. candida:* Mojave Glossy Snake, 53 to 73 narrow blotches.

– *A. e. eburnata:* Desert Glossy Snake, slightly colored with 53 to 83 narrow small blotches.

– *A. e. noctivaga:* Arizona Glossy Snakes, blotches on the body are slightly wider or equal to the spaces between them.

– *A. e. occidentalis:* California Glossy Snakes, from 51 to 75 dark brown blotches.

– *A. e. philipi:* Painted Desert glossy Snake, 53 to 83 blotches.

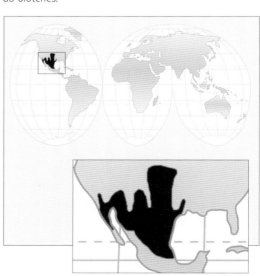

(Linnaeus, 1758)

American Racer

COLUBER CONSTRICTOR
FAMILY **COLUBRINAE**

Coluber constrictor
(American Racer).
Adult specimen

Coluber constrictor (American
Racer). Young specimen.

DESCRIPTION

This snake has a thin agile body that moves quickly, and can reach up to seven feet in length.

The head is narrow but still well differentiated from the body with a few superciliary edges and large eyes with round pupils.

It has 17 rows of scales in the middle of the body and a divided anal scale.

The coloration of the body varies greatly and can be uniformly black, blue, brown, or greenish on the back, while the ventral part is white, cream, or gray. The chin and the neck tend to be a light color. The young have a different, much more marked color: they are gray with dark spots on the flanks and gray, brownish-gray, or reddish blotches on the middle line of the body. The tail is always brown. This coloration disappears in one or two years.

HABITAT

Prairies and zones with scattered bushes.

Open forests with rocky outcrops, also abandoned fields.

Sometimes also in more humid zones like swamps or lakeshores.

It is fairly widespread and can be found in a large number of environments except in high mountains or in warmer deserts.

It climbs well even though it is a mainly terrestrial species.

BEHAVIOR

• When bothered it makes a loud sound by shaking the tip of its tail, and brushing against dry vegetable remains, producing a sound similar to that of a rattlesnake. If its predator continues to approach it, it coils up hiding its head or even raises its tail in a threatening fashion, and puffs strongly.

Coluber constrictor (American Racer).
Emerged out of its egg.

• When handled it bites repeatedly, discharges the contents of its cloaca, and moves its body with such force that its tail, used like a whip, can sometimes even break.

• Although it is not venomous, its bites can cause very painful wounds.

• It is diurnal and it looks hard for its prey, raising its head in order to better see it.

• It hunts rodents, birds, lizards, frogs, and even large insects that it does not kill by constriction; rather it flattens its prey by squeezing its body against the floor.

REPRODUCTION

They mate in spring and lay three to 32 oval eggs often hidden in a mammal's uninhabited burrow. It often lays communal clutches.

When born, the young measure 15 inches. The males reach sexual maturity in one or two years, and the females in two or three.

STATUS

It is not protected federally, but it is protected by some states' laws as in Iowa, where it is illegal to kill and collect this species.

The pesticide residues are dangerous for the insectivorous young.

The habitat reduction due to agriculture and suburban development, as well as the direct extermination of this species by humans, constitute the main dangers for its populations; they are nonetheless still abundant.

DISTRIBUTION

Southern Canada, all of the continental states of the United States except for Alaska; Mexico, and Guatemala, with ten to 11 slightly defined subspecies.

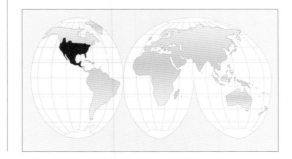

COLUBER HIPPOCREPIS

SUBFAMILY **COLUBRINAE**

 Linnaeus, 1758

 Horseshoe Snake

Coluber hippocrepis (Horseshoe Snake). Adult specimen.

DESCRIPTION

A thin slender snake from three to five feet long. The head is relatively small but wide and well defined.

The eyes are fairly prominent, with round pupils.

It is the only European colubrid that has a series of small scales (subocular) between the eyes and the supralabials. Another distinct characteristic is that the ventral scales are narrower, more like the Viperidae than other colubrids from the Old World.

The dorsal background color is whitish or yellowish, with large brown dark or black rhomboidal or round blotches in regular intervals all along the back. Other similar but smaller blotches alternate on both sides. An open V-shaped or horseshoe-shaped blotch stands out on top of the head with its vertex pointing towards the front part. In front of this, there is another blotch that appears as a wide inter-ocular stripe. The dorsal blotches on the tail and on the flanks form three dark longitudinal lines. It has lower whitish, yellowish, or orangish parts.

The coloration of the young tends to be more whitish with dark blotches separated by light colored stripes.

HABITAT

Plains and scrubland covered with bushes or few trees, and rocky zones.

It also likes to hide in abandoned or uninhabited rural buildings.

In Europe it is a thermophile and xerophile species typical of dry Mediterranean surroundings characterized by maquis scrubland.

They live in more mountainous zones in northern Africa, up to 6, 890 feet in elevation.

BEHAVIOR

• Diurnal, quick, and agile.

• When frightened it attempts to flee, but if cornered, raises its body and tries to bite hard repeatedly. At the same time, it emits whistles and snorts of different intensities.

• Thanks to the anchoring of its ventral plates, it could be the European species that moves the best on sand.

• It normally hunts actively, and is frequently seen entering rodents' burrows in search of prey.

• The young feed on saurians and the adults, aside from rodents, also feed on birds and, less often, eggs.

REPRODUCTION

In the southern part of the Iberian Peninsula females lay eggs in May and July.

The clutches have five to ten white and elongated eggs, which measure around two inches in length and .8 inch in width. They place the eggs under rocks or in the sandy terrain of abandoned burrows.

STATUS

The Berne Convention of the European Community has protected it in Spain since 1982.

In Spain it is most common in lower Andalusia and Levant, and much rarer in the peninsular center and in Catalonia.

It is also rare on the island of Sardinia.

DISTRIBUTION

Northern Morocco, Tunis and Algeria, Portugal, southern Spain and its Mediterranean coast, and Sardinia.

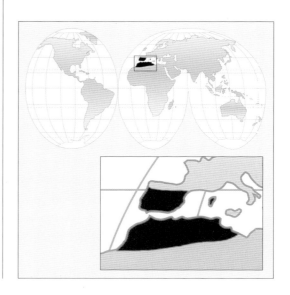

Lacepede,1789

 Western Whip Snake

COLUBER VIRIDIFLAVUS

FAMILY **COLUBRINAE**

Coluber viridiflavus
(Western Whip Snake).
Adult specimen.

DESCRIPTION

Slender with a strong, quick, and agile appearance.
The adults can reach a total length of seven feet, but
they normally do not exceed five feet. The males tend
to be larger than the females.

The head is small, but well distinguished from
the rest of the body; the tip of the snout is obtusely
rounded.

Large bright and colorful eyes with round pupils
and a dark iris.

Has 19 rows of smooth dorsal scales, and typically
has 8 supralabial scales on each side; the fourth and
fifth are in contact with the eye.

It may have two liveries: one yellow–green and one
black. The yellow–green phase consists of a yellowish
colored background crossed in the first part of the
trunk by borders and dark green stripes; the second
half of the body is much darker, lined with parallel
black or greenish brownish gray lines. The lower part
is whitish or yellowish–white. In the black phase, the
coloring of the upper parts of the body is black, but
the labial, gular, and mental scales tend to be gray.
The lower parts of the body are whitish. The young
are very different from the adults: they are a pale olive
green color with a black head, brightly and colorfully
dotted in yellow.

HABITAT

Lives in perennial and caducous forests in a
Mediterranean climate.

It prefers sunny places in plains and hills with
bushes, rocks, or stony areas.

It is considered to be the most ubiquitous European
species of the genus Coluber, and although it prefers
warm zones, it can adapt to cooler zones, from sea level
to an elevation of 6,562 feet (in the Alps).

It is sometimes found in the Pyrenees bound to
thermal zones. It takes advantage of the micro-climate
in these areas to proliferate in a not especially favorable
environment.

BEHAVIOR

• This snake is diurnal, extraordinarily fast and agile,
and can easily climb trees and bushes.

• When captured it aggressively tries to bite.

• It is guided by its vision when hunting and kills the
largest prey by constriction.

• It feeds on micromammals, reptiles, and birds.

Coluber viridiflavus (Western Whip Snake).
Young specimen. Detail of the head.

REPRODUCTION

The ritual combats in spring between the males are
very spectacular because of the strength that the
contenders employ and the strong lashes they give
with their tail.

Coupling takes place preferably in May; the male
holds onto the female's neck and nape with its mouth.

Incubation varies between six to eight weeks.

It lays between five and 15 eggs, in crevices and
holes in the floor.

When born the young measure one to ten inches.

STATUS

European law protects it.

It is a common species in Italy.

In the north and northeast of the Iberian Peninsula,
it is a rare species confined to less favorable climates
(cooler and mountainous), maybe due to competition
with other species such as *Malpolon monspessulanus*.

DISTRIBUTION

Northeastern Spain, Andorra, central and southern
France, southern Switzerland, all of Italy, eastern
Slovenia, Croatian Coast, Sicily, Sardinia, Corsica.

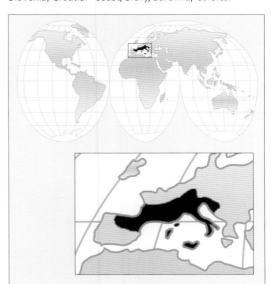

CORONELLA AUSTRIACA

SUBFAMILY **COLUBRINAE**

 Laurenti, 1768

 Smooth Snake

Voronella austriaca (Smooth Snake). Adult specimen.

DESCRIPTION

Small to medium-size, which generally does not exceed 24 inches, although there are specimens that reach 28 inches in length.

This snake has a cylindrical body with a small head, a pointed snout, and small brownish-gray reddish brownish-gray, or yellowish eyes with round pupils.

Relatively large rostral scale that is higher than it is wide, and the third and fourth supralabial scales in contact with the eye. Smooth dorsal scales forming 19 rows on the center of the body.

It has a fairly variable general color: grayish or brownish-gray, yellowish, or less frequently blackish, with irregular, somewhat numerous dark brownish-gray or black blotches distributed along the back sometimes forming faint stripes. A large dark blotch often protrudes on the nape of the neck. Another dark stripe joins the eye to the commissure of the mouth and in some, extends forward toward the nasal scales. The lower parts tend to be gray, reddish brown, or blackish, either uniform or with fine back dots.

The young have a brighter coloring with more marked ornamentation than the adults.

The oldest may completely lack blotches. Altino and melanic animals have been found.

HABITAT

In clearings and the margins of low forests, along the borders of paths, and in stony areas with scarce plants.

It prefers the dryer and sunnier climates, although is sometimes found in humid zones.

In zones with Atlantic or Continental climates, it lives in perennial and caducous forests, from sea level to 7,874 feet in the Alps.

It is a mountainous species in zones with Mediterranean climate.

It is adapted to the temperate and cool climate of Europe.

CORONELLA AUSTRIACA (Smooth Snake).
Adult specimen. Pattern and coloration of the scales.

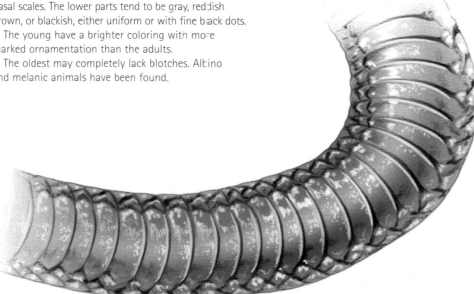

BEHAVIOR

• It sleeps for a fairly long time in winter, according to the climactic conditions of the place.

• Although it is diurnal, it tends to hide and is normally found below trunks and stones avoiding very hot weather, above all in summer.

• It moves quite slowly and develops great strength when coiling up.

• If bothered it may adopt a defensive attitude similar to a viper, very often trying to bite.

• Another means of defense are the fetid secretions it expels from its cloacal gland when bothered or handled.

• It lies in wait to catch its prey.

• It mainly feeds on reptiles, above all on lizards, although also on pikes and small colubrids.

• Its mouth hardly enlarges and does not allow it to swallow very large prey.

REPRODUCTION

Possibly an ovoviviparous colubrid, as an adaptation to the basically cold climate it lives in.

It can give birth to up to 15 young in August or at the beginning of September; at birth they usually measure five to eight inches.

STATUS

National and European law (Berne Convention) protects it.

Many peasants and hikers confuse it with the viper, which is why many of the snakes are killed.

It seems to be seriously endangered in Great Britain.

DISTRIBUTION

Europe, aside from the majority of the southern Iberian Peninsula, northern and central Scandinavia, and a large part of Great Britain.

Towards the east it is also found beyond the Urals and in Turkey.

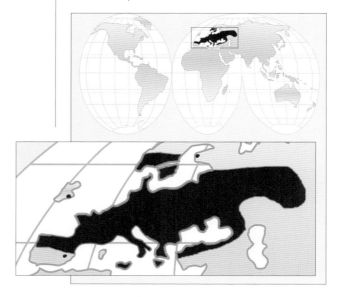

(Daudin, 1803)

 Southern Smooth Snake

CORONELLA GIRONDICA

SUBFAMILY **COLUBRINAE**

Coronella girondica
(Southern Smooth Snake)
Adult specimen.

DESCRIPTION

Small snake; adults tend to reach 20 to 26 inches and larger ones are in the minority.

The body is thin, smooth, and cylindrical with a small but well differentiated head; the eyes are small with round pupils; the snout is prominent in respect to the lower mandible.

The rostral plate is wider than it is high; it has eight supralabials and the fourth and fifth are in contact with the eye.

The scales form 19 to 21 rows on the center of the body.

The tail represents one quarter of the total length.

The back is brown, grayish, yellowish, or pink, with darker blotches in transversal stripes. There are much blurrier blotches on the flanks. It has characteristic dark stripes that join the eyes at the height of the prefrontals and continue down on both sides of the face until slightly after the commissure of the mouth. On the back of the neck it tends to have a bright and colorful blotch in the form of a V, U, or Y. The lower parts are whitish or yellowish, sometimes with pinkish tones and characteristic quadrangular black blotches generally forming two lines.

It differs from *Coronella austriaca* by the distinct configuration of the rostral scale and the dark ventral lines that the aforementioned does not have.

HABITAT

Prefers arid Mediterranean ecosystems where it is commonly found.

Inhabits scrubland and perennial forests.

It is found in open and barren forests, between bushes, heaped up branches, dry tree trunks, and stone walls.

BEHAVIOR

• It is a terrestrial species that is active during the day in spring while in summer it appears to be more active at sunset or in the morning hours.

• It moves slowly and rarely bites, although sometimes when handled expels a fetid substance from its cloaca.

• Its diet consists mainly of lizards, baby micro-mammals, and small snakes, even of its own species.

REPRODUCTION

Mating takes place in May and the species can be oviparous or ovoviviparous, depending on the climatic characteristics of its habitat.

The eggs are laid in July and the young are born between August and September and measure from four to seven inches.

STATUS

Its population density is very variable, depending on the zones, and although it may be common locally, it often goes unnoticed.

It is protected by European law.

The greatest danger for its populations comes from the degradation of its habitat where it lives.

It is not considered an endangered species.

DISTRIBUTION

Northern Tunisia, Algeria, and Morocco; Portugal, Spain (with the exception of the northern regions), southern France, Italy, and Sicily.

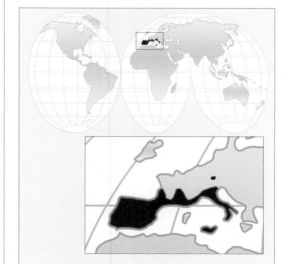

CORONELLA GIRONDICA
(Southern Smooth Snake)
Ventral pattern.

DRYMARCHON CORAIS

SUBFAMILY COLUBRINAE

 (Boie, 1827)

Indigo Snake

Drymarchon corais
(Indigo Snake).

Drymarchon corais
(Indigo Snake).

BEHAVIOR

• A species associated with the gopher turtle *Gopherus poliphemus*, (in the United States), because it is a guest of the turtles' abandoned dens in winter and spring to hide, change location, or to lay its eggs.
• It also uses armadillos' burrows.
When frightened it prefers to flee, but if cornered, it vertically flattens its neck, puffs, and makes its tail vibrate like a rattlesnake; although if trapped, it rarely tries to bite.
• During winter it stays active, especially if the temperatures are higher than 50ºF.
• It leads a diurnal life and actively looks for prey.
• It is not a constricting species and immobilizes its prey with its mandibles.
• It eats a wide variety of prey: rats, birds, frogs, lizards, small turtles and snakes, even venomous ones (it is immune to them).

REPRODUCTION

It mates from November to March in the United States. The clutch, laid from March to July, consists of three to ten eggs. The young are born from May to October.

STATUS

The North American subspecies are considered to be endangered and are protected by law.
This decline is a result of: the loss and fragmentation of its habitats, the attack of domestic dogs, collection for trade, death from being run over by cars, the decline of the population of turtles, and the large concentration of toxic insecticides in its environment (reserves in Georgia).

DISTRIBUTION

In the United States: Florida, Georgia, and Texas. From Mexico to northern Argentina.

■ Eight subspecies.

DESCRIPTION

Strong looking snake that can measure up to ten feet, making it the largest colubrid in the New World.
The body has a triangular cross-section, with scales that are normally flat, although some large males have some slightly keeled dorsal scales.
The scales are distributed in 17 rows on the middle part of the body.
The hemipenis is bilobed.
The anal scale is not divided.
The body coloration of the eight subspecies is very variable; it can vary from an iridescent blue on the chin and a reddish throat on the Eastern Indigo Snake, to the yellow, beige, pale coffee, or pale gray color of the other subspecies.
Some individuals or subspecies are a uniform color while others have a different coloring on the front part

and on the back part. The Texas Indigo snake *D. c. erebennus*, is a good example of this; the front part of the body is a brownish-gray or a reddish brownish-gray.

HABITAT

This snake has an eminently tropical distribution.
It inhabits a wide variety of ecosystems, from open forests, savannahs with palm trees, plains, and oak forests, to agricultural zones for North American species.
The southernmost species inhabit caducous jungle, the medium subperennial jungle, apple fields, land under cultivation, pastures, and stay close to water-courses.

Cope, 1861

 Beauty Snake

ELAPHE TAENIURA

SUBFAMILY COLUBRINAE

DESCRIPTION

This snake is relatively strong and slender with a long tail. It can be up to eight feet in total length in some populations, while in others it is only four feet. The head is flat and narrow and well differentiated from the body. The eyes are of a moderate size, with round pupils and a gold or grayish iris.

There is so much variability in the snakes' coloration in its wide area of distribution that it is considered to have two large populations: the Indochina, characterized by the brownish yellowish to olive gray dorsal color and dark dorsal blotches in the form of an H or in two rounded parallel lines; and the Indomalaysian body color varies between cream and gray, with just one reticule of dark individual scales along the body. In both, however, the back part of the body and tail have a characteristic clear vertebral stripe and two wide lateral lines, also very light in color, as well as a prominent straight black line behind the eyes.

The number of ventral scales varies between 225 and 305 (up to 265 in the Indochina population and more than 265 in the Indomalaysian), and it has between 84 and 125 subcaudal scales.

HABITAT

Boundaries of tropical forests, scrubland regions close to the water, rocky outcrops between vegetation, carstic caves, bamboo forests, cultivated areas and even inside inhabited areas (leafy gardens, borders of paths).

The majority of subspecies live from sea level to 3,281 feet in elevation although some (like *E. t. yunnanensis*) live in areas up to 9,843 feet.

BEHAVIOR

• This snake is as active during the day as at night. It tends to move with agility on the substrate, although sometimes it may climb trees and bushes.

• Although not venomous, it is very aggressive, and when in danger, it raises the front part of the body from the floor, inflates its neck, folds itself in the form of an S and hisses threateningly.

• Sometimes it also expels a foul liquid as a dissuasive measure.

• It feeds on rats, bats (some populations that live in caves are specialists in capturing bats), birds, and chicks found in their nests.

REPRODUCTION

They are oviparous; the females lay between five and 25 eggs, although usually no more than 15.

The incubation period is from 55 to 77 days and the newborns are generally very similar to the adults (in some subspecies however, they have a somewhat different pattern).

E. taeniura frisei. Adult specimen's head.

STATUS

Not very much is known about the current state of its populations in its natural surroundings, although it seems to be common in many regions.

All the subspecies except *E. t. schmackeri* have been successfully raisec in captivity.

DISTRIBUTION

Southeast Asia, Indonesia, and East Asia to the foot of the Himalayas to the east of China and Taiwan.

■ Up to seven different subspecies are distinguished:

- *E. t. taeniura:* Eastern China.

- *E. t. friesi:* Island of Taiwan.

- *E. t. mocquardi:* South of continental China, the island of Hainan, and northern Vietnam.

- *E. t. schmackeri:* Archipelago of Ryu-kyu (Japan).

- *E. t. yunnanensis:* Central and southern China, northeastern India and northern Burma, Laos, Thailand, and Vietnam.

- *E. t. grabowskyi:* Sumatra and Borneo.

- *E. t. ridleyi:* Peninsula of Malacca (Malaysia and Thailand).

E. TAENIURA
(Stripe-tailed Snake).
Adult specimen.

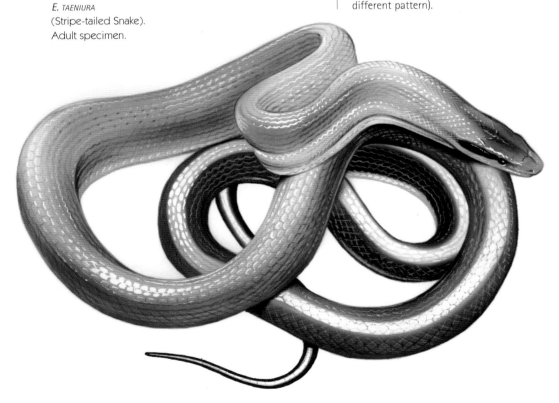

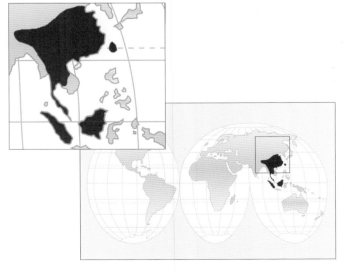

ELAPHE GUTTATA

SUBFAMILY **COLUBRINAE**

 (Linnaeus, 1766)

Corn Snake

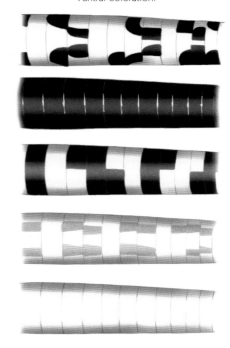
ELAPHE GUTTATA (Corn Snake). Adult specimen.
Ventral coloration.

Elaphe guttata (Corn Snake). Adult specimen.

DESCRIPTION

This species represents small or medium-sized snakes within the genus Elaphe, given that it only reaches two to five feet maximum (depending on the subspecies). The head is flat and well different ated from the body, the snout blunt and rounded, and the eyes have dark circular pupils.

The body is an orangish, pinkish, yellowish, brownish, or grayish color, with large black, reddish, brown, or grayish blotches along the back, and other smaller ones along the flanks.

The stomach is a creamy color and except in *E. g. rosacea*, it has large black rectangular marks irregularly distributed that turn into stripes on the tail's underside.

There is a stripe between the eyes that goes down towards the neck; it is the same color as the rest of the body's blotches.

The dorsal scales are smooth and slightly keeled while the ventral scales have a fairly pronounced keel. It has between 197 and 245 ventral scales and between 47 and 84 subcaudal scales.

HABITAT

In semidry open or slightly humid ecosystems, frequently on sandy or grassy floors of pine forests.

Also in rocky hillsides and close to small watercourses, lagoons, or ponds. It can sometimes be observed in caves as well as close to inhabited zones: gardens, abandoned buildings, country houses, etc.

From sea level up to a maximum elevation of almost 6, 562 feet.

BEHAVIOR

• Mainly a nocturnal species but can also be seen frequently at sunset or in the early hours of the morning.

ELAPHE GUTTATA (Corn Snake).
Adult specimen's head.   Side view.

Upper view.

• It spends many hours hidden under leaves on the floor, under rocks, buried in sand, or inside hollow tree trunks.

• Although it is considered a terrestrial snake, it can climb trees (it has been seen in trees taller than 33 feet high).

• It feeds on rats, bats, birds (on adults, eggs, and chicks) lizards, and frogs.

REPRODUCTION

Oviparous, the female lays up to 30 eggs (normally from 12 to 25) during the months of June, July, or August.

When born, the young measure between eight and 14 inches in length and look similar to the adults.

STATUS

It is a fairly common snake in a good part of its area of distribution and, in general, is not considered endangered. The subspecies *E. g. rosacea* is, however, considered to be endangered, threatened by the urban development in its extremely reduced zones of distribution, and, therefore protected in the state of Florida.

The fact that it has been able to live for more than 20 years in terrariums proves that it adapts very well to being in captivity; it has hardly any problems reproducing and even allows people to handle it with no real objection.

DISTRIBUTION

Central and eastern United States continuing south to northeast Mexico.

■ Up to three subspecies are recognized. (although *E. g. rosacea* is not accepted by many authors, including *E. g. guttata*):

- *E. g. guttata*: From the southernmost part of New Jersey to Louisiana and Florida.

- *E.g. emoryi*: From southern Nebraska and Illinois to the east until Utah and to the south up to New Mexico and Texas, always to the west of the Mississippi River. It extends to the eastern half of Mexico to north of Queretaro and Veracruz.

- *E. g. rosacea*: Is an insular subspecies that only inhabits a few of the Florida Keys: Big Pine, Key West, Ramrod, Stock Island, Summerland, Vaca Key, and a few others.

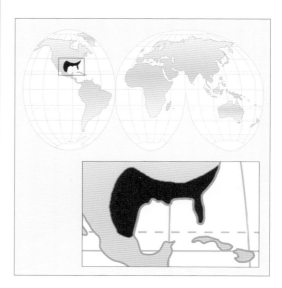

(Laurenti, 1768)

Aesculapian Snake / Aesculapian Rat Snake

ELAPHE LONGISSIMA

FAMILY **COLUBRINAE**

DESCRIPTION

This species has a long slender body; a narrow, well defined head, round pupils, and smooth flat dorsal scales.

The ventral scales are slightly keeled, with a small keel on each side. There are from 195 to 250 (normally 210 to 248) ventral scales and from 60 to 104 (generally 60 to 90) subcaudal scales.

The adults' back is a uniform color, but the tonality is very variable: yellowish, brownish-gray, greenish, grayish, or blackish.

The lateral area of the neck and the labial scales are much lighter in color. A light colored vertebral stripe appears on some specimens that extends along the entire body, and on others, there may be four dark stripes on both sides of the vertebral region and on the flanks.

The ventral zone is whitish or yellowish, with dark fairly spread out spots.

It can reach a length of seven feet including the tail, although, in general, it does not exceed 55 to 67 inches. The males are larger than the females.

HABITAT

Usually found in temperate environments in stony or rocky areas where there is some vegetation, in scrublands, or in the margins of pasturelands and forests, but it can also be found in hedges that demarcate areas under cultivation, stone walls, ruins, haylofts, and even below the roof of country houses.

From sea level to an elevation of 6, 562 feet, although the majority of the populations do not tend to go above 4,101–5,246 feet.

It is, however, a mountainous species in the southern area of its distribution.

Side view.

Upper view.

ELAPHE LONGISSIMA
(Aesculapian Snake). Adult specimen's head.

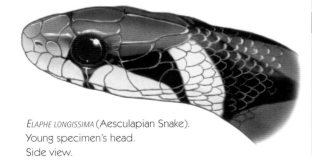

ELAPHE LONGISSIMA (Aesculapian Snake).
Young specimen's head.
Side view.

Elaphe guttata (Aesculapian Rat Snake).
Adult specimen.

BEHAVIOR

• It moves well on land where it appears quick and agile, and is a regular swimmer, but above all, it is a species with an arboreal preference; it climbs with ease, even up vertical tree trunks.

• It appears to be active during the day (sometimes also at twilight), but it distances itself from the excessive heat in the middle of the day.

• When bothered, it may bite, but normally it only tends to expel a fetid secretion from its anal glands.

• The young individuals mainly feed on lacertids and insects (crickets, grasshoppers), while the adults prefer to capture rodents, birds (especially chicks and eggs) and small reptiles.

• This snake hibernates from October to March or April in rock crevices or in mammals' abandoned burrows.

REPRODUCTION

Reproduces oviparously, laying from five to 20 eggs (usually from five to eight) in rock fissures, holes in trees, stone walls, dunghills, beneath the moss, or in accumulations of vegetation, and in moist earth.

The young that are born in the month of September measure eight to ten inches in length.

STATUS

It is an emblematic species from time immemorial. It was worshiped as a representative of Aesculapius, the Greco-Roman god of medicine and healing who carried a magic staff. Today, it is the symbol of medicine.

Although its exact state is poorly known in many parts of its area of distribution, it is definitely a more protected European snake.

DISTRIBUTION

From central and southern Europe, through the Caucasus, down to the coasts of the Black Sea, to northern Iran.

■ Two subspecies are known:

- *E. l. longissima*: Spain (only on the most northern side of the southern Pyrenees), central and southern France, southern Germany and Poland, The Czech Republic and Slovakia, Austria, Switzerland, Italy, former Yugoslavia, Albania, Hungary, Romania, Bulgaria, Greece, Moldavia, the Ukraine, Georgia, Russia, Turkey, and northeastern Iran (it is possible that the populations of this country constitute another third subspecies, but the topic is still being discussed).

- *E. l. romana*: Only in the southern half of Italy and Sicily.

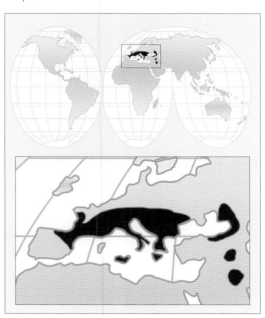

ELAPHE MANDARINA

SUBFAMILY COLUBRINAE

 Cantor, 1842

 Mandarin Rat Snake

Side view.

ELAPHE MANDARINA
(Mandarin Rat Snake).
Adult specimen's head.

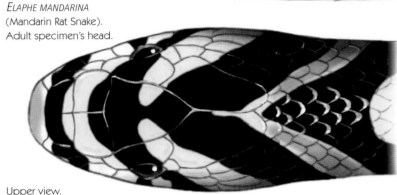

Upper view.

Elaphe mandarinus (Mandarin Rat Snake).
Adult specimen.

DESCRIPTION

It is a medium–sized species; it normally measures between 40 and 47 inches maximum, although some exceptionally large specimens reach up to almost 67 inches.

The head is compact but well differentiated from the body, and the snout very rounded.

The eyes are small with round dark pupils, that are almost black like the tongue.

Its coloring is very bright and striking: the dorsal zone varies from gray to brown, going through a greenish color, but the most characteristic is the presence of a series of oval yellow black–edged blotches, along the entire body, from the neck to the tip of the tail.

It has a black V–shaped stripe on the back part of the head, a black line between the eyes that reaches the commissure of the mouth, and another black line that crosses the snout.

The stomach is a creamy or whitish color with large quadrangular black blotches that sometimes extend from one side of the body to the other.

The scales are small and smooth except on the tip of the tail where they are slightly keeled.

The frontal shield is quite large.

It has between 200 to 241 ventral scales and between 59 to 82 subcaudal scales.

HABITAT

It is generally a mountainous species that can be found in areas up to an elevation of 9,843 feet. It mainly frequents open forests and rocky areas with an abundance of bushes.

It is not unusual for it to appear in areas under cultivation (mainly in mountain rice fields).

BEHAVIOR

• It is basically a terrestrial species that can easily climb small trees and bushes; it is active at twilight and is clearly diurnal, especially in spring and at the beginning of fall.

• During the maximum insolation hours it tends to remain hidden under rocks or in abandoned burrows of subterranean mammals.

• Mostly feeds on micro-mammals (rats, shrews), which it often captures underground.

• The prey is held by the mouth and suffocated by constriction with one or two loops of the snake's coils.

• It is not very aggressive; when it senses danger it adopts a threatening posture, makes the tip of its tail vibrate, and flees quickly towards the closest hole it can find.

• Sometimes, when people try to grab it with their hand, it may bite without hesitation.

• It is not venomous.

STATUS

Its exact current state in nature is unknown, but, due to the fact that a good part of its area of distribution is in not very populated areas, it does not seem to be in serious danger.

Rarely held in captivity, it has problems adapting and has not managed to be bred very often.

REPRODUCTION

It reproduces oviparously little is known about its reproductive behavior in nature.

In captivity the females lay three to eight eggs, from which the young are born after 42 to 55 days of incubation at 77 to 82.4⁰F.

When the young are born they measure 12 inches in length and their coloration is almost identical to that of the adults.

Sexual maturity can be reached at two to three years of age.

DISTRIBUTION

Central, southern, and eastern China, the Island of Taiwan, and the extreme north of southeast Asia (northern India, Burma, and Vietnam).

■ In some works it has been recognized as two distinct subspecies: the common *E. m. mandarina*, and *E. m. takasago*, from central China; they have some differences in coloration and in number of scales, although these are generally not recognized.

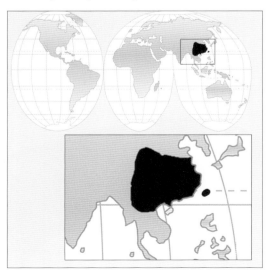

Side view.

Upper view.

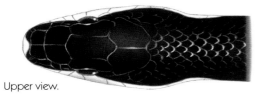

ELAPHE OBSOLETA (black). Head.

 (Say, 1823)

 Common Rat Snake
Chicken Snake

ELAPHE OBSOLETA
SUBFAMILY **COLUBRINAE**

Elaphe obsoleta (Common Rat Snake).
Adult specimen.

DESCRIPTION

This snake has a long robust body, and is the largest species of the genus *Elaphe* that lives in the New World; it can measure up to eight feet in length, although it generally does not exceed six feet; the most common length varies between four feet and five feet.

Its head is small, elongated, and not very differentiated from the body.

The snout is round and the pupils dark and circular.

The body scales are small and smooth but the ventral scales have well developed keels. It has between 218 and 258 ventral scales and between 63 and 102 subcaudal scales.

The dorsal coloration is variable but three predominant patterns can be distinguished:

- uniform: dark brown or black, with or without some light irregular marks along the body (*E. o. obsoleta*).

- striped: reddish, orangish, yellowish, grayish, or greenish with four dark longitudinal lines (*E. o. quadrivittata* and *E. o. rossalleni*).

-blotched: grayish, yellowish, or brownish with large dark dorsal blotches and other smaller ones on the flanks (*E. o. lindheimeri* and *E. o. spiloides*).

The color of the stomach is always uniformly whitish, yellowish, orangish, or grayish, although some specimens appear lightly spotted.

HABITAT

Very varied: forests, scrubland areas, wooded canyons, rocky outcrops, marshy areas, areas of cultivation, and even semi-urban areas and abandoned rural houses, both in considerably humid conditions as well as in other much dryer ones.

They live from sea level to an elevation of 4,265 feet.

BEHAVIOR

• It is a diurnal species especially active at sunrise and sunset, becoming nocturnal during the summer months.

• It is an efficient climber that climbs trees frequently (it has been found up to 59 feet above the ground), and is also an excellent swimmer.

• It mainly feeds on rats, birds, but can also capture many other types of prey such as small rabbits, squirrels, young prairie dogs, eggs, lizards, frogs, and invertebrates.

• It hibernates between October to April in caves, in rock crevices, holes in trees, and in old abandoned buildings, sometimes communally.

REPRODUCTION

It reproduces between May and August.

The clutches consist of between ten to 20 eggs (sometimes up to 30 or 40).

It is not unusual for various females to use the same place to lay their eggs.

STATUS

It is a very common snake that has great geographic variability and even individual variability, which often makes it very difficult to correctly identify the different subspecies.

Hybridization is also common in this species, which is why the exact distribution is unknown for certain subspecies.

It has lived for more than 20 years in captivity.

Side view.

Upper view.

ELAPHE OBSOLETA. (orange). Head.

DISTRIBUTION

The mid-eastern part of the United States and a small zone south of Canada.

■ Five different subspecies tend to be distinguished:

- *E. o. lindheimeri*: The states of Texas, Oklahoma, Mississippi, Louisiana and Kansas.

- *E. o. obsoleta*: Almost all of the northern and central part of the United States east of the Rocky Mountains, and some zones close to lakes Erie, Huron, and Ontario in Canada.

- *E. o. quadrivittata*: Coastal plaines of North Carolina, South Carolina, Georgia, and Florida.

- *E. o. rossalleni*: Only in the south of Florida state: Everglades and Big Cypress Swamp.

- *E. o. spiloides*: From the southernmost part of Illinois and Indiana to the coastal plains of the Gulf of Mexico from Louisiana to Florida.

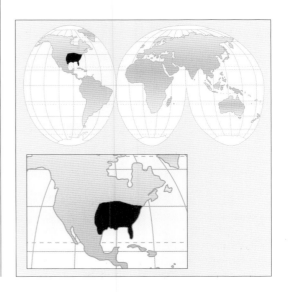

ELAPHE QUATUORLINEATA

SUBFAMILY **COLUBRINAE**

 (Lacépède, 1789)

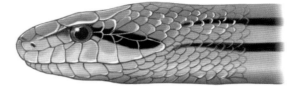 Four-lined Snake
Four-lined Rat Snake

ELAPHE QUATUORLINEATA
Adult specimen. Head

Side view.

Upper view.

Elaphe quatuorlineata
(Four lined Rat Snake).
Adult specimen.

DESCRIPTION

It is a large and slender snake although fairly solid, more robust than other colubrids in its area of distribution.

Its head is wide and somewhat pointed, with an obtuse snout that protrudes slightly over the mandible, well differentiated from the body.

It has large eyes, round pupils, and dark irises.

The body scales are oval or rhomboidal; they may be slightly keeled, above all on the posterior part, which gives it a rough looking appearance. It has between 185 to 234 ventral scales (normally 195 to 230), and 49 to 90 subcaudal scales (on average 55 to 85).

The color of the body is usually brownish-gray, of a greenish, grayish, or whitish sort, but more commonly (especially in adults of western populations) a yellowish brownish-gray.

A black stripe between the eye and the commissure of the mouth stands out on the head.

Individuals of the western populations are characterized by four longitudinal parallel black stripes that stand out along the body, from the neck to the base of the tail. Eastern populations, on the other hand, lack stripes, the back having more than 40 large blotches bordered in black, often joined in a zigzag.

The stomach is a yellowish or whitish color without blotches.

The largest specimens can reach up to 8.5 feet in length, but normally do not exceed five feet.

HABITAT

Frequents both perennial and caducous forests, scrubland, hedges, rocky hillsides covered with vegetation, margins of land under cultivation, and is even found in stone walls, stables, abandoned buildings, and country houses.

At some periods of the year they can also be found in marshy areas, and close to watercourses.

From sea level to an elevation of 8,202 feet (in Europe, however tend not to go above 1,969 feet).

BEHAVIOR

• An agile colubrid although rather slow. Active during the day; moves well both on land and in the trees and bushes; it is also a good swimmer.

• In its adult state it feeds on water rats, shrews, young hares, rabbits, topillos, squirrels, birds and their eggs (which they swallow whole) and small reptiles. The young prefer micro-mammals, saurians, and insects.

REPRODUCTION

The females are oviparous and lay from 3 to 18 eggs under tree roots, at the base of bushes, or under stones. They incubate for 45–62 days.

The newborns weigh .5–1 oz and measure between eight and 16 inches. They have a blotched pattern like that found on adults in eastern populations.

STATUS

It is a common species in many zones in its area of distribution, but they have always been widely hunted (for dietary reasons in some regions in Asia Minor), which is why they are on the way to extinction in countries such as Romania and certain places in Italy and former Yugoslavia.

ELAPHE QUATUORLINEATA
Young specimen. Head.

Side view.

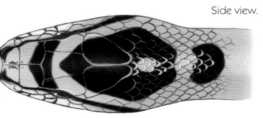

DISTRIBUTION

From Italy and southeastern Europe to the northern coasts of the Black and Caspian Sea, Turkey, Syria, Lebanon, Israel, and northern Iran.

■ Three subspecies are known:

- *E. q. quatuorlineata*: From the Island of Sicily, and Italy in southern Europe (Albany, Bulgaria, Greece, and former Yugoslavia) to the Balkans.

- *E. q. sauromates*: From east of the Balkans to north of the Aral Sea to Turkey, Syria, Lebanon, and southern Israel.

- *E. q. muenteri*: Only on the Cyclades Islands (Greece).

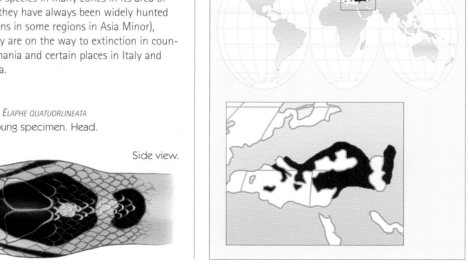

Side view.

Upper view.

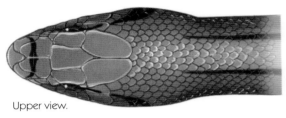

ELAPHE SCALARIS
(Ladder Snake).
Adult specimen. Head.

Elaphe scalaris
(Ladder Snake).
Adult specimen.

 (Schinz, 1822)

 Ladder Snake

ELAPHE SCALARIS

FAMILY **COLUBRINAE**

DESCRIPTION

This snake has a solid body that is considerably long: it can reach up to seven feet although, generally, the adults do not exceed five feet. Males are much smaller than the females.

The head is wide, robust, and well differentiated from the body, and the snout fairly pointed.

The tail is short, the pupils round, and the body scales small and smooth. It has between 198 and 228 ventral scales, and between 48 and 68 subcaudal scales. The anal plate is divided.

In comparison with other representatives of the genus *Elaphe*, the ladder snake has a large prominent triangular rostral scale that is very similar to that found in members of the genus *Pituophis*.

The adults have a uniformly colored body (reddish brownish-gray, yellowish brownish-gray, or grayish brownish-gray) with two dark longitudinal lines on the back that spans from the beginning of the trunk to the tail.

The head has dark blotches between the labial scales and a dark stripe between the eye and the commissure of the mouth.

HABITAT

Generally found in sunny places that are often stony, always with some kind of vegetation: open forests, scrublands, limits of cultivated fields, pasturelands, vineyards, hedges, and stone walls.

From sea level to 4,921 feet in Spain or 6,070 feet in the Coastal French Alps, although they are not usually found above an elevation of 2,297 feet.

BEHAVIOR

• It is an agile, quick, and vigorous snake that demonstrates mainly diurnal activity, although it also tends to be active during twilight or even at night at the end of summer and fall.

• Due to its adaptable habits, can be considered both a terrestrial and arboreal species.

• The young individuals prefer to feed on arthropods and small reptiles, while the adults capture small mammals (bunnies, rats, shrews), medium-sized birds (Swallow, Rock Thrush, Petronia, Sand Martin), chicks (Coracias, Merops, etc.), lizards (*Acanthodactylus, Podarcis, Psammodromus*) and another lizard (*Lacerta*).

• Although it is not venomous, it is a fairly aggressive species that whistles loudly when it feels threatened and cannot escape. It bites hard if trapped.

REPRODUCTION

Coupling takes place between the months of April and June.

The clutch is deposited one month after in holes in the ground, abandoned burrows, or beneath leaves. It is made up of five to 24 eggs (normally five to ten).

The incubation lasts between five and 12 weeks depending on environmental conditions.

The young measure eight inches when born and have a very characteristic coloration this is where the species' name comes from: a series of black transversal blotches stand out on the back with a whitish gray or cream background. The blotches are found from the neck to the tip of the tail, and their layout is similar to rungs of a ladder.

STATUS

One of the more common snakes in the moderately-humid Mediterranean environments in the south and center of the Iberian Peninsula.

Due to the important role that it plays as a controller of rodent populations, it is a species protected by law in countries such as Spain.

DISTRIBUTION

Portugal, Peninsular Spain (except for the northern border), the Island of Minorca, southeastern France (including the small islands of Hyères de Bagaud, Port-Cros, Porquerolles, Pomègue and Ratonneau) and a small zone to the extreme northeast of Italy that reaches Trucco (Liguria).

■ There are no subspecies.

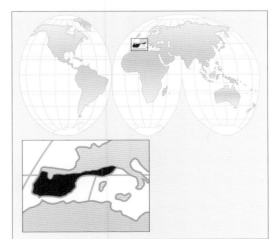

GONYOSOMA OXYCEPHALA

SUBFAMILY **COLUBRINAE**

(Boie, 1827)

Red-Tailed Rat Snake

Gonyosoma Oxycephala
(Red-Tailed Rat Snake).
Adult specimen.
Detail of the head.

DESCRIPTION

A fairly large snake, normally between five and six feet, although specimens are known that reach eight feet

The head is well distinguished from the body and the eyes are large with greenish yellow irises.

The tongue is dark blue.

The body is thin but strong, with a characteristic cross section that is taller than it is wide, and the tail is long.

The coloration is generally light green, yellowish green, or dark green.

The labial scales are also green, except in the specimens from Indonesia, whose scales are yellow.

The skin between the scales has black and white areas that are visible when the body inflates.

The tail contrasts vividly with the rest of the body which is orange-brown, yellow-brown, or gray.

A dark line extends from the angle of the mouth between the eyes.

The ventral scales are green, a diffuse green, or yellow in some specimens from Indonesia.

Individuals that are totally yellow, brownish-gray, or orange brownish-gray can be found. Also, some specimens that are typically green have blue blotches distributed along the body.

HABITAT

Exclusively arboreal.

It prefers trees and bushes to the primary or secondary rainforest.

Also close to swamps or mangrove swamps.

They are also found in rubber plantations and in gardens and parks, from sea level to an elevation of 2,461 feet.

BEHAVIOR

• They are very rarely found on the ground. Normally they are coiled up and perfectly camouflaged on tree branches at a fairly high elevation.

• They drink the rainwater that slides on their body or which is retained in a hole in the trunks.

• If bothered, it vertically inflates the front part of the body raising itself in the form of an S; therefore it is capable of repeatedly biting hard.

• Sometimes its tongue may be curved back and move slowly up and down. It is assumed that this is done to disconcert and scare a potential enemy.

• It may also excrete a smelly liquid from its anal glands if handled.

• Mainly eats arboreal rats and squirrels, but also birds and bats, which it is capable of hunting even when they are in flight on account of its extraordinarily quick movements.

REPRODUCTION

The reproductive period seems to take place during an entire year; there are different mating periods.

The clutch generally consists of 5 to 8 cylindrical eggs.

The eggs may be laid in a tree hollow or even in the ground, taking advantage of a crevice in the humid substrate.

In captivity with a temperature of 79° to 86° F, the eggs take 87–125 days to hatch.

The newborns are 16 to 22 inches long.

STATUS

No information is known about the status of its populations.

Although it has a very wide area of distribution, there are numerous zones where specimens have still not been collected.

Many regions it inhabits may be affected by the uncontrolled cutting of trees.

DISTRIBUTION

Inhabits an ample area in southeast Asia; Burma (Myanmar), Thailand, Cambodia, Indonesia, Laos, Malaysia, Singapore, the Philippines, Vietnam, and the Indian Islands of Andaman and Nicobar.

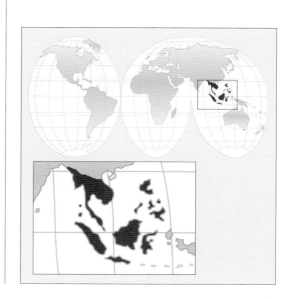

(Brown, 1901)

 Gray Banded King Snake

LAMPROPELTIS ALTERNA
FAMILY **COLUBRINAE**

Lampropeltis alterna
(Gray Banded King Snake).
Adult specimen.

DESCRIPTION

With a size between 20 and 35 inches, it is a medium-sized snake, although individuals may be found up to 58 inches in length.

It has between 210 to 232 ventral scales, a characteristic that differentiates it from the Royal Mexican Snake *Lampropeltis mexicana*, a very close species that has 190–212 ventral scales.

The head is gray with a few black blotches. A band that is also black joins the eyes through the parietal scales. The eyes are relatively large and bulging with a silver iris. The dorsal pattern has a series of alternative gray or red bands separated by narrow black stripes bordered in white. The body's gray bands are the most repeated characteristic of this species; these, however, are quite variable.

The typical variety *alterna* has between 15 and 39 black rings, while the variety *blairi* alternates between 9 and 17. Some individuals may have very darkened gray stripes and show a certain tendency towards melanism.

The specimens in which the gray bands acquire bluish tones are especially bright, colorful, and attractive.

The extension of the red bands is also very variable, sometimes of a smaller size on the posterior part of the body. The ventral part is a light color, almost white or cream, with black bands that almost cross the stomach.

HABITAT

The Gray Banded King Snake preferably inhabits rocky and limestone hills in regions with scarce vegetation in a dry or semi-humid climate.

BEHAVIOR

• During the day it hides in the crevices of rocks and during the night it actively searches for its prey or mate.

• It is found in broad daylight on rare occasions, and it is most active from sunset to midnight.

• When handled, it has the tendency to spasmodically shake itself and expel a foul smelling liquid.

• It feeds mainly on saurians, but frogs and small mammals also make up a part of its diet.

• Its favorite prey are the lizards of the genus *Sceloporus*.

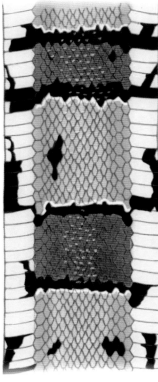

Upper view.

LAMPROPELTIS ALTERNA
(Gray Banded
King snake).
Adult specimen.
Coloration

REPRODUCTION

Mating takes place during the month of June and at the end of this month pregnant females can already be found.

Copulation lasts about 20 minutes.

The eggs measure approximatedly .2 x .4 inches.

The eggs take 55–70 days to hatch in captivity at a temperature of 80.6° F.

The babies' size varies from nine to 11 inches and weight from .2 to .3 oz.

STATUS

In the past it was thought to be a rare species, it is found very infrequently as it leads a discreet life.

It is currently considered an abundant species.

It is not protected by international law.

In the North American State of Texas its capture is allowed with a prior paid license.

DISTRIBUTION

It extends from southeastern Texas to northern Mexico, in the states of Coahuila and Durango: it has recently been found in the southernmost part of the state of New Mexico.

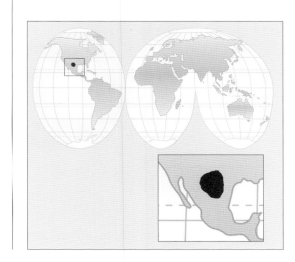

LAMPROPELTIS CALLIGASTER

SUBFAMILY COLUBRINAE

 (Harlan, 1827)

Prairie King Snake

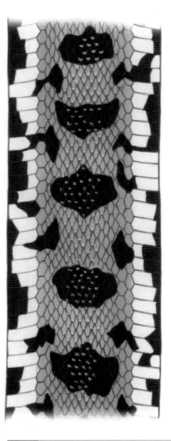

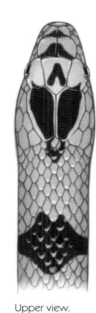

Upper view.

*LAMPROPELTIS
CALLIGASTER
RHOMBOMACULATA*
Adult specimen.
Coloration.

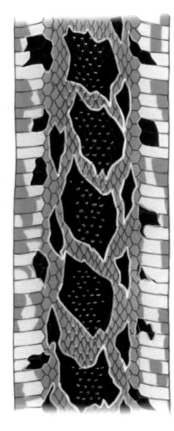

Upper view.

*LAMPROPELTIS
CALLIGASTER
CALLIGASTER*
Adult specimen.
Coloration.

DESCRIPTION

It is a slender medium–sized snake that reaches 52 inches.

Its coloration is variable, and changes according to the individual, the age, and the geographic zone. Generally its dorsal coloration consists of a gray-brown color with a pattern in the form of a reddish saddle. There are also some small lateral blotches the same color as the dorsal ones. The background color may vary with the age, normally becoming darker, while the pattern may tone down.

It has a V-shaped mark that is, fairly distinguished on the upper part of the head. The ventral color is normally yellow or whitish with a few scant brown blotches.

Three subspecies are distinguished:

L. c. calligaster. It normally has close to 60 reddish or blackish dorsal blotches and 23 to 27 rows of dorsal scales.

L. c. rhombomaculata. It rarely has more then 56 reddish-brown dorsal blotches and 21 to 23 rows of dorsal scales. The progressive darkening with age is characteristic of this species, virtually leaving the snake a uniform brown color.

L. c. occipitolineata. Is distinguished by the adults' large number of dorsal blotches (78 to 79). It has 21 rows of dorsal scales.

The last two teeth on the maxilla are not larger, opposite from *L. getula.*

Lampropeltis calligaster
(Prairie King Snake).
Adult specimen.

HABITAT

Open fields, prairies, cultivated land, rocky hills, and cleared forests.

BEHAVIOR

• It has a very discreet life and is rarely seen outside except for after dark, an intense rain, or on very hot summer nights.
• It spends most of its time under rocks or trunks or buried in the soft substrate.
• It is not aggressive.
• It feeds on small mammals, amphibians, birds, lizards, and on other snakes and insects.

REPRODUCTION

The clutches consist of 6 to 17 eggs with an average of 11, and are laid between June and July in an underground cavity.

The babies are born in 49 to 77 days and measure seven to 12 inches.

STATUS

It is rarely seen although its populations are not considered to be endangered. It may sometimes be confused with the Great Plains Ratsnake *Elaphe guttata emoryi*, but this species has keeled scales and a divided anal plate.

DISTRIBUTION

■ Three subspecies are known:
- *L. c. calligaster*: Lives in the western part of its area of distribution in Indiana, towards the west, to Nebraska, towards the south through the Mississippi Valley, to the east of Texas and west of Louisiana.
- *L. c. rhombomaculatus*: from Maryland to northern Florida, to the west up to Tennesse and southeast to Louisiana.
- *L .c. occipitolineata*: only known in Okeechobee and Brevard on the Florida peninsula.

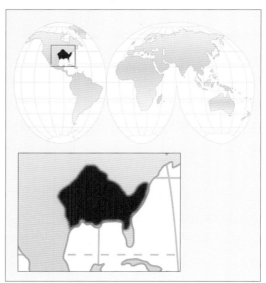

(Linnaeus, 1766)

 Common King Snake

LAMPROPELTIS GETULA

FAMILY COLUBRINAE

Lampropeltis getula
(Common King Snake).
Adult specimen.

DESCRIPTION

This species that can reach a length of six feet has a small head that is slightly differentiated from the body, eyes with round pupils, and a rather short tail.

Its body is cylindrical and its scales smooth and bright.

It has 198 to 255 ventral scales and 37 to 63 subcaudal scales.

The hemipenes are characteristically somewhat bilobed.

Its coloration greatly varies depending on its geographical distribution; seven subspecies are recognized:

California King Snake *L. getula californiae*: it has a wide variety of phases, but its most characteristic coloration consists of a black background color with transversal white or cream bands.

Florida King Snake *L. g. floridana*: also has a very variable coloration, but the most common is a brown or black background with many yellow-centered scales; also has 40 to 68 transversal bands.

Eastern King Snake *L. g. getula*: has a brown or black background with 20 to 45 white or cream scales that characteristically join on each flank forming a line.

Speckled King Snake *L. g. holbrooki*: has a uniform brown or black coloration, but the majority of scales have a yellow dot.

Mexican Black King Snake *L. g. nigritus*: uniformly brown, dark, or black.

Black King Snake *L. g. niger*: the dorsal part is black with a few scant yellow dots on the flanks, ventrally white, yellow, or black.

Desert King Snake *L. g. splendida*: has a black head, a black or dark brown background with lateral, very yellow blotched scales. It may have narrow transversal bands on its back (42 to 97).

HABITAT

Prefers dry regions, although it is a fairly adaptable species.

It is found in stony zones in semidesert regions, grassy valleys, conifer forests, plains scrubland, and along the edges of cultivated fields.

BEHAVIOR

• It is mainly diurnal but in the warmest periods is found in the open by night, while during the day it stays hidden in rock crevices or in animal burrows safe from the sun's rays.

• It kills its prey by constriction, strangling them with its coils.

• It is known to feed on other snakes, even if venomous; it seems to be immune to their venom. However, it is not a strictly ophiophagous, but also feeds on lizards, rodents, birds, and amphibians.

REPRODUCTION

Mating takes place between May and June and the female lays five to 24 white or yellowish, elongated eggs that adhere to one another.

The clutch is laid underground in a hole that is kept humid.

The newborn babies measure from nine to 11 inches.

STATUS

It is an abundant species in many areas of its distribution and respected for it ability to hunt venomous snakes.

Due to its docile character it is one of the most abundant snakes in captivity, where it is bred easily.

DISTRIBUTION

The United States: central and southern areas of the East and West Coast, and midwestern and southern states. Northern Mexico.

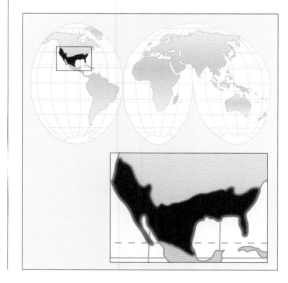

LAMPROPELTIS PYROMELANA

SUBFAMILY **COLUBRINAE**

 (Cope, 1866)

 Sonora Mountain King Snake

Lampropeltis pyromelana (Sonora Mountain King Snake). Adult specimen.

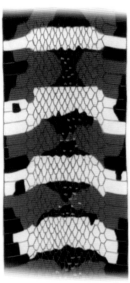     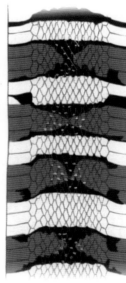

Upper view.

Upper view.

LAMPROPELTIS PYROMELANA PYROMELANA (Arizona Mountain King Snake). Adult specimen. Coloration.

LAMPROPELTIS PYROMELANA INFRALABILIS (Utah Mountain King Snake). Adult specimen.

BEHAVIOR

• This snake leads a discreet life; it prefers to be outside in the early morning hours or at twilight.

• It is normally active from the end of April to the end of September.

• It shows more surface activity after rain.

• It eats lizards, small mammals, and probably other snakes, which it kills by constriction.

REPRODUCTION

The reproductive period tends to start at the beginning of April and taper off toward the end of May. Copulation tends to last less than 5 minutes.

The period of egg formation tends to last two months and the clutch consists of three to six eggs.

They are maintained at 80.6° F and the eggs hatch after 70 days.

STATUS

It is hunted by mammals and birds, above all by owls, and other preying birds.

Humans kill it because they mistake it for the Coral Snake or because they hit the snakes on highways or on roads.

Uncontrolled collecting causes its populations to decline.

DISTRIBUTION

■ Four subspecies are known:

- *L. p. infralabialis*: found in northern Arizona, central Utah, and eastern Nevada.

- *L. p. knoblochi*: region of Mojarachic, Chihuahua, Mexico.

- *L. p. pyromelana*: Chihuahua and Sonora, Mexico and Arizona (United States).

- *L. p. woodini*: restricted to the Huachuca Mountains in southern Arizona and the border area of Mexico.

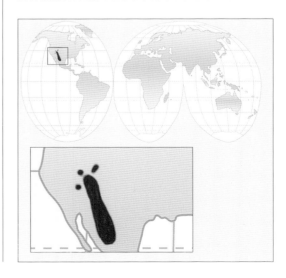

DESCRIPTION

A medium snake that can reach a maximum length of 41 inches, although most tend to measure much less.

Cylindrical snake with a fairly wide head.

The last two teeth on the maxilla are usually larger and sharper than the rest.

The snout is white or yellowish or with a few black dots. Right above the snout there is a black blotch on the head that covers the eyes and almost reaches the nape.

The dorsal pattern consists of a series of alternating black and red rings separated by more than 40 white rings.

The black bands often disappear on the flanks. The scales are flat and have 23 to 25 rows of scales on the middle of the body and 210 ventral scales.

The anal scale is not divided.

Four subspecies are distinguished:

Arizona Mountain King Snake *L. p. pyromelana*: has 10 infralabial scales and 43 white bands.

Hauchuca Mountain King Snake *L. p. woodini*: has fewer than 42 white bands; the black bands are very narrow and disappear when descending the flanks. It may have a few red dots on the black cephalic blotch.

Utah Mountain King Snake *L. p. infralabialis*: has 9 infralabial scales (the other subspecies have 10); and 42 to 57 white rings. The white rings are complete around the body.

Chihuahua Mountain King Snake *L. l. knoblochi*: its white rings join laterally in two longitudinal bands that span the flanks, leaving the dorsal blotches, in the shape of red and black saddles, completely isolated.

HABITAT

It is usually found in mountainous regions.

It inhabits regions 3,281–8,858 feet in elevation in pine, fir, juniper, and chaparral forests. It likes flowing water and is usually found close to heaps of rock where it often finds refuge.

Some specimens have also been cited to be found in prairies, normally next to a watercourse.

It tends to prefer colder climates than other similar colubrids.

DESCRIPTION

It is a hard snake to define due to the great variability of its populations; there are around 25 known subspecies.

Its size may vary between one and 14 inches.

The head is almost undistinguishable from the nape of the neck.

The back teeth on the maxilla are larger and sharper than the front ones.

The body is cylindrical, with flat bright scales distributed in 19 to 23 rows.

The dorsal coloration is a combination of brown, gray, and red blotches, or red, black, yellow, or white bands.

There are fewer than 30 white or yellow rings and they tend to widen close to the stomach. Sometimes on the ringed forms, the red rings are penetrated by the black.

The livery of the two most recognized species is:

Sinaloan Milk Snake *L. t. sinaloe*: has intense colors with a black head and a red snout lightly dotted white. The sequence of the rings is: red, black, white or yellow, black, red. The red bands are about three times wider than the black-white-black bands. The number of red rings alternates between 10 and 16. The dorsal coloration is paler than the ventral.

Scarlet King Snake *L. t. elapsoide*: has a red head with a black stripe on the posterior part.

The red rings vary from 12 to 22. The white or yellow ring on the ventral zone expands until it is wider than the black one.

(Lacepede, 1788)

Milk Snake

LAMPROPELTIS TRIANGULUM
FAMILY COLUBRINAE

Lampropeltis triangulum sinolae (Milk Snake). Adult specimen.

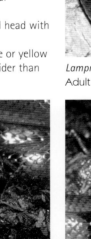

HABITAT

Very diverse, semi-arid, marshy zones, in the foothills of the Rocky Mountains, tropical jungles, pine forests, open forests, rocky hills, prairies, area with dunes, fields under cultivation, and suburban areas.

From sea level to 8,038 feet.

BEHAVIOR

• It is often found under trunks or stumps, and is normally hard to find outside except at night.

• It is very docile and never bites.

• Eats snakes, lizards, reptile eggs, small birds and small mammals, which it kills by constriction.

• Dietary preferences vary greatly between populations.

• Its coloration may be considered mimetic in respect to venomous snakes, imitating the Copperhead *Agkistrodon contortrix*, in the northern area of its distribution, and in the south the Coral Snakes of the genus *Micrurus*.

REPRODUCTION

In the United States, mating takes place in spring.

It lays 2 to 17 elliptical eggs, usually beneath tree trunks.

Incubation lasts six to nine weeks and the young measure five to 11 inches and are more vividly colored than the adults.

STATUS

Its populations are not endangered.

The most common name in English is Milk Snake, because of the myth that these snakes went to the stables to drink directly from the cattle's udders.

DISTRIBUTION

It is one of the species of snakes with a wider area of distribution that reaches 3,579 miles extension; from the south of Ontario to Ecuador and the Venezuelan coastal mountain range.

■ In total, there are 25 subspecies, nine of them in the United States.

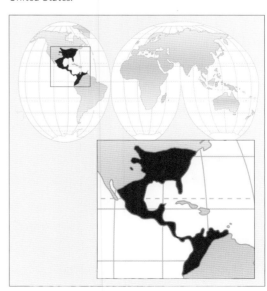

LAMPROPELTIS ZONATA

SUBFAMILY **COLUBRINAE**

 (Lockington, 1876)

Mountain King Snake

Lampropeltis zonata
(Mountain King Snake).
Adult specimen.

STATUS

Its capture is regulated by laws of the State of California where it is classified as a *Species of Interest* (County of Los Angeles).

DESCRIPTION

A small-sized snake whose length varies between 20 and 40 inches.

It generally has a tricolor coloration with triads of white, black, and red rings. The red rings always have black rings on both sides. In some subspecies, like *L. z. herrerae* or in some individuals of *L. z multicincta*, the red rings disappear, leaving a livery very similar to that of the California King Snake *L. getulus californiae*, but in the *L. zonata* the white rings do not widen when they reach the stomach.

The snout is a uniform black or black with red blotches.

The scales are flat and distributed in 23 rows.

The anal plate is not divided.

The last two teeth are larger and solider than the front ones.

Upper view.

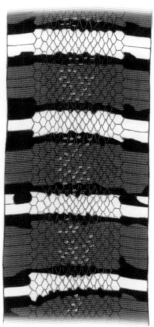

LAMPROPELTIS ZONATA MULTIFASCIATA
(Mountain King Snake).
Adult specimen.
Coloration.

DISTRIBUTION

It covers isolated zones of the states of Oregon and California in the United States, Baja California, and the Todos los Santos Island.

■ Seven subspecies are distinguished although some of them are difficult to identify despite the animal's area of origin being known:

The following are found in Mexico: *L. z. agalma*, San Pedro King Snake, and *L. z. herrerae*, Todos los Santos Island King Snake.

In the states of Oregon and California: *L. z. multicincta*, Sierra Mountain King Snake, and *L. z. zonata*, St. Helena Mountain King Snake.

In the state of California: *L. z. multifasciata*, Coastal Mountain King Snake, *L. z. parvirubra*, San Bernardino Mountain King Snake, *L. z. Pulchra*, San Diego Mountain King Snake.

HABITAT

Lives in humid pine forests. From sea level (Todos los Santos Island) to 7,784 feet in the San Gabriel Mountains, in the county of Los Angeles. It is also found in the chaparral.

• Sometimes, according to various observers, its bright and colorful livery may be used as a lure; it may provoke birds that are defending their nests to attack them; in this way, the snake finds and captures the chicks. It is a good climber.

• It feeds on rodents, lizards, snakes, birds, and their eggs.

BEHAVIOR

• This snake leads a discreet life; it hides under fallen tree trunks, stones, or leaf piles, often close to the mountain torrents.

• It is mainly diurnal but is also active on hot summer nights.

REPRODUCTION

The eggs are laid from June to July in clutches of three to eight eggs.

The young are born in nine to ten weeks and measure close to eight inches in length.

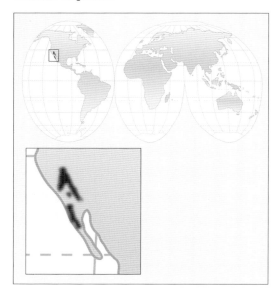

(Shaw, 1802)

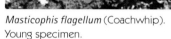
Coachwhip

MASTICOPHIS FLAGELLUM

SUBFAMILY COLUBRINAE

Masticophis flagellum (Coachwhip).
Young specimen.

Masticophis flagellum (Coachwhip).
Adult specimen.

DESCRIPTION

It can reach 8.5 feet in length, which is why it is one of the largest snakes in North America.

It is slender with flat scales, and stands out for its very long tail that can move incredibly fast.

The head is large and angular and the eyes, with round pupils, are protected by the supraocular shields. The body scales are found on the middle of the body, distributed in 17 rows.

The coloration is different depending on its geographic origin; the western races generally have liveries in which yellow, brownish-gray, gray, or pink predominate with dark bands on the nape of the neck. This individual's head and nape are a dark almost black brown, while the tone on the posterior part of the body is closer to a lighter brown. There are a few totally black specimens. The ventral coloration is normally brown or pink. The transversal bands and blotches tend to be more conspicuous on the young specimens.

HABITAT

These snakes are found mainly in dry open places: deserts, prairies, dunes. Also in open and chaparral forests. From sea level to an elevation of 7,054 feet.

BEHAVIOR

• It moves very quickly (velocities of 3.6 miles per hour have been registered); it is also an excellent climber.

• It looks for food mainly in the morning and at sunset.

• It is a nervous animal, and when surprised, tries to hide between the rocks, in the vegetation, or in teh borrow of a mammal, but when it feels cornered it puffs strongly and tries to use its long tail to hit its enemy's face. If handled, it moves nervously, expels a smelly liquid, and tries to bite hard.

• While it looks actively for food, it can keep its head raised to find its prey more easily.

• Its diet includes all types of small vertebrates, many of them rodents that infest certain areas and venomous snakes.

• When the prey is captured, it is quickly swallowed live.

REPRODUCTION

Mating takes place in spring and the eggs are laid in summer.

They lay four to 16 eggs on the rough surface, which hatch in six to 11 weeks.

The newborns measure 11 to 16 inches long.

STATUS

In general, it is not considered endangered; its local populations are abundant, although some subspecies, like the San Joaquin Whipsnake are very aggressive.

M. f. rudducki, is listed as a "Species of special Concern."

This species name comes from the braid-like appearance of its scales similar to the whips that old stagecoach drivers used.

DISTRIBUTION

Wide distribution that covers the entire south of the United States including Florida, Baja California, and a large part of northern Mexico.

■ It includes six subspecies:

- *M. f. flagellum*, Eastern coachwhip.

- *M. f. cingulum*, Sonora coachwhip.

- *M. f. fulginosus*, Baja California coachwhip.

- *M. f. lineatulus*, Linned coachwhip.

- *M. f. piceus*, Red coachwhip.

- *M. f. ruddocki*, San Joaquin coachwhip.

- *M. f. testaceus*, Western coachwhip.

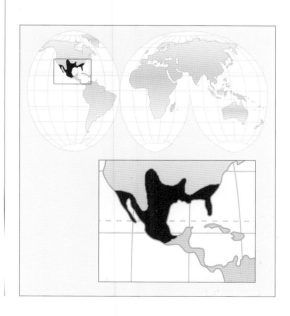

PITUOPHIS MELANOLEUCUS

SUBFAMILY COLUBRINAE

(Daudin, 1803)

Gopher Snake
Bull Snake

Pituophis melanoleucus sayi (Gopher Snake). Adult specimen.

DESCRIPTION

It can measure up to eight feet; it is one of the longest snakes in the United States.

It is a strong snake with large eyes, and a head that is slightly differentiated from the neck.

Its snout is slightly pointed with an enlarged rostral scale that extends upwards between the internasal scales.

It has four prefrontal scales. The scales are keeled and distributed on the body in 27 to 37 rows. The anal scale is not divided.

The body is lightly colored: beige, white, cream, yellow, red-orangish with numerous brownish-gray, black, or reddish marks on the back, more spaced out towards the tail and smaller towards the sides.

A characteristic dark band crosses the forehead in front of the eyes.

The ventral face is white or yellowish, generally somewhat blotched black. The distribution and tone of these blotches varies greatly among the recognized 15 subspecies, and even in a subspecies such as *P. m. mugitus*, the blotches may disappear, displaying a practically uniform livery.

In the past, some subspecies were considered a different species such as *P. Catenifer*, but now, they are all under the same taxonomy.

HABITAT

Fairly varied although it prefers dry environments: it inhabits pine or oak forests, prairies, zones of scrubland, rocky deserts, chaparral, and cultivated zones from sea level to 8,858 feet.

BEHAVIOR

• This species spends a lot of time underground in tunnels it burrowed or in burrows made by other animals like turtles. Generally diurnal, it may, however, be active nocturnally in hot weather.

• When in danger, it unleashes an elaborate system of defense: it inflates its body to look larger, opens its mouth, raises its body into an S shape and makes its tail repreatedly vibrate. It also expels accumulated air, producing a loud snort, and accompanied by attacks. It uses this strategy to try to scare its enemy, producing a few disconcerting moments which it takes advantage of to flee and quickly save itself.

• Normally, it is not a species that bites when handled.

• It hunts a large number of rodents, rabbits, birds and their eggs, and occasionally lizards and insects.

• It often enters the rodents' burrows where it kills them by compressing them against the tunnel walls with its coils. However, it normally kills by constriction.

REPRODUCTION

Mating takes place in spring.

It lays one or two clutches per year of three to 24 cream-colored or white eggs.

STATUS

It is sometimes exterminated because it is confused with the rattlesnake on account of its coloring and intimidating posture.

Being a great exterminator of rodents, some farmers often introduced it to granaries and stocks of food.

It is not on the list of endangered animals.

DISTRIBUTION

All the West Coast and Midwest of the United States, points south of Canada (south of Alberta, and British Columbia), south to New Jersey, Florida, Virginia, Kentucky, Tennessee, Alabama, Georgia, the Carolinas, and northern Mexico.

■ 15 subspecies, ten of them in the United States.

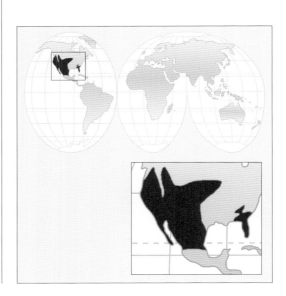

(Linnaeus, 1758)

Mole Snake

PSEUDASPIS CANA

SUBFAMILY COLUBRINAE

Pseudaspis cana (Mole Snake).
Adult specimen.

DESCRIPTION

The South African specimens can exceed seven feet. Others from the same area of distribution rarely exceed 53 inches.

It has a cyclindrical compact body, particularly in large individuals, with a short, thick, and pointed tail.

The head is comparatively small and almost indistinguishable from the neck. It has a pointed snout that is somewhat hookshaped. The eyes are medium-sized with round pupils. The scales are flat and distributed in between 25 to 31 rows. The anal plate is divided.

The coloration is variable. The adults are uniform, generally with a light grayolive colored back with all tones of brown and reddish brown and even black on the specimens of the province of the South African Cape. Some scales with black margins often appear on individuals with light coloration. The young individuals differ greatly from the adults; they have a light reddish-brown pattern with four lines of darker blotches on which the two interior blotches may join together to form a zigzagged line. Some individuals maintain the infantile coloration when they are adults.

HABITAT

Very varied, they include cultivated areas, savannah zones, prairies, mountain, and desert zones.

BEHAVIOR

• The common name comes from its habit of burrowing tunnels in the soft substrate. They are often found with half their body or their head sticking out on the surface, and the rest of the body buried.

• They also exploit burrowing mammals' burrows to hide and search for food.

• When bothered, they react aggresively, puffing and attacking.

• If handled, it violently shakes and may cause painful bites.

• Once in captivity, it tends to lose a large part of its aggressiveness.

• Adults prefer to eat rodents and other small mammals while the less subterranean young mainly feed on lizards in rocky areas. Some individuals also feed on eggs.

REPRODUCTION

The males fight among themselves during the mating season and can bite with ferocity.

It is ovoviviparous.

They mate at the end of spring (October) and between March and April; between 25 to 40 (sometimes more than 95) babies are born.

The newborns measure about eight inches.

STATUS

It is one of the most common snakes in the dry zone of the South African Cone.

It is well received in agricultural zones; to sustain itself it eats a large quantity of rodents.

DISTRIBUTION

South Africa, Angola, Kenya, Tanzania and Zaire.

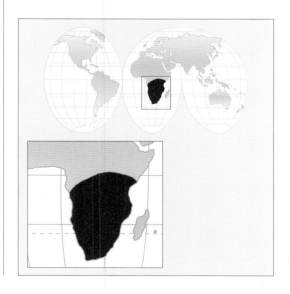

PTYAS MUCOSUS

SUBFAMILY COLUBRINAE

 (Linnaeus, 1758)

📄 Dhaman

Ptyas mucosus (Dhaman). Adult specimen.

PTYAS MUCOSUS (Dhaman). Adult specimen.
Detail of the head.

Side view.

Upper view.

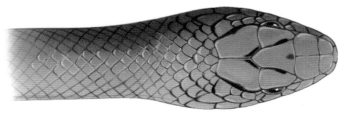

PTYAS MUCOSUS (Dhaman).
Adult specimen.
Coloration.

DESCRIPTION

A large species, it is one of the largest colubrids.

The majority of individuals measure from six to seven feet, but some specimens have been found to measure more than 12. Males are larger than the females.

The body is robust and its thickness diminishes towards the end parts of the body; it has a long tail that measures close to one-fourth of the body's total length. The head has large eyes and is elongated, well distinguished from the rest of the neck.

The coloration is fairly uniform; it is an olive brown, a dark brownish-gray, or with lighter tones like yellow or sepia. The posterior part of the body is marked by thin black lines that sometimes form rhomboidal patterns. The lips and ventral scales are bordered in black. The ventral scales are gray, whitish, or cream.

HABITAT

It is a species that mainly inhabits lower zones, although it has been found a few times at an elevation of more than 5,906 feet.

It is diurnal although difficult to observe in broad daylight in inhabited zones.

It is found in different habitats in its area of distribution, both in semidesert zones with a few bushes as well as in forests.

It swims, dives, and climbs with great ease.

BEHAVIOR

• Normally it tries to escape, but if cornered it defends itself with determination. It maintains the head slightly erect and the body in an S-form, then it compresses the body with the spine arched and the throat markedly widened.

• When bothered it often produces a sound similar to a cat's meow, at the same time making the tip of its tail vibrate rapidly. It may bite repeatedly and hard.

• It feeds mainly on amphibians, frogs and toads, but it can capture almost any prey such as reptiles, salamanders, water turtles, scindidae, agamidae, snakes, birds, and mammals.

REPRODUCTION

During rut, the males enter into very ritualized combat in which individuals coil their bodies together on the floor or with the body half raised.

The breeding period varies with the climate.

They lay six to 14 eggs and the female coils up on them to protect them. The newborns measure 12 to 16 feet.

They reach sexual maturity when they are three years old.

STATUS

It is a common snake within much of its area of distribution.

It is sometimes confused with the cobra and therefore pursued in some zones.

It is captured for food in Kerala and Malabar.

There is a false belief that this species is the male cobra. Another false belief is that it sucks cow's udders.

It is included in Appendix II of CITES.

DISTRIBUTION

India, Sri Lanka, Burma. It extends towards the east to Afghanistan and Turkestan and south and east China.

It is also cited in Java and Sumatra.

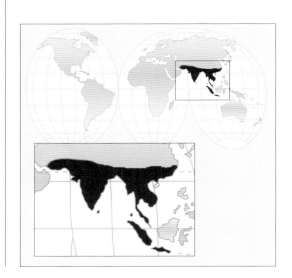

 (Schlegel,1837)

 Royal or Diadem Snakes

SPALEROSOPHIS DIADEMA

SUBFAMILY **COLUBRINAE**

Spalerosophis diadema
(Royal or Diadem Snakes).
Adult specimen.

DESCRIPTION

It can reach seven feet in length, but the most common size is around five feet. The females are larger.

It is slender looking with a very oval defined head.

It has eyes with a round pupil and a yellow iris.

The body scales are slightly keeled and the cranial scales are divided into a few smaller ones. It has a small line of scales between the supralabial scales and the eyes.

The background color is gray, yellowish, ochre, and reddish. It has reddish or brownish-gray transversal blotches in the form of a diamond. On the flanks it has two rows of dark alternate blotches. It has various dark transversal lines on its front. A dark line joins the eyes with the bucal commissures; its specific name refers precisely to this characteristic.

This species with an ample distribution is divided into three or four subspecies with important differences as far as body coloration; some of these subspecies are considered by other authors as different species.

HABITAT

It inhabits arid or semi-arid zones with a considerable thermal contrast between day and night.

It hides in the crevices of rocks, under stones, or in burrows.

During the first hours of the day during the first months of spring, it can be seen basking in the sun, remaining alert and hiding itself at the slightest sign of alarm.

It is found on the plains and on mountainous massifs up to an elevation of 6,562 feet.

BEHAVIOR

• It is active during the day in spring and nocturnally in summer.

• It is always alert and is quick and agile.

• When cornered it bites hard.

• It has been observed at times in treetops, where its coloration acts as camouflage as below on the ground.

• It may be confused in the more eastern part of its area of distribution with *Daboia ruselli*, but this viper has a typically triangular head, a different distribution of the scales, and a vertical pupil.

• It eats lizards, snakes, rats, and birds, although rodents seem to be the base of its diet. It does not hesitate climbing trees for hunting when necessary.

REPRODUCTION

Little is known about its reproductive habits, but it is believed to lays its eggs between May and June, after a winter resting period.

It lays three to 15 eggs and the new young are observed starting in October. Their measurements are 16 to 20 inches.

STATUS

No information is known about its populations, although it does not seem to be endangered.

DISTRIBUTION

Northern Africa to Arabia, Asia Minor, Pakistan, and northeast of India.

- *S. d. cliffordi*: Northern Africa to Egypt, Israel, and Syria.

- *S. d. dolichospila*: the easternmost point of Morocco, Tunisia, Algeria (some authors consider it a different species).

- *S. d. diadema*: in the species' eastern distribution.

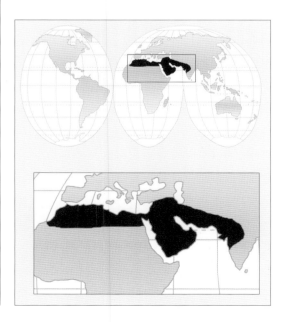

SPILOTES PULLATUS

SUBFAMILY **COLUBRINAE**

 (Linnaeus, 1758)

 Tropical Rat Snake

Spilotes pullatus
(Tropical Rat Snake).
Adult specimen.

DESCRIPTION

Very large colubrid that measures between 8.5 feet and 10 feet, which makes it one of the largest colubrids of the neotropics.

The head is well differentiated from the rest of the body; it is laterally compressed and has a striking appearance.

The tail is thin and pointed.

The dorsal scales are enlarged and keeled with two apexes. The vertebral column is usually well defined. It has 16 rows (18 as an exception) of dorsal scales and 217 to 241 ventral scales (207–228 on the males and 215–241 on the females). Its anal plate is undivided.

The head is yellow or brownish-gray with very irregular black blotches.

The eyes are large and black.

The general coloration is made up of oblique black and yellow stripes; black irregularly filters into the yellow areas. The yellow stripes dissipate towards the back of the body until they disappear, then there is a uniformly black coloration with a few transversal dark gray or dark brownish-gray bands.

The ventral face is a uniform yellow is marked with lateral black blotches.

HABITAT

It is mainly an arboreal species even though it can often be seen on the floor.

It inhabits warm and temperate zones, and prefers humid areas close to water currents with an abundance of trees and scrublands.

It frequents the rainforest, the secondary forest, and the gallery forests that follow the courses of rivers.

Also close to towns and farms.

BEHAVIOR

• It is called a quick moving colubrid and therefore is called the flying colubrid in some areas.

• It is also a great swimmer.

• When it feels threatened it is highly aggressive, displaying a bright and colorful threatening posture; it lifts the front part of its body in the form of an S, inflates the neck area adopting an appearance similar to a cobra and makes the tip of its tail vibrate. If the aggressor gets too close, it may bite repeatedly.

• Its diet consists of birds and small mammals that it hunts both on the floor and in the treetops.

• It is often found close to cattle-raising areas in search of rodents.

• Prey is killed by constriction.

REPRODUCTION

It is ovoviviparous and can lay from eight to 25 eggs. The newborns feed on frogs and lizards.

STATUS

Abundant species.

In Brazil it is called the henhouse snake because it tends to be installed on the farms to exterminate the rodent population.

In rural areas, the myths about this snake say that it places the tip of its tail in a nursing baby's mouth like a pacifier) to replace the nipple of its sleeping mother's breast.

DISTRIBUTION

From southern Mexico, Central and South America, to Argentina.

■ Five subspecies are known.

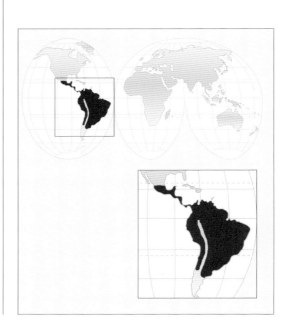

(Linnaeus, 1758)

AMPHIESMA STOLATA

SUBFAMILY NATRICINAE

 Buff-Striped Keelback

Amphiesma stolata
(Buff-Striped Keelback).
Adult specimen.

DESCRIPTION

It can reach a maximum length of 30 feet, and the females are considerably larger than the males.

It has keeled scales.

The body is short and the tail proportionally very long; it is approximately one-fourth of the entire length.

The neck is clearly differentiated from the head.

The eyes are large with a round yellowish-gold spotted pupil.

The tongue is orangish with black spots.

The last tooth on the upper mandible is differentiated into a fang, possibly linked to a venomous gland (opisthoglyphous dentition).

The coloration of the body is fairly variable, although two yellow lines tend to stand out that extend along the dorsal sides from the neck to the tip of the tail; they stand out on an olive green or brownish-gray background. There are also some irregular dark blotches on the front part of the body. The chin and throat are white, yellow, or orange, and some individuals have black spots on their stomachs.

HABITAT

It is diurnal and predominantly terrestrial.

It is found along riverbanks and at the edges of marshes.

In the rainy season it can often be found in open fields, prairies, and cultivated zones close to water, always in areas with an abundance of food (frogs and toads).

It seems particularly abundant during the rainy season.

BEHAVIOR

• During the driest and warmest period, it hides in holes in the ground or in the walls of wells or drains.

• In northern India it retreats to hibernate during winter.

• When alarmed, it flattens the nape of its neck and the front part of the body and takes deep inhalations to show the bright blue color at the base of its scales.

• It almost exclusively eats frogs and toads although it is rarely found in water.

REPRODUCTION

Mating takes place during summer and the eggs are laid from May to September in some kind of shelter in the earth.

The females often remain next to the eggs.

The eggs are white and adhered together.

There are normally from three to 12 eggs and the babies are born during the rainy season.

It is a totally harmless species.

STATUS

It seems very abundant, and is especially visible during the monsoon season when a large number can be found both during the day and at night.

It is less abundant in higher zones.

DISTRIBUTION

Pakistan, India, Sri Lanka, Andaman Islands, Burma, Thailand, Vietnam, Laos, Taiwan, China, Kampuchea, and Nepal.

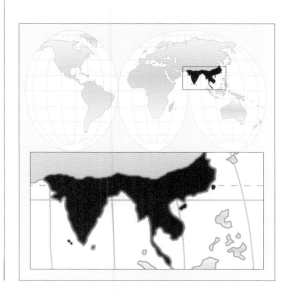

NATRIX MAURA

SUBFAMILY NATRICINAE

 (Linnaeus, 1758)

 Viperina Snake

Natrix maura (Viperina Snake) Detail of the head.

Natrix maura
(Viperina Snake)
Adult specimen.

REPRODUCTION

It is in heat twice a year: in spring and fall.

Mating may last for more than an hour and there are no ritualistic fights between the males. The female lays between four and 24 eggs in hollows, crevices between rocks, or under roots next to the water's shore.

Incubation lasts between one and a half months to three months, and the first are born in August.

DESCRIPTION

Is a small to medium-sized snake that, although it can reach three feet in length, usually does not exceed 28 inches.

The head is well differentiated with a short snout that is rather rounded.

Large eyes with round pupils and a gold colored iris.

The tail makes up about one-fifth of the total length.

It has keeled dorsal scales that form 21 rows on the center of the body. It generally has two postocular and preocular scales.

The background color of its body is a brownish-gray, gray, greenish, yellowish, and even reddish, or orangish color. Two series of dark alternate blotches span the back and often join, forming one zigzagged stripe. There are a series of blotches on the sides that may have the shape of an ocellus.

There is another typical design that consists of a dark background color on which two light-colored dorsal parallel lines stand out.

A dark inverted V-shaped blotch often appears on the nape of the neck. The stomach and the lower parts of the tail may be a yellowish-white color with dark subquadrangular blotches often arranged like a chessboard.

HABITAT

This species is closely linked to water, more so than the Collar Snake.

It is found in a wide variety of water environments; lagoons, marshes, ponds, irrigation ditches, streams, etc.

It can handle a certain level of salinity.

Much more abundant in large water currents.

BEHAVIOR

• It is not very agile on land while in water it moves very quickly; it can also remain underwater for a long time without coming up for air.

• It lives in groups and spends a large amount of time underwater with the head sticking out of the water.

• When it feels threatened it may take on the intimidating posture of the vipers that have a somewhat similar livery. Therefore, it widens the mandibles, giving the head a clearly triangular shape, and at the same time, it emits forceful snorts and projects its head forwards, never biting.

• When handled, its cloacal glands release fetid secretions.

• It mainly feeds in the water, and its diet consists of fish, amphibians, salamanders, newts, frogs, toads, as well as their larvae, and on invertebrates.

• It often takes its prey out of the water to swallow it.

STATUS

It is very abundant, and in some regions, like that of the Iberian Peninsula, it is the most common ophidian.

DISTRIBUTION

Libya, Tunisia, Algeria, Morocco, Portugal, Spain, France, northern Italy.

The Balearic Islands, Sardinia.

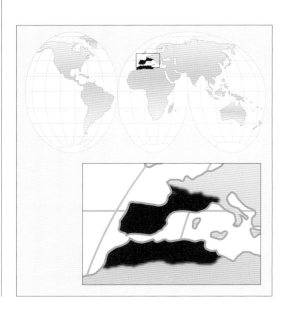

(Linnaeus, 1758)

Grass Snake

NATRIX NATRIX

SUBFAMILY NATRICINAE

Natrix natrix (Grass Snake). Adult specimen.

DESCRIPTION

This snakes generally does not grow longer than three feet although females have been known to reach seven feet.

It is a thick colubrid as an adult, with a wide and rounded snout, and a large, well differentiated head, widened posteriorly on the adults, especially on the females.

Large eyes with a black, brownish-gray, or reddish brownish-gray iris.

Keeled dorsal scales forming 19 rows along the center of the body. It normally has one preocular scale and three postocular scales.

The background color of the upper parts is fairly variable and on average, is a grayish, greenish, or olive brownish-gray that is basically uniform with small dark blotches that vary greatly in number and in distribution.

There are dark blotches on the upper parts of the scales' sutures.

Both sides of the neck and the nape are covered with a light colored blotch, followed by a blotch in the form of a dark crescent shape.

The young have a yellowish white collar bordered in black that completely disappears on the adults.

There are melanic individuals distributed throughout all the populations.

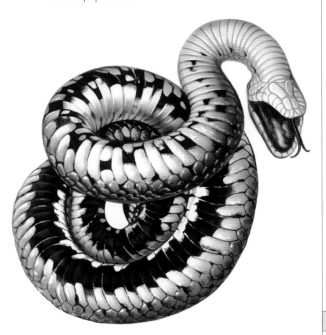

Female Grass Snake, *Natrix natrix*.

HABITAT

Semiaquatic species, normally found close to water, in rivers, marshes, ponds, artificial lakes, or irrigation ditches. Sometimes the adult animals inhabit dryer places such as prairies, hedges, or forests.

BEHAVIOR

• This snake moves fairly quickly on the floor and is a very good swimmer; it can remain underwater for a rather long time (more than 30 minutes).

• If bothered, it may display elaborate behavior that consists of playing dead. To do so, it fills its stomach with air, relaxes the muscles, writhes, turns over, and sticks out its tongue. It may even expel drops of blood from the mouth.

• Another type of conduct that it may use is, when captured, it defends itself by expelling a fetid liquid from the cloaca, spraying whoever holds it.

• The adult females can also take on defensive attitudes that are similar to vipers, although, naturally it is a harmless species that does not bite.

• It can hunt both on land and in water, preferably in the morning or in the late afternoon hours. It feeds on frogs, toads, newts, salamanders, and fish.

REPRODUCTION

Up to two periods of heat may occur, in spring and fall.

Copulation may be collective, with one or two participating females and 5 to 10 males.

They generally lay between 11 and 53 eggs, although sometimes they may lay even more. Incubation lasts between three and 11 weeks, depending on the climate.

On average, the babies tend to be born in September and measure from four to nine inches long.

STATUS

It is thought to be the most abundant snake of Europe, but it is scarcer in the southern regions. It is almost extinct in Cyprus.

DISTRIBUTION

Tunisia, Algeria, and Morocco.

All of Europe except for Ireland and northern Scandinavia.

Asia Minor and Central Asia.

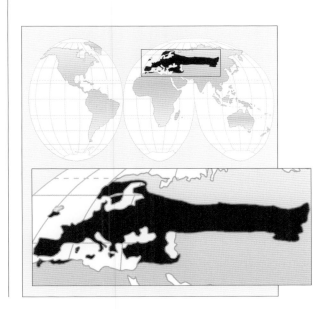

NATRIX TESSELLATA

SUBFAMILY NATRICINAE

 (Laurenti, 1768)

Dice Snake

Natrix tessellata (Dice Snake).
Adult specimen on water.

DESCRIPTION

The adults may exceed three feet in length, but generally measure less than 30 inches.

This snake has a fairly triangular girth, narrow and pointed, with a round pupil and a yellowish or reddish iris.

The dorsal scales are very keeled, forming 19 rows on the central part of the body. It generally has two preocular scales and three postocular scales.

The background color on the upper parts is fairly variable, usually grayish or brownish-gray, and less yellowish and greenish. It often has two groups of dark, regularly distributed blotches that may be large or small, or join and form dark stripes on the back and on the sides in a mosaic form.

There is sometimes a mark in the shape of an inverted V on the nape of the neck. The lower parts are whitish, pink, squared, with dark wide whitish-yellow bands that may also be completely black.

Melanic individuals may be found.

The young animals have the same coloring as the adults, but the colors are more vivid and contrasted.

HABITAT

More aquatic than even the Viperina Snake; it prefers lakes, swamps, and river estuaries. It is also found in other sources of water such as rivers, torrents, ponds, wells, artificial lakes, rice fields, and coastal zones.

BEHAVIOR

• It hibernates in rock crevices or under rocks close to the water, alone or in groups of up to 200 individuals.

• It spends the majority of its active time in the water, coiled up at the base of rocks along the shores.

• It is an excellent swimmer and can even be found in salt water a fair distance from the coast.

• If handled, it empties the contents of its intestines and releases a smelly liquid secreted by the cloacal glands while whistling loudly. It is, however, a totally harmless snake.

• It mostly feeds on fish, which constitute 70% of its diet. It also eats frogs, toads, newts, tadpoles, and sometimes baby rodents. In some coastal zones it may feed in the sea.

REPRODUCTION

The mating period is in May or June.

The females lay four to 35 eggs in June or July; these eggs are stuck together, forming one mass containing small embryos.

The eggs are laid on the floor under the rocks.

The babies are born in the middle of August or at the beginning of September; they measure between 6 and 9 inches and weigh between .014 and .018 oz.

STATUS

They are very abundant at the estuaries of large rivers as well as in lakes and swamps in a large part of their area of distribution.

They are thought to be endangered in some countries in Central Europe like Germany and Switzerland, where they are protected.

DISTRIBUTION

Italy, southeastern Europe, Asia Minor, countries that border the Caspian and Black Seas, central Asia, and Pakistan.

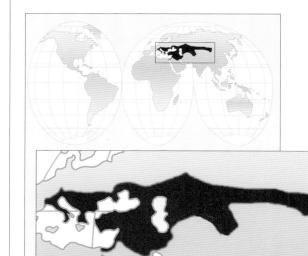

📄 (Linnaeus, 1766)

📄 Southern Water Snake

NERODIA FASCIATA

SUBFAMILY NATRICINAE

Nerodia fasciata (Southern Water Snake).
Adult specimen.
Detail of the head.

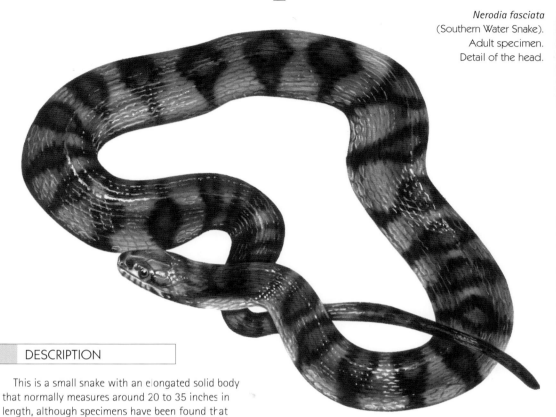

Nerodia fasciata (Southern Water Snake).
Adult specimen.

DESCRIPTION

This is a small snake with an elongated solid body that normally measures around 20 to 35 inches in length, although specimens have been found that measure up to 59 inches.

The tail is long and thin, and the head is small with a rounded snout.

It always has a black stripe that goes from the eyes to the commissure of the lips.

The back is a reddish, brownish, yellowish, or grayish color with a series of dark bands along the entire body and thin light colored strias on some subspecies' flanks.

The old specimens tend to loose the bands and become uniformly dark.

The stomach is yellow with fairly marked transversal red blotches.

The body's scales are keeled and are arranged in 21 to 25 rows.

The anal plate is divided.

Nerodia fasciata (Southern Water Snake).
Adult specimen. Ventral zone.

HABITAT

All types of fresh and brackish water: lakes, marshes, wetlands, rivers, or streams.

It inhabits coastal or fluvial valleys, and is only found from sea level to an elevation of 984 ft.

BEHAVIOR

• This species has aquatic habits; it swims quickly and agilely, both along the surface and underwater.

• It frequently moves on land and can even be seen on the tree branches that project out over the water.

• It is active during the day and at night, and it feeds on small fish, frogs, tadpoles, salamanders, and crabs.

• When in danger it may expel a smelly substance from its anal glands, but it also defends itself by raising the front part of its body, whistling, and biting decisively.

REPRODUCTION

It is ovoviviparous.

The female gives birth to 25 to 30 already perfectly formed young (although figures of more than 50 have been reported), from 8 to 10 inches in length.

STATUS

It is a common species in the majority of humid medium in its zone of distribution. It is found in decline in some areas due to the drying of the aquatic zones and the destruction of the forests along the riverbank (for example, in Illinois).

It is often kept as a pet, and tends to live between five and eight years in captivity, although some animals have been kept in captivity for up to 15 years.

DISTRIBUTION

Eastern part of the United States, from North Carolina to the Florida Keys, and in the south to western Texas, and the northern part of southern Illinois.

There is a small population in the northern part of the island of Cuba.

■ Six different subspecies are distinguished:

- *N. f. fasciata*: coastal plains of both Carolinas, Georgia, Florida, and Alabama.

- *N. f. clarki*: states in the Gulf of Mexico, from Florida to Texas.

- *N. f. compressicauda*: southern Florida, the Keys, and northern Cuba.

- *N. f. confluens*: from Alabama to Texas and in the Mississippi Valley up to the southernmost part of Illinois.

- *N. f. pictiventris*: Florida Peninsula. Introduced into Brownsville (Texas).

- *N. f. taeniata*: Florida Coasts, form Daytona Beach to Vero Beach.

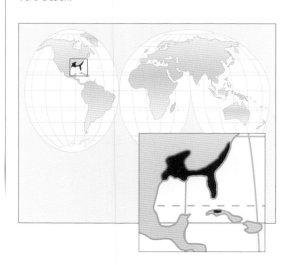

NERODIA SIPEDON

SUBFAMILY **NATRICINAE**

 (Linnaeus, 1758)

Northern Water Snake

Nerodia sipedon
(Northern Water Snake).
Adult specimen.

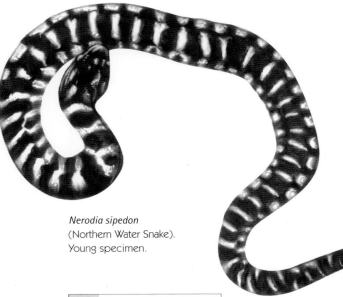

Nerodia sipedon
(Northern Water Snake).
Young specimen.

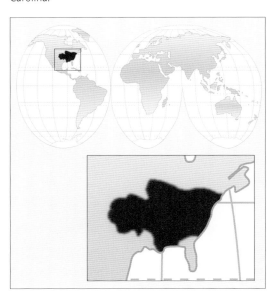

DESCRIPTION

Is a medium-sized robust but slender snake; the largest specimens do not exceed 59 inches in length, and the average for the adults is between 24 and 47 inches.

The head is small and rounded and there is no black line from the eyes to the commissure of the mouth.

The dorsal color is a reddish, brownish, or grayish color with a series of dark bands behind the neck that alternate in the middle of the body and extend along the flanks. All the marks become darker with age until turning almost black in practically all of the subspecies. The stomach is whitish, yellowish, or grayish with a reticle of small reddish or black blotches with very varied patterns.

The body scales are markedly keeled and are arranged in 21 to 25 rows. The anal plate is divided.

HABITAT

Any fresh water environment: lakes, ponds, swamps, wetlands, marshes, reservoirs, canals, streams, rivers, and even in water that is highly saline in certain marshes close to the coast.

It adapts well to a moderate human presence demonstrated by the fact that it can colonize aquatic zones within urban parks.

It lives from sea level to an elevation of 4,757 feet.

NERODIA SIPEDON
(Northern Water Snake).
Young specimen. Detail of the head.

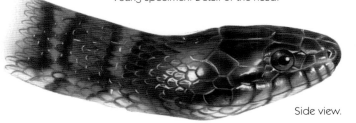

Side view.

BEHAVIOR

• With aquatic habits, it is an excellent swimmer, both on the surface and underwater. It is active during both the day and at night.

• It mainly feeds on tadpoles, frogs (that it captures during the day among the vegetation along the water's edge), and small fish (it usually hunts these by lying in wait or surprising the fish during the night while sleeping in their refuge), although, it can also eat salamanders, baby sea turtles, small birds, insects, crustaceans, and micro-mammals.

• When in danger, it tends to escape by swimming quickly. It can also defend itself by expelling a smelly liquid, but if cornered, it inflates itself and attacks hard.

• Although it is not venomous, when biting, it inflicts wounds that tend to bleed profusely due to an anti-clotting substance found in its saliva.

• During the warm months, it is a fairly sociable species (this can be proved when surprising numerous individuals basking in the sun together on a large rock or on a sandy shore); when fall comes, they are solitary again.

REPRODUCTION

It reproduces ovoviviparously, and coupling takes place between April and June.

The females normally give birth to 20 to 40 already formed babies between July and September.

The babies which measure from six to 12 inches long at birth, appear similar to adults.

STATUS

In spite of being a harmless species, it is often confused with venomous species and also with the aquatic *Agkistrodon piscivorus*; this is why it is quickly eliminated when found.

Although it is a very common and abundant snake in almost its entire area of distribution, laws in states like Iowa protect it.

DISTRIBUTION

Central and eastern United States and southeastern Canada.

■ 2 subspecies are known:

- *N. s. sipedon*: Ontario and Quebec in Canada, and in the United States, from Maine to eastern North Carolina towards the west between Tennessee and Indiana, up to Minnesota and Colorado.

- *N. s. insularum*: Only on a few of Lake Erie's small islands.

- *N. s. pleuralis*: From South Carolina and Georgia to Louisiana, to the north up to Indiana and Illinois and to the west, to Oklahoma.

- *N. s. williamengelsi*: Only on a few small islands and the coastal region close to a small area of North Carolina.

(Schlegel, 1837)

Red-Necked Keelback

RHABDOPHIS SUBMINIATUS
SUBFAMILY NATRICINAE

Rhabdophis tigrinum is a species close to *Rhabdophis subminiatus*. Adult specimen.

Rhabdophis subminiatus (Red-necked Keelback). Adult specimen.

DESCRIPTION

It can reach 51 inches in length.

It has keeled and overlapping scales.

The head is an olive–green color, the sides are yellow, and the neck and the front part of the body are a reddish color.

The eyes are large and dark.

The majority of individuals have a dark line that joins the eyes and the supralabial scales. The back is a gray green or a green brownish-gray color, with black and yellow spots, with a reticulated weft, or with a line in the middle of the back.

The young are a different color than the adults, with a very bright livery and a characteristic yellow–black collar on the neck that disappears when it reaches maturity.

HABITAT

Forested lowlands with abundant sources of water and hills up to an elevation of 5,869 feet.

Also close to rivers, swamps, irrigation ditches, or rice fields.

Rhabdophis subminiatus (Red-necked Keelback). Adult specimen. Detail of the head.

BEHAVIOR

• Diurnal and crepuscular habits.

• It mimics cobras, and when alarmed, raises the front part of its body and flattens its neck, spreading a hood that shows a bright coloration.

• The skin on the nape of the neck contains venomous glands that can cause a bad irritation if the venom touches the mucous zones of any potential enemy.

• The Red-necked Keelback, just like the other twelve species of the genus *Rhabdophis*, has opisthoglyphous dentition; that is, an enlarged rear fang that is in contact with a venom-producing gland.

• Although it is hardly aggressive and bites on very rare occasions, its bite has been said to induce very severe poisoning, as well as other species of the genus, like *Rhabdophis tigrinum* (denominated Yamakagashi in Japan), whose bites have been fatal on more than two occasions. Animals kept in captivity as pets have inflicted these bites.

• It is amphibious.

• It feeds on frogs, toads, and fish, which it paralyzes with the venom from its rear fang.

REPRODUCTION

The clutch consists of five to 17 eggs that hatch after eight to ten weeks of incubation.

The young are five to eight inches long.

STATUS

It is not protected by international law.

DISTRIBUTION

Thailand, Indochina, northern parts of peninsular Malaysia, India (Sikkim), southern China (Hainan, Yunnan, Fujian, western Hong Kong), Indonesia (Java and Borneo).

■ Two subspecies: *R. s. helleri* and *R. s. subminiatus*.

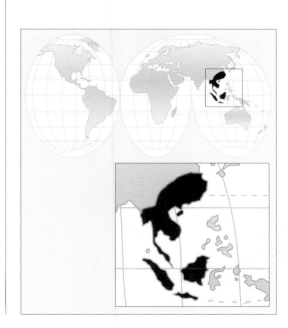

THAMNOPHIS ELEGANS

SUBFAMILY **NATRICINAE**

 Baird & Girard, 1853

 Western Terrestrial Garter Snake

Thamnophis elegans
(Western Terrestrial Garter
Snake). Adult specimen.

Thamnophis elegans
(Western Terrestrial Garter Snake).
Adult specimen. Detail of the head.

DESCRIPTION

It is a small snake, no more than 42 inches in length.
The general coloration of its body and the marks are extremely variable, although they tend to be grayish. The three dorsal and lateral stripes may be a very conspicuous yellow or orangish color, or more subdued and distorted with dark brownish blotches along the entire body.

It has eight supralabial scales. The internasal scales are not pointed forwards like in other species; the body scales are keeled and distributed in 19 to 21 rows; and the anal plate is not divided. The ventral scales vary slightly in number, close to 167, and it has around 57 subcaudal scales.

HABITAT

Generally in humid environments close to rivers, streams, marshes, wetlands, lakes, but also in dryer areas like grassy prairies or along the borders of forests.

It lives in some towns, even in dry areas with very little water and seasonal droughts (there are isolated populations that live in sand dunes).

It lives from sea level to an elevation of 10,499 feet.

STATUS

Like almost all garter snakes, it is an abundant animal in many parts of its area of distribution and is not endangered.

BEHAVIOR

• With semi-aquatic and diurnal habits, it tends to escape by swimming quickly across the water's surface when bothered.

• In respect to its dietary habits, it is an opportunistic species, capable of taking advantage of all available resources; it can eat small fish, tadpoles, frogs, salamanders, aquatic invertebrates, worms, slugs, snails, small lizards, rodents, and birds.

• It captures its prey with the mouth and then swallows it whole, killing it by suffocation in the digestive track (although it also seems that its saliva may be slightly toxic).

• Its natural enemies are abundant; it forms a part of many hunting animals' diet: wading birds, predator fish, aquatic turtles, birds of prey, foxes, skunks, raccoons, coyotes, and ophiophagous snakes (that is, snakes that eat smaller snakes) like *Agkistrodon*, *Micrurus*, and *Lampropeltis*.

REPRODUCTION

It is ovoviviparous.

The females give birth to between four and 19 young, each measuring between seven and nine inches, during the months of July, August, or September, depending on the latitude. They may reach sexual maturity when they are two years old, although it is more common when they are three.

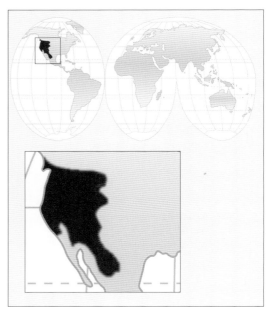

DISTRIBUTION

Southeastern Canada, western United States, and northern Mexico.

■ Up to five different subspecies are recognized:

- *T. e. elegans*: Western Nevada, Sierra Nevada and in the coastal mountain range of California to the Cascade Mountains, in western Oregon.

- *T. e. biscutatus*: Southern Oregon and the northeasternmost part of California.

- *T. e. terrestris*: Western coast of southern Oregon up to the county of Santa Barbara, California.

- *T. e. vagrans*: Southeast of Manitoba, British Columbia, Alberta, Saskatchewan, and the island of Vancouver in Canada, and in the United States, from North Dakota to Oklahoma and towards the west through California, Oregon, and Washington.

- *T. e. errans*: Only in northern and central Mexico.

(Linnaeus, 1766)

 Eastern Ribbon Snake

THAMNOPHIS SAURITUS

SUBFAMILY NATRICINAE

Thamnophis sauritus
(Eastern Ribbon Snake).
Adult specimen.

DESCRIPTION

It is one of the thinnest, most slender, and agile ribbon snakes that exist, even though it has a modest length of no more than three feet.

The tail is very long, almost one third that of the total length.

The color of the body is dark and it has three light-colored, very marked longitudinal lines that stand out; they are generally yellowish, although they are bluish on some subspecies.

The scales are markedly keeled and are arranged in 19 rows. The anal plate is not divided.

HABITAT

Always close to water, it alternates from grassy prairies to marshes, wetlands, lagoons, lakes, rivers, and streams.

BEHAVIOR

• It is a semi-aquatic species that is often seen basking in the sun on the rocks that protrude from the water; it is also tends to bask on bushes and on accumulated vegetation found along the water's edge.

• When it feels threatened it immediately hurtles itself into the water and escapes by swimming quickly. Unlike the authentic aquatic snakes that swim underwater, the garter snakes swim by slithering along the surface.

• It has mainly diurnal habits although some southern populations may save the majority of their activity for nighttime, according to the seasons.

• Certain southern populations may be active during the entire year, but the most northern ones hibernate for long periods of time in subterranean dens

(sometimes up to six months) to be able to survive the adverse climactic conditions of the winter months.

• They may hibernate together with other individuals of its species, but not in such a large number as other species of Thamnophis.

• It basically feeds on tadpoles, frogs, salamanders, and small fish, but can also capture snails, worms, and aquatic invertebrates, and even birds and rats.

REPRODUCTION

It is ovoviviparous and between two and 26 small snakes from seven to nine inches in length are born during the months of July and August.

Sexual maturity is reached at two or three years of age.

STATUS

Like all species of the genus Thamnophis, it is a common snake in the larger part of reasonably conserved aquatic zones, and some species may have significant problems due to excessive urban or infrastructure development only in certain areas.

Although a certain number of specimens are kept and bred in captivity, it is not as habitual with this species as with others.

DISTRIBUTION

The eastern part of the United States and small areas of southern Canada.

■ Four subspecies are known:

- T. s. sauritus: From Indiana, Ohio, Pennsylvania, New York, and New Hampshire towards the south to Florida and Louisiana.

- T. s. nitae: It is only found in a small area in the Gulf of Mexico in Florida, from Wakulla County to Withlacoochee River.

- T. s. sackeni: Southernmost part of South Carolina, southeastern part of Georgia, and the Florida peninsula.

- T. s. septentrionalis: South of Canada (Ontario), Michigan and Indiana towards the east, to Maine and New Hampshire.

THAMNOPHIS SIRTALIS

SUBFAMILY NATRICINAE

 (Linnaeus, 1758)

 Common Garter Snake

Thamnophis sirtalis (Common Garter Snake).
Adult specimen.

Thamnophis sirtalis
Capturing a frog.

DESCRIPTION

This snake has a slender body and can measure up to 51 inches, although it generally does not exceed three feet.

The head is small and slightly differentiated from the body, the snout is blunt, and the eyes have a round pupil.

The dorsal coloration may be dark brown, black, green, or olive greenish, with a light colored vertebral stripe from the base of the neck to the tip of the tail and two other longitudinal stripes, parallel to the previous, on the flanks. Between the dorsal and lateral stripes, there are numerous small black and reddish blotches.

The body scales are keeled and arranged in 19 rows. The anal plate is not divided in two. It normally has seven supralabial scales.

HABITAT

Riverbanks, streams, lakes, ponds, reservoirs, or irrigation canals; also in humid prairies, farms, and even in suburban parks.

In plains and mountains at an elevation of up to 8,038 feet.

BEHAVIOR

• It is fundamentally terrestrial, but always lives close to water in which it moves skillfully and agilely.

• It is mainly active during the day, and is found during the early morning hours basking in the sun on rocks or fallen tree trunks.

• Its considerable sociability can be seen mainly when hibernating with a large quantity of its kind in communal dens (in certain places thousands of specimens may congregate in the same place, and their reappearance on the surface in spring has become, in some areas, a real tourist attraction).

• Its diet consists of worms, frogs, tadpoles, small fish, and micro-mammals.

REPRODUCTION

It reproduces ovoviviparously and the females give birth to between seven and 25 young each time (sometimes up to more than 60), between six and ten inches long.

STATUS

It is the most widespread species of snakes in North America and also most habitually found in many places in its very extensive area of distribution.

Thamnophis sirtalis (Common Garter Snake).
Adult specimen. Detail of the head.

DISTRIBUTION

A good part of the United States and southern Canada.

■ Due to the extreme geographic variability that it has throughout its extensive territorial environment, 12 different subspecies have been established, although there is a certain controversy about the validity of them and of many others that have been described:

- *T. s. sirtalis*: From Ontario (Canada), Minnesota and New York to eastern Texas and southern Florida.

- *T. s. annectans*: Texas and in the surrounding area of Oklahoma.

- *T. s. concinnus*: Oregon and the southwesternmost area of Washington.

- *T. s. fitchi*: From the center of California, Nevada, and Utah up to Montana, Idaho, and Washington, following the East Coast through British Columbia (Canada) to the southernmost part of Alaska.

- *T. s. infernalis*: The California coast, between Humboldt and San Diego Counties.

- *T. s. dorsalis*: From western Texas along the Rio Grande Valley to southern Colorado.

- *T. s. pallidula*: Coastal Canadian provinces, Quebec, and areas next to New England.

- *T. s. parietalis*: From southern Canada (British Columbia, Alberta, Saskatchewan, Manitoba) through the region of large prairies to the border between Texas and Oklahoma.

- *T. s. pickeringi*: Vancouver Island, the British Columbia coast, and northern Washington.

- *T. s. semifasciatus*: Around Chicago, between southern Wisconsin and northern Illinois and Indiana.

- *T. s. similis*: North of the Florida Peninsula from Wakulla county to the Withlacoochee River.

- *T. s. tetrataenia*: San Mateo County, California.

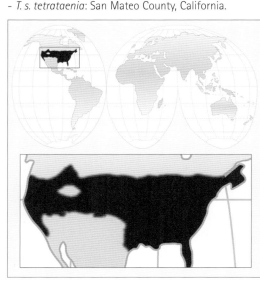

(Schneider,1799)

Schneider's Smooth Water Snake
Rainbow Water Snake

ENHYDRIS ENHYDRIS

SUBFAMILY **HOMALOPSINAE**

DESCRIPTION

The males measure 35 inches and the females 38 inches.

This snake has flat bright scales and looks somewhat solid.

The mouth is rounded and the snout slightly elongated.

The nostrils are located on the top part of the head as an adaptation to aquatic life.

The eyes are small with a yellow-spotted iris and a vertical elliptical pupil found high up and focused upwards.

The nasal scales are in contact with the rostral ones. It has 21 to 22 rows of scales on the middle of the body.

The tail is short.

The head is brown with two light-colored lines that meet at the mouth. The dorsal color is an olive green, brown, or gray. It may have two lighter longitudinal stripes that go along the entire body, bordered in black. This color changes abruptly on both sides of the body and on top of the supralabials, making the color of the body much lighter. The stomach is a lemon yellow and is bordered by dark lines.

Enhydris enhydris (Schneider's Smooth Water Snake). Adult specimen.

HABITAT

It is an aquatic species found in fresh and salt water, often found in rivers, estuaries, lakes, marshes, rice fields, and irrigation ditches.

It is sometimes found out of water.

BEHAVIOR

• It normally tries to go unnoticed, looking for shelter always close to the water, in the nooks and crannies along jagged shores or in the vegetation.

• This colubrid has opistholglyphous dentition and a calm disposition; it does not tend to bite if handled. If it does bite it provokes a slight local inflammation that lasts close to an hour.

• The fresh water fish and frogs constitute its main source of food.

REPRODUCTION

Mating takes place in the month of October and the babies are born in March.

It is ovoviviparous and gives birth to four to 18 babies that measure 5.5 inches.

STATUS

It is not a common species, except in India.

DISTRIBUTION

Northeastern India, southern China, Indochina, and Malaysia.

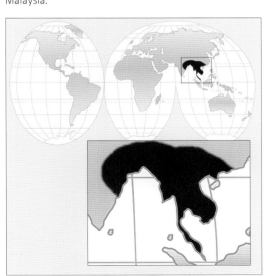

Enhydris enhydris (Schneider's Smooth Water Snake). Adult specimen.

ERPETON TENTACULARUM

SUBFAMILY **HOMALOPSINAE**

 Lacepede, 1800

Tentacled Snake

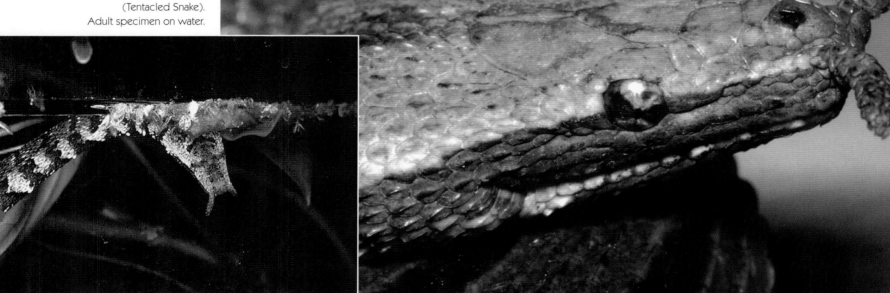

Erpeton tentaculatum
(Tentacled Snake).
Adult specimen on water.

DESCRIPTION

It is a small-sized snake that can reach 28 inches.
Its appearance is unmistakable; it is the only one that has extensions that look like a pair of two to three inch tentacles that protrude over the snout. Their purpose is unclear, they may have been used as bait to capture fish, or as sensitive organs to find prey, or to camouflage.
Its head is differentiated from the body, forming a trapezoid if observed from above.
The head has large scales interspersed with other smaller ones.
The lower mandible is relatively rigid.
The dorsal scales are very keeled and the ventral scales are very reduced and doubly as keeled.
The scales are rough to the touch.
The body color may vary from dark to light brown or gray. The lighter colored animals tend to have brown, reddish-brown, or black longitudinal dorsal lines and lateral lines. The ventral part is a yellow-brown.
This snake has such specialized adaptations for an aquatic life that a specific membrane and a stretched glottis can be inserted inside the internal part of the nostrils to close them off.

HABITAT

Exclusively aquatic, they are found in rivers, streams, ponds, swamps, and rice fields, always in fresh or salt water that is acid and calm.

BEHAVIOR

• It is a totally aquatic species that cannot move out of water due to the stunted development of the ventral scales.
• In water its coloration, as well as the form of its body, are totally cryptic; it goes unnoticed because it looks like a soaked branch.
• If handled, it tenses the body and remains completely rigid even though it is taken out of the water, maybe to look even more like a wet branch.
• It exclusively eats small fish, shrimps and other small prey; it waits for them, completely still, until they approach the snake.

REPRODUCTION

It is ovoviviparous and gives birth to five to 13 babies that measure from eight to nine inches and look like the adults.

STATUS

The state of its population is unknown.
Sometimes it is marketed as a pet, although it almost always arrives in very bad condition due to the long trip out of water in the sacks.

DISTRIBUTION

South and central Thailand, Cambodia, and Vietnam.

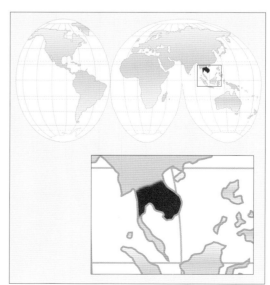

Dasypeltis scabra
(African Egg-Eater Snake).
Adult specimen. Detail of the head.

 (Linnaeus,1758)

 African Egg-Eater Snake

DASYPELTIS SCABRA
SUBFAMILY **DASYPELTINAE**

Dasypeltis scabra (African Egg-Eater Snake).
Adult specimen in its natural habitat.

DESCRIPTION

Normally 20 to 28 inches in length; exceptional cases may reach 47 inches.

It is a slender colubrid with a short head slightly differentiated from the neck, and a rounded snout.

The tail is short.

The scales are rough and very keeled; the lower lateral scales are serrated.

The anal plate is not divided.

The coloration is very variable from one region to another and tends to imitate the coloring and patterns of venomous snakes, as well as the color of the floor where it inhabits.

The back is gray, light brownish-gray, or grayish brownish-gray, marked with dark rhomboidal or squared patterns. The flanks have dark brownish-gray, almost black, vertical bands. The ventral face is whitish or yellowish, smooth with small black dots. The head is marked with one or two thin marks in the shape of a V, aimed towards the mouth, and another similar but larger one on the nape of the neck.

HABITAT

Mainly in plains, savannahs, and open forests.
Only absent from the desert and the enclosed tropical jungle.

BEHAVIOR

• It is partially arboreal and hides under rocks or tree trunks or in the same nests where it eats birds' eggs.

• It is totally harmless and imitates both the coloring and the threatening acts of venomous snakes. Just like the Saw Scaled Viper, the vipers with serrated scales of the genus *Echis*, who rub the serrated lateral scales together in undulatory body movements, producing a characteristic noise.

• In other zones where it does not coincide with this

viper, it imitates the nocturnal viper, Night Adder, *Causus*, inflating its body, puffing hard, pretending to attack with an open mouth.

• It feeds exclusively on birds' eggs. The buccal cavity can widen extraordinarily and the eggs are swallowed whole; the shell breaks when going through the highly developed apophyses of the cervical vertebrae. The contents of the egg then empty out into the esophagus and the shell remains are regurgitated.

• The species mainly receives nourishment during birds' reproductive period.

• It prefers fresh eggs and if it swallows one with an embryo it will regurgitate it with the shell.

Dasypeltis scabra
(African Egg-Eater Snake), feeding.

REPRODUCTION

It lays 6 to 25 cream-colored eggs that are surprisingly not deposited all at once but over the course of one or more days in different places.

The babies take from 80 to 90 days to hatch.
When born, they measure .8 to 1 inch.

STATUS

It seems to be fairly abundant although it is rarely seen.

DISTRIBUTION

Northern Africa, Egypt, Somalia; very rare in Morocco, South of Arabia to western Gambia and from there to the South African Cape.

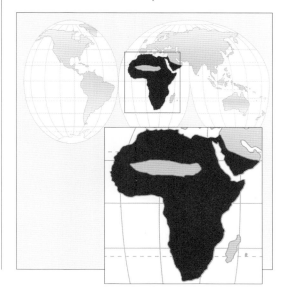

BOAEDON FULIGINOSUS

SUBFAMILY LYCODONTINAE

📄 (Boie, 1827)

📄 Brown House Snake

BOAEDON FULIGINOSUS
(Brown House Snake)
Adult specimen.

Boaedon fuliginosus
(Brown House Snake)
Adult specimen.

DESCRIPTION

It normally measures between 24 and 35 inches, with a maximum of 60 inches.

It has a slightly flattened head that is somewhat differentiated from the neck, and a slightly elongated mouth.

The eyes are fairly small with a vertical and elliptical pupil.

The body is cylindrical, rather slender, and has a moderately long tail.

The scales are flat, bright, and fairly small, distributed in 27 to 39 rows on the central part of the body.

The color of the body varies and oscillates between a yellowish brown, a reddish or dark brown, and a mahogany color. The larger adults turn almost black. The individuals in the southern zones of their area of distribution are marked by two light lines on both sides of the head: the one located higher extends from the snout to the upper part of the head's base; the lower one joins the eyes with the commissure of the mouth. These lines sometimes extend towards the front part of the body. On the most southern specimens these lines are less apparent and they may even be absent.

The stomach is white or yellowish-white.

The males have prominent hemipenes.

Some authors place this species within the genus *Lamprophis*.

HABITAT

It lives in the savannah as well as in prairies and in more arid zones. However, it is found in all types of environments, even in ones that are most inhabited by man, and less in the driest deserts and dense jungle.

BEHAVIOR

• Nocturnal slow-moving species that always moves on the ground and never in the trees.

• The large specimens can bite with ease when trapped, although they become tame quickly in captivity.

• The adults feed mainly on young rats that they can hunt around human dwellings.

• It occasionally eats rats and birds.

• It prefers to eat lizards in the dryer zones.

• It kills its prey by constriction.

REPRODUCTION

It is oviparous and deposits 8 to 10, with a maximum of 16, eggs that measure 1 x .5 inches. They are deposited under decomposing vegetables or in cracks between stones.

They are born after 60 to 90 days of incubation, and the newborns measure from 8 to 10 inches. They can lay various clutches during the breeding season.

STATUS

It is an abundant snake that exploits human populations to look for food.

It is a great rodent controlling species, which is why it is highly beneficial.

It is very scarce in Morocco.

DISTRIBUTION

Isolated points in the south of Morocco, and in almost all of sub-Saharan Africa.

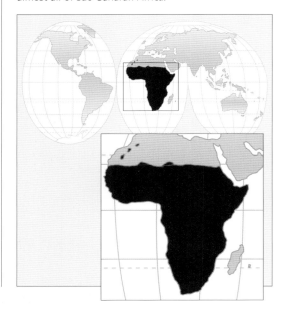

(Holbrook, 1836)

Mud Snake

FARANCIA ABACURA
SUBFAMILY LYCODONTINAE

DESCRIPTION

Can reach seven feet in length, although the most common size is between 40 to 54 inches.

The head is not differentiated from the neck, the iris is red with a round pupil, and the tongue is small.

The body is cylindrical, covered in flat bright scales (except the supra-anal region) arranged in 19 rows.

The anal plate is usually divided.

The tail ends in a pointed scale in the shape of a spine.

The body is black or a dark shiny blue.

The stomach has bright and colorful red bands that extend upwards on the flanks.

■ Two subspecies are known:

- Eastern Mud Snake F. a. abacura: it has 53 or more, red bands on the stomach that extend in triangular forms upwards on the flanks.

- Western Mud Snake F. a. reinwardti: it has 52 or less red bands on the stomach that extend in a rounded form towards the flanks.

HABITAT

Swamps, margins of lakes with plentiful vegetation, slow flowing rivers and streams with muddy bottoms, and flooded plains.

BEHAVIOR

• It has nocturnal habits and a reserved life; the few times it is seen, it is buried in the mud.

• It can be found at night during the rainy season along the highways.

• When surprised, it rotates the back part of its body, exposing the bright and colorful coloration of the ventral scales in an attempt to surprise its potential predator.

• When handled it does not bite, rather it tries to hit the hands of the attacker with its caudal spine.

• It feeds mainly on sirenidae and amphiumas, which it traps, helped by its large curved teeth. Also on frogs and some fish.

Farancia abacura
(Mud Snake).
Adult specimen.

REPRODUCTION

It lays a large number of eggs, from 11 to 60, in July and August.

The females dig a hole in the sandy floor and stay coiled around the clutch.

Sometimes they lay the eggs in alligators' nests, therefore obtaining the protection of the female cayman.

Farancia abacura (Mud Snake).
Adult specimen.
Detail of the head.

STATUS

It is not endangered.

This snakes feeds many popular legends, which, naturally, are false. One of them says that this snake can inject venom with the corneous tip of its tail, when, in reality, the tail is not strong enough to puncture the skin.

Another legend is that it can hold the tip of the tail in the mouth and roll down the surrounding hills like a tire.

DISTRIBUTION

Southeast of the United States, F. a. abacura; found from Virginia to Florida towards the west up to the southeast of Alabama. F. a. reinwardti, Alabama to the eastern part of Texas and in the Mississippi Valley to southern Illinois.

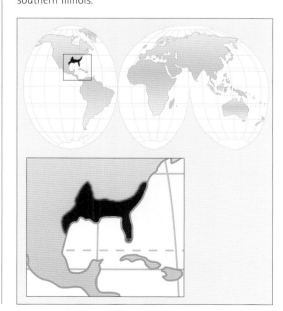

Farancia erytrogramma
(Rainbow Snake) is a
species that is close to
those who share its habitat.

LEIOHETERODON MADAGASCARIENSIS

SUBFAMILY **LYCODONTINAE**

 (Dumeril & Bibron 1854)

 Madagascar Giant Hognose Snake

Leioheterodon madagascariensis (Madagascar Giant Hognose Snake). Adult specimen.

DESCRIPTION

Can reach 5 feet in length.

The females are larger than the males.

This species, just like the other two of its genus, is characterized by its keeled rostral scales, slightly flattened and pointed upwards.

The head is differentiated from the rest of the body; it has large eyes with round pupils. A few large supercilliary scales protect the ocular globules.

It has 23 rows of scales on the back. It has eight yellow supralabial scales bordered in black on the upper part of the head.

The anal scale is not divided.

The color of the body is a gleaming black. On the head and on the front part of the body towards the back are yellow marks that become more numerous towards the back, alternating yellow or gold bands with black ones.

The stomach is yellow and this hue extends at least along the front part of the body by a few triangles on the flanks.

HABITAT

It is fairly territorial and can be found in prairies, plains, savannahs, the primary jungle, dry forests, as well as close to human settlements, occupying zones with sandy floors.

BEHAVIOR

• It has diurnal and terrestrial habits and may sometimes hide in holes that it digs; it is a good burrower.

• When in danger, it tries to escape quickly.

• If cornered, it raises the front part of the body while also spreading the neck area, displaying a small hood, and puffing forcefully.

• It rarely bites, but if it does, can inflict painful wounds.

• It eats mainly lizards and amphibians.

• It is often seen looking for food close to the highways in broad daylight.

REPRODUCTION

Its clutches consist of more than twelve 2 x 1.3 inch eggs that take two to three months to hatch. The newborns measure about 13 inches.

Leioheterodon madagascariensis (Malagasy Giant Hognose Snake). Adult specimen. Detail of the head.

STATUS

It is fairly common.

In Madagascar it is called Menarana.

DISTRIBUTION

It is distributed on the entire island of Madagascar.

It is common on the Perinet and Berenty reserves, and it also frequents the central west coast and the Kirindy Forest in Morondava.

It is also found in Comoros, where it was probably introduced.

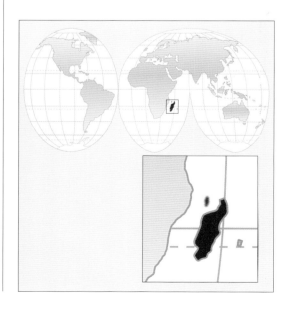

(Linnaeus, 1758)

 Common Wolf Snake

LYCODON AULICUS

SUBFAMILY **LYCODONTINAE**

Lycodon aulicus
(Common Wolf Snake)
Adult specimen.

Lycodon aulicus (Common Wolf Snake)
Adult specimen. Detail of the head.

DESCRIPTION

It reaches a maximum of 30 inches.

This snake has a slender body with a somewhat rounded flat head that is slightly differentiated from the rest of the body.

The eyes are black with a vertical pupil.

It has flat bright scales with 17 rows in the middle of the body.

The tail makes up one fifth or one sixth of its entire length.

The body color and marks are fairly variable.

At least two subspecies are recognized:

- *L. a. aulicus*: The body is a light or dark brown with transversal yellow bands and a yellow collar or two white blotches on the neck. The bands widen on the flanks with isolated blotches that are the same color as the background color. The number of bands may vary between 9 and 18 and cover the entire body, or just the front part.

- *L. a. capucinus*: The base color is a dark brown or purple with characteristic white or yellow reticules.

The labial scales are yellow and the stomach is white. In both races, specimens have been cited without marks and uniformly brown.

They are called Wolf Snakes because of their well-developed front teeth.

HABITAT

It is mainly active at night and inhabits rocky valleys, and dry forests with a large number of stones.

It also inhabits fields under cultivation and the inside of man-made buildings.

BEHAVIOR

• It spends the day hidden in cracks, under rocks, or under rooftops of human settlements.

• It is a great climber that can climb practically vertical walls.

• Although it may bite with ease if trapped, it normally reacts to being provoked by coiling up and hiding its head between one of the body's coils, remaining like this, even if thrown in the air.

• It mainly eats lizards of the family Geckonidae, although sometimes it may feed on lizards, frogs, or baby rodents.

REPRODUCTION

It is ovoviviparous and can lay from four to 11 eggs.

When born, the babies measure from seven to seven-and-onehalf inches long and grow to be double this length in the first year.

It reaches sexual maturity when it is two years old.

STATUS

It is very abundant and has taken advantage of the humanized environment.

A large number can even be found in large cities, living inside dwellings.

Sometimes it is confused with the very venomous kraits (*Bungarus*), due to its similar coloration and its enlarged front fangs.

Its bite causes panic, but the Wolf Snake is harmless.

DISTRIBUTION

Sri Lanka and India, southern China, towards the south through all of Indochina, west of Indonesia and the Philippines.

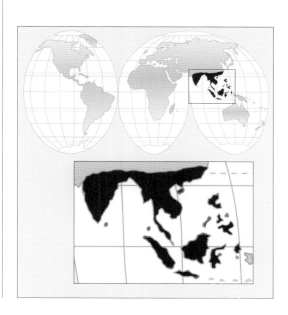

CALAMARIA LUMBRICOIDEA

SUBFAMILY CALAMARINAE

 Boie, 1827

Variable Reed Snake

Calamaria lumbricoidea
(Variable Reed Snake).
Adult specimen.

DESCRIPTION

It can reach 26 inches in length.
It has a cylindrical body and a short tail; this is why it is called the *Reed Snake*.
The head is hardly differentiated from the body although the scales are enlarged.
The eyes are of moderate size with round pupils.
The tail is thick and ends abruptly forming a pointed tip.
With only 13 rows of scales on the middle part of the body, it has the fewest rows of scales in the entire subfamily.
The body is dark brown or iridescent black on the back part, with or without thin light-colored blotches. The first or second line of lateral scales that are in contact with the ventral scales are yellow, and the stomach is yellow with or without a few transversal black bands.
The body color varies depending on the elevation at which it is found; there are two varieties: one at an elevation of 3,281 feet and the other from this elevation to sea level.

HABITAT

It is terrestrial and nocturnal.
It can be found in lowlands and in hills in wooded zones at an elevation of up to 4,593 feet.

BEHAVIOR

• It is a burrower that hides below the layer of humus and vegetable remains in the forest, leading a primarily subterranean life.
• Its relatively short tail ends with a pointed scale that allows it to anchor itself inside the dens.
• It is only found on the surface outside its hidden refuge at night or after a strong rain.
• It preys on frogs, earthworms, and other invertebrates.

REPRODUCTION

It lays eggs.

STATUS

It seems to be abundant in wooded hills but rare in lowlands.

DISTRIBUTION

South of Thailand, east of Malaysia, Singapore, Indonesia, east of Sulawesi, and the Philippines.

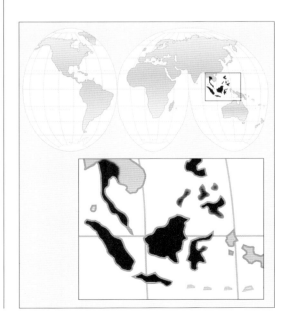

DESCRIPTION

Can measure up to 26 inches.
Slender body.
Has a rounded head that is well differentiated from the rest of the body and covered in small scales except for the nasal scales. It has a large number of labial scales (20 on each side) and a small rostral scale, both with a normal appearance. It is the only species that has differentiated dorsal scales. Following the vertebral column, it has a chain that consists of groups of three enlarged scales surrounding a smaller scale. It has an ample series of small and irregular scales on both sides with two longitudinal lines of large scales.
The color of the body is a light brown that is slightly lighter in color on the ventral side.

HABITAT

It lives in very soft and humid ground.
Swamps, tropical jungle (up to 3,609 feet in elevation) and rice fields.

BEHAVIOR

• It is an amphibian, its diet consisting mainly of frogs.

REPRODUCTION

It is oviparous and lays two to four eggs.

 Reinhardt, 1836

 Strange-Scaled Snake

XENODERMUS JAVANICUS
SUBFAMILY XENODERMINAE

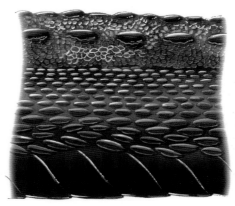

(Strange–Scaled Snake) arrangement of the atypical scales. *Xenodermus javanicus*.

DISTRIBUTION

Malaysia, Sumatra, Java, and Kalimatan.

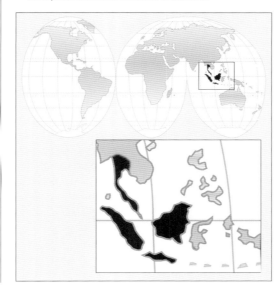

DESCRIPTION

Can measure up to 32 inches.
Has a cylindrical slender body covered with flat scales, a relatively differentiated head, and eyes with round pupils.
The tail is very long.
The mouth has small, numerous teeth that are cramped.
The head is red or dark brown on the front part, black on the back. The body is a brown-gray or brown with a vertebral stripe in the form of a light yellow or

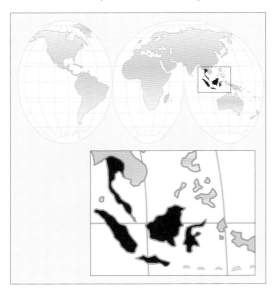

 (Gray, 1835)

Malayan Many-Toothed Snake

SYBINOPHIS MELANOCEPHALUS
SUBFAMILY SYBINOFINAE

brown ladder with darker bars or transversal dots.
The body becomes darker towards the tail.

HABITAT

Close to the streams in the tropical jungle lowlands up to 3,609 feet.

BEHAVIOR

• Has diurnal and terrestrial habits and feeds on lizards, frogs, tadpoles, and grasshoppers, which it hunts in the grass and in the bushes.
• Is totally harmless.

Sibynophis melanocephalus (Malayan Many-Toothed Snake). Adult specimen.

REPRODUCTION

Oviparous.

STATUS

Fairly common.

DISTRIBUTION

South of Thailand, Malaysia, Singapore, and Indonesia.

HETERODON NASICUS
SUBFAMILY **XENODONTINAE**

 Baird & Girard, 1852

Western Hognose Snake

Heterodon nasicus
(Western Hognose Snake).
Adult specimen.
Detail of the head.

DESCRIPTION

Its size varies from 16 to 35 inches in length.

The body looks solid and squat with a thick neck and a short tail. The head is also thick, short, and slightly differentiated.

The head ends with a hognose snout with a very enlarged rostral scale that is keeled on the upper part.

The dorsal scales are keeled and arranged in 23 rows.

It has enlarged teeth that are linked to a venomous gland situated on the rear part of the upper mandible (the generic name *heterodon*, means different tooth).

The anal plate is divided. Small scales separate the prefrontal scales.

The Eastern Hognose Snake, *Heterodon platirrinos,* is a lighter color, generally a yellowish-brown or a gray-yellow with dark blotches distributed on the back, and various rows of rounded blotches on both sides. The stomach and tail are black with white or yellow spots.

BEHAVIOR

• An efficient burrower that hides underground, protecting itself from the noontime heat and the chill of the night.

• It is not very quick or agile, but is very skillful in the construction of subterranean corridors. It shows signs of spreading the hood less frequently and less spectacularly than the Eastern Hognose Snake; instead, it spreads the head and neck slightly, puffing and trying to escape as quickly as possible. This is why it is called the Puff Adder.

• However, when the animal feels cornered it plays dead or turns over, showing its stomach.

• It mainly eats lizards and frogs although small mammals and chicken also make up a part of its diet.

REPRODUCTION

The animals mate from March to May.

It lays four to 23 eggs with a thin shell in the loose sand from June to August.

They are born 7 to 9 weeks later.

HETERODON NASICUS
(Western Hognose Snake).
Adult specimen.
Scale pattern and
coloration.

DISTRIBUTION

Southeastern Canada, southern central United States, and northern Mexico.

■ Three subspecies:

- Dusty Hognose Snake, *H. n. gloydi.*

- Plains Hognose Snake, *H. n. nasicus.*

- Mexican Hognose Snake *H. n. kennerlyi.*

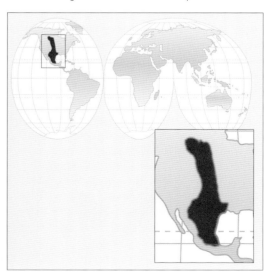

HABITAT

Found in prairies with isolated trees, and in flood plains close to a river's course.

It is also found in the East in semidesert environments or in a canyon layer.

It requires loose sandy floors for excavating.

Lives from sea level to an elevation of 8,038 feet.

Heterodon nasicus. Adult specimens.

STATUS

In general it does not seem to be endangered, although many populations along the limits of its area of distribution are isolated and are relic populations.

Some are subject to official protection, like those in Illinois.

Sometimes is confused with the rattlesnake due to its defensive postures.

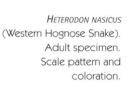

HETERODON PLATYRHINOS

SUBFAMILY XENODONTINAE

(Latreille, 1801)

Eastern Hognose Snake

Heterodon platyrhinos
(Eastern Hognose Snake).
Adult specimen. Detail of the head.

Heterodon platyrhinos (Eastern Hognose Snake). Adult specimen.

HETERODON PLATYRHINOS
(Eastern Hognose Snake). Adult specimen.
Scale pattern and coloration.

DESCRIPTION

It can vary in size from 20 to 45 inches.

It is a solid looking snake with a short head, ample neck, and pointed snout slightly turned upwards.

The scales are keeled, distributed in 23 to 25 rows. The anal plate is divided.

Its color is extremely variable: yellow, brown, gray, olive green, and orangish. Dorsally is has square dark blotches and on the flanks it has various rows of round blotches. In some geographic zones individuals with a totally black back are common. The stomach is gray or green (rarely black), spotted with yellow, gray, or pink. The tail is always lighter than the body, and it lacks the black pigmentation of the Western Hognose Snake *H. nasicus.*

HABITAT

It prefers sandy areas in the prairies or the hills with isolated trees and cultivated fields.

It lives from sea level to an elevation of 2,460 feet.

BEHAVIOR

• It is a good burrower, active during the day.

• Looks for refuge during the winter, burying itself in the sand.

• This species' defensive behavior is very notable and spectacular. When bothered, it flattens the neck like a cobra and at the same time inflates its body and puffs forcefully, charging hard at the predator, although generally with the mouth closed. If the aggressor keeps insisting on bothering the snake, it will then suddenly collapse, turn the body compulsively onto the back showing the stomach, while opening the mouth, leaving the tongue hanging out, and emptying the smelly contents of its cloaca before having one last convulsion and remaining totally immobile. This behavior is used to try to play dead with the idea that many predators will reject the decomposing and smelly meat.

• Eats frogs and toads that it digs up fairly deep in the ground.

• The teeth located on the rear part of the upper mandible inject venom that is fairly active on the prey once it has been seized.

• On very rare occasions, it has bitten people.

REPRODUCTION

It is oviparous and lays 4 to 61 thin-shelled elongated eggs in cavities in the sandy floor.

Mating takes place in spring or in autumn.

The eggs are laid in June or July and the young are born in 39 to 65 days, measuring from 6 to 9.5 inches.

STATUS

It is not endangered.

DISTRIBUTION

A great part of the eastern zone of the United States, from the center of Minnesota, to the north up to the southernmost point of New Hampshire and Florida to the south from eastern Texas, and western Kansas.

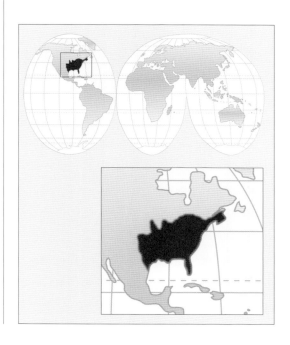

HYDRODYNASTER GIGAS

SUBFAMILY XENODONTINAE

 (Dumeril, Bibron & Dumeril 1854)

 False Water Cobra

Hydrodynaster gigas
(False Water Cobra).
Adult specimen.
Detail of the head.

Hydrodynaster gigas
(False Water Cobra).
Adult specimen.

DESCRIPTION

Generally five to seven feet, although specimens have been found that measure more than 9 feet long. It has a strong constitution and an impressive appearance. Its head is clearly distinguished from the rest of the body.

The dorsal scales are not keeled and are found in 19 rows along the body. The anal plate is divided.

The base color of the body is gray, light brown, or yellowish-green, with irregular transversal bands and darker dots. The adults' colors tend to become darker and can acquire tonalities that are almost uniformly dark green. The females generally have a lighter-toned dorsal coloration. The males' stomach is a blotched yellow or it has black or brownish-gray lines. On the other hand, the females have a brownish-gray stomach with a few barely visible black blotches.

HABITAT

Secondary jungles close to slow watercourses, cultivated fields, coastal areas with marshes and mangrove swamps.

Also in dryer areas with bushes and cactus.

BEHAVIOR

• It is diurnal and terrestrial.
• When bothered it may spread its widened parietal scales and a hood similar to the cobra's, although it keeps its body in a horizontal not a vertical position, and at the same time emits threatening snorts to scare potential predators.
• It actively looks for food, which consists mainly of frogs, toads, and fish, but in dryer zones, small mammals and fish are also included.
• It is generally voracious and although it partially constricts, tends to swallow its prey alive. While swallowing the prey, it injects a venom produced by the Duvernoy gland which is in contact with the two large rear fangs on the upper mandible; these fangs are not canaled and the poisoning comes more from the entrance of the saliva into the wound than by injection into the prey's body.
• With an aggressive temperament, it readily bites, and although it is very difficult for it to poison an animal or person, it should be handled with great care.

REPRODUCTION

It is ovoviviparous and can deposit more than three dozen eggs per clutch.

STATUS

This trade of this species is regulated in Appendix II of CITES.

DISTRIBUTION

Eastern Bolivia, northern Argentina, Paraguay, Brazil, and Guyana.

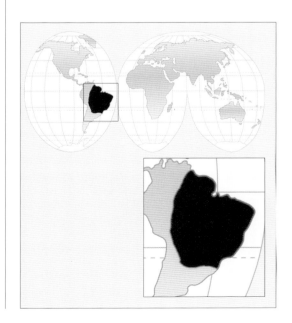

(Laurenti, 1768)

 Argentine Green Hognose Snake

PHILODRYAS BARONI

SUBFAMILY XENODONTINAE

Philodryas baroni
(Argentine Green Hognose Snake).
Adult specimen.
Detail of the head.

DESCRIPTION

This species can exceed three feet in length.
The head is well-distinguished from the body, but very narrow (three times longer than wide).
The rostral scale along with other small scales, prolongs upward and in front of the snout. The obliquely arranged dorsal scales are smooth and lanceolated.
The eyes are large with a round pupil.
It has eight or nine supralabial scales, the fifth and sixth create the eye's lower border.
There are 12 to 15 teeth on the maxilla; they increase in size towards the back, followed by a diastema and a pair of canaled fangs located at the height of the eye's posterior angle (opisthoglyphous dentition).
The caudal plate is divided and the tail is very long.
The dorsal coloration is bright and colorful; it is green from the head to the tip of the tail, with a black vertebral line as wide as a scale that becomes less defined on the back part of the body. There is a dark brown line on the flanks that is not as well defined. The supralabial plates are white bordered in black on the upper part of the body. It is a light green or a yellowish color on the ventral side.
Some specimens (fusco-flavescens) have a light chestnut dorsal coloration with a black line on the back and an even lighter chestnut-colored stomach.

HABITAT

It frequents stony areas with isolated trees in temperate mountainous zones.
It does not frequent the tropical jungle or especially warm areas.

BEHAVIOR

• It is mainly terrestrial; it hides under cracks in the rocks, although it also has certain arboreal tendencies.
• It has an aggressive and restless temperament; when it is trapped it defends itself with force, but there are no exact references about the local reactions provoked by its bite.
• It mainly eats lizards, frogs, and chicken, which it captures in the treetops.

REPRODUCTION

It is oviparous.

STATUS

It is considered common in the province of Cordoba.

DISTRIBUTION

In northeastern Argentina: Tucuman, Santiago del Estero, southeast of Catamarca, and in the southern part of the province of Cordoba.

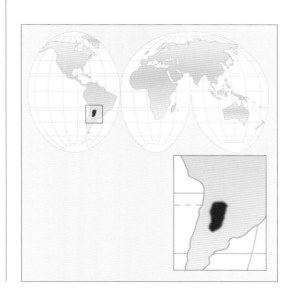

DIPSAS BICOLOR

SUBFAMILY **DIPSADINAE**

  (Guenther, 1895)

Snail-Eating Snake

Dipsas bicolor (Snail-Eating Snake).

DESCRIPTION

Reaches 16 inches in length.

Its body is very laterally compressed and the head very differentiated from the short and wide neck; it has large eyes with a vertical pupil.

It has 11 to 19 rows of smooth dorsal scales; the vertebral row is considerably larger.

The maxillary teeth (upper mandible) increase in size towards the back of the mouth; the teeth on the mandible do exactly the opposite; the front teeth are larger than the back ones. The anal plate is not divided.

Its coloration is made up of a series of light and dark rings; the light rings have red stripes in the center. The upper part of the head is black.

HABITAT

It is found among the low vegetation of the rain forest.

BEHAVIOR

• Active at night.

• Its diet is very specialized with the hunting of mollusks (with or without shells). Its specialized cranium allows the lower mandible or maxilla to move forward and backward, independently of the upper mandible.

• When it traps a snail, it extracts the latter from its shell with its large curved teeth found on the front part of the lower mandible.

• It is an example of an evolutive convergence with the Pareatinae, with which it shares the same diet.

REPRODUCTION

It is oviparous.

DISTRIBUTION

From Honduras to Costa Rica.

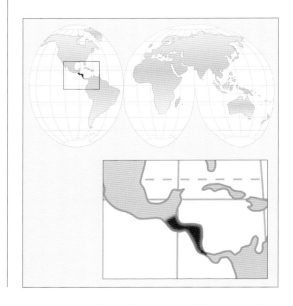

ELACHISTODON WESTERMANNI

SUBFAMILY **ELASCHISTODON**

Reinhardt, 1863

Indian Egg-Eater Snake

Elachistodon westermanni
(Indian Egg-Eater Snake).

DESCRIPTION

It measures 32 inches.

The head is not differentiated from the rest of the body. It has a very reduced dentition; there are teeth only on the rear part of the upper mandible.

Like *Dasypeltis*, the neck's vertebral hypophyses are differentiated into an egg-cutting apparatus.

The dorsal scales are flat and the vertebral row is widened.

The eyes have a vertical pupil.

The body is an olive green or a blackish color with yellowish-white dots and two white stripes that go from the rostral scale to the lip to above the eye. The stomach is a whitish color with brown blotches on the borders of the ventral scales.

BEHAVIOR

• There is no information about its ecology or biology.

• It exclusively eats eggs, forming a case of evolutive convergence with the African snakes (*Dasypeltis*).

• It is extremely rare and the only ten specimens known are kept in museums.

REPRODUCTION

It is oviparous.

DISTRIBUTION

North of the state of Bengal (India).

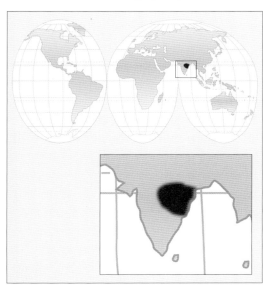

Wagler, 1830

Keeled Slug Snake

PAREAS CARINATUS

SUBFAMILY PAREINAE

Pareas carinatus
(Keeled Slug Snake).
Adult specimen.

DESCRIPTION

It can reach two feet in length.

Its body is very laterally compressed with slightly keeled scales arranged in 15 rows; the vertebral row has wider scales.

The head is short and wide, with large eyes and an elliptical pupil.

The maxillary teeth are small and there are only four; those on the mandible and the palatine are larger than the front ones and become gradually smaller towards the back of the mouth. The lower mandible is more rigid than that of the other colubrids; it is reinforced because the chin scales are joined together by a suture that forms a line dividing the lower part of the mandible in two.

The body is brown with dark blotches, forming a network of thin transversal lines. A black line starts at each eye and moves towards the back forming a mark in the shape of an X on the neck. It is ventrally whitish with a few irregular brown dots on each scale. The anal plate is not divided.

HABITAT

Humid tropical jungles up to an elevation of 5,577 feet.

BEHAVIOR

• It has nocturnal and semi-arboreal habits but, although it seeks protection in the trees, it can also be found on the ground looking for food.

• It has a very specialized diet based on mollusks with or without shells. For this it has marked adaptations: the lower mandible is rigid and strong, reinforced by scales that are joined together without the typical fold on the chin, allowing the mouth to open very wide. It also has some very large sharp curved front teeth.

• When it finds its prey it grips it in its mandibles, and without crushing the shell, grasps the snail, making it turn its head with its sharp front teeth until extracting it from the shell.

REPRODUCTION

It is oviparous and lays three to five eggs. The young reach maturity in less than a year.

STATUS

It seems to be a fairly common species.

DISTRIBUTION

Thailand, Malaysia, and towards the south of the Indo-Australian archipelago.

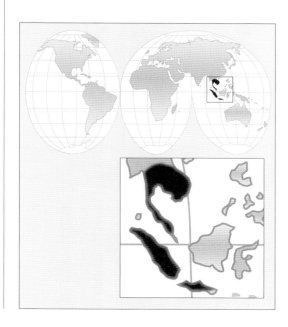

AHAETULLA PRASINA

SUBFAMILY BOIGINAE

 (Boie, 1827)

 Oriental Whip Snake

Ahaetulla prasina
(Oriental Whip Snake).
Adult specimen.
Detail of the head.

Ahaetulla prasina
(Oriental Whip Snake).
Adult specimen.

DESCRIPTION

The females can reach seven feet while the males do not tend to exceed five feet.

This snake has an extremely elongated, thin, and slightly laterally compressed body.

The head is thick in relation to the body, slightly flattened vertically, and ends in an elongated snout with a slightly flexible tip.

The eyes are large and the pupil a gold color in the form of a horizontal 8; it is aligned with the cleft in the snout in order to facilitate vision. The vision is binocular in 45% of the field of vision; this is fundamental for measuring distances and precisely perceiving the relief in a wooded environment.

It has a divided anal plate.

The color on the upper part of the animal is a leaf green and the ventral area is a lighter green. These two colors are separated by a thin pale yellow stripe. Locally, the snake's color may vary with populations that are gray, and others that are yellow and orange.

On many occasions snakes of the genus *Ahaetulla* are cited as being the genus *Dryophis*.

HABITAT

It lives in the highest part of the trees, in the jungles where there are monsoons, and tropical humid jungles in the plain regions, often close to rivers.

Also found in gardens and plantations.

BEHAVIOR

• Its green coloration allows it to go unnoticed among the trees' leaves and branches. It spends long periods of time immobile or simulating the swaying of the branches produced by the wind.

• When resting or moving it does not form tight coils with its body, rather it undulates in large loops and seems to slither very quickly between the foliage.

• The skin between the scales is a pale blue.

• When the animal is alarmed, it inflates the front part of the body to look larger and separates the scales to show the stated tonality. It also opens its mouth in a threatening fashion.

• The prey it captures in the foliage tends to be small mammals, birds, lizards, and arboreal frogs.

• It has opistholglyphous dentition and injects venom into its prey when proceeding to swallow them. The venom produces localized symptoms of swelling, pain, and numbness of extremities in humans.

REPRODUCTION

It is ovoviviparous and gives birth to seven to ten young during each labor.

Apparently, the babies are born at any time of the year.

When the young are born, they measure around 9.5 inches and feed on small lizards and frogs.

STATUS

It seems to be abundant in its entire area of distribution.

It is often found infested with parasites in animal shops; this is why adopting it as a pet may prove to be problematic.

DISTRIBUTION

India, Burma, Thailand, China, Western Malaysia, Singapore, the Philippines, and Indonesia.

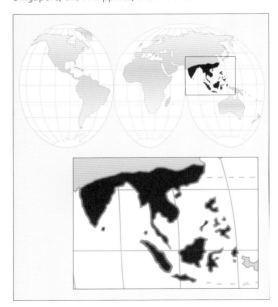

 (Hallowell, 1844)

Blanding's Tree Snake

BOIGA BLANDINGI

SUBFAMILY **BOIGINAE**

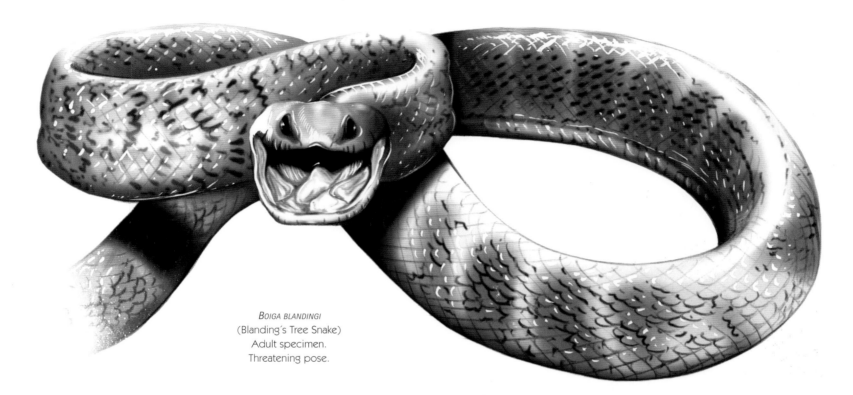

BOIGA BLANDINGI
(Blanding's Tree Snake)
Adult specimen.
Threatening pose.

DESCRIPTION

It can reach eight feet, but the average size is .7 inches.

The head is large, wide, leveled, and well differentiated from the neck, with large prominent eyes and a round pupil.

It has a very concave rostral scale. The nostrils are large.

The body is relatively thin, laterally compressed, has a rubbery texture, is flexible, and has flat, narrow, elongated scales that are arranged in 21 to 25 rows on the middle part of the body.

The vertebral line of scales is very enlarged. The ventral scales are laterally keeled. The anal plate is divided.

The body color is varied and may oscillate between a grayish-yellow and an olive brownish-gray, or a dark blue, with faint whitish transversal blotches. There are some individuals (mainly males) that are completely black. The scales on the lower lip are whitish, often with dark borders. The ventral part of the body is a yellow tinged with black. The color of the skin between the scales is a bluish gray.

HABITAT

It can be found in forests but also in wooded savannahs and in prairie areas with trees and gallery forests in savannahs as well as in trees close to human settlements, and even in gardens and parks within cities located in forested zones.

BEHAVIOR

• It leads an arboreal life and has an excellent ability for climbing up the tallest trees.

• It is mainly nocturnal and remains inactive during the day between bunches of leaves or in tree holes.

• It can be found on the floor crossing highways and other open spaces.

• When bothered it inflates the body, levels the head, and lifts the front part of the body forming a coil in the shape of an S. If it is still bothered, it opens its mouth widely, showing its insides covered in a bright and colorful pink or blue color; then it may charge and hit, although not generally at the objective. This behavior is normally just a resource to scare the aggressor.

• This snake looks actively for its prey, made up of birds (which it tries to catch by surprise while resting in their nests), arboreal birds' eggs, and arboreal saurians like chameleons and agamids. It also hunts rodents and bats. At sunset it waits at bats' caves for them to leave in search of food.

• It has potentially dangerous venom, although no serious poisonings are known of thus far.

REPRODUCTION

It lays seven to 14 eggs that are approximately .8 x 1.6 inches.

STATUS

There is no information about its populations, although it is assumed not to be endangered.

DISTRIBUTION

Equatorial Africa: Ghana, Togo, Nigeria, Zaire, Uganda, Kenya, Zambia, Angola, Southeast of Sudan.

In western Africa, from Sierra Leona to Guinea and Togo.

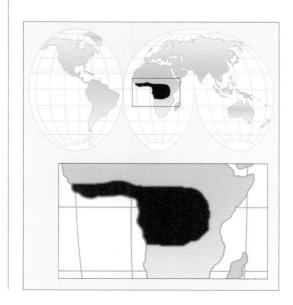

BOIGA DENDROPHILA

SUBFAMILY BOIGINAE

 (Boie, 1827)

Mangrove Snake

Boiga dendrophila
(Mangrove Snake).
Adult specimen.

DESCRIPTION

This snake can reach eight feet.

This large colubrid has a clearly triangular head, well-differentiated from the body, with large eyes and a vertical pupil.

The body is elongated and flattened laterally with a transversal triangular profile.

The neck is narrower.

The scales are flat.

It has an easily identifiable body coloration that consists of a bright and lustrous black color with thin lateral yellow bands that may or may not converge on the vertebral line with the band from the other side. The number of marks and their size varies among the seven subspecies that are recognized and can oscillate from between 21 to 80 bars. The head is black with a yellow throat and yellow supralabial scales bordered in black. The stomach is blackish or a dark gray, sometimes marked with yellow.

HABITAT

It typically inhabits the mangrove swamps as well as the margins of the jungle and the forests along the riverbanks.

BEHAVIOR

• It prefers to be arboreal; during the day it remains coiled up in tree branches and from these, it hangs itself over the marshes or rivers.

• It remains active during twilight and at night.

• The body's coloration can be considered mimicry of the very venomous Banded Krait, Bungarus fasciatus, which evidently instills respect and fear in its possible enemies.

• It has a rather calm temperament during the day, while at night it may easily become aggressive; it often displays a threatening posture that consists of throwing the head back and forming a front ring of defense, while opening its wide mouth. Then it may bite. However, its venom is not very strong and only produces local effects on people.

• Although it is not exactly thought to be a very dangerous snake, it should always be handled with care.

• It feeds on a wide variety of prey, including snakes, lizards, and frogs, but mostly prefers small mammals.

REPRODUCTION

It is oviparous and can lay up to three clutches a year. The clutches consist of 4–15 eggs that can be deposited in holes, in tree trunks, or in the ground. The newborns measure 14 inches.

STATUS

It is relatively common in pet shops.

Many specimens arrive at pet shops infested with parasites; it is difficult for them to become acclimatized.

DISTRIBUTION

- B. d. melanota inhabits the Malaysian Peninsula and Sumatra.

- B. d. dendrophila in Java.

- B. d. annectans in Kalimatan (Borneo).

- B. d. gemmicincta on the Celebes Islands, the other three forms inhabit the Philippines.

- B. d. multicincta in Palawan.

- B. d. divergens in Luzon.

- B. d. latifasciata in Mindanao.

 (Daudin, 1803)

Mussurana

CLELIA CLELIA
SUBFAMILY BOIGINAE

Clelia clelia (Mussurana).
Young specimen.

Clelia clelia (Mussurana).
Adult specimen.

DESCRIPTION

A large snake that can reach a length of eight feet.

The head is not very differentiated from the neck, with large eyes, a vertically elliptical pupil, and a rostral scale that is much wider than it s high; it is visible from above.

The body is cylindrical with a moderately long and sharp tail.

The smooth dorsal scales, with pits on the apexes, are distributed in 19 longitudinal rows. The ventral scales are round. The cloacal plate is not divided. There are between 67 to 76 divided subcaudal scales on the males and from 57 to 70 on the females.

The coloration of the body completely varies depending on the animal's age.

When born and in the neoteric stage, it has a bright and colorful red color on the entire body, with the upper part of the head and the nape of the neck black and separated by a white and yellow band. The body gets darker with age and when it reaches three feet in length turns a uniform indigo, black, or brown with or without a cephalic transversal band. The ventral band is whitish without blotches.

It has 12 to 15 irregular maxillary teeth, the last two canaled and separated by a diastema; they are located towards the vertical line of the eye's upper border.

HABITAT

It inhabits the primary and secondary forest as well as prairies and savannahs in zones with dry or humid tropical climate.

BEHAVIOR

• It is terrestrial and crepuscular; looks for food and hides in mammals' burrows, in the fallen leaves, or in fallen tree trunks.

• The colors on the young presumably imitate that of the Coral Snakes in an attempt to scare potential predators; however, it is a calm species that rarely bites when handled.

• It feeds mainly on other snakes, although it is not strictly ophiophagous and rodents are included in its diet.

• It is immune to the rattlesnake's very toxic venom. It bites it on the neck, then coils up around it.

• It kills its prey by combining constriction with the effect of venom from its rear fangs.

REPRODUCTION

It is oviparous.

The females lay more than 40 eggs, about 50 days after mating.

The incubation period lasts about 120 days.

STATUS

Peasants systematically kill the young that are called Blood Vipers, because they confuse them with Coral Snakes.

In general, peasants are fond of this species because it preys on venomous snakes.

It is included in Appendix II of CITES.

DISTRIBUTION

■ There are Two subspecies from the Yucatan Peninsula (Mexico) extending downward to the north of Argentina.

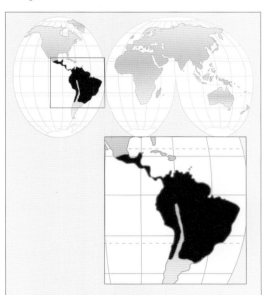

CHRYSOPELEA ORNATA

SUBFAMILY **BOIGINAE**

 (Shaw, 1802)

 Golden Tree Snake

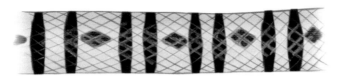

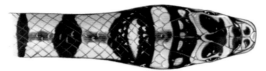

Upper view.

Side view.

Upper view.

CHRYSOPELEA ORNATA
(Golden Tree Snake).
Body pattern and head details of two types. Coloration.

Chrysopelea ornata (Golden Tree Snake).
Adult specimen. Detail of head.

REPRODUCTION

It is oviparous.
It lays six to 12 eggs that hatch close to 65 days after.

STATUS

It seems to be an abundant species in Indochina and Sri Lanka, but is rare more in India.
When found in pet stores it is usually very infested with parasites and rarely survives.

DISTRIBUTION

South of China, India, Sri Lanka, north of the Malaysian Peninsula, Myanmar (Burma) and the rest of Indochina.

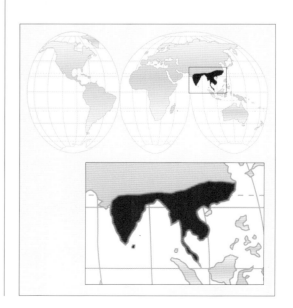

DESCRIPTION

It can measure up to five feet.
The head is well differentiated from the body with a depressed snout and large eyes with a round pupil.
It is slender although not as slender as other Tree Snakes.
The neck is compressed.
The lateral crested extensions of the ventral scales are characteristic; they coincide with a the neck on each side, forming a suture that longitudinally spans the entire stomach, as well as an enlarged row of scales on the vertebral zone.
The tail is one-fourth the entire body length.
The crested subcaudal scales are arranged in two rows, with the same groove as the rest of the stomach.
The head is black, marked with transversal bands and yellow dots with yellow labial scales. The back is a yellowish-green with a black line in the center of each scale. There may or may not be groups of yellow scales shaped like dots, arranged in a vertebral line with faint bands formed by completely black scales. The ventral face is yellowish with black dots close to each lateral groove.
In Sri Lanka and in the south of India, there is another type called the flowered snake; this may have a vertebral line of large red or orange dots in the form of a flower, as well as intervals of black transversal bands that are much more marked.

HABITAT

It inhabits forests and jungles as well as isolated trees in forest clearings or in city gardens.

BEHAVIOR

• It is essentially arboreal, but it is also found in the grass or in low shrubs.
• It is active during the day and much more active during the rainy season.
• The snakes of the genus *Chrysopelea* have the unique ability to intentionally fall from one branch to another or towards the floor: to do this they flatten and puff up their body, using the extension of their ventral scales.
• The body is kept rigid and horizontal and can glide across large distances like this.
• It is also an excellent climber; it can practically vertical tree trunks.
• It mainly eats geckos, other lizards (*Draco*), as well as other snakes. In captivity it sometimes accepts newborn rats.

DESCRIPTION

Although it is usually a smaller size, it can sometimes exceed seven feet.

The head is elongated and short, very differentiated from the thin neck, and the eyes are large with a round pupil.

The body is extremely elongated and slender, slightly compressed, and covered in very narrow, oblique and keeled scales that are distributed in 17 to 21 diagonal rows.

The coloration is fairly varied due to the existence of regional variations, as well as different colorations in both sexes. The females are frequently a uniform yellowish-gray or olive color. Although in some regions the males are uniformly black or brown, they may also be vividly colored, varying from a bright green to an orangish, or blue color. The body's scales may often be bordered in black. The young individuals have a similar coloration to a small-sized stalk with blue blotches on the front part of the body.

The head is a dark brown on top and white underneath.

It has emerald green eyes and a yellow throat.

HABITAT

Dry and humid savannahs, gallery forests.

It is only absent in the mountain prairies of the arid deserts, as well as in the dense jungle of the Congo basin.

Especially close to rivers, streams, and lakes.

BEHAVIOR

• It is a diurnal and arboreal species, capable of moving quickly in the treetops.

• It is also a great swimmer.

• When bothered, it greatly inflates its neck, displaying a bright coloring between the scales, while sometimes, at the same time, it leaves its tongue hanging and moves it up and down.

• It has excellent vision that helps it find its prey. It preys on chameleons, birds, small mammals, and even frogs.

• It may actively look for prey or may capture its prey after remaining still for a long time and waiting for it to come closer. It traps its prey with its mandibles and chews it to kill it with its powerful venom before swallowing. It does not constrict.

• Although timid, it may bite. The wide opening of the mouth as well as the somewhat frontal position and size of the venomous fangs help the snake to inject venom, although the snake needs to hold onto the victim for a few seconds.

• The venom is extremely powerful; it has LD50 on a rat that weighs only 0.72 mg, with a potent blood-destroying agent. There is an effective serum to counter this venom.

 (A. Smith,1829)

 Boomslang

DISPHOLIDUS TIPUS
FAMILY BOIGINAE

D spholidus tipus (Boomslang). Adult specimen. Detail of head.

Dispholidus tipus (Boomslang). Adult specimen. Detail of head. Different colorations.

REPRODUCTION

It lays up to 25, 1.6 x 1 inch eggs below decomposing tree trunks or on the forest floor.

The babies are born after 60 to 79 days and measure 11 to 13 inches.

STATUS

It populations are not considered endangered.

DISTRIBUTION

From sub-Saharan regions to the South African Cape area.

Not found in the Congo basin or in arid deserts.

■ Three subspecies are known:

- D. t. tipus: is the most widely distributed.

- D. t. kivuensis: rift region, north of Zambia to southeast Kenya.

- D. t. punctatus: north of Angola, west of Zaire and northeast of Zambia.

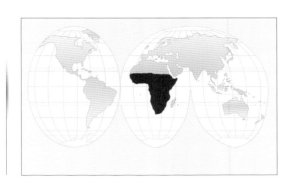

ERYTHROLAMPRUS BIZONUS

SUBFAMILY **BOIGINAE**

  Jan, 1863

📄 False Coral Snake

Erythrolamprus bizonus
(False Coral Snake).
Adult specimen.

DESCRIPTION

Reaches a length of three feet, although the average size is 28 inches.

The body is cylindrical and the tail long. The head is slightly differentiated from the body.

The eyes are of moderate size with a round pupil.

It has 15 rows of smooth dorsal scales and no pits on the apexes. The anal plate is divided as are the subcaudals.

It has 10 to 15 teeth on the upper mandible, plus two canaled ones separated from the rest by a diastema; these are located on the vertical line of the eye's rear border.

Pairs of black rings separated by a white ring make up the body's color. In the spaces between the pairs of black rings, there are a lot of red borders slightly spotted in black. The neck has two well-defined black rings separated by one white or yellow ring. The supralabial scales have outer black borders. They also have a black ocular band. The snout is white but spotted in black.

HABITAT

Found from sea level up to an elevation of 3,281 feet.

BEHAVIOR

• It is a nervous snake with quick movements that may be aggressive when handled.

• It should be handled with care; the canaled teeth on the upper mandible are in contact with a venom-producing gland, but the venom does not seem to seriously effect humans.

• It has terrestrial habits and a fairly discreet life (they are rarely found). It hides under fallen tree trunks, among fallen leaves, and the ground humus, as well as among partially visible root systems.

• Active mainly at twilight and after rains, to feed on small snakes, lizards, and small rodents.

REPRODUCTION

Oviparous.

It lays its eggs in the fallen decomposing trunks.

The babies measure from six to eight inches and are adults when they reach 30 inches.

This species is very similar to snakes of the genus *Micrurus*, Coral Snakes, and even more so to the colubrids, Milk Snakes *Lampropeltis triangulum*.

According to Marten's theory about mimicry, the one that most closely imitates the totally harmless Milk Snake is the irritable and moderately poisonous *Erythrolamprus*. A meeting with one of these could be very disagreeable but not lethal; as with the true Coral Snakes, the victim may remember the danger that facing a snake with colors like the always fatal Coral Snake entails.

STATUS

The state of its population is unknown.
It appears affected by progressive deforestation.

DISTRIBUTION

From Costa Rica to Colombia and Venezuela.

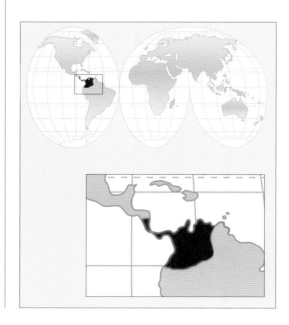

 (Geoffroy, 1827)

 False Smooth Snake

MACROPROTODON CUCULLATUS

SUBFAMILY **BOIGINAE**

Macroprotodon cucullatus
(False Smooth Snake).
Adult specimen.

DESCRIPTION

Small colubrid that does not exceed 26 inches.
It has a well-defined head with a leveled snout and a flattened head.
The eyes are small and located in an upper-frontal position on the head, and the pupil is oval in low light.
Smooth and bright scales generally arranged in 19 to 25 rows on the middle of the body.
The upper parts have a very variable but fairly pale gray, or brownish-gray coloration, with small dark blotches that may form faint bars or stripes. The majority have a blackish collar around the neck that may extend to the upper part of the head. It also has dark lines that go from each nostril, to the eyes, to the buccal commissures, and a blotch in the form of a V, located on the upper part of the head. The ventral zone is whitish, grayish, pale brownish-gray, or pink, with slight dark blotches, or a shiny black square pattern.

HABITAT

Open forests and not very dense scrubland areas.
Above all, in stony areas with low vegetation, and in stone walls.
It frequents dry and warm zones.
From sea level to an elevation of 1,312 to 1,640 feet, in Europe, and up to 5,906 feet, in Morocco.

MACROPROTODON CUCULLATUS
(False Smooth Snake).
Adult specimen. Detail of the head.

Side view.

BEHAVIOR

• It has terrestrial habits and is active mainly during twilight or at night; during the day, it tends to be inactive and stays hidden under rocks, crevices, or in a den.
• It normally moves slowly, but may be quite fast and agile if bothered.
When threatened, and if it cannot escape, it throws its head back and lowers the snout so that the nape of the neck and the neck's dark ornamentation are made visible.
• Although it tries to bite when handled, its mouth is very small and the fangs are too far back in the mandible to be able to inject any venom.
• It mainly feeds on small reptiles like lizards, salamanders, or small blind green dragons, and a lesser number of reduced micro-mammals.
• Some prey is captured while resting in its habitual places.
• In some areas, with very favorable conditions, it does not hibernate at all during the year.

REPRODUCTION

It lays from three to seven eggs in June, below the rocks on sandy terrain.
The incubation lasts from 49 to 63 days.
The newborn babies measure from four to five inches long.

STATUS

It is one of the Iberian Peninsula's most unusual species, and its population density only supassed on the Balearic Islands (where it was introduced).
Locally it is also abundant in areas in southern and central Spain.
European and Spanish laws protect it.

DISTRIBUTION

Southern Spain and Portugal. Balearic Islands. Southern Italy (Lampedusa Island), and Morocco, Algeria, Tunisia, Libya, and Egypt. Southwestern Israel.

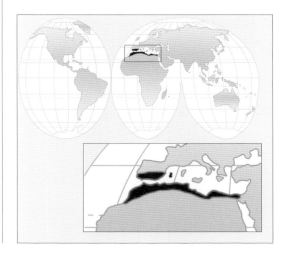

MALPOLON MONSPESSULANUS

SUBFAMILY BOIGINAE

 (Hermann, 1804)

Montpellier Snake

Malpolon monspessulanus
(Montpellier Snake).
Adult specimen.

Malpolon monspessulanus (Montpellier Snake).
Adult specimen. Detail of the head.

DESCRIPTION

Large colubrid that can reach eight feet, although the males normally measure around three feet and the females five feet.

The head is large, narrow, and somewhat pointed, with prominent supraocular scales that extend from the snout in the form of two defined crests with a depression between them; this, together with two large eyes, gives it a threatening expression.

The back has large scales that are arranged in 17 or 19 rows on the middle of the body, and a central longitudinal groove that becomes more obvious with age.

The background is generally a uniform olive green, to a brown, or grayish color. There tends to be a dark area that takes up part of the front region of the trunk and that, in some cases, extends back by means of a thin lateral border. The ventral coloration is very variable, although the most common is a yellowish color spotted with dark pigment.

The newborns have a green or uniform brownish-gray back with a complex pattern with whiter and darker blotches. This coloration sometimes remains at different levels on the adults, above all on the females.

HABITAT

This colubrid is very adapted to the Mediterranean climate where it occupies a wide variety of biotopes. It lives in coastal dunes up to elevations of more than 6,562 feet, both in lightly forested zones, scrublands, and in clearings.

It may also frequent cultivated zones, irrigated crops, and even dumps and abandoned lots in large cities.

BEHAVIOR

• It is diurnal and mainly terrestrial, although it can also climb trees very efficiently and swim.

• When scared it hisses strongly while leveling its body and widening its neck. It can bite ferociously, although it very rarely injects the venom from its rear fangs. If it did (a few cases have been cited) it would provoke slight poisoning with neurotoxic syndromes.

• It is a very active colubrid and it hunts guided by vision, patrolling in search of prey or remaining still. Sometimes it spends a long time with the head raised, moving it from left to right to find prey that moves in its surroundings.

• It eats a wide variety of prey, from other reptiles to small mammals and birds.

REPRODUCTION

Reproduction starts after a winter rest.

Copulation takes place from April to June, and 4 to 20 eggs are deposited one month later.

The young are born 45 to 60 days after and measure from eight to 11 inches.

STATUS

In general, it is an abundant species, not only capable of coping with human presence but also taking advantage of it.

It is often directly attacked or hit; it has the habit of basking in the sun on the asphalt.

European laws protect it.

DISTRIBUTION

Portugal, Spain (except in the Atlantic area), Mediterranean France, northeastern Italy, Croatia, Greece, Albania, southern Bulgaria, Turkey, Morocco, Algeria, Tunisia, northern Egypt, Iran, Syria, Israel, Jordan, and some republics of the former USSR.

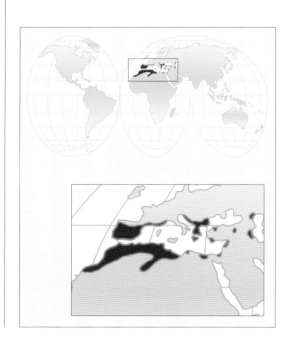

(Daudin, 1803)

 Green Vine Snake

OXYBELIS FULGIDUS

FAMILY BOIGINAE

DESCRIPTION

It can reach up to four feet in length.

This snake has an extremely slender and elongated body that is somewhat laterally compressed.

The elongated head is well differentiated from the body and ends in a pointed snout.

The eyes have a golden-yellow iris with a round pupil.

The tail is very long.

There are 15 rows of obliquely arranged smooth or keeled scales with pits on their apexes. The anal plate is divided just like the subcaudal ones.

The back is a bright green with a thin longitudinal yellow line on the borders of the ventral scales along the entire body down to the lower part of the tail. The stomach is a yellowish green.

It has 20 to 25 maxillary teeth with larger rear teeth; the three rear teeth are canaled. The front mandibular teeth, except for the first two or three, are considerably longer than the rear ones.

The species, the Mexican Vine Snake (*Oxybelis aeneus*), is very similar, but is a grayish color.

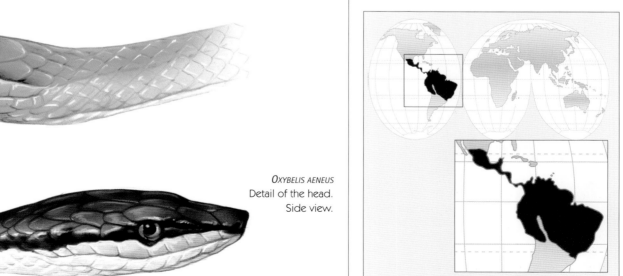

Oxybelis fulgidus (Green Vine Snake). Adult specimen.

HABITAT

It mainly frequents tropical humid or very humid forests as well as gallery forests, and transitionary ones in the middle of the mountain.

In Panama from sea level to an elevation of 4,101 feet, and in areas with an average temperature of 67 °F to more than 82 °F.

BEHAVIOR

• Arboreal and diurnal, its form allows it to go virtually unnoticed among the tree branches and leaves.

• This mimicry is accented because it spends a long time rigid and immobile in a large number of positions, held up only by the back part of its body.

• Sometimes it imitates the swaying of the leaves in the wind with a rhythmic, almost unperceivable movement.

• When threatened it opens its mouth wide, showing the palate, even though it does not usually bite hard.

• It is an absolute specialist in taking advantage of immobility for hunting purposes; it remains still and waits for its prey to come closer.

• It is specialized in preying on lizards, although sometimes it captures birds; some specimens are specialized in hunting hummingbirds and, for this, they remain still, close to the flowers.

• It also eats Anura and small mammals.

• The adaptation to the same type of life and biotype has made the snakes of the genus Oxybelis experience an adaptive convergence with the Asian genus, *Ahaetulla*: both genera have notably similar behavior and physical appearance, although their evolutive origin is different. However, among other obvious differences, *Ahaetulla* is ovoviviparous.

REPRODUCTION

The species is oviparous and lays up to 10 eggs.

STATUS

Like other species bound to the jungle, the disappearance of large masses of trees may cause the decline of its populations.

DISTRIBUTION

From Mexico to Brazil.

OXYBELIS FULGIDUS (Green Vine Snake) Detail of the head. Side view.

OXYBELIS AENEUS Detail of the head. Side view.

PSAMMOPHIS SIBILANS

SUBFAMILY **BOIGINAE**

 (Linnaeus, 1758)

 African Hissing Sand Snake

Psammophis sibilans
(African Hissing Sand Snake)
Adult specimen.

DESCRIPTION

This species can reach six feet in length.
Elongated, thin, and cylindrical body.
The head is of medium size, markedly differentiated from the rest of the thin body, with somewhat large eyes and round pupils.
It has somewhat prominent superciliary crests.
The scales are flat and arranged in 17 rows around the middle of the body. The anal scale may be whole or divided.
The tail is very long and consists of 72 to 109 caudal scales.
The coloration is variable, characterized by thin longitudinal strips that are lighter than the background towards a reddish brown, light olive or dark olive. It has a thick yellowish vertebral band that is flanked with thinner stripes located on the upper part of the sides. Between the pale longitudinal lines and the flanks, there is a pattern of small blotches. The head has a uniform coloring or an irregular pattern of blotches.
The blotches may disappear or change depending on the different individuals or subspecies. The stomach is white and may sometimes have gray blotches.

HABITAT

Varied. Subspecies from the North of Africa inhabit the areas of open desert, stone deserts, dune areas, or desert steppes with a scarce vegetation of thorny bushes. However, it does not inhabit the most extreme desert areas.
The southern subspecies inhabit the arid savannahs and the prairies of the mountainous zones.

BEHAVIOR

• It is a diurnal, terrestrial, timid, and quick snake.
• It is only active during the day, even in the middle of summer. During winter it does not really hibernate, but only decreases its activity.
• It has good vision and looks for prey with the front part of its body somewhat raised; it lifts the head, which widens the field of vision.
• It feeds on small mammals, rats, lizards, frogs, and birds.
• It holds onto its prey with chewing movements without releasing the animal at any time.
• When surprised, it escapes quickly, traveling 33 feet before stopping and remaining still, hidden in a small bush or below the branches.
• When trapped, it bites immediately; the venom injected by its rear-grooved teeth is not mortal, but may cause a lot of pain, vomiting, and swelling in humans.

REPRODUCTION

It is oviparous and has a high rate of reproduction; it can lay up to 30 eggs.
The young measure .8 to 1 inch in length.

STATUS

They are often found crossing highways.
There is no information about its populations, although it is not expected to be endangered.

DISTRIBUTION

■ Three subspecies are recognized with very separated areas of distribution:

- *P. s. sibilans*: Morocco, Northern Africa, Egypt. Mauritania, Mali, Senegal, and Nigeria.

- *P. s. Leopardinus*: Namibia and Angola.

- *P. s. brevirostris*: South Africa and Zimbabwe.

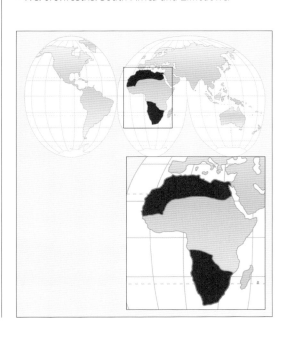

Baird and Girard,1853

Southeastern Crower Snake

TANTILLA CORONATA

SUBFAMILY BOIGINAE

Tantilla coronata
(Southeastern Crower Snake)
Adulto specimen.

DESCRIPTION

Small snake that measures six to 12 inches.
The head is undifferentiated from the body and it has small eyes and a round pupil.
There are 15 flat dorsal scales. The anal plate is divided.
It is a tan or reddish color with a black head and chin. The black color extends to the side of the commissure of the mouth–afterwards there is a white stripe followed by another black one on the neck, made up of 3 to 5 scales. The black part of the head's upper section extends almost to the mouth. The stomach is a uniform white, yellow, or pink color.

HABITAT

Old pine and oak forests.
Around the swamps and in the sandy hills with a soft floor.
They live from sea level to an elevation of 1,969 feet.

REPRODUCTION

Mating takes place between April and May.
It lays from one to three eggs.
The female seems to ovulate a large number of eggs in the oviduct, but only the cited ones are laid.
The newborns measure about three inches.

STATUS

It seems to be a somewhat rare species in some states.

BEHAVIOR

• It is nocturnal and found underneath fallen tree trunks, in the forest's humus or below rocks.
• It is rarely found on the surface in the middle of the day.
• It is a very good burrower.
• This species eats worms, slugs, and insect larvae that it finds underground.

DISTRIBUTION

From Louisiana to western Florida.

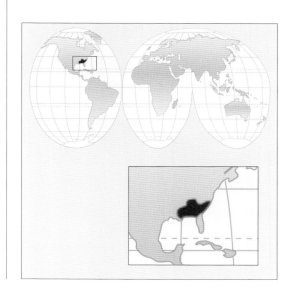

TELESCOPUS FALLAX

SUBFAMILY BOIGINAE

(Fleischmann, 1831)

Mediterranean Cat Snake

Telescopus fallax (Mediterranean Cat Snake). Adult specimen.

DESCRIPTION

It measures 24 to 28 inches in length, though, it can occasionally reach three feet. It has a delicate looking appearance with smooth and shiny scales.

It has a small, triangular, flat, well-differentiated head, with medium but very conspicuous eyes with a vertical pupil and a gold iris.

The head is thinner towards the neck.

The dorsal scales are distributed in 19 rows on the central part of the body. The frontal scales are very large. Its loreal scale is very elongated and generally touches the eyes' front border.

It has a gray, yellow, grayish, or yellowish brownish-gray background color. The dorsal pattern is made up of 40 to 57 dark elliptical transversal blotches. The flanks are covered with narrower blotches. The blotch on the nape of the neck is generally darker than the rest of the body and may form a point that tapers towards the head. The stomach is a whitish, yellowish, or flesh color, dotted in gray or blackish-gray.

HABITAT

Zones with calcareous floors and a large number of stones and rocks, covered with scrubland, bushes, or Mediterranean perennial forest.

It is also found close to man-made walls and ruins.

The mountainous zones may reach an elevation of 4,921 feet.

BEHAVIOR

• A slow-moving species that is habitually terrestrial, even though it can climb perfectly.

• It prefers to move around during twilight; during the day it hides under the rocks or in rock crevices.

• When bothered, it adopts similar postures to the vipers and, if handled, tries to bite ferociously; it usually does not inject its venom, which is very lethal to saurians, but has only a weak local effect on humans.

• It has been confirmed that the peat bog lizard, *Lacerta vivipara*, dies instantaneously when bitten.

• It mainly feeds on lacertids, which it hunts by approaching them with considerable caution (a habit which has given it its name in many languages). In general, it keeps the prey in its mouth, but if it is very large, it traps it with its body's coils and paralyzes it with its venom.

• It also eats rats and chickens.

REPRODUCTION

It lays between five and seven eggs at the base of the bushes or in rock crevices. The eggs hatch at the end of summer.

The babies measure from six to eight inches.

STATUS

It is protected in Bulgaria and in some republics of the former Yugoslavia.

DISTRIBUTION

■ Seven to nine subspecies are recognized.

Northeast Italy, the west coast of Croatia, Montenegro, Macedonia, Albania, Greece and on many of its islands, Cyprus, Turkey, Caucasian republics of the former USSR, Libya, Iran, Iraq, and northern Israel.

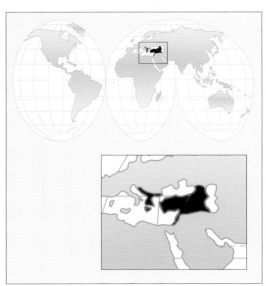

A. Smith,1849

 Savannah Vine Snake

THELOTORNIS CAPENSIS
SUBFAMILY **BOIGINAE**

Thelotornis capensis
(Savannah Vine Snake).
Adult specimen.

DESCRIPTION

Can exceed three feet in length, although it normally measures between 24 and 32 inches.

The head is elongated and narrow, arrow-shaped, and well differentiated from the neck.

The eyes are large and have the characteristic form of a horizontal 8. A thin groove that begins at each eye and reaches the tip of the snout allows for binocular vision.

The body is cylindrical, exceptionally elongated and narrow, with a very large tail.

The scales are slightly keeled, narrow, and elongated; they are distributed in 19 rows along the middle of the body. The anal shield is divided.

The body is a gray or brownish-gray color with dark blotches that form oblique transversal bands. The upper part of the head is a bluish gray and is usually more dotted with black and pink dots. There are one or two conspicuous black blotches on each side of the neck. The supralabial scales are white and form a border of this color. The tongue is a bright red with black tip. The stomach is a pinkish-gray with numerous dark gray blotches.

Previously it was thought to be a subspecies of *Theletornis kirtlandi*, although today it is believed to be a different species.

HABITAT

This species inhabits fairly dry savannahs and also gallery forests that follow the course of the river.

BEHAVIOR

• It is a throughly arboreal species that can move very quickly above the trees. It often remains immobile with a part of the body projecting out into the space, looking like a branch; this camouflage allows it to avoid drawing the attention of prey and its own predators.

• When bothered, it moves its colorful tongue up and down, and, if it cannot escape, it greatly inflates its neck, showing the black stripes on its throat, in an attempt to look menacing.

• It is thought that its bright and colorful tongue may be used to attract and hunt birds. It also eats chameleons, frogs, other snakes, and even bats, which it traps with its mouth and injects them with venom, without constricting. It swallows its prey in a very characteristic position: downward with the head hung from a branch.

• This snake rarely bites, and although it would have to bite hard and for a long time, (because its rear fangs only have one canal) various lethal poisonings have been cited, such as when the famous herpetologist, Robert Mertens, was affected due to a mix-up in 1975. Its venom contains a powerful hemotoxin that can cause very serious coagulopathy. There is currently no serum to combat this venom.

REPRODUCTION

It lays ten elongated eggs that take three months to hatch.

STATUS

No information is known about the state of its populations, although it does not seem to be endangered.

DISTRIBUTION

■ Three subspecies are known:

- *T. c. mossambicanus*: Mozambique, Kenya, and Somalia.

- *T. c. capensis*: South Africa and Botswana.

- *T. c. oatesii*: Namibia, Angola, Botswana, Zaire, and Zimbabwe.

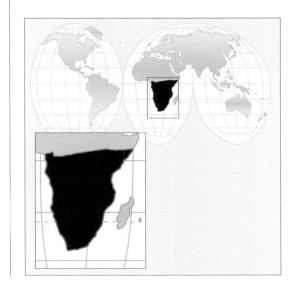

TRIMORPHODON BISCUTATUS

SUBFAMILY BOIGINAE

 (Dumeril & Bibron 1854)

📄 Lyre Snake

Trimorphodon biscutatus
(Lyre Snake).
Adult specimen.

DESCRIPTION

It can measure up to four feet in length.
It has a slender body, a wide head, and a narrow neck that gives the head a triangular form.
The eyes are prominent and have vertical pupils.
The scales are flat and arranged in 21 to 27 rows. The anal plate may be whole or divided.
The common name, Lyre Snake, comes from the V-shaped mark on the upper part of its head. There may be another V-shaped mark in front of this one that reaches above the eyes.
The body is a pale brown, gray, or reddish brown, with large clear-centered dark blotches on the back, and smaller dark blotches on the flanks. The stomach is white or cream colored, blotched with brownish dots.
The young individuals are a similar color to the adults, but much more contrasted.

HABITAT

Rocky hills, canyons, mountainous areas with a preferably arid climate.
Also in perennial and chaparral forests.
It lives from sea level to an elevation of 7,382 feet.

BEHAVIOR

• It is mainly a nocturnal species that remains inactive during the day, hiding in deep crevices.
• It becomes alarmed easily and then raises its body from the floor and shakes its tail, puffing, charging, and trying to bite the intruder.
• This behavior together with the body pattern and its elliptical pupils, make it easily confused with rattlesnakes; this is an example in which the mimicry of a less dangerous species adopts not only a similar physical appearance but also a series of acts analogous to those of a much more dangerous species.
• It looks for its prey in rock crevices.
• It feeds on bats, small rodents, lizards, and probably chickens that build their nests on the floor.
• It has two canaled fangs on the rear part of the upper mandible that are in contact with a venomous gland that injects hematic venom into the prey once the snake has trapped and bitten it with its mandibular teeth.
• This venom is presumably harmless to humans.

REPRODUCTION

It is oviparous and deposits clutches of six to 20 eggs in fissures below the rocks.
The babies are born after three months of incubation.

STATUS

This species has never been found in large numbers. The habit people have of moving rocks to find snakes for the pet market may ruin this species' habitat in the most exploited areas.

DISTRIBUTION

From southeast California and southern Texas to southern Costa Rica.
■ Six subspecies are recognized, three of them n the United States:

- Sonora Lyre Snake *T. b. lamdba* in California, Arizona and Sonora (Mexico).

- Texas Lyre Snake *T. b. vilkinsoni*, in Texas and Chihuahua.

- California Lyre Snake, *T. b. vandenburghi* in southern California and Baja California (Mexico).

- The Central American Lyre Snake *T. b. quadruplex* inhabits western Guatemala to the south of Costa Rica.

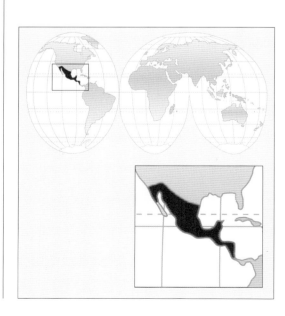

F. Aparallactidae or Atractaspididae

10 GENERA / 60 TO 65 SPECIES

This family is found in an uncertain taxonomic situation; sometimes it is classified as a subfamily Colubridae, or Viperidae, or even Elapidae.

This family's main characteristics are:

• A small head that is undifferentiated from the neck, with very small eyes and a round pupil.
• Cephalic shields may often be joined and are therefore fewer in number.
• The loreal scale is always absent.
• The body is round, cylindrical, and sometimes very long and thin.
• The scales are flat and unpitted on the apexes.
• There are dark colored, discreet species and others that are brightly colored.
• Has a wide variety of fang forms, linked to highly developed venomous glands; it usually has rear fangs similar to colubrids, but the front ones are so large that they jut out laterally when the mouth is closed. In other species the fangs can rotate forwards as in the Viperidae.
• Many are harmless, although some may be dangerous.
• They are all ground dwellers.
• Some use insect or mammals' tunnels or dens and others burrow their own tunnels in the loose earth.
• They usually have specialized diets.
• All but one species in the genus, *Amblyodipsa*, are oviparous.

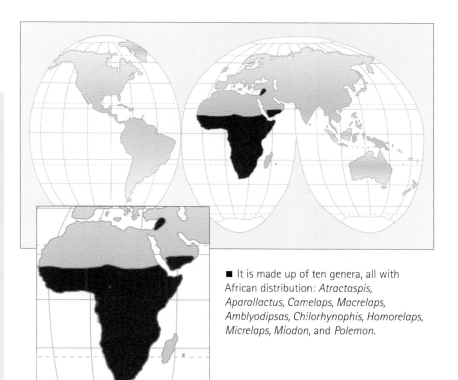

■ It is made up of ten genera, all with African distribution: *Atractaspis, Aparallactus, Camelaps, Macrelaps, Amblyodipsas, Chilorhynophis, Homorelaps, Micrelaps, Miodon,* and *Polemon.*

Aparallactus capensis (Cape Centipede Eater). Adult specimen in its habitat.

APARALLACTUS CAPENSIS

 (A. Smith, 1849)

 Cape Centipede Eater

Aparallactus capensis
(Cape Centipede Eater). Adult specimen.

DESCRIPTION

This snake reaches a maximum length of 18 inches although the majority of specimens do not exceed ten inches.

The head is small, undifferentiated from the neck, with a wide round snout and very small eyes with a round pupil.

The mental scale separates its first lower labial scale. There are five lower labial scales.

The body is fairly thin, cylindrical with a moderately short tail; the scales are flat and are arranged in 15 rows with 126 to 186 round ventral scales. The anal shield is not divided.

The color varies from a yellowish-brown to a reddish-brown or gray-brown, with a thin dark line that extends from the neck to the tail. The upper part of the head is black with a black thick collar and neck. The stomach is uniformly white.

It has two relatively large fangs on the maxilla, approximately above the eyes (opisthoglyphous dentition).

HABITAT

It is found in a wide variety of habitats, from high lands and mountain prairies to savannahs and coastal scrubland.

BEHAVIOR

• This small burrowing snake is found under rocks, tree trunks, plant remains, or in soft humus.

• It is also found in old termite nests where it sometimes meets up with a large number of individuals in search of warmth, refuge, and food.

• When handled, it fights forcefully and tries to bite, although its minute teeth are harmless.

• It feeds exclusively on centipedes that it traps and chews, injecting them with venom that is poisonous to them. In spite of its small size it confronts large centipedes, which it overpowers in fights that may last up to 15 minutes.

STATUS

The status of its population is unknown, although it is not thought to be endangered.

REPRODUCTION

It lays two to four very elongated eggs about 1.3 inches long and .2 inches wide.

DISTRIBUTION

■ These centipede-eating snakes are distributed in all of sub-Saharan Africa and comprise 11 species.

Cape Centipede Snake is specifically distributed from Port Elizabeth to Zimbabwe, north of Botswana and Mozambique (except in the south).

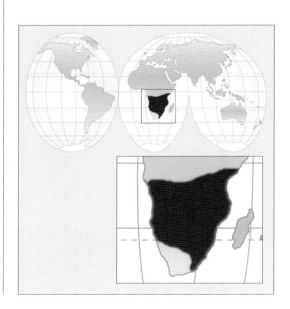

Smith,1849

 Bibron's Burrowing Asp

ATRACTASPIS BIBRONI

Atractaspis bibroni
(Bibron's Burrowing Asp).
Adult specimen.

DESCRIPTION

Small snake that can reach 28 inches, although it normally measures from 12 to 20 inches.

The head is small, wedge-shaped, compressed, and undifferentiated from the neck. It has small eyes, a round pupil, and is covered with large scales in contra-position to the small scales associated with the Viperidae.

The body is cylindrical and relatively slender, with a short tail and a spiny tip.

It has smooth and bright scales arranged in 19 to 25 rows in the middle of the body. The anal plate is not divided.

The back may be brown, gray, or blackish, often with purple highlights. The stomach may be brown, white, or a pale color with a series of darker blotches. When it is white, this color may extend to the two rows of lower scales on the flanks.

The large front fangs that inject venom are visible even when the mouth is closed.

In comparison to the small mouth, this species has relatively large front fangs that inject venom. The fangs are so large that the mouth cannot be open to straighten them. For biting, the fangs are moved over the lower mandible that catches and digs into the prey by a lateral movement of the head, without the necessity to open the mouth.

Sometimes it also catches its prey completely in the center of the lower mandible and bites with the two fangs.

HABITAT

Semidesert zones, savannahs, and forests.

BEHAVIOR

• This snake has nocturnal habits; it mainly lives in the subsoil, usually underground, under rocks, or under fallen tree trunks.

• It can also often be found under opencast skies after rainfall.

• When bothered it is prone to move itself almost convulsively, shaking, arching its neck and hanging its head down while trying to bury itself in the floor.

• The small caudal spine provides firm support for exerting pressure when digging.

• It is responsible for a large number of envenoma-tions in certain zones.

• Many of its victims are peasants that have been bitten on their feet close to settlements. In other instances, accidents happen because the victims think the snake will not bite if they hold it by the neck; this is not true.

• The venom is highly toxic, but because it is injected in a small quantity, symptoms are normally not too serious. This venom causes intense pain and edema and also has a cardiotoxic effect.

• No fatal cases have been cited, although some fairly serious ones have been.

• It often bites because people confuse it with the harmless Purple-glossed Snake of the genus *Amblyodipsas.*

• It probably eats other small snakes, lizards, and newborn rats.

REPRODUCTION

It is oviparous and lays from six to seven eggs.

STATUS

The state of its population is not recognized, although it does not seem to be endangered.

DISTRIBUTION

■ South Africa, Botswana, Namibia, Zimbabwe, Malawi, Zambia, Zaire, Angola, Mozambique, Tanzania, and Kenya.

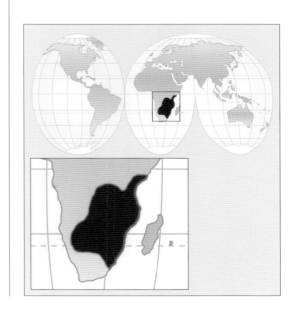

F. ELAPIDAE

MORE THAN 250 SPECIES

The Elapidae is a family of venomous snakes that inhabit warm zones with a middle latitude on all continents except Europe, as well as a significant part of the world's temperate and tropical oceans.
All the venomous snakes that live in places like Australia belong to this family; it includes two–thirds of indigenous species of ophidians (Australia is the one continent where venomous species predominate over nonvenomous ones).

Its venom inoculation apparatus is found on the front part of the maxilla (proteroglyph); it is more perfected than in snakes where it is found on the posterior position (opysthoglyph), but not as evolved as in the Viperidae (solenolgyph).

The Elapidae's toxins are very varied, although those that affect the nervous system (neurotoxic) predominate; these damage mainly the tissues and the circulatory system (hemotoxic).

The venom gland produces a secretion that accumulates in a reserve cavity located above the teeth. The venom is injected by specialized muscles that compress the reserve and penetrate the wounds made by the fangs. Thanks to certain modifications in the fangs, some species can even project the venom a few feet away.

This family is made up of more than 250 species in almost 70 genera and has terrestrial, arboreal, amphibian, and above all, marine representatives; some of the most poisonous species in the world are found in this family, such as cobras, Coral Snakes, mambas, and sea snakes.

Except for the characteristics of its dentition and the system it uses for injecting venom, it differs very little anatomically from the Colubridae. In fact, some authors may classify these two families as one.

It is divided into two subfamilies: *Elapinae*, the terrestrial Elapidae, Hydrophiinae, and the sea Elapidae.

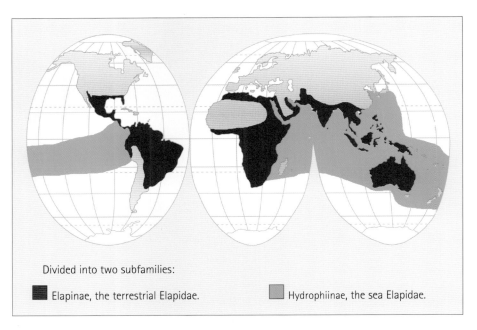

Divided into two subfamilies:

■ Elapinae, the terrestrial Elapidae.   ▩ Hydrophiinae, the sea Elapidae.

Naja mossambica (Mozambique Spitting Cobra). Adult specimen in its habitat.

GENERAL CHARACTERISTICS

• The head is not at all or is only slightly differentiated from the body, covered with large scales. The loreal scale is absent.
• The upper maxilla is short with front fangs and some small back teeth.
• The fangs are proportionally short, canaled, and fixed on the front part of the mouth.
• Mandible with small curved teeth on the front part.
• The maxillary bone is only still moveable in some genera such as *Dendroaspis or Oxyuranus.*
• There are hypophyses on the trunk's vertebrae.
The hemipenes' spermatic reserve is always forked.

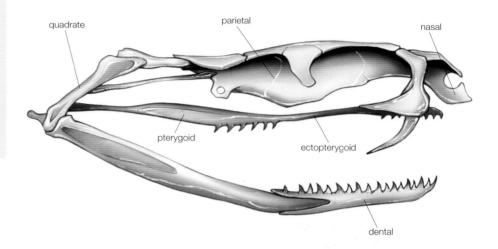

COBRA. Cranium. Side view.

quadrate

parietal

nasal

pterygoid

ectopterygoid

dental

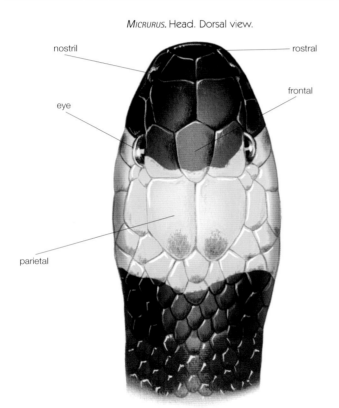

MICRURUS. Head. Dorsal view.

nostril

rostral

eye

frontal

parietal

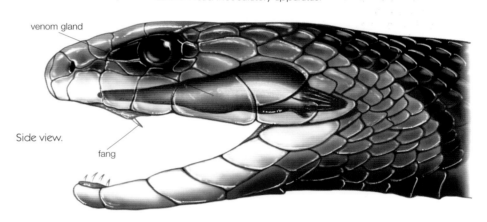

ELPIDAE. Head Incoculatory apparatus.

venom gland

Side view.

fang

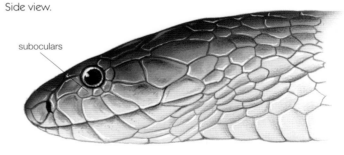

COBRA. Head. The loreal scale, characteristic of the Elapidae, is visibly absent, as well as varius subocular scales.

Side view.

suboculars

Maritime Snake's nostrils closed during immersion.

Other snakes do not have subocular scales, but do have a loreal scale.

Cobra's scales.

■ In Africa, the most characteristic genera are:
- *Boulengerina*: African water cobras; the one Elapinae that is truly aquatic.
- *Dendroaspis*: mambas, a large extremely venomous snake with arboreal habits.
- *Hemachatus*: a South African collared snake.
- *Naja*: the majority of the species of this genus are authentic cobras and popularly known for their dangerous and intimidating stance of rising up and inflating the skin on the neck.
- The following are also African: *Walterinnesia*, *Pseudohaje*, *Paranaja*, *Elapsoidea*, and *Aspidelaps* (the last two are known as African Coral Snakes).

■ Aside from the various species of cobras of the genus *Naja*, the following stand out in the Asian region:
- *Bungarus*: bungurus feeds primarily on other snakes.
- *Maticora*: maticoras, brightly colored and often longitudinally striped.
- *Ophiophagus*: king cobra.
- *Calliophis*: called Asiatic coral snakes.
- *Hemibungarus*.

■ Only three genera are found in America: *Micrurus*, *Micruroides*, and *Leptomicrurus*, but they are represented by close to 60 species. They are fiercely venomous coral snakes.

■ The Australian region (Australia, New Guinea, and nearby islands) is home to more genera than the rest of the world. Without any type of competition with the Viperidae, they have undergone a large irradiation that has enabled them to live in a wide spectrum of ecologic niches. The following terrestrial or semiburrowing species are found: *Acanthopis*, *Cacophis* or *Denisonia*; arboreal species such as *Hoplocephalu*, aquatic species such as *Austrelaps*, territorial species like *Notechis*, *Oxyuranus*, *Pseudechis*, *Pseudonaja*, *Suta*, or *Tropidechis*. Other genera that are present: *Micropechis*, *Parapistocalamus*, *Pseudapistocalamus*, *Toxicocalamus*,

SUBFAMILY **ELAPINAE**

Elapins

50 GENERA / 200 SPECIES

• The majority of species are oviparous, some are ovoviviparous and only very few, like the Australian *Denisonia*, are authentically viviparous.
• They are terrestrial and arboreal snakes (some are burrowers); there is just one species that has aquatic habits, the African *Boulengerina annulata*, and some, like the *Bungarus* and the Australian species *Austrelaps superbus*, frequent swamp areas.
• Although the majority are small or medium-sized, there are large species that reach 13 feet (*Dendroaspis*) and even 19 feet (*Ophiophagus*).
• Many species like the Coral Snakes have bright and colorful colorations with a base of color rings, transversal bands, longitudinal stripes, or peculiar patterns.
• The small species feed on arthropods and reptiles, especially on geckos, and the small blind culebrids, while the larger ones also capture frogs, toads, small mammals, and terrestrial birds. Some species (*Ophiophagus*, *Bungarus*) are ophiophagous, that is, they almost exclusively eat other snakes.
• There are nocturnal, crepuscular, and other strictly diurnal species.

Maticora bivirgata. Adult specimen in its habitat.

Demansia, *Aspidomorphus*, *Acalyptophis*, *Drysdalia*, *Echiopsis*, *Elapognatus*, *Furina*, *Hemiaspis*, *Loveridgelaps*, *Ogmodon*, *Rhinoplocephalus*, *Salomonelaps*, *Vermicella*, and *Simoselaps* (these last two are known by the name Australian coral snakes).

■ Two different groups are distinguished in this subfamily that some authors classify as two different subfamilies within the Elapidae:

- The Laticaudinae, are not quite as exclusively adapted to aquatic life; they spend part of their time on land. They still have overlapping scales and reduced ventral plates. Their nostrils are not as high up as in the Hydrophiinae, which proves that they are less adapted to aquatic life. It is oviparous, and goes on land to deposit the clutch in the beach's sand. Only three genera are known: *Laticauda*, *Aipysurusm*, and *Emydocephalus*.

- The Hydrophiinae are absolutely aquatic. They have granular and juxtaposed scales and no ventral plates (their ventral scales are small and very similar to the dorsal scales). The nostrils are located higher up on the head than in the Laticaudinae. They are ovoviviparous and give birth to already formed babies in the water, generally close to the river's mouth. This group is made up of the genera *Ephalophis*, *Parahydrophis*, *Hydrelaps*, *Acalyptophis*, *Astrotia*, *Disteira*, *Enhydrina*, *Hydrophis*, *Kerilia*, *Kolpophis*, *Lapemis*, *Leioselasma*, *Pelamis*, *Thalassophina*, and *Thalassophis*.

■ The phylogenetic origin of these two groups is difficult to discern, although they seem to have different origins; studies have recently linked the Hydrophiinae to the terrestrial Asian Elapidae (*Calliophis*, *Maticora*) and the Laticaudinae to the Australian snakes (*Demansia*).

SUBFAMILY **HYDROPHIINAE**

Sea Snakes

18 GENERA / 50 SPECIES

• Is characterized by an extraordinary adaptation to water; it is so adapted that many of these snakes are incapable of moving on land, and spend their entire lives in the ocean.
• They can remain submerged for a long time, their tail has dorsally been made narrower to facilitate swimming, the nostrils can seal off below water while swimming and they have glands on the bottom of the mouth (Hydrophiinae) or in pits located between the premaxilla and the septomaxilla (Laticaudinae), that eliminate excess salt.
• They exclusively feed on fish, although the species of the genera, *Emydocephalus* and *Aipysurus*, are specialized in eating their clutches.
• They generally live in fairly shallow coastal water and in estuaries of large rivers. However, some species may live in fresh water: *Enhydrina schistosa*, that inhabit the large Lake Tonle Sap, in the center of Cambodia, and two endemic subspecies, *Hydrophis semperi*, that live in Lake Taal on Luzon Island (Philippines) and *Laticauda crockeri*, in Lake Tegano, on Rennell Island of the Solomon archipelago.
• They are habitually found along the coasts of the Indian Ocean, the coasts of Southeast Asia, the American coasts of the Pacific Ocean, the eastern coasts of Africa and in the surroundings of Madagascar. They are not found in the Atlantic Ocean.
• Some species may be found in large numbers in certain zones during breeding season, and others may travel in

Pelamis platurus
Adult specimen in its habitat.

spectacular runs of thousands of individuals during the migrations out at sea.
• The sea snakes' venom is one of the most powerful known; it has strong neurotoxic affects, although human bites are the exception.

(Shaw and Nodder, 1802)

Common Death Adder

ACANTHOPHIS ANTARCTICUS
SUBFAMILY **ELAPINAE**

Acanthophis antarcticus
(Common Death Adder).
Adult specimen.
Detail of the head.

REPRODUCTION

It is ovoviviparous; it gives birth to up to
30 perfectly developed babies, although the litter
is usually made up of fewer.
The newborns measure six inches in length and
already have adult coloration.

STATUS

The exact state of its populations is unknown; due to
its camouflaged coloration and its almost subterranean
habits, it often goes by unnoticed.
In some zones it seems to be in decline due mainly
to the changes in its habitat.
The introduction of the sea toad, *Bufo marinus*, for
example, has been very detrimental to it; numerous
specimens have been found dead with these large
toads in their mouth.

DISTRIBUTION

Eastern and southern Australia, except in the southeasternmost area, surrounding the central desert
regions.
Also in New Guinea and adjacent islands, towards
the west up to Ceram Island.
It is substituted by *Acanthophis praelongus* in the
northern part of the continent, while *Acanthophis
pyrrhus* lives in the central and eastern parts.

■ No subspecies have been described.

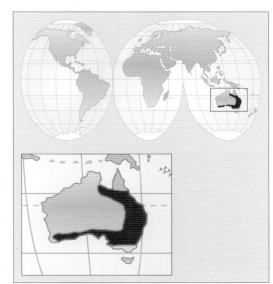

DESCRIPTION

It is a robust, solid, small snake that does not tend
to exceed 32 inches in length, and reaches a maximum
of three feet.
The head is large, wide, triangular, and well differentiated from the body, and the eyes have vertical pupils,
which makes this Elapidae look very similar to the
authentic vipers.
The tail is shorter, thinner, and has a very thin pale-
colored tip.
The dorsal coloration is very variable, although the
gray and reddish-brownish phases predominate, with a
series of pale bands arranged all along the body. The
ventral region is a grayish or cream color with irregular
dark blotches.
The scales on the center of the body may be smooth
or slightly keeled and are arranged in 21 rows, sometimes 23. There are between 110 and 138 ventral scales
and between 35 and 50 undivided subcaudal scales.
The anal plate is not divided.

HABITAT

Prefers dry zones and the soft ground of open
forests, pastures, shrub like regions, and rocky
outcrops, but may also inhabit jungles and humid sclerophyll forests close to the coast.

BEHAVIOR

• Has mainly crepuscular habits; also active during
warm nights.
• It is a sedentary and semiburrowing species that
buries itself under loose ground or among accumulations of vegetation.
• Thanks to its cryptic coloration, it is completely
camouflaged among fallen leaves on the ground,
where it remains still, only leaving the tip of its tail
visible; this moves like a worm to attract the micro-
mammals, birds, amphibians, and small reptiles upon
which it feeds.
• It is absolutely not a venomous goad, as popular
belief claims.
• However, due to its behavior, it is one of the most
dangerous Australian snakes. It is very easy to step on
without seeing; this provokes it to attack and bite. It
also has very long fangs in proportion to its small size,
and its neurotoxic venom is extremely powerful,
leading to a 50% mortality rate. This is why it is called
by its well-known name, Common Death Adder.

Acanthophis antarcticus
(Common Death Adder).
Adult specimen.

BUNGARUS CAERULEUS

SUBFAMILY ELAPINAE

 (Schneider, 1801)

Indian Krait, Blue Krait, Common Krait

Bungarus caeruleus
(Indian Krait). Adult specimen.

DESCRIPTION

A terrestrial snake with a cylindrical body, a head that is slightly differentiated from the body, and a short tail.

It has small eyes, a black iris, and an indistinguishable pupil.

Scales are bright and the large hexagonal vertebral scales characteristic.

It is a medium snake and reaches a maximum length of six feet.

The back is black, metallic blue, or dark brown, with a series of bands or double white stripes along the body; sometimes these stripes are hardly visible or totally absent on the front part. It may have a preocular blotch. The stomach and lower part of the head are white or cream colored.

It has between 195 and 225 ventral scales, and between 37 and 56 subcaudal scales.

HABITAT

It lives in a wide variety of biotypes, from cultivated fields, scrubland areas, and open forests to the proximities of inhabited zones, where it may even enter dwellings.

Often found close to or in water.

BEHAVIOR

• Has mainly nocturnal habits; during the day it remains hidden underground, under accumulations of vegetation, in termite nests, or inside mammals' abandoned burrows.

• Feeds mainly on other snakes, although sometimes it may also capture rats, frogs, and lizards.

• Cannibalism has been confirmed on different occasions.

• It is a dangerous species for humans, and every year causes a certain number of deaths. During the day it is timid and not very aggressive (if it is perturbed, it reacts by hiding its head under the body's coils), while at night it appears to be nervous and irascible, readily willing to bite, even without provocation.

• When it bites, it holds onto the prey for quite awhile, thereby inoculating a significant quantity of venom. The venom is powerfully neurotoxic and in a few hours paralyzes the nervous system and collapses the respiratory system.

REPRODUCTION

It is oviparous; the female deposits a clutch of six to 15 eggs between May and July that measure .8 x 1.4 inches.

The eggs are usually laid below a fallen trunk or among accumulations of vegetation, and the female protects the eggs by coiling up around them; this however, cannot be considered true incubation, like that observed in pythons, for example.

The babies, which have the same coloration as adults, measure ten to 20 inches when they hatch. The males are larger, with a proportionally longer tail.

STATUS

A fairly common species in many zones in its area of distribution and does not appear to be threatened.

DISTRIBUTION

It occupies the entire Indian subcontinent and bordering areas.

■ Although not always accepted, two different subspecies can be distinguished:

- *B. c. caeruleus*: Sri Lanka, India, Nepal, and Bangladesh.

- *B. c. sindanus*: Northwestern India, Pakistan, and the southeasternmost regions of Afghanistan.

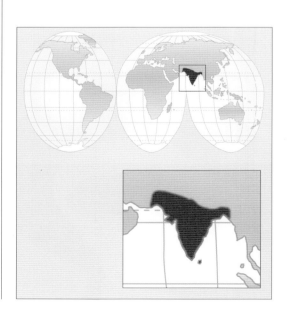

BUNGARUS FASCIATUS
(Banded Krait). Adult specimen.
Head

Side view.

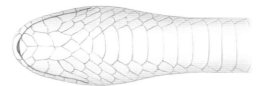

Upper view.

Ventral view.

📄 (Schneider, 1801)

📄 Banded Krait

BUNGARUS FASCIATUS

SUBFAMILY ELAPINAE

Bungarus fasciatus (Banded Krait). Adult specimen.

DESCRIPTION

It is of considerable size, although it normally measures between four and six feet; some specimens have reached more than seven feet in length.

It has a fairly solid body, the head is wide and depressed, somewhat differentiated from the body, the snout short, the eyes black, and the pupil subtly bordered with yellow.

The tail is short and its tip is narrow and blunt.

It has a marked dorsal crest, giving the body a triangular form.

The body's scales are smooth and bright, and the vertebral scales are fairly large and hexagonal. It has between 214 and 230 ventral scales. The anal plate is not divided.

It has an unmistakable coloration, and alternating thick black and yellow rings on the body and tail. The head is predominantly black, although it has a yellow mark in the form of a V on the upper part, and the labial scales, the snout, and the throat are also yellow. Some rare specimens have longitudinal stripes in the same chromatic pattern instead of the typical transversal bands.

The young are born the same color as the adults but with less contrast and a paler tonality.

HABITAT

It prefers open zones such as pasturelands, prairies, and cultivated fields, generally not too far from water.

It can also be found in low forests and is seen with a certain frequency in the surroundings of inhabited zones.

It lives at sea level and higher up to an elevation of 7,546 feet.

BEHAVIOR

• It is predominantly nocturnal and is usually also active during the day after intense rain. It usually rests during daylight hours, hidden in the grass, in underground holes, and even in slightly flooded zones.

• Its main source of food is constituted by other species of snakes, although it may also prey on small mammals, lizards, eggs, birds, frogs, and even fish.

• When the captured prey is very large, it can regurgitate a part of it while digesting the rest over the course of one or two days, then will swallow the remaining part again.

• It is timid and moves slowly during the day; when it feels threatened, it reacts by immobilizing itself and hiding its head.

• In fact, the Banded Krait is the least aggressive of all because it almost never bites. It is so calm that in many zones in its area of distribution, the inhabitants that share its habitat do not think it is poisonous.

• In reality, its powerful neurotoxic venom may be lethal for humans; however, its pacific behavior makes the bites true exceptions.

REPRODUCTION

The clutch contains four to 14 eggs that are deposited among the vegetation or in protected hollows in the floor.

The female remains coiled up around them for quite awhile.

The babies are born after 60 days, and when they hatch, measure between ten and 14 inches.

They reach maturity when they are three years old, at which point they are already more than 35 inches long.

STATUS

It frequents northeastern India, Assam, and Bangladesh; it is rarer in the west.

It is also abundant in the south of southeast Asia where the Banded Krait is the most abundant species.

In China, on the other hand, it is a threatened and protected species; those who use it in traditional medicine also consume it.

DISTRIBUTION

A good part of Southeast Asia: northeastern India, Burma, Thailand, Cambodia, Laos, Vietnam, south of China, Malaysia, and Indonesia (Sumatra, Java, and Borneo).

■ No subspecies have been described.

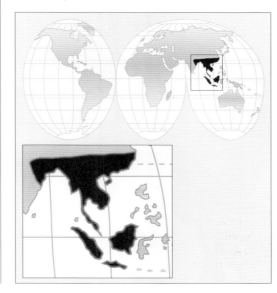

DENDROASPIS ANGUSTICEPS

SUBFAMILY **ELAPINAE**

 (Smith, 1849)

Eastern Green Mamba

Dendroaspis angusticeps
(Eastern Green Mamba).
Adult specimen. Detail of the head.

DESCRIPTION

A snake of considerable size, but slender and light with a long thin tail; it can measure up to eight feet long, although the average size varies between five and seven feet.

The head is long and thin, the eyes are of medium size, and the scales are smooth.

It has between 17 and 21 rows of scales on the central area of the body, and between 201 and 232 ventral scales.

The back is a bright green with yellowish tones on the sides and a paler, greenish tone on the ventral part; it is bright and colorful in a terrarium but completely cryptic in its natural environment.

The babies are a bluish-green when born, and do not take on the adult coloration until they reach a minimum of 24 inches in length.

HABITAT

Tropical rainforests and other dryer wooded zones with abundant vegetation, like savannahs with shrubs, and coastal or gallery forests.

Tends to frequent fruit plantations and sometimes even goes inside houses.

It lives from sea level to an elevation of 4,921 feet.

BEHAVIOR

• It is an agile snake with almost completely arboreal habits; in fact, the word *Dendroaspis*, of Greek origin, means tree snake.

• It is fundamentally active during the day and it sleeps in the treetops, often quite high up.

• It feeds on small climbing mammals, birds, chicks, eggs, arboreal frogs, geckos, chameleons, and bats.

• It has an even worse reputation than the cobras; the mamba is considered more fearsome than the cobra. Aside from the high toxicity of its venom it does not show any warning signs before attacking, and its fangs are much longer; they are curved and can reach a very frontal position due to the great mobility of the maxilla.

• In spite of this, attacks on humans are rare, even though its neurotoxic venom can cause death or serious paralysis if the victim is not treated quickly.

REPRODUCTION

It is an oviparous species that lays eight to 17 eggs (that are two to 2.4 inches) in the spaces between the tree's roots or among accumulations of vegetation.

The eggs are laid between October and November, and the babies are born three months later.

The babies already measure 12 to 16 inches in length when they hatch.

STATUS

It leads a discreet life and has almost entirely arboreal habits; it tends to go unnoticed in many places and is more abundant than it seems.

In some coastal regions of Kenya and Tanzania for example, concentrations of two or three animals per hectare have been counted, and up to five specimens have been found in just one large tree.

DISTRIBUTION

Eastern Africa, from central and southern Kenya to the east coast of the Republic of South Africa, through Tanzania, Mozambique, Malawi, and the east of Zimbabwe.

Isolated populations have been encountered in the nearby forests of Mount Kilimanjaro, Chyulu and the region of Kibwezi, Kenya, as well as the Usumbaras, in Tanzania.

■ No subspecies are known.

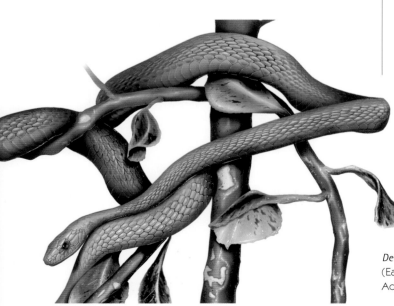

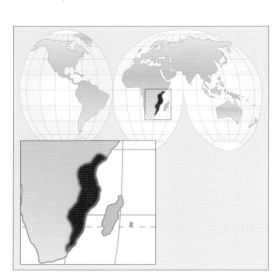

Dendroaspis angusticeps
(Eastern Green Mamba).
Adult specimen in its habitat.

Gunther, 1864

Black Mamba

DENDROASPIS POLYLEPIS

SUBFAMILY ELAPINAE

DESCRIPTION

This is a long thin snake with rapid, agile movements, a long flattened head, the inside of whose mouth is black.

The body is cylindrical and the tail long and thin.

It is considered the largest venomous snake in Africa; although its average length is eight feet, it can reach more than 12 feet, and some specimens have been known to reach up to 14 feet.

It has between 23 and 25 rows of scales on the ventral area of the body, and between 248 and 281 ventral scales.

It is of uniform dark color on the back: it varies between olive green, brownish-gray, and gray, but it is never completely black despite its name. The ventral zone is pale with irregular dark blotches that are more concentrated on the posterior tip.

The babies are a greenish color that becomes darker as the animal matures.

HABITAT

It is primarily abundant in the humid wooded savannahs, found at moderate elevations, mainly in the surroundings of fluvial valleys.

It is also found in open forests and riverbank forests, although not in the dense jungle; it is even found in semidesert zones with large isolated trees or rocky outcrops where this large snake can take shelter and lie in wait for its prey.

It lives from sea level to an elevation of 5,906 feet.

BEHAVIOR

• This mamba has the most terrestrial habits of all, even though it can also climb and move easily in the trees and bushes.

• In reality, it should be considered a semi-arboreal snake.

• Aside from sleeping on branches, it also tends to sleep in termite nests, mammals' burrows, and spaces between rocks, or in trees.

• It often has a preferred den that becomes almost permanent.

• It is very fast and can reach a velocity of up to seven miles/hour, even in the densest weeds.

• It is active during the day and feeds on all types of small mammals (rats, squirrels, bats), birds, lizards, and other snakes.

• It is less timid than the green Dendroaspis; when it senses danger, it opens the mouth threateningly, emits a disconcerting and prolonged whistle and is even capable of slightly inflating its neck.

• Its neurotoxic venom, which also has cytological and even hemotoxic effects, is very powerful and leads to a certain number of deaths within the population that shares its habitat.

• In fact, it is one of the most feared snakes in Africa; in some regions it is called the seven-step snake because that is believed to be the maximum distance that a victim can walk after being bitten by this animal.

Dendroaspis polylepis (Black Mamba).
Adult specimen.

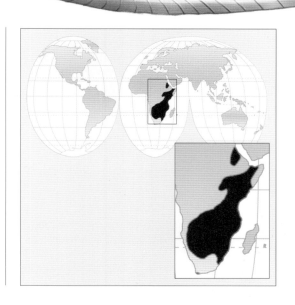

DENDROASPIS POLYLEPIS (Black Mamba).
Adult specimen. Ventral view.

REPRODUCTION

The females lay six to 18 eggs, often in mammals' abandoned burrows.

The babies measure between 16 and 24 inches in length when they hatch (six weeks after they are laid).

Right from the beginning, the babies are restless and aggressive and their venom lethal.

STATUS

The exact state of their populations is unknown, but this species does not seem to be endangered.

DISTRIBUTION

South and East Africa.

■ Two subspecies are distinguished:

- D. p. polylepis: from southern Kenya and Tanzania, towards the south to Swaziland, Lesotho and the Transvaal, in the Republic of South Africa, and towards the west to Angola, Zaire, Botswana, and Uganda.

- D. p. antinorii: Somalia, Eritrea, Ethiopia, southeastern Sudan, Uganda, and northern Kenya.

DENDROASPIS VIRIDIS

SUBFAMILY **ELAPINAE**

 (Daudin, 1803)

West African Green Mamba

Dendroaspis viridis (West African Green Mamba). Adult specimen.

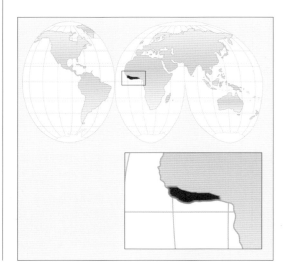

DENDROASPIS VIRIDIS (West African Green Mamba). Adult specimen.

DESCRIPTION

It is a long and slender snake that can reach up to eight feet in length, although it normally measures between five and seven feet.

The head is long and thin, the eyes of medium size, and the pupil round.

The scales are smooth and arranged in 13 rows on the center of the body. The dorsal scales of this central zone are proportionally larger.

The back is an emerald green color, sometimes with small dark blotches; the scales have a blackish border, which makes the animal appear to have thin oblique strias all along the body. The stomach is a yellowish or a pale green color with ventral scales that are also bordered in black. The labial scales are yellowish and the long narrow tail is a brownish-gray.

HABITAT

Tropical jungles, riverbank forests, and densely wooded savannahs with shrubs.

Often found in suburbia and parks in populations where the original forests have recently been eliminated.

BEHAVIOR

• It is diurnal and arboreal, moving among the trees' branches with great agility; it has an extraordinary talent for climbing.

• Sometimes, however, it descends and moves on the jungle floor.

• It sleeps and rests in the treetops, often at a considerable height.

• Its green color gives it an extraordinary ability to mimic, making it very difficult to detect among the tree branches where it lies in wait for its prey: birds, chicks, eggs, and all type of arboreal vertebrae.

• It is timid and not very aggressive, but because it does not show any warning signs before attacking, and because it lives at a certain height, the frequent accidental encounters with this species have very serious consequences; its neurotoxic venom may lead to a rapid collapse of the respiratory system, and even worse, it usually bites on the head or the chest, inflicting wounds for more serious tan those to the extremities.

REPRODUCTION

It is oviparous and has not been widely studied; the exact size of the clutch and average dimensions of the eggs are unknown.

The babies measure from 14 to 18 inches when born, and they are dangerous right from the start.

As with other venomous species, the young have less, more concentrated venom, than the adult individuals.

STATUS

This species is more abundant than is thought; although it is often present, it can go completely unnoticed.

In certain well-conserved forested regions, it is one of the most common snakes.

DISTRIBUTION

West Africa, from the south of Guinea to Ghana. To the west of this central zone of its area of distribution, small isolated populations are known in Gambia, and in Guinea-Bissau, and to the east of Togo, Benin, Nigeria, and the island of Santo Tome.

■ No subspecies are known.

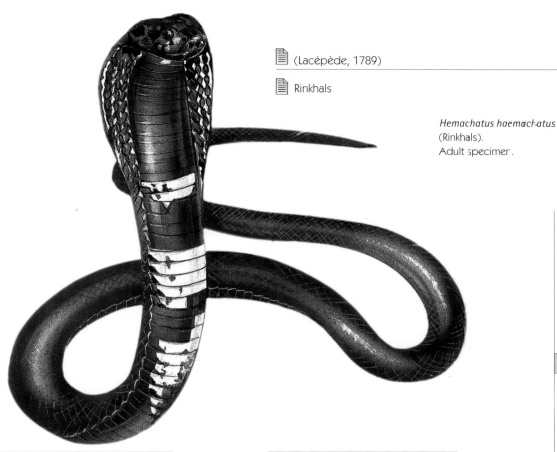

📄 (Lacépède, 1789)

📄 Rinkhals

HEMACHATUS HAEMACHATUS
SUBFAMILY ELAPINAE

Hemachatus haemachatus
(Rinkhals).
Adult specimen.

• Although its neurotoxic venom may be lethal for human beings, it is not as deadly as that of the species of the genus *Naja*, and this species causes very few deaths.
• The venom that this snake spits tends to reach the height of the eyes and most often produces ocular lesions.

REPRODUCTION

It is the only species of African *Elapidae* that gives birth to perfectly developed babies.

Between January and March ten to 30 babies are born, although in exceptional cases, more than 60 have been counted.

The newborns measure between six and seven inches.

STATUS

This species is not endangered, and it is even particularly abundant in some places, like the southern part of Transvaal in the Republic of South Africa.

DISTRIBUTION

Republic of South Africa, Lesotho, west of Swaziland, and an isolated population in Zimbabwe (Inyanga Highlands).

■ Only species of the genus *Hemachatus* that does not have subspecies.

DESCRIPTION

Although this cobra is closely linked to those of the genus *Naja*, its keeled scales, the absence of strong teeth on the maxilla, and its giving birth to already perfectly formed babies distinguishes it.

It is a medium snake that reaches a maximum of 60 inches in length, but normally does not exceed 35 to 39 inches.

It is robust with a short tail, a pointed head that is slightly differentiated from the neck, and its skin can spread in the form of a hood when the animal feels threatened.

It has between 17 and 19 rows of scales on the middle of the body, and between 116 and 150 ventral scales.

Its dorsal coloration may be black or a dark uniform brown, blotched or with irregular pale bands all along the body, while the stomach is a dark gray or blackish color. All specimens have one or two white bands on the front part of the neck.

The more bright and colorful young individuals have 40 black bands on a yellow background and their head is completely black. They also have white bands on the neck.

HABITAT

Humid or somewhat arid regions such as savannahs, pastureland, scrublands, mountainsides, and rocky outcrops.

It is often found close to human settlements.

It lives from sea level to an elevation of 8,202 feet.

BEHAVIOR

• It is basically active at night although it likes to bask in the sun during the day.
• Its prey consists mainly of toads and rats, although it also captures frogs, birds, eggs, lizards, and other snakes.
• It usually takes shelter inside termite nests, burrowing mammals' dens, in underground holes, or between tree roots.
• Like other species of cobras, it can play dead in extremely threatening situations.
• It is also a spitting species that can project its venom far thanks to the special adaptation of its fangs; it is a true specialist in this.

Hemachatus haemachatus
(Rinkhals).
Adult specimen playing dead.

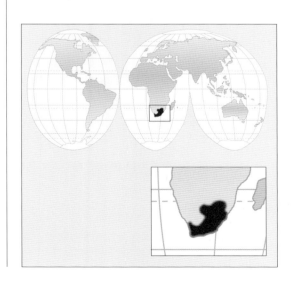

MICRUROIDES EURYXANTHUS

SUBFAMILY ELAPINAE

 (Kennicott, 1860)

 Western Coral Snake, Arizona Coral Snake, Sonoran Coral Snake

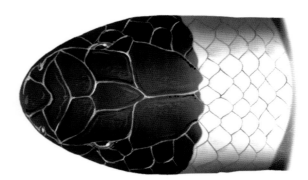
Upper view.

Ventral view.

Micruroides euryxanthus (Western Coral Snake). Adult specimen.

MICRUROIDES EURYXANTHUS (Western Coral Snake). Adult specimen. Detail of head.

DESCRIPTION

Small slender snake that normally measures between 12 and 16 inches in length, and reaches a maximum of 22 inches.

The head is small and undifferentiated from the body, the snout is round, and the mouth and teeth are a discreet size.

The scales are smooth and bright, arranged in 15 rows on the center of the body. It has between 205 and 245 ventral scales and between 19 and 31 subcaudal scales. The anal plate is divided.

As in all coral snakes, the coloration is very bright and colorful; it has alternating red, black, and yellow or white (these are narrower) bands all along the body. The tip of the head is completely black.

Some authors think that this species should not be separated from the rest of the coral snakes in its genus, and they classify it as *Micrurus euryxanthus*.

HABITAT

Typical of dry and semidesert areas populated with saguaro cactus. It prefers rocky zones and mountainsides close to small watercourses, always with sandy or loose ground.

It lives from sea level to an elevation of 5,906 feet.

BEHAVIOR

• Predominantly active at night; it spends the day hiding in abandoned mammals' burrows, under rocks, or in rock crevices.

• However, it tends to move in broad daylight on cloudy days, when it rains, or after a storm.

• It feeds mainly on small, blind colubrids of the genus *Leptotyphlops*, lizards, and other small snakes.

• When bothered or attacked by a predator, it hides its head under the body's coils and raises the tail, showing the colorful lower part.

• It may also expel a smelly cloacal liquid.

• Its neurotoxic venom is very powerful and may be fatal, producing rapid paralysis and a collapse of the respiratory system, but due to its small size and its discreet habits, there have been very few cases of bites from this animal.

• Of all the harmless colubrids that imitate the coral snakes' contrasted coloration, *Lampropeltis triangulum elapsoides*, could be the one that most resembles this venomous species.

REPRODUCTION

It is oviparous and not very much is known about this. The female lays two to three eggs at the end of summer in underground holes or under rocks.

After ten weeks of incubation, the babies are born already measuring six to eight inches in length.

STATUS

The fact that it is generally considered a rare species could be attributed more to the fact that it easily goes unnoticed rather than to its true scarcity.

In reality, it is a fairly common species in many regions of its area of distribution.

DISTRIBUTION

Southern area of the United States and northeastern Mexico.

■ Six different subspecies are distinguished:

- *M. e. euryxanthus*: Arizona and New Mexico, United States. Chihuahua, north of Sonora and Tiburon Island, Mexico.

- *M. e. australis*: Southeast of Sonora and north of Sinaloa, Mexico.

- *M. e. neglectus*: Only in northern Mazatlan (Sinaloa), Mexico.

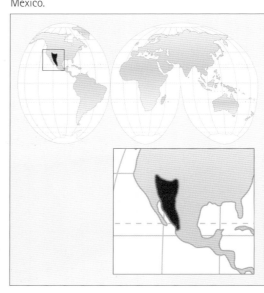

(Dumeril, Bibron & Dumeril, 1854)

Southern Coral Snake

MICRURUS FRONTALIS
SUBFAMILY **ELAPINAE**

DESCRIPTION

A small snake that normally measures between 28 and 35 inches long, although in exceptional cases, specimens have been found that measure more than 36 inches.

The head is small, round, and not very differentiated from the body.

The tail is short and blunt.

It has smooth and shiny body scales, and between 194 and 244 ventral scales and 15 to 32 subcaudal scales. The anal plate is divided.

Its coloration is spectacular, with complete rings around the body arranged in triads and separated by thick red bands; each triad is made up of three black rings separated by two white or yellow ones.

Simophis rhinostoma is a totally inoffensive colubrid that has an almost identical mimetic coloration.

It is the species with the most southern distribution of the entire genus *Micrurus*.

HABITAT

Jungles and tropical and subtropical forests close to swamps, lakes, and small water currents.

Also in sandy and stony zones, prairies, savannahs, and even in areas under cultivation. It lives at sea level up to an elevation of 4,265 feet.

BEHAVIOR

• It has discreet and nocturnal habits; tends to take shelter during the day in subterranean burrows or under accumulated vegetation.

• Some subspecies manage to become true burrowers that move in tunnels built in the humus of the jungle floor.

• It feeds mainly on snakes and other small reptiles, although it may also hunt micromammals, frogs, and even fish.

Micrurus frontalis (Southern Coral Snake). Adult specimen.

• Although its neurotoxic venom is very dangerous, its calm nature and very short fangs make it so that there are almost no instances of bites on the local population.

• When it feels threatened, it hides its head under the body, adopts a devious posture and raises the tail coiling up its tip to show the bright red coloration of its underside.

REPRODUCTION

It is oviparous and lays between three and seven eggs in underground holes, generally protected by vegetation, rocks, fallen tree trunks, or even inside termite and ant nests.

The incubation varies according to the temperature and other environmental factors, but is generally around 80 days.

STATUS

The exact state of its populations is unknown, but does not seem to be in danger in many areas of its zone of distribution.

DISTRIBUTION

Southeast of South America.

■ Eight different subspecies are distinguished:

- *M. f. frontalis*: Southern Brazil, Paraguay, and northern Argentina.

- *M. f. altirostris*: Southern Brazil, Uruguay, and north-eastern Argentina.

- *M. f. baliocoryphus*: Argentina (Entre Ríos, Corrientes, and Misiones) and Brazil (Santa Catarina).

- *M. f. brasiliensis*: Brazil (Bahía, Minas Gerais, and Goiás).

- *M. f. diana*: Bolivia (Serranía de Santiago).

- *M. f. multicinctus*: Brazil (south of Saô Paulo to the north of Rio Grande do Sul).

- *M. f. pyrrhocryptus*: Brazil (Mato Grosso), west of Bolivia, Paraguay, and Argentina (Santa Fe and Mendoza).

- *M. f. tricolor*: Brazil (Mato Grosso) and Paraguay.

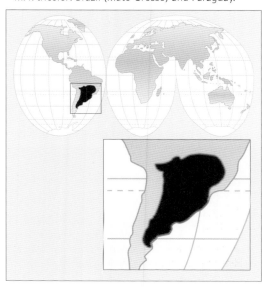

Micrurus frontalis
(Southern Coral Snake).
Adult specimen.
Defensive posture.

MICRURUS FULVIUS

SUBFAMILY **ELAPINAE**

 (Dumeril, Bibron & Dumeril, 1854)

Eastern Coral Snake, Harlequin Coral Snake

Micrurus fulvius (Eastern Coral Snake).
Adult specimen.

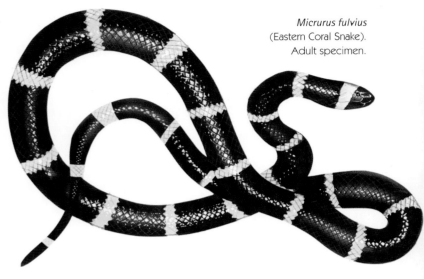

Micrurus fulvius
(Eastern Coral Snake).
Adult specimen.

DESCRIPTION

Like all coral snakes, it is a small snake that measures between 20 and 32 inches long.

It has a slender body, the head is not differentiated from the body, the eyes are small and the scales are smooth and shiny, arranged in 15 rows. The anal plate is divided.

It has an alternating red, black, and yellow ringed coloration, very similar to *Micruroides euryxanthus*, although in this case, the red bands almost always have irregular black blotches. The tip of the head is always black.

Various species of colubrids imitate the colors of this dangerous species, such as *Cemophora coccinea* and the subspecies of the milk snake, *Lampropeltis triangulum elapsoides*.

HABITAT

It prefers open forested areas and scrubland zones in dry areas, although it is occasionally found in wetlands and marshes.

It is also found in rocky outcrops and fluvial canyons.

BEHAVIOR

• This species has very discreet, mainly diurnal habits. It is not observed often, due to its semisubterranean behavior; it spends most of its time buried underground, below tree trunks, or under accumulations of leaves or rocks.

• It has also been found inside burrowing mammals' subterranean dens and even in a gopher turtle's burrow.

• It is only found moving on the surface in the early morning hours or in the late afternoon hours in spring and fall.

• It prefers to feed on small snakes and lizards, although it may also eat birds, frogs, fish, and large insects.

• Cases of cannibalism have been observed.

• It has powerful neurotoxic venom but its small mouth and short fangs make it not very dangerous to humans, unless handled.

• An important benefit is also obtained from this snake: its venom is often used in the making of anti-bite serums for venomous snake bites and is also employed in the research of drugs that help combat illnesses such as cancer or AIDS.

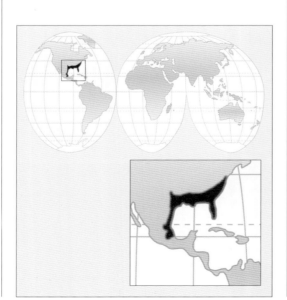

REPRODUCTION

The female lays from two to 13 elongated eggs in hollows in the ground, almost always protected below rocks or accumulations of vegetation.

The eggs hatch in 60 to 90 days and the snakes measure seven to nine inches at birth.

STATUS

This seems to be a scarce species in many zones, and is even considered rare; this is due more to the fact that it goes by unnoticed than to its actual numbers.

In fact, it is used to living in urban areas without being detected.

In fact, it is more common than it seems; it is not threatened and the most serious danger it faces is the destruction of its habitat.

DISTRIBUTION

Mexico and the southern part of the United States.

■ It is classified in five different subspecies:

- *M. f. fulvius*: The United States (from North Carolina to southern Florida and to the west up to the Mississippi River).

- *M. f. fitzingeri*: Mexico (from Queretaro and Guanajuato to Morelos).

- *M. f. maculatus*: Mexico (Tamaulipas).

- *M. f. microgalbineus*: Mexico (from the southwest of Tamaulipas and the central and eastern part of San Luis Potosi to the center of Guanajuato).

- *M. f. tenere*: The southern part of the United States (west of the Mississippi, from Louisiana, Arkansas, and Texas) and northern Mexico (Coahuila, Nuevo Leon, and Tamaulipas).

Naja haje (Egyptian Cobra).
Adult specimen.

 (Linnaeus, 1758)

 Egyptian Cobra

NAJA HAJE

SUBFAMILY **ELAPINAE**

Naja haje (Egyptian Cobra).
Adult specimen. Detail of the head.

DESCRIPTION

One of the largest cobras on the African continent; can reach up to ten feet in length, although it does not normally exceed five feet.

It has a thick and robust body, the head is wide and slightly differentiated from the neck, and the tail considerably longer.

The hood, without ocellus, can reach six to seven inches in width when it spreads.

Smooth dorsal scales arranged in 17 to 21 rows in the m ddle of the body. It has 191 and 220 ventral scales The anal plate is not divided. It is the only cobra that has small subocular scales directly below the eye.

The coloration is very variable: the back may be brownish-gray, grayish, or blackish, while the ventral zone tends to be yellowish or cream-colored, sometimes with random blotches. Some specimens have alternate light and dark wide bands all along the body. It often has a black band on the lower part of the neck.

The young individuals may be yellowish, gray, orangish, or reddish, with a dark ring on the neck that stands out; some of them have a series of thin black strias on the back.

HABITAT

It avoids wooded regions and lives mainly in savannahs, pasturelands, semidesert zones, cultivated areas, and other open zones, although not in the true desert.

From sea level to an elevation of 8,202 feet in some mountains in Ethiopia and Saudi Arabia.

BEHAVIOR

• Although essentially terrestrial, it is capable of climbing trees and swimming fairly well.

• It may appear active during the day, but it is active mainly at twilight and at night.

• When it rests, it tends to take shelter inside termite nests, cracks in rocks, or holes in the floor.

• It feeds on small mammals, eggs, birds, toads, lizards, other snakes, and even on fish.

• It is used to frequenting inhabited zones and going inside houses and farmyards in search of domestic birds and rodents.

• It is not an aggressive species, and it prefers to escape if faced with danger. However, if it is cornered it raises the front part of the body, inflates its hood and may even throw itself against its enemy.

• In extreme situations, it is capable of playing dead.

• It has very powerful neurotoxic venom; a dose o 15 to 20 mg is enough to kill a human.

• Its bite produces a progressive paralysis that causes the respiratory system to quickly collapse.

• The lethal characteristics of this cobra are so well-known that this species is also known as the Cleopatra Cobra; it is thought to have been used by the famous Egyptian queen to kill herself.

REPRODUCTION

This snake is oviparous and lays between 8 and 3 eggs that measure approximately 2 x 1 inches.

The young cobras are born after 48 to 70 days, depending on the incubation temperature.

When born, they measure eight to 17 inches in length and weigh about one-half ounce.

STATUS

Overall, it does not appear to be threatened; there are regions where it is fairly abundant (such as in Zimbabwe and the Transvaal), while in others it is becoming rarer (e.g., in western Africa).

DISTRIBUTION

A large part of Africa: Morocco, Algeria, Tunisia, Libya, northern Egypt, from Senegal to central Somalia, from Angola and Namibia to Mozambique, and in the southern part of South Africa.

Beyond the African continent, it is found only in the southwesternmost point of the Arabian Peninsula.

■ It is classified into four different subspecies:

- *N. haje haje*: northern, eastern, and western Africa. It has 21 rows of scales on the middle of the body.

- *N. h. anchietae*: Namibia, Angola, Botswana, and Zambia (17 rows).

- *N. h. annulifera*: South Africa, Botswana, and Zimbabwe (19 rows).

- *N. h. arabica*: Southwest of the Arabic Peninsula.

- Although a fifth subspecies, *N. h. legionis*, Valverde 1989, is not always recognized, it has been described through specimens from western Morocco.

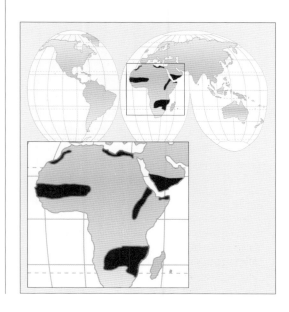

NAJA MELANOLEUCA

SUBFAMILY **ELAPINAE**

 Hallowell, 1858

Forest Cobra

Naja melanoleuca
(Forest Cobra).
Adult specimen.

DESCRIPTION

A large and robust snake that can measure a maximum of 9 feet, although its average length is five to six feet.

The tail is long and narrow.

The head is large with considerable eyes and round pupils.

The scales are flat, bright, and distributed in 19 to 21 rows on the central part of the body. The ventral scales vary between 201 and 214. The anal plate is not divided.

The coloration is very variable, but three main forms are distinguished: in the northern part of its area of distribution it has a black back and the ventral part is white or cream with blotches and dark bands; the sides of the head have thin black and white stripes that extend up to the labial scales; in the savannahs in western Africa its back has alternate black and yellowish bands, the tail is black and the head is yellowish brown; in the coastal zones of eastern Africa, the back is a dark brownish-gray with paler sides and a yellow stomach or cream-colored with black blotches.

Melanic specimens, that is, those totally black, sometimes appear in western Africa.

HABITAT

This species is found mainly in forests, tropical jungles, open forests and savannahs, although it may also inhabit rocky areas with little vegetation.

It is also capable of adapting to life in fruit plantations, where it usually lives in the trees.

It lives at sea level up to an elevation of 9,186 feet in humid jungle mountains.

BEHAVIOR

• Although it is basically a terrestrial snake that lives in forests, it can also be considered fairly aquatic; it has accustomed itself to living fairly close to the water.

• It is quick and agile both on the floor and in the water, and can climb trees easily where it has been found at heights of up to 33 feet.

• It is both diurnally and nocturnally active; it goes to sleep inside large termite nests, holes in trees or rocks, and among dense, shrub-like vegetation.

• It feeds on toads, frogs, small mammals, lizards, and on other snakes and fish that it captures underwater and brings to land before swallowing.

• It is fairly aggressive and tries to bite when bothered. It takes on the typical intimidating posture of the cobras that charge and spread the neck's hood when irritated or threatened.

• Until rather recently, this species held the longevity record for a snake in captivity: 28 years.

• Although its neurotoxic venom is fairly powerful and the species is commonly found close to human populations, there have been very few human victims.

REPRODUCTION

The female lays ten to 26 eggs at the beginning of summer that measure from about one to two inches. She usually lays them between tree roots or among accumulations of vegetation.

The incubation lasts between 55 and 70 days, depending on the temperature, and the babies measure between eight and 14 inches long at birth.

STATUS

Fairly common in the majority of its area of distribution and is not considered a threatened species.

DISTRIBUTION

Forest regions in sub-Saharan Africa, from Senegal and Mali to the west up to southern Sudan, Ethiopia, and Somalia in the east, then towards the south along the eastern coast up to Mozambique and northeastern South Africa.

In general, no subspecies are recognized, although some authors have described up to three based on the different phases of coloration: *N. m. melanoleuca*, *N. m. aurata*, and *N. m. subfulva*.

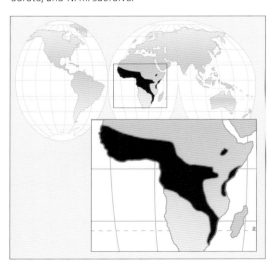

Peters, 1854

 Mozambique Spitting Cobra

NAJA MOSSAMBICA
SUBFAMILY **ELAPINAE**

Naja mossambica
(Mozambique Spitting Cobra).
Adult specimen.
Detail of the head.

DESCRIPTION

A medium cobra with a long tail; it normally measures between 32 and 47 inches, and it can reach a maximum of 60 inches in length.

The head is wide, the snout round, and the eyes medium, with a round pupil.

The scales are smooth and arranged in 23 to 25 rows n the center of the body. It has between 177 and 205 ventral scales. The anal plate is not divided.

The back color is normally brownish-gray, gray, or a reddish color, while the stomach is a pale brown, pinkish, or grayish color.

There are numerous random black bands and blotches on the neck, throat, and first third of the ventral part of the body; some specimens only have small blotches while others are completely black.

The young individuals tend to be olive green and the lower part of the neck is often a salmon color.

HABITAT

It can be found in savannahs, regions with shrubs, coastal forests, rocky areas, and semidesert zones.

It ives at sea level up to an elevation of 5,906 feet.

BEHAVIOR

• t is mainly terrestrial; however, is usually found close to permanent water sources.

• Likewise, it frequently and agilely climbs trees and sleeps in the treetops.

• The adult animals have nocturnal habits, although during the day they can be seen taking sunbaths close to their lairs (under rocks, in termite nests, between tree roots or vegetation, or in holes in the ground).

• The young, on the other hand, tend to be diurnal; therefore they do not compete for food with their elders and, at the same time, avoid being eaten by them.

• It feeds on rats, lizards, small snakes, frogs, birds, eggs, and even on large invertebrates. It is often found in the proximities of inhabited zones, such as in parks and large gardens, to where it frequently travels in search of rodents.

• When bothered it raises the front part of the neck, spreads its hood, and hisses threateningly.

• This species also forms part of the group of spitting cobras, that is, of those capable of projecting venom to a distance of almost 10 feet, thanks to a modification of the inoculating fangs.

• It is not only capable of spitting venom when raised, but can also do so from ground level or from inside its refuge.

• The venom has little neurotoxic effect; its effect i= seen mainly by swelling and loss of skin on the affected zone (cytotoxic); mortal cases are therefore exceptional.

• It spits venom only to defend itself, not for hunting; it always captures its prey by biting them.

• As a system of defense, it can also play dead to confuse its enemies.

REPRODUCTION

The clutch laid in summer consists of ten to 36 egg= that measure approximately one inch.

At birth, the babies measure from eight to ten inch= in length.

STATUS

Due to its small size and discreet habits, it is an abundant species in a good part of its area of distrib - tion, although it may go unnoticed.

In fact, in some zones, it is one of the most comm=n snakes (for example, in eastern Botswana and its capital, Gaborne).

DISTRIBUTION

Southeastern Africa: southern Tanzania, Zanzibar and Pemba island, Malawi, Mozambique, southern Zambia, Zimbabwe, southeastern Angola, northern Namibia, Botswana, Swaziland, and the Republic of South Africa (Natal and Transvaal).

Previously, this species, just like the pale cobra, *N. pallida*, and the spitting cobra from Eastern Africa, *N. katiensis*, were considered subspecies of the black-necked cobra, *N. nigricollis*, but the four are currently classified as separate species.

■ No subspecies of the Mozambique spitting cobra are recognized.

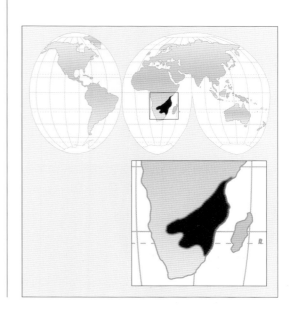

NAJA NAJA

SUBFAMILY **ELAPINAE**

 (Linnaeus, 1758)

 Indian Cobra, Spectacled Cobra

Naja Naja (Indian Cobra, Spectacled Cobra).
Adult specimen.

DESCRIPTION

This species of cobra best represents the typical image of these well-known and dangerous animals.

It is a robust yet slender snake that normally measures between 51 and 63 inches, although some specimens can reach up to 96 inches in length.

The head is slightly differentiated from the neck, but can widen into the form of a hood when the animal is threatening. This spreading is possible due to the mobility and notable length of the frontal ribs; when it raises its body, it tenses the soft skin and relaxes the neck. The spectacle-like ocellus on the back part of this hood stand out, even though some specimens from Pakistan and northwestern India do not have them.

The cephalic scales are large and there is the characteristic presence of a small scale cradled between the 4th and 5th infralabial scales. Another distinct characteristic is that the preocular scale is in contact with the internasal scale.

The coloration is variable, generally of a uniform black, grayish, or brown tonality, but there are specimens with blotches or white bands all along the body.

HABITAT

Very variable; the sole habitats in which they are not found are in arid deserts and mountainous zones above an elevation of 5,906 feet; otherwise in jungles, open forests, cultivated areas, and even within populated areas.

BEHAVIOR

• It is fundamentally active at twilight and at night. It tends to rest during the day inside termite nests, hollows in the floor, or between large tree roots.
• Although it basically prefers dry regions, it also frequents water currents and is a good swimmer.
• It is generally timid and not very aggressive, but when it feels threatened, it adopts its characteristic threatening position, raising the front part of the body and spreading the neck's hood.
• It mainly feeds on rats, but also on birds, eggs, frogs, toads, fish, lizards, and snakes, including other smaller cobras.
• It is a very dangerous species due to its powerful neurotoxic venom that leads to quick respiratory collapse that can cause human death in less than one hour.

• Although it is responsible for a considerable number of such deaths throughout its area of distribution, it is one of the species that snake charmers most frequently employ in their shows.

REPRODUCTION

It is oviparous; between the months of April and July it lays from 12 to 30 elongated eggs in holes in the ground. They hatch after any time between 48 to 69 days.

The newborns measure between eight and 12 inches and their venomous glands are active from the start.

STATUS

This species is still fairly abundant in the majority of its area of distribution, although lately it has been excessively hunted–its different spectacle patterned skin is a very valued leather. For this reason, the Indian government directly controls the exportation of skins and the number of animals captured per year.

For the latter reasons, and due to its similarity to other more threatened species of Asian cobras, it is classified in appendix III of CITES.

DISTRIBUTION

Sri Lanka, India, Pakistan, Nepal, Bhutan, and Bangladesh.

Until a few years ago, all the Asian cobras were thought to belong to this species that was divided into numerous different subspecies.

Today, the majority are considered different species (*N. kaouthia, N. atra, N. sumatrana, N. sputatrix, N. samarensis, N. philippinensis, N. sagittifera, N. oxiana*).

■ No subspecies of the Indian Spectacled Cobra are recognized.

Hood with ocellus, *Naja kaouthina.*

Hood of *Naja naja.*

Hood without ocellus, *Naja oxiana.*

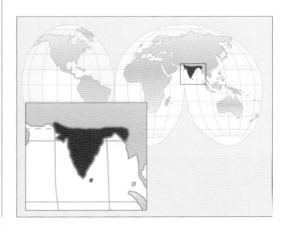

Reinhardt, 1843

Black-necked Spitting Cobra

NAJA NIGRICOLLIS

SUBFAMILY ELAPINAE

DESCRIPTION

A large solid snake that can reach eight feet in length, but normally measures between four and six feet.

The head is wide, the body cylindrical, the scales smooth, and the tail long and narrow.

It may have between 17 and 25 rows of scales on the center of the body, although generally there are 21. The number of ventral scales varies depending on the subspecies.

It is one of the cobras that has a greater variability in coloration. Therefore, from the normal form, N. n. nigricollis, two distinct phases of color are distinguished: one has a dark brownish-gray back, a paler stomach, and brown blotches on the neck; another has a black or dark gray back with red blotches on the stomach and on the neck; the subspecies, N. n. nigricincta, is characterized by having a gray, brown, yellowish, or reddish body, spectacularly marked with a series of black bands that almost reach the tip of the tail (this pattern is why this type is known by the name, Spitting Zebra Cobra); the subspecies N. n. woodi, on the other hand, is completely black both ventrally and dorsally, although some specimens have bright blue blotches on the ventral scales.

HABITAT

It mainly lives in savannahs, but in the extremes of its area of distribution it penetrates semidesert zones and tropical forests.

It appears close to towns and cities with a certain frequency.

It lives from sea level to an elevation of 5,906 feet.

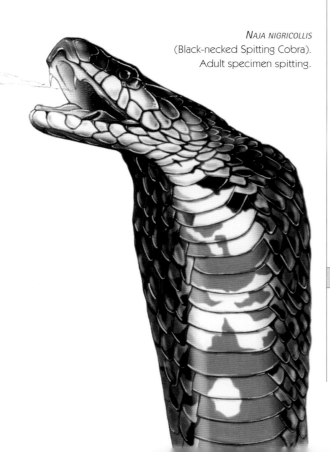

NAJA NIGRICOLLIS (Black-necked Spitting Cobra). Adult specimen spitting.

Naja nigricollis (Black-necked Spitting Cobra). Adult specimen. Detail of head.

BEHAVIOR

• This species is timid, with discreet habits; it seeks refuge in termite nests, cracks in rocks, or in mammals' burrows.

• It is mainly terrestrial and is usually found in the surrounding areas of streams, rivers, and marshes.

• It is a good climber found fairly frequently in trees and on large rocks.

• It feeds on frogs, toads, small birds, eggs, lizards, other snakes, and small mammals.

• The adults basically have nocturnal habits, although they tend to bask in the sun in the early morning hours or at sunset, while the young are more active during the day.

• It is not very aggressive and tries to escape or play dead before attacking.

• Just like other spitting cobras of the genus Naja, it can project its venom a certain distance, whether in an upright position with the hood spread or directly from the ground. This venom mainly has cytotoxic effects, producing necrosis of tissues, although neurotoxic consequences have also been described.

• As in all spitting snakes, its glands produce a large amount of venom, but this venom does not usually cause death–the animal needs to bite for this.

• This animal usually spits venom at eye level; this causes temporary loss of vision due to a severe irritation of the cornea–if it is very serious, it can lead to a permanent blindness.

REPRODUCTION

It lays from eight to 24 eggs that measure 1 x 1.6 inches between April and May; they hatch after 60 to 70 days.

The young measure eight to 10 inches long when born, and tend to have very different colorations from the adults.

STATUS

It is not a threatened species, and in some regions of its wide area of distribution, is a fairly abundant snake.

DISTRIBUTION

In all of sub-Saharan Africa, except in tropical humid jungles, and in the southeasternmost part of the continent.

■ Three different subspecies are recognized:

- N. n. nigricollis: From Senegal in the east, through western Africa to Sudan, Ethiopia, and Somalia in the west, and towards the south through Kenya, Tanzania, and Zambia to Zaire, Congo, and Angola.

- N. n. nigricincta: Southwestern Angola and northern Namibia.

- N. n. woodi: Republic of South Africa (northeast of the Cape province) and south of Namibia.

- The other two subspecies, N. n. atriceps and N. n. crawshayi, have been described but are not accepted by the majority.

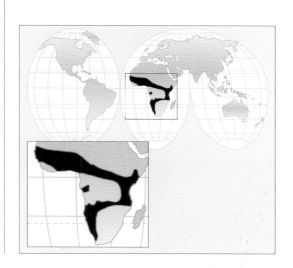

NOTECHIS SCUTATUS

SUBFAMILY ELAPINAE

 (Peters, 1861)

Common Tiger Snake

Notechis scutatus (Common Tiger Snake). Adult specimen.

DESCRIPTION

It is a robust medium snake that does not tend to exceed five feet in length.

The head is wide, leveled, and slightly differentiated from the neck. The eyes are small, the iris dark, and the pupil round.

It has 15 to 19 rows of scales on the central part of the body, between 140 and 190 ventral scales, and between 35 and 65 undivided subcaudal scales. The anal plate is not divided.

The dorsal coloration is extremely varied: grayish, greenish, olive green, brownish-gray, brown, or black, almost always with numerous light cream or yellow colored bands all along the body. The stomach is yellow, greenish, or gray with dark random blotches.

Sometimes specimens without bands are found as well as melanic animals. Although albinos exist, they are much more unusual.

HABITAT

It shows a clear preference for living in humid environments close to marshes, wetlands, and water currents. A large number of these snakes are often concentrated in these places.

However, they can also be found in dryer zones and in areas under cultivation.

BEHAVIOR

• It is mainly diurnal and terrestrial and has a certain ability to climb trees and bushes.

• It tends to become seminocturnal during the hot season.

• It feeds mainly on amphibians, but it can also capture all types of small and medium animals: fish, lizards, birds, and micromammals. Ecologically, it actu-

ally behaves like a water colubrid or like the amphibian, *Agkistrodon*.

• During its resting hours, it hides under rocks, tree trunks, or in accumulations of leaves, in the abandoned burrows of mammals, lizards, large crustaceans, and on some islands of penguins.

• It is generally calm and prefers to escape when it senses danger. But if infuriated it may appear very aggressive, hissing and inflating its neck (in the form of a small hood) and its entire body before attacking, somewhat like the cobras, but without lifting its body from the ground.

• It has a powerful neurotoxic venom that is also cytotoxic and coagulopathic; it is one of the species with the largest number of victims in Australia. This could be attributed to its southern distribution that coincides with the continent's most populated area.

REPRODUCTION

It is an ovoviviparous species that gives birth to up to 40 babies at each birth (although as an exception, the large-sized females have given birth to up to 100 babies).

When born, the small tiger snakes measure six inches in length and already have the same coloration and pattern as the adult animals.

STATUS

It is fairly common; in certain places it is very abundant.

DISTRIBUTION

Southern Australia.

■ Two subspecies are distinguished:

- *N. s. scutatus*: Southeastern Australia (New South Wales, Victoria, southern Queensland, and the southeastern area of southern Australia.

- *N. s. occidentalis*: Southwesternmost area of the continent, in Western Australia.

Notechis scutatus (Common Tiger Snake). Adult specimen.

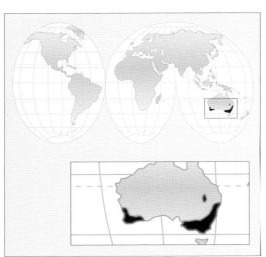

Cantor, 1836

King Cobra, Hamadryad

DESCRIPTION

The largest venomous snake in the world, it easily reaches 13 feet, some specimens exceeding 18 feet; some have even reached 20.

Its body is slender and robust and its head leveled and very large.

The snout and pupil are round.

The venom gland is large and stores a lot of toxin.

It is less toxic than that found in the genus *Naja*, but because it injects a large amount of venom, its bite can lead to the death of a person in 15 to 20 minutes.

Its uniform coloration is very variable throughout its area of distribution; it is light green to dark brown with 32 to 43 lighter bands on the body that decrease to 11 to 13 around the tail; they stand out much more on the young specimens.

The head's hood is narrow and often has a dark border that crosses the light blotch on the neck.

HABITAT

Tropical jungles, bamboo forests, dense scrubland, and estuary areas.

BEHAVIOR

• In spite of its size and the high toxicity of its venom, the King Cobra causes fewer human deaths than other species of venomous snakes. This is because it is not very abundant, is generally timid and evasive, and always inhabits natural zones, not towns and rice fields which other much more dangerous species of cobras inhabit (like the Indian Cobra, who is responsible of so many more mortal attacks).

• It does not become irritated easily, except when breeding. When it breeds it lifts the front part of the body (which can reach more than three feet in height) and spreads the skin on the neck in the form of a hood. In this aggressive position, it keeps the neck straight, not curved as does the Spectacle Cobra.

• Its diet is based on other snakes, both harmless, (young pythons, large terrestrial colubrids such as those of the genus *Ptyas*) and venomous ones (among them, other species of cobras), as well as, although less frequently, monitor lizards, lizards, birds, and mammals.

Ophiophagus hannah (King Cobra).
Adult specimen. Defensive posture.

Ophiophagus hannah
(King Cobra).
Detail of the head.

OPHIOPHAGUS HANNAH
(King Cobra).
Young specimen.

REPRODUCTION

It is the only snake that builds a nest to deposit its clutch, which can consist of more than 50 eggs.

The nest is made up of a mass of vegetation that the female piles up using her head.

Once the eggs are laid, the female remains close to the nest, and stays there watching them during their incubation; they are incubated from the heat of the sun and by the energy liberated in the decomposition of the nest's plant material.

When the babies leave the shell they already measure about 20 inches in length and are almost black with very conspicuous white bands.

STATUS

In some places within its area of distribution, the King Cobra is considered a sacred animal and is protected as one, while in other zones it is very often hunted because of its potential danger.

It is not as abundant a species as a predator that occupies the highest level of the trophic chain in its natural environment should be, but it does not particularly seem to be in danger.

Snake charmers often employ it.

It is classified in appendix III of CITES in India.

DISTRIBUTION

Southeastern Asia: India, Bangladesh, Burma, Thailand, Laos, Cambodia, Vietnam, southern China (Fukien, Kwangtung, and Kwangei), Malaysia, Indonesia (Sumatra, Java, Borneo, Sulawesi) the former Celebes and some other small islands, the Philippines, (Balabac, Jolo, Luzon, Mindanao, Mindoro, Negros, and Palawan).

■ No subspecies are known.

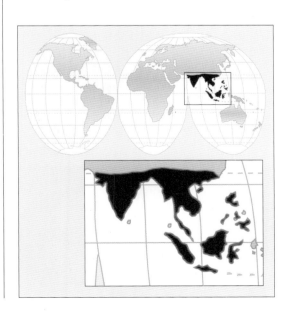

OXYURANUS SCUTELLATUS

SUBFAMILY **ELAPINAE**

 (Peters, 1867)

 Taipan

Oxyuranus scutellatus
(Taipan). Adult specimen.

OXYURANUS SCUTELLATUS (Taipan).
Lateral view.

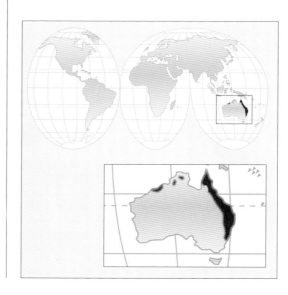

DESCRIPTION

A large slender snake with a cylindrical body that tends to reach more than six feet in length, but in some cases has reached even more than ten feet.

It is very similar to the mambas, although neither the adults nor the young Taipans have arboreal tendencies.

The head is large, long, and well-differentiated from the neck.

The mouth has large fangs that its moveable maxilla allows to place rather upright.

It has both smooth and keeled scales. The scales are arranged in 21 to 23 rows on the center of the body. It has between 220 and 250 ventral scales, and between 45 to 80 subcaudal scales with an undivided anal plate.

The dorsal coloration is a somewhat dark brownish color than can be almost black, with cream-colored flanks and stomach; the stomach often has yellow or orangish blotches. Some specimens have a uniform orange tone over the entire body.

HABITAT

Although it is very varied, it tends to prefer grass valleys, savannahs, and other open zones, as well as both humid and dry coastal forests.

OXYURANUS SCUTELLATUS
Detail of the head. Side view.

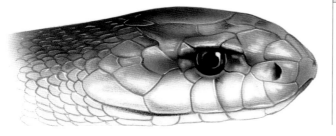

BEHAVIOR

• It is terrestral and known for its rapid movements. During spring, it tends to be diurnally active, at sunrise and at sunset, although in summer it tends to be more nocturnal.

• It takes shelter in mammals' abandoned burrows, under rocks, in crevices, under accumulations of vegetation, or among large branches and fallen tree trunks.

• Its main diet consists of small mammals, previously marsupials, but today more often rats.

• It also eats lizards and terrestrial birds.

• In the regions where it lives, it is a very feared species due to the length of its fangs and the strength of its neurotoxic venom that is said to be able to kill a horse in five minutes.

• This venom also has cytotoxic effects that produce inflammations and necrosis in the wound's immediate area.

• Its bite tends to be fatal for humans, although mortal accidents produced by this species are less common than thought.

• Its exaggerated reputation of aggression is not true either; when it feels threatened, it first tries to escape and hide, and only if it is unsuccessful does it become aggressive and try to bite.

• Also, before attacking, it uses its elaborate threatening behavior: it moves its tail up and down, inflates the head, and lifts part of its body from the ground.

REPRODUCTION

One of the few oviparous Australian *Elapidae*, the majority give birth to already developed babies.

The clutch contains 6 to 25 eggs that are deposited in hollows in the floor or under rocks.

The incubation lasts from 60 to 70 days.

When the little ones are born, they measure two feet in length.

STATUS

The state of its population is unknown.

DISTRIBUTION

New Guinea, northern and eastern Australia.

■ Two subspecies are distinguished:

- *O. s. scutellatus*: Queensland, the northernmost point of the Northern Territory and eastern New South Wales, Australia.

- *O. s. canni*: Southeastern New Guinea.

Pseudonaja textilis
(Common Brown Snake).
Adult specimen.

(Duméril, Bibron and Duméril, 1854)

Common Brown Snake,
Eastern Brown Snake

PSEUDONAJA TEXTILIS

SUBFAMILY **ELAPINAE**

- Although its fangs and venomous gland are small, its venom is neurotoxic, which also has a strong coagulant and harmful effect on the blood system, making it one of the most dangerous and lethal Australian snakes.
- The fatal encounters with this species are not common, but they occur with a certain regularity.

REPRODUCTION

Also an oviparous species whose clutches may consist of up to 35 eggs.

The incubation lasts 11 weeks and the newborns measure from 10 to 12 inches.

There is a direct relation between oviparous reproduction and the presence of divided subcaudal scales; all the Australian *Elapidae* with undivided subcaudal scales give birth to already developed babies, although the reasons behind this phenomenon are unknown.

STATUS

It is not exactly known but it seems that the clearing of the forests and scrubland zones for agricultural purposes have helped it; it is quite abundant in cultivated areas, to which it is attracted by the abundance of rats.

DISTRIBUTION

Central and eastern Australia.

■ Two different subspecies are recognized:

- *P. t. textilis*: All eastern Australia, from Cape York, in Queensland, to New South Wales and Victoria, and towards the west through the Northern Territory and southern Australia.

- *P. t. inframacula*: Only on the Eyre and Yorke Peninsulas, in southern Australia.

DESCRIPTION

Is a large cylindrical snake that reaches five to eight feet in length and is similar in constitution and habits to the large terrestrial African cobras.

The head is not differentiated from the neck, and the tail s long and narrow.

The scales on the center of the body are arranged in 17 rows. It has between 185 and 235 ventral scales and between 45 and 75 subcaudal scales that are divided, as is the anal plate.

The dorsal coloration is variable and may be orangish, brownish-gray, or grayish, while the ventral zone is a cream, yellow, or light brownish-gray color with a series of dark random blotches. The upper part of the young one's head is blotched black, and has a black border on the neck; it tends to have dark bands all along the body that disappear with age.

HABITAT

It lives in a wide variety of habitats, but prefers dry and semi arid areas.

It does not usually frequent the jungles, humid sclerophyll forests, or the mountain zones.

BEHAVIOR

- It is terrestrial, agile, and moves quickly; it is mainly active during the day.
- It feeds on a wide variety of prey: small mammals, birds, reptiles, and amphibians.
- When bothered it is extremely aggressive and readily attacks.
- It adopts the characteristic threatening posture of raising the front part of the body in the shape of an S.

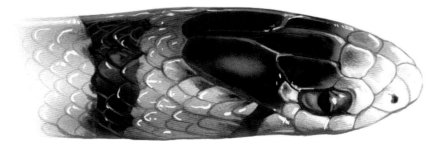

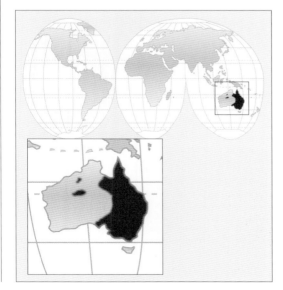

Pseudonaja textilis
Young specimen. Head.
Side view.

WALTERINNESIA AEGYPTIA

SUBFAMILY ELAPINAE

 Lataste, 1887

 Black Desert Cobra

Walterinnesia aegyptia
(Black Desert Cobra). Adult specimen.

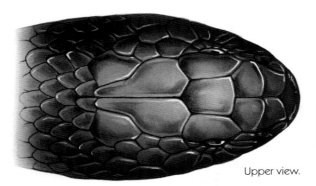

Upper view.

Side view.

WALTERINNESIA AEGYPTIA. (Black Desert Cobra).
Details of the head.

DESCRIPTION

This is a medium snake with a cylindrical body; it normally measures between 32 and 35 inches, but can reach up to five feet.

The head is wide and short, slightly differentiated from the body, and the tail is long and narrow, ending in a point.

The scales on the front part of the body are smooth and the back part and the tail are keeled. It has between 180 and 200 ventral scales, and between 40 and 53 subcaudal scales. The loreal scale is absent, and the anal plate is divided.

The fangs are large and fixed in their position. There are none of these teeth on the maxilla.

It is uniformly black both dorsally and ventrally, and on the latter, there are almost bluish tones, although some specimens are dark brown or gray.

HABITAT

It is found in semidesert areas with soft ground or in sandy or rocky deserts, both in flat and mountainous areas.

It often approaches cultivated zones and irrigated areas, and even appears close to or within towns located on the borders of desert regions.

BEHAVIOR

• It is a calm and discreet burrowing species that feeds on rodents and other small mammals, lizards, snakes, birds, eggs, toads, and frogs.

• It is generally nocturnal; during the day it tends to take shelter in mammals' subterranean burrows and in lizards' burrows of the genus *Uromastyx*.

• It is active even during very cold nights; it takes advantage of this climactic factor to easily capture lethargic diurnal lizards.

• In spite of being a cobra, it does not raise its body from the floor or inflate its neck when angry like many of its most well-known relatives of the genus *Naja*; rather, in this situation, it hisses loudly and decidedly attacks, although often with the mouth closed.

• Its venom is neurotoxic and has led to cases of human death, but these are very unusual and always happen at night when the snake is accidentally stepped upon.

REPRODUCTION

Not much is known.
Oviparous.
The babies measure between 12 and 16 inches long when they hatch.
The young animals in Egypt and in the majority of the Near East are just like the adults, but those in Iran have wide cream-colored or pinkish bands all along their body.

STATUS

The state of its populations is unknown, although it does not seem to be a very abundant species.

DISTRIBUTION

It is the species of *Elapidae* with the widest distribution in the Near East.

It is found in northern Egypt, Israel, Lebanon, Syria, Jordan, Iraq, Iran, Kuwait, and Saudi Arabia.

■ This is the only species that represents its genus; no other subspecies have been described.

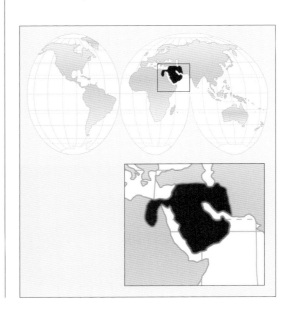

DESCRIPTION

This is a medium snake that tends to measure between three and four feet, reaching a maximum of five feet.

The front part of the body is elongated and subcylindrical, and is laterally swelled and compressed towards the back part.

The tail is leveled in the form of a paddle.

The head is large and wide, the neck apparent, and the snout short, but it is characterized by the form of the rostral scale that is projected downwards exceeding the supralabial scales, giving the impression of a small beak.

It has a greenish iris.

Large cephalic plates.

The body scales are slightly keeled. The 230 to 361 ventral scales are small and slightly differentiated; they often appear divided. The scales form between 49 and 69 rows on the center of the body. There is no mental scale.

The adults are gray, bluish, olive green, or brownish-gray on the back; they are much paler on the ventral part with 43 to 49 dark ringed bands all along the body–these are wider on the back than on the stomach. This pattern is much more marked on the young animals; it fades with age, and is lost in the oldest specimens.

The body's skin appears loose and baggy, similar to the Asian aquatic snakes of the family Acrochordidae.

HABITAT

It is a typical species of shallow and coastal water; it prefers to occupy coral reefs and submerged rocky areas close to the beaches.

It is often found in the turbulent boggy waters close to a river's mouth.

It also frequents estuaries and can even swim upriver a certain distance in fluvial currents (for example, a specimen captured close to Calcutta is worth mentioning; it was captured 80 miles from the sea).

BEHAVIOR

• It is an excellent swimmer and is totally aquatic; generally, it never leaves the sea. It is not, however, completely incapable of moving on solid land; it can slowly and clumsily slither on land.

• It feeds almost exclusively on fish, and is specialized in capturing catfish in water with very little visibility.

• Although it is not especially aggressive, it readily bites when bothered and there have been instances when it has bitten swimmers that got too close to the animal without noticing it.

• In fact, it is one of the sea snake species that causes the largest number of mortal accidents in a good part of Southeast Asia. Its neurotoxic venom is one of the most powerful that exists; it is ten times more powerful than the cobras, producing a respiratory collapse in a few hours.

 (Daudin, 1803)

Beaked Sea Snake, Hook-Nosed Sea Snake
Boie's Sea Snake

ENHYDRINA SCHISTOSA
SUBFAMILY HIDROPHIINAE

Enhydrina schistosa (Beaked Sea Snake).
Adult specimen.

REPRODUCTION

From February to May a minimum of three to a maximum of 33 babies are born (normally from four to ten); they are already perfectly developed when their mother expels them from her body, and measure 10 to 12 inches long.

STATUS

It is abundant in certain regions such as the coasts of Pakistan and in southern India, but it is rarer towards the east.

It uncommon in the waters of Madagascar.

ENHYDRINA SCHISTOSA.
(Beaked Sea Snake). Adult specimen.
Detail of the head. Side view.

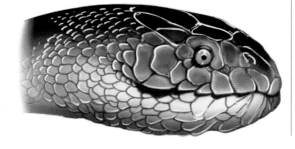

DISTRIBUTION

From the Persian Gulf to the south up to the Seychelles Islands and Madagascar, and towards the east, through India, Sri Lanka, and Southeast Asia to Vietnam, along with the northern coasts of New Guinea and Australia.

■ It has no subspecies and, in general, is recognized as the only species of its genus. However, other authors distinguish a second species, the sea snake Zweifel, *Enhydrina zweifeli*.

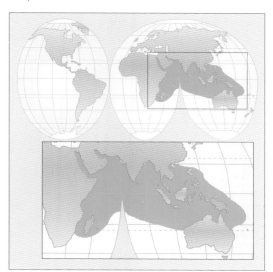

HYDROPHIS CYANOCINCTUS

SUBFAMILY **HIDROPHIINAE**

 Daudin, 1803

Annulated Sea Snake, Chittul

Hydrophis cyanocinctus
(Annulated Sea Snake).
Adult specimen.

DESCRIPTION

It is an elongated, medium snake that normally measures between 51 and 61 inches in length, although some specimens may be larger, up to six feet.

The front part of the body is slender and cylindrical, but swells and becomes compressed laterally towards the back.

The tail is long and paddle-shaped.

The head is wide and small, somewhat differentiated from the body, and the snout is large and extended forwards.

It has five to eight maxillary teeth behind the developed fangs.

The 290 to 398 ventral scales are small. The ones on the center part of the body, in 37 to 49 rows, are slightly keeled and sometimes even differentiated into two or three tubercles. It has large cephalic scales on the upper part of its head. The triangular, relatively large mental scale is always present.

The dorsal color varies from a light greenish to a grayish-blue color, and always has a few characteristic dark transversal bands all along the body (between 41 and 70). On the large adult specimens, these bands become indistinguishable. The ventral zone is a yellowish-brownish-gray, although it sometimes has a ventral black border. The young animals are yellow with extremely marked ring-shaped blotches, and a dark yellow blotch in the form of a horseshoe on the upper part of the head. The males tend to have a more contrasted coloration, the tail is thicker, and the scales more markedly keeled.

BEHAVIOR

• It is a nocturnally active and a rapid and agile swimmer. It feeds on all types of small fish, including eels and those that jump from the mud.

• It also has a certain prehensile capacity on the upper part of the body, which allows it to anchor to rocks in order to lie in wait for its prey.

• Therefore, it is known by divers for its ability to coil around the most varied man-made objects submerged at the bottom of the sea.

• They do not usually leave the water voluntarily, but if they do, they can slither clumsily on solid land; this is something other species of sea snakes cannot do.

• Its habits of staying close to the surface make it more dangerous because it is often caught in local fishermen's nets. This provokes a certain number of mortal accidents because its neurotoxic venom, that also has myotoxic effects, is very strong, and can cause human death in four or five hours if proper treatment is not received.

• Luckily, it is not very aggressive and does not usually bite anything aside from fish and, when it does, tends to inoculate little or no venom.

HABITAT

It is habitually found in shallow water, almost always close to the coasts.

It is very frequently found in coral reefs and not very often found in the open sea.

It tends to be seen at night swimming around the piers and ports.

REPRODUCTION

It is an ovoviviparous species, the female giving birth to two to 16 babies directly in the water that measure 14 to 16 inches in length.

STATUS

It is an abundant species, the most common in the Arabian Gulf; also one of the most habitual ones all along both coasts of the Indian subcontinent and Sri Lanka.

It is one of the few marine snakes that have been successfully maintained in captivity in a few zoos and aquariums in Asia and in the United States.

DISTRIBUTION

Indian and Pacific Oceans, from the Persian Gulf, along the Indian coasts, Sri Lanka, and Southeast Asia, to the Philippines, the southern islands of Japan, and Papua New Guinea.

■ No subspecies are known.

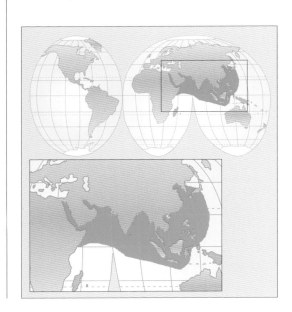

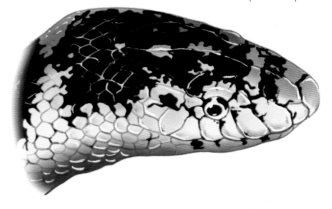

HYDROPHIS CYANOCINCTUS
(Annulated Sea Snake).
Detail of the head. Side view.

(Schneider, 1799)

Banded Sea Snake, Yellow-Lipped
Sea Krait, Schneider's Sea Krait

LATICAUDA COLUBRINA

SUBFAMILY HIDROPHIINAE

Laticauda
colubrina
(Banded Sea
Snake).
Adult specimen.

DESCRIPTION

Medium 60 inch long snake, with a cylindrical, elongated body, a head that is hardly differentiated from the body, and large cephalic scales and round pupils.

Its nostrils are located on both sides of the snout (not on the upper part of its head as in other sea snakes), the body scales are smooth and the tail vertically depressed in the form of a paddle.

Unlike other marine snakes, it has large ventral scales (195 to 240) to facilitate movement on land. It has 21 to 25 rows of scales on the central part of the body and 30 to 45 divided subcaudal scales. The anal plate is likewise divided. The mental scale is small and round.

The color of the body is a metallic bluish-gray and has 24 to 64 black or brownish-gray rings along the body, with three to five more bands on the tail. The head is black, and the front part of the face and the labial scales are yellow, cream, or a light gray color. The ventral zone is yellowish in the spaces between the black bands. The coloration of the young ones is practically identical to that of the adults. The females are larger than the males.

BEHAVIOR

• Although it spends the majority of its life in the ocean, it may go on land to rest and take refuge in rock crevices or in caves, which is necessary for reproduction, given that it deposits its eggs on land.

• It is nocturnally active, feeds exclusively on fish and eels–conger eels and moray eels are its preferred prey in many areas of its distribution.

• It is timid and withdrawn but the strength of its neurotoxic venom is very significant and can cause a person to die within five hours.

• However, fatal accidents from this species are extremely rare, and also, in the case of an accidental bite, it tends to inoculate a very small amount of venom.

STATUS

During the reproductive period, large quantities of these snakes are concentrated in certain favorable places. This is why, in certain areas, their populations are often overexploited during this critical period, such as in the Philippines, where this species is very valued for its meat and skin.

It also seems to be a fairly common species in many other regions.

DISTRIBUTION

East coast of India, Sri Lanka and the Bay of Bengal towards the east along the coasts of Indochina, Indonesia, and the Philippines to Australia, Melanesia, and Polynesia.

Also in the waters of New Zealand.

■ No subspecies are known.

HABITAT

It is a typical inhabitant of shallow waters, habitually found living in coral reefs, atolls, flooded mangrove swamps, and in the surroundings of small rocky islands, where a large number are concentrated during the mating season.

REPRODUCTION

It is an oviparous species that lays five to nine eggs between June and August, buried on land in the moist sand in cracks, crevices in rocks, or in other somewhat protected places that are found above the upper tide line.

Laticauda colubrina (Banded Sea Snake). Adult specimen out of water.

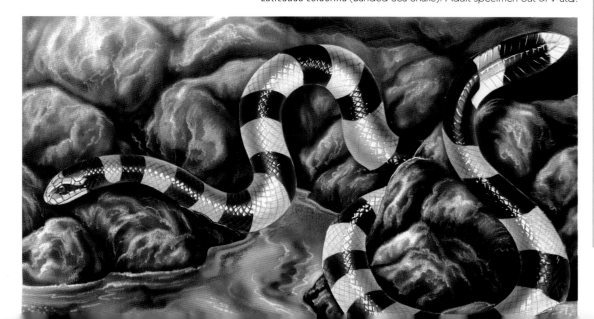

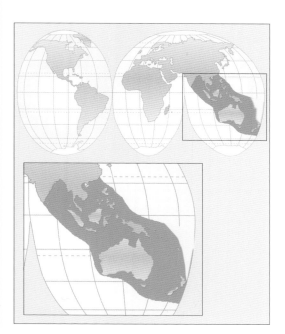

PELAMIS PLATURUS

SUBFAMILY **HIDROPHIINAE**

 (Linnaeus, 1766)

Pelagic Sea Snake

Pelamis platurus (Pelagic Sea Snake).
Adult specime .

DESCRIPTION

Small elongated snake that measures no more than 35 inches in length.

The head is narrow, long, and leveled, the snout long, and the neck well-defined.

The body is laterally depressed in its entire length with a marked dorsal crest, more evident on the central zone and on the stomach, forming a type of obtuse keel.

The coloration is unique among sea snakes: the back is a dark brown or black and the flanks and the stomach are a vivid yellow, sometimes orangish color.

On some specimens, however, it is a very pale brown or cream colored (there are never dark rings as on the majority of species).

The paddle-shaped tail, is yellow with irregular black or brown blotches.

There are completely melanic animals (black) and some xanthophyll snakes (yellow).

The ventral scales are small, almost vestigial, and are arranged in 280 and 340 rows. The anal plate is divided into four small shields.

PELAMIS PLATURUS
(Pelagic Sea Snake).
Adult specimen.
Different tail patterns.

HABITAT

Although it is occasionally found in coastal waters, its habitual environment is in open water, where it tends to be found close to or under a type of floating material; a lot of pelagic fish are concentrated there.

BEHAVIOR

• Although it is an excellent underwater swimmer, it is a pelagic species that spends a lot of its time on the water's surface, where it usually searches for fish.

• It is generally diurnal.

• It is ichthyophagous, feeding on all types of small fish.

• It is totally aquatic and probably the snake species best adapted to sea life.

• It has a great ability for cutaneous respiration (directly absorbing oxygen from the water) and can remain under water for more than three hours.

• On the other hand, on solid ground, it cannot move very much and dies shortly after being taken out of water.

• In spite of being a very venomous and dangerous species, it is a harmless snake when swimming freely and only tries to bite if it feels seriously threatened.

• Its bite has neurotoxic and myotoxic effects and can cause a person to die in little more than two hours if proper treatment is not received.

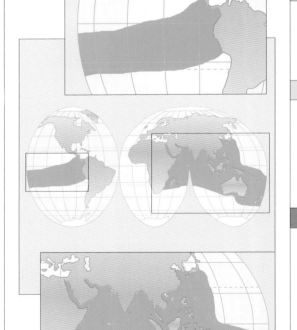

REPRODUCTION

In spring, the females give birth to two to ten already formed babies directly in the water.

The period of gestation varies between five or six months.

STATUS

It is an abundant species in many areas of its zone of distribution and common in the majority of them.

Large concentrations of specimens of this species are often observed in certain favorable places.

DISTRIBUTION

It is very widely distributed–it is the sea snake with the most extensive distribution, found from the eastern coasts of the South African Republic to the north up to the Persian Gulf and to the east through the Indian and Pacific Ocean to the west coast of Central America.

It is found as far south as the waters close to New Zealand and as far north as the eastern waters of China, the Philippines, and Japan.

■ It is the only representative of its genus. No subspecies are known.

F. Viperidae
(VIPERS OR ADDERS)

+180 SPECIES

The Viperidae is a family of venomous snakes found in Europe, Asia, Africa, America, and the Indo–Australian archipelago, although not in Australia where all the existing venomous species belong to the Elapidae family.

These snakes inhabit temperate and even cold regions (in Europe, for example, *Vipera berus* reaches the Arctic Circle), but its population is most diverse in the tropical zones.

The venom inoculating apparatus in these solenoglyph snakes is more evolved; due to the special availability of bones in the mouth, the large hollow fangs found on the maxilla are horizontally distributed when the mouth is closed, but, when it opens, the fangs lift and move 90° forward.

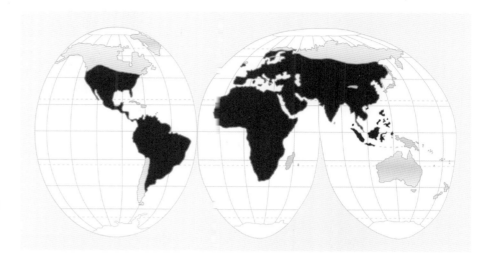

■ The family Viperidae consists of 188 species, up to 26 genera, and is divided into three different subfamilies: Viperinae, Crotalinae, and Azemiopinae.

Bitis nasicornis (Rhinoceros Viper). Adult specimen.

GENERAL CHARACTERISTICS

• Has a solid body, a head that is well-differentiated from the body, large eyes with vertical pupils, and a short tail.

• The body scales are keeled and overlapping.

• The upper maxilla is short, vertically elongated, and swings over the prefrontal articulation with two long canaled fangs.

• The mandibular bones, the ectopterygoid, and the quadrate are very long; the latter is obliquely aimed backwards.

• The spermatic groove is always forked.

• The retina has two differing types of cells.

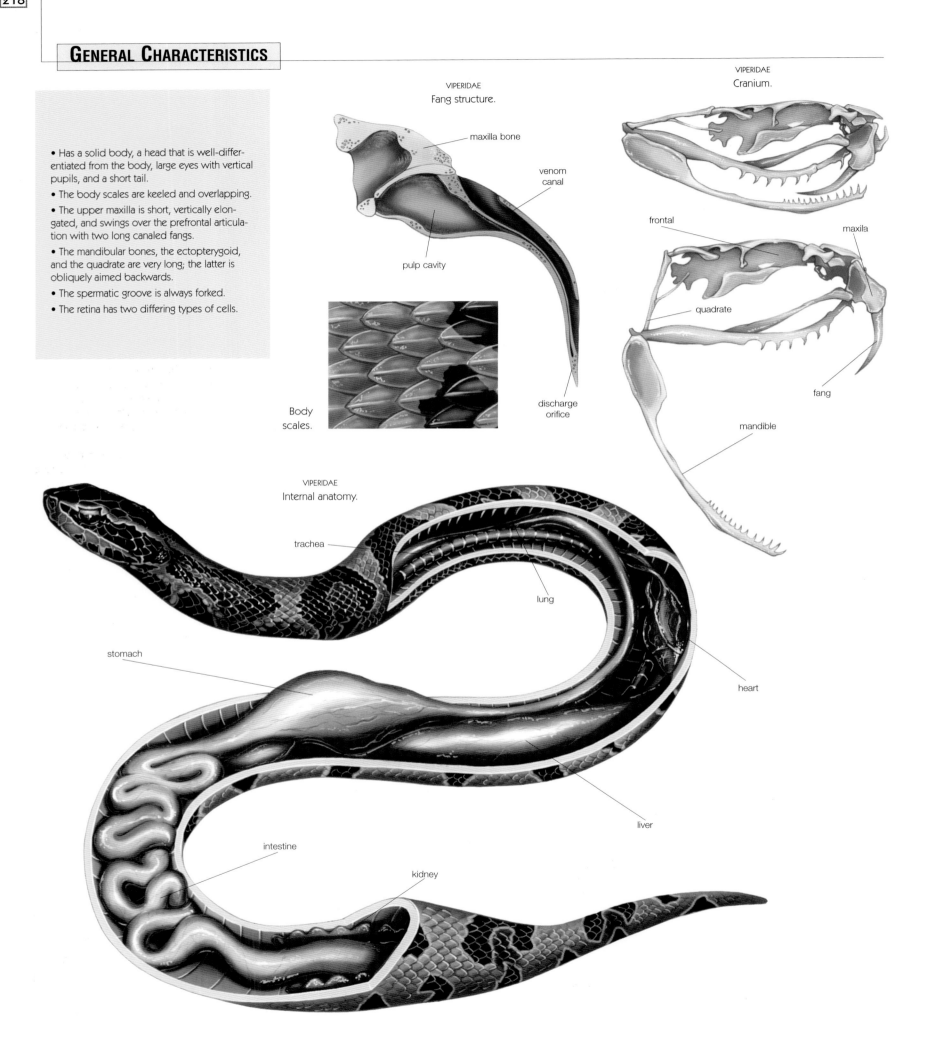

VIPERIDAE
Fang structure.

maxilla bone

venom canal

pulp cavity

discharge orifice

Body scales.

VIPERIDAE
Cranium.

frontal

maxila

quadrate

fang

mandible

VIPERIDAE
Internal anatomy.

trachea

lung

stomach

heart

liver

intestine

kidney

VIPERIDAE
Cephalic scale structure
Head.

Side view.

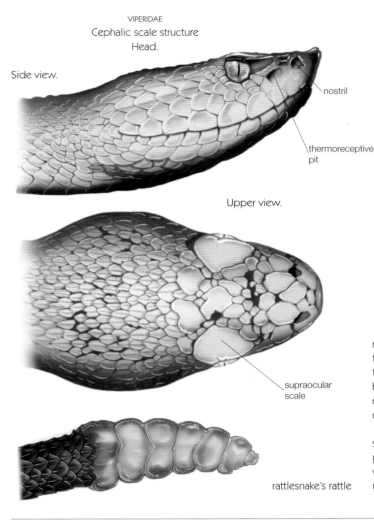

nostril

thermoreceptive pit

Upper view.

supraocular scale

rattlesnake's rattle

VIPERIDAE
Inoculating apparatus. Head.

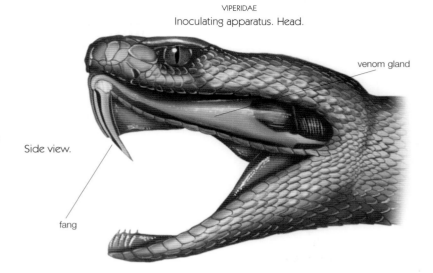

venom gland

Side view.

fang

When it bites, the venomous gland above the mouth compresses, expelling its contents towards the canals found inside the fangs. In this manner, the venom is directly injected into the victim as if by a hypodermic needle. All of this makes its bite extraordinarily effective and these snakes truly dangerous.

However, in spite of its perfect inoculating system, these animals also have a series of fairly primitive characteristics (like the structure of the vertebrae or the hemipenes, for example), which makes us think they more likely originated from a group of primitive Colubridae instead of from one of the evolved Elapidae, as often thought.

Paleontology does not help much in clarifying its origin; the first known fossils belong to the European Oligocene and are perfectly recognizable Viperidae.

They are small or medium-sized snakes that may be oviparous or ovoviviparous, and according to some authors, in some cases even viviparous.

In general, they are terrestrial, although there are quite a lot of arboreal species and a few semiaquatic ones.

SUBFAMILY **VIPERINAE**

Russell's Viper

Daboia russelli. Adult specimen in its habitat.

Exclusively in the Old World, found in Europe, Asia, and Africa, although absent in Madagascar and Oceania. Abundant in Africa (where this subfamily's center of dispersion is probably located), common in Europe and the Near East; a few species reach Southeast Asia and Indonesia.

■ The family consists of 10 genera:

The following are found in Africa:
- *Adenorhinus*, with only one arboreal species that lives in Tanzania.
- *Atheris*, seven species of usually green arboreal vipers with prehensile tails.
- *Bitis*, the puffing vipers: ten species that live in the jungle and the savannahs

10 GENERA / 45 SPECIES

• The majority of species inhabit tropical zones, but many do so in temperate regions and some even in cold areas.
• It is characterized by a triangular-shaped head and by smaller scales on the upper part of the head.
• The upper maxilla is very short and has no groove to hold a sensory organ.
• There are no sensory pits between the eye and the nostril.
• The dorsal scales are always somewhat keeled.
• The dorsal coloration often has a longitudinal zigzag, rhomboidal, or barred pattern.
• A few species have a uniform color without conspicuous marks.
• It basically feeds on micro mammals, although some species also capture birds, amphibians, reptiles, and even large invertebrates.
• Its hunting technique consists of attacking by surprise, envenoming its prey, allowing it to escape, and following it using its extraordinarily developed sense of smell.

with a bright and colorful coloration that helps them camouflage themselves among the fallen vegetation on the floor.
- *Cerastes*, two species adapted to living in desert zones, one of them also distributed in Arabia and the Near East.
- *Causus*, six species characterized by their large cephalic plates and their appearance that is more similar to the Colubridae than to the Viperidae.
- *Echis*, two species that are also found on the Arabian Peninsula and towards the east of India and Sri Lanka.

Two genera live in Asia:
- *Pseudocerastes*, just one species, typical in desert zones, characterized by the existence of a specific sensory organ in the nostrils.
- *Eristicophis*, lives in the deserts in Iran, Afghanistan, and Pakistan.

Two genera inhabit Europe, Asia, and Africa:
- *Vipera*, the true vipers.
- *Daboia*; many authors do not recognize it as such, rather they consider it only a subgenus of the genus *Vipera*.

15 GENERA / 142 SPECIES

• Has generally a solid appearance and stands out with its clearly triangular and leveled head that is differentiated from and much narrower than the neck.

• The size varies from 1.6 feet in the smallest *Crotalus transversus*, *Crotalus pricei* to 12 feet in *Lachesis muta*, or 8.2 feet in *Crotalus adamanteus*.

• It has two types of cephalic scales: *Sistrurus*, *Agkistrodon*, *Calloselasma*, and some *Trimeresurus* have large cephalic plates, while the rest have small irregularly arranged cephalic scales.

• The tail is short, although the arboreal genera like *Trimeresurus* or *Bothriechis* have a prehensile tail as an adaptation to life in the trees.

• The solenolglyph fangs on the front part of the upper mandible may be erect; these fangs are protected by a sheathing when the mouth is closed. They may have a series of replacement fangs located right behind the functional fangs.

• Its venom generally has strong hemotoxic effects aside from some species such as *Crotalus durissus*, which has strong neurotoxic effects.

• Some genera such as *Crotalus* and *Sistrurus*, with more than 30 species, have an organ that is unique among reptiles–the presence of an appendage called a rattle, capable of emitting a characteristic sound when the snake becomes alarmed or threatened. This organ forms from the accumulation of remains from successive moltings.

• They are crepuscular and nocturnal.

• They are generally terrestrial although some species, like *Agkistrodon piscivorus*, are amphibian; many others are arboreal: *Trimeresurus*, *Bothriechis*, etc. Some have conquered the desert: *Crotalus cerastes* and others have adapted to mountainous terrain; *Glodyus himalayanus*, is habitually found between 6,562 and 11,483 feet.

• The majority of the genera are ovoviviparous, although some, such as *Lachesis*, *Calloselasma*, and a few *Trimeresurus* and *Ovophis*, are oviparous.

SUBFAMILY **CROTALINAE**

They are also called pit vipers because they are characterized by the existence of a cavity or a thermoreceptive pit found on each side of the head, between the nostril and the eye. This organ can perceive variations in temperature up to .001°, which is very important in nocturnal orientation and in hunting.

Crotalus atrox. Adult specimen in its habitat.

Western diamondback rattlesnake

The family's taxonomy is still debated; before, few genera were recognized with many species, and currently, they are usually separated into smaller genera.

The following genera have been found in the New World: *Agkistrodon*, *Crotalus*, *Lachesis*, *Sistrurus*, *Bothrops*, *Bothriechis*, *Bothriopsis*, and *Porthidium* (these last three genera were previously placed within the genus *Bothrops*).

In Asia: the genera, *Trimeresurus*, *Tropidolaemus*, *Ovophis* (these last two were previously included in *Trimeresurus*), *Calloselasma*, *Deinagkistrodon*, *Glodyus* (these three were previously included in *Agkistrodon*) and *Hypnale*.

SUBFAMILY **AZEMIOPINAE**

Fea's Viper

It is considered the most primitive subfamily of the Viperidae. It has intermediary characteristics between the Viperidae and the Colubridae.

They are oviparous and hibernate in winter.

They live in humid mountainous and wooded zones in the foothills of the Himalayas, between the north of Burma, south of China, in southeastern Tibet, and in Vietnam.

1 SPECIES

• Their head is covered with large scales in a way similar to the Colubridae.

• The body is elongated and the head is slightly round or triangular.

• The fangs and venom sacks are small.

Azemiops feae. Adult specimen in its habitat.

(Hallowell, 1854

Green Bush Viper,
Common Bush Viper

ATHERIS SQUAMIGER

SUBFAMILY VIPERINAE

Atheris squamiger
(Green Bush Viper).
Adult specimen.

DESCRIPTION

A relatively large arboreal viper that can reach a maximum length of 32 inches, although it normally measures 20 inches. Females are larger than males.

Its body is slender, but the large specimens are moderately robust, and it is covered with small very keeled overlapping scales that are somewhat raised in their center, giving it a rough appearance similar to the scales on a pineapple. The dorsal scales are arranged in 15 to 25 rows on the middle part of the body.

The tail is relatively large and very prehensile.

Compared with the size of the body, the head is extremely large and wide, covered with the same type of very keeled scales.

The coloration is very variable in some populations while in others it is more uniform. The majority of individuals have green tonalities, but may vary from a greenish-yellow to a bluish hue. The body has numerous yellow scales that can form close to 30 transversal, somewhat marked, bands. The stomach may vary from yellow to a dark green. The neck is yellow and the tip of the tail is a whitish color.

HABITAT

Rainforest.
Mainly in low dense flowery shrubs.
It can also be found in wooded areas around the jungle's border.
They live from sea level to an elevation of 6, 234 feet.

BEHAVIOR

• A typically arboreal and mainly nocturnal species.
• During the day it remains immobile, basking in the sun on a bush where its body coloration allows it to go unnoticed.
• It is an expert climber, often found more than 20 feet high.
• At night it descends towards the forest floor and, by keeping its head down, hanging from a low branch, it waits for its prey to pass on the ground below.
• Its diet mainly consists of small rodents, although it also feeds on lizards, frogs, chameleons, and small birds.
• The tail is usually yellow or white and can also be used as a lure to attract its prey.
• The venomous fangs are long and sharp. This snake is irascible, but even so, there have been few cited cases of envenomation. Its venom has a hemotoxic effect and though classified as moderately dangerous, various deaths have been cited from this species' bites.

REPRODUCTION

It is ovoviviparous and gives birth to seven to nine babies that measure six to 6.6 feet when born.

STATUS

May sometimes be confused with the rough-scaled bush viper *Atheris hispidus* that shares its habitat, but *A. squamiger* has smaller eyes, more middle dorsal scales, and less elongated scales.

DISTRIBUTION

- *A. s. squamifer*: is widely distributed in tropical Africa from Ghana, Gabon, Cameroon, and the Republic of Congo in the west, to the center of Zaire and northern Angola, up to eastern Uganda and eastern Kenya. It is also found on Bioko Island.

- Subspecies *A. s. robustus*: is limited to the Ituri jungle in the eastern part of Zaire.

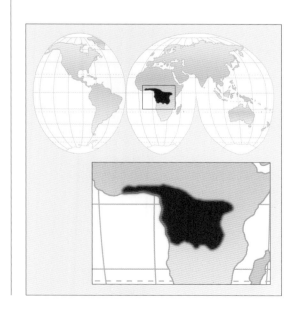

BITIS ARIETANS

SUBFAMILY VIPERINAE

 (Merren, 1820)

Puff Adder

Bitis arietans
(Puff Adder).
Adult specimen.

Bitis arietans
(Puff Adder).
Adult specimen.
Detail of head.

DESCRIPTION

Normally from 32 to 43 inches, although a 75-inch specimen has been cited in Somalia. The females are considerably larger than the males.

The body is solid and ends with a short tail that is wider at the base and longer on the males than on the females.

The head is large and flattened, covered in small keeled overlapping scales that are much wider than those on the narrow neck.

The snout is round with large upward-facing nostrils.

It has from 29 to 41 rows of scales on the middle of the body.

The coloration of the dorsal zones is very variable; it can be yellow, reddish-brownish-gray, or a blackish-gray, with a series of V-shaped transversal light and dark bands. In general, the coloration is dull, aside from a few very colorful male specimens in South Africa and other regions in eastern Africa. It has from two to six transversal bands alternating between white and dark close to the tail. It generally has one well marked dark blotch on the upper part of the head and two oblique dark bands on each side of the head, under and behind the eyes.

HABITAT

Found in a wide variety of habitats, but prefers savannah or pastureland areas with scarce shrublike vegetation.

It is absent only in zones with a marked Mediterranean climate in northern Africa, in the extreme desert, and in the tropical humid jungle.

It is found from sea level up to an elevation of 11,483 feet.

BEHAVIOR

• It is terrestrial and moves clumsily and slowly; it often moves in a straight line like a worm.

• It is mainly active at twilight or at night.

• It spends a long time without moving, confiding in its body's coloration which allows it to go unnoticed on the substratum.

• When bothered and cannot escape, it inflates its body in spectacular fashion and puffs noisily while adopting its characteristic posture: with the neck and front part of the body slightly raised in an S form and the head slightly pointed downward, it is ready to attack.

• It is quite aggressive and readily bites, it is responsible for many serious cases of envenomation mainly because its camouflage colors and its habit of basking in the sun on paths make it go unnoticed by the passers-by that step on it. The venom is relatively toxic: 100 mg is fatal for human beings. With just one bite, it can inject from 100 to 350 mg; however, the deaths caused by this species' bite are exceptional and only occur in five to ten percent of the cases. The venom is hemotoxic and cytotoxic and has almost no neurotoxic effect.

• It feeds on rodents, birds, lizards, and even on other snakes that it catches by surprise when they pass nearby.

REPRODUCTION

It is ovoviviparous and extremely prolific. It generally has between 20 and 40 babies at one time, but a large female in eastern Africa is cited to have given birth to 156 babies.

At birth, the babies measure between five and eight inches.

STATUS

It is perhaps the most characteristic snake of tropical Africa, where it is very common in some regions.

DISTRIBUTION

It is found at certain points in southern Morocco and on the Arabian Peninsula. It is absent in the Saharan zone and present on the rest of the continent, except in the tropical rainforest zones of the equatorial areas and in some spots in the Namibian desert.

■ Two subspecies are recognized:

- The nominal *B. a. arietans*, widely extended.

- *B. a. somalica*, in Somalia, northern Kenya, and eastern Ethiopia; it differs from the typical form because of its keeled subcaudal scales.

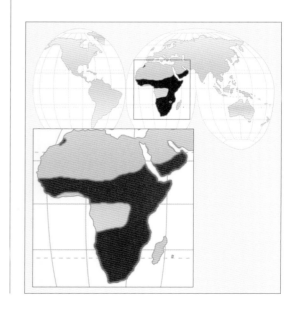

(Duméril y Bibron, 1854)

Gabon Viper

BITIS GABONICA
SUBFAMILY VIPERINAE

Bitis gabonica
(Gabon Viper).
Adult specimen.

DESCRIPTION

Large viper that can exceed 6 feet in length, although the majority of specimens measure around 4 feet.

The large individuals, natives of west Africa, can weigh more than 19 pounds.

The head is very large, wide, and leveled. It is covered with small scales and has two nasal appendages; in the subspecies, B. g. rhinoceros, they are very evolved.

The body is solid, the tail short, and the scales are distributed in 28 to 41 rows in the middle of the body; all of them are keeled except for the three or four rows that border the ventral scales.

The body's coloration is very beautiful, bright, and colorful, and creates a notable camouflage among the humus and the fallen leaves in the tropical jungle; it consists of yellowish rectangles, forming a vertebral line that alternates with triangles that have opposite vertices. The flanks are covered with a pattern that

consists of a group of opposite-facing interwoven triangles that are brownish-gray, purple, or pink.

The head is a light pinkish color or a suede color with a somewhat dark line; and on each side, there is a brownish-gray chocolate line that starts obliquely from the eye; on B. g. gabonica, there are two of these bands that are separated by a light area between them, while on the B. g. rhinoceros, there is just one.

The ventral face is a pinkish color or a suede color, with dark gray blotches.

HABITAT

It typically inhabits tropical jungles.
Found in clearings and along the limits of rainy jungles with thick vegetation.

BEHAVIOR

• It is nocturnal; it spends many hours inactive and unnoticed, half-buried in the forest's floor, protected by its camouflage coloration.

• It is slow-moving, extremely calm and lazy, and rarely tries to bite.

• If bothered, it only inflates itself and puffs noisily.

• It feeds mainly on rodents, although the older animals may hunt larger animals such as monkeys or mongooses.

• It waits patiently, completely still for its prey to approach then quickly charges at it; unlike many Viperidae, it does not release its prey until it is dead.

• This species stands out for the enormous size of its venomous fangs that can reach a length of just over two inches. Although its venom is relatively low in toxicity, the large amount that it can inoculate in just one bite (from 450 to 600 mg) is potentially mortal. However, due to its calm nature and the fact that it is limited to the primary tropical jungle, its bites are very rare. The venom, like that of other similar vipers, has hemotoxic and cytotoxic effects.

REPRODUCTION

It is ovoviviparous and quite prolific; it has been cited to give birth to close to 60 babies.

The newborns are large, measuring from ten to 13 inches, with a very vivid coloration.

The females breed every two or three years.

STATUS

In the primary tropical jungle it can be very abundant.

This habitat has been seriously altered in recent years from deforestation and the uncontrolled hunting of many of the animals in the tropical forest.

The effects of the serious degradation that is taking place in a large part of its area of distribution are unknown on the populations of this impressive snake.

The populations in the Southern Cone of Africa are very vulnerable and are in decline.

In South Africa there have been reintroductions of animals born in captivity in their natural environment.

DISTRIBUTION

From Guinea to southern Sudan through the north to Uganda, western Kenya, southeastern Tanzania, Zambia, Zaire, and northern Angola.

There are also populations in the Southern Cone of Africa: Zululand (South Africa), Zimbabwe, and Mozambique.

The subspecies B. g. rhinoceros is limited to the jungles of Guinea, Togo, and Ghana.

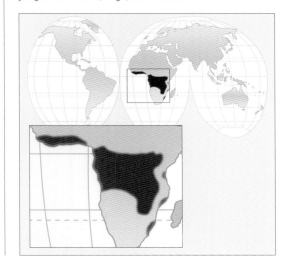

BITIS GABONICA RHINOCEROS
Detail of the head.

Side view.

B.TIS GABONICA GABONICA
Detail of the head.

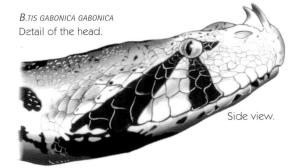

Side view.

BITIS NASICORNIS

SUBFAMILY VIPERINAE

 (Shaw, 1802)

Rhinoceros Viper

Bitis nasicornis
(Rhinoceros Viper).
Adult specimen.
Detail of the head.

BITIS NASICORNIS (Rhinoceros Viper).
Adult specimen. Detail of the head. Upper view.

DESCRIPTION

The maximum size is four feet although very large specimens are exceptional; the most common size is between two and three feet.

This viper has a heavy appearance with the triangular fairly narrow head that is covered with small overlapping very keeled scales. At the tip of the snout there are two or three pairs of horn-shaped scales; the front pair are larger, and due to this characteristic, this snake is called the common name, Rhinoceros Viper. The eyes with vertical pupils are relatively small and found in a fairly frontal position.

Other characteristics that stand out are the section of the body that is markedly triangular and the pronounced narrowing in the neck area. The tail is short. The body scales are very rough and keeled like in the cephalic area; these can cause small wounds when the animal twists upon handling. The scales are arranged in 31 to 43 rows on the middle part of the body.

The coloration is very bright and attractive. The background color is a dark olive with a complicated pattern of different geometric rhomboidal triangular forms or in the shape of a butterfly; they can be blue, red, yellow, or white.

It has a dark mark on the upper part of the head in the form of an arrow framed by a white, blue, or yellow line that goes above the eyes and joins the tip of the snout with the back part.

The specimens from the central and western part of their area of distribution tend to have a more bluish tone than the specimens from the east that are more greenish.

HABITAT

It strictly lives in humid jungles and is almost never found outside of the forest's vegetation. It lives in zones close to water, even in partially flooded zones.

BEHAVIOR

•It is mainly terrestrial, although it sometimes likes to climb trees or bushes where it basks in the sun. It has predominantly nocturnal habits; during the day it remains still under the fallen leaves of the forest's floor. Its apparently very bright coloration is very disruptive allowing it to be perfectly camouflaged among the fallen vegetation and the chiaroscuro of the diffused light. When feeding, it generally remains completely still for a long period of time waiting for the prey to come close enough so that it can charge without warning. Although its diet consists mainly of good-sized mammals, primarily rodents and insectivorous mammals, amphibians and fish have also been cited as an integral part of its diet.

•Normally it has a good character, unlike the aggressiveness of the Puff-Adder *Bitis arietans*, but if repeatedly bothered, it is capable of puffing more powerfully than any African snake, and, it can also inflate its body to be almost double the size of its normal resting size.

•This species' bites are rare; the composition and toxicity of its venom is somewhat unknown; however, it is known to be slightly less toxic than the Puff-Adder, *Bitis arietans* and the Gaboon Viper, *Bitis gabonica*. It has hemolytic and necrotic effects on its victims.

REPRODUCTION

Sometimes it has given birth to more than 40 babies, although normally the number of babies varies from six to 30.

The babies are born during the rainy season and measure from seven to ten inches.

STATUS

This species exclusively lives in the forest, which limits its possibilities of spreading and makes it vulnerable to the increasing deforestation of the humid African jungle. The populations in some areas tolerate its presence, even letting it stay close to their rooms.

DISTRIBUCIÓN

East coast of Africa: Liberia, Guinea, Ghana; central Africa: southern Uganda, Eastern Kenya, Zaire, The Republic of the Congo, Equatorial Guinea, Gabon, Cameroon, southern Nigeria.

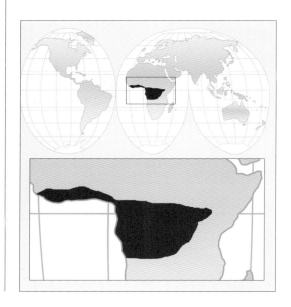

DESCRIPTION

This snake reaches 35 inches in length, although its size normally varies between 12 and 24 inches.

This small viper has different characteristics than the majority of species in the family, and its appearance is more similar to a Colubrinae.

The head is only slightly differentiated from the rest of the body, with a round snout, and eyes with a round pupil.

The upper part of the head is covered in fairly large cephalic plates that are symmetrical, unlike many Viperidae.

The body has a solid appearance and is covered with slightly keeled scales that do not look rough; these are located in 15 to 23 rows on the middle part of the body.

The body's background color is generally brown, gray-brown, pinkish-brown, or olive-green.

There are 20 to 30 dark rhomboidal blotches on the back, bordered by the whitish scales, and oblique bars or black blotches are found on the flanks. The body's patterns may be very variable and there may also be individuals that completely lack marks (especially in populations in some zones in Zimbabwe) or whose vertebral marks are even joined together in one dark line. All these variations may make these snakes more difficult to identify.

There is a characteristic V-shaped dark blotch on the head that is in a central position between the eyes and extends back on each side of the neck.

The lower part of the body is whitish, yellowish, or light gray, with black dots.

HABITAT

Savannah, prairies, and marshes, and generally in humid zones with abundant vegetation.

It can also be found in dryer zones, but always near a source of water.

Normally, it hides in termite nests or in mammals burrows.

Sometimes it is found not far from settlements.

 (Lichtenstein, 1823)

 Rhombic Night Adder

CAUSUS RHOMBEATUS
SUBFAMILY **VIPERINAE**

Causus rhombeatus
(Rhombic Night Adder)
Adult specimen.

BEHAVIOR

• Although, as its common name indicates, it is predominantly nocturnal or crepuscular, it is not unusual to be found active in broad daylight.

• It is predominantly terrestrial, but it may enter water or climb small shrubs in pursuit of amphibians, on which it mainly feeds.

• When frightened, it responds by inflating the body and puffing hard in a high-pitched and insistent way. If still bothered it may raise the front part of the body, flatten the neck (so that it looks like a cobra) and, sticking out its tongue, charge powerfully.

• It feeds mainly on frogs and toads; they are often swallowed alive before feeling the full effects of the venom.

• The fangs are relatively short and are not moveable as in other vipers, but are linked to large venomous glands (close to four inches), that extend along each side of the neck.

• What we know about the composition of the hemotoxic venom leaves little doubt about its serious danger to humans.

REPRODUCTION

It is an oviparous species.

The female lays seven to 26 eggs with a rough-looking appearance; they take two-and-one half months to hatch.

STATUS

It seems to be abundant in some parts of its area of distribution.

At first sight, it may be confused with the Common egg-eater, *Dasypeltis scabra*, but this one has vertical pupils.

DISTRIBUTION

Through eastern South Africa, Zimbabwe, Zambia, eastern Angola, and southern Zaire, Kenya, and eastern Nigeria. Also in elevated areas in Ethiopia and central Sudan.

Currently, western African populations are considered another species called the West African Night Adder, *Causus maculatus*. Some populations in South Africa, with a different coloration and two dorsal lines, called the Two-striped Night Adder, *Causus bilineatus*, are also considered to be a separate species.

Causus rhombeatus
(Rhombic Night Adder)
Adult specimen
catching an amphibian.

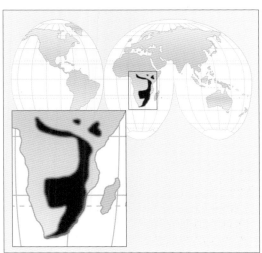

CERASTES CERASTES

SUBFAMILY **VIPERINAE**

 (Linnaeus, 1758)

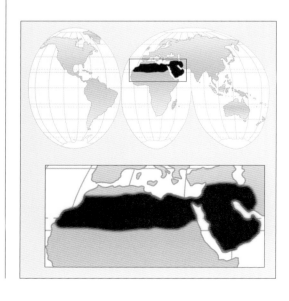 Horned Viper

Cerastes cerastes
(Horned Viper)
Adult specimen.

has significant cytotoxic effects. Its bite causes nausea, vomiting, hemorrhages, and necrosis on the directly affected zone, but is rarely mortal.

REPRODUCTION

It is an oviparous species.

The female deposits between ten and 23 eggs between July and August that may be joined together forming a type of conglomeration.

The babies, which hatch after six to eight weeks of incubation, measure from four to six inches in length.

DESCRIPTION

Small snake that is 20 to 24 inches in length and sometimes measures up to 32 inches.

Has a solid body and a very short tail.

The head is wide, leveled, triangular, and is clearly differentiated from the body. The eyes have a vertical pupil.

It is characterized by having a pointy little horn above each eye, made up by only one scale, although sometimes specimens without horns have been found.

The body scales are keeled and distributed in 25 to 37 rows on the middle part of the body. The scales on the head are also keeled. The scales on the sides of the body are saw-toothed. It has between four and five rows of subocular scales between the lower border of the eye and supralabial scales that vary between 12 and 15. The ventral scales are laterally keeled and the subcaudal scales are divided.

The dorsal coloration is grayish, yellowish, brownish-gray, or reddish, with a series of dark rectangular blotches arranged transversally along the body. The flanks have small dark blotches that overlap the dorsal scales. There is no mark on the upper part of the head, but there is a thin dark narrow one that goes from the eyes to the commissure of the mouth. The ventral zone is a whitish color without blotches. Many individuals have a black tip.

Cerastes cerastes
Detail of head of two types. Side view.

STATUS

Due to its inhospitable natural environment, its general status is unknown; but in many places it is still fairly common.

DISTRIBUTION

All of northern Africa, the Sinai Peninsula, Israel, Jordan, southern Iraq, Iran, and the Arabian Peninsula.

■ Two different subspecies are recognized:

- *C. c. cerastes*: Morocco, Mauritania, Mali, Nigeria, Sudan, Algeria, Libya, Egypt, and southern Israel.

- *C. c. gasperettii*: The Sinai Peninsula, Israel, Saudi Arabia, Jordan, Iraq and Iran (some authors consider this subspecies to be its own species, the Horned Viper of Arabia, *Cerastes gasperettii*).

BEHAVIOR

• It is predominantly active at night; during spring, it may show activity during the early morning and late afternoon hours.

• It hibernates during several months of the year and feeds on micromammals, reptiles, and birds.

• To hunt its prey, it almost completely buries itself in the sand, leaving only the upper part of its head sticking out and sometimes the tip of the tail.

• It is not aggressive at all and tends to flee rapidly when it senses danger. It can move on the sand somewhat quickly with a characteristic undulatory movement, leaving typical marks in its wake. When it wants to be threatening it may rub its spiny lateral scales against one another, creating a characteristic humming as a warning.

• It has very powerful neurotoxic venom that also

HABITAT

It lives almost exclusively in sandy and rocky deserts, preferring places where there is shrublike vegetation.

It lives from sea level to an elevation of 4,921 feet.

(Linnaeus, 1758)

Common Sand Viper
Sahara Sand Viper

CERASTES VIPERA

SUBFAMILY VIPERINAE

Cerastes vipera
(Common Sand Viper).
Adult specimen.

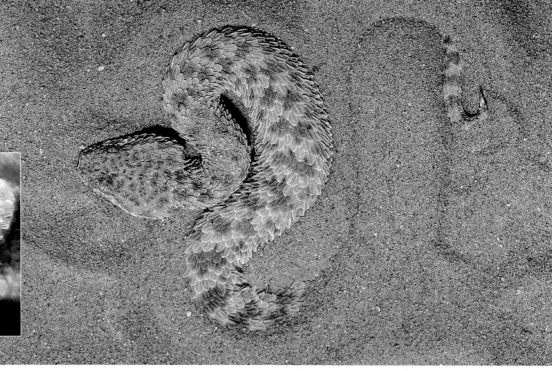

Cerastes vipera
(Common Sand Viper).
Adult specimen.
Detail of the head.

DESCRIPTION

A small robust snake that measures only eight to 14 inches long, reaching a maximum of 20 inches.

The head is wide, flattened, triangular, very well differentiated from the body, and the tail very short and thin.

It does not have horns above the eyes like *Cerastes cerastes*, and unlike this species, which has very laterally positioned eyes, its eyes are obliquely aimed upwards.

The body's scales are rough, very keeled, and are arranged in 23 to 27 rows on the central part of the body. The keeled scales on the flank look saw-toothed. There are between three to four rows of subocular scales between the eyes' lower border and the supralabial scales (ten to 12). The ventral scales are laterally keeled and the subcaudal ones divided.

The dorsal coloration is brownish-gray, creamy, or of yellowish color, with a series of dark transversal bands and small alternating blotches that extend all along the body. The upper part of the head does not have a pattern; the closest to a pattern is a few dark isolated scales. The ventral zone is a light uniform yellow and the tip of the tail is black on the females and on the males; on the males it may be ringed with brownish-gray borders.

HABITAT

It generally lives in sandy deserts and prefers zones with dunes and scattered shrubs.

BEHAVIOR

• It is predominantly nocturnal and terrestrial and tends also to be active during twilight.

• During the day it rests buried in the sand or in subterranean mammals' abandoned burrows.

• Just like the horned viper, *Cerastes cerastes*, it completely buries itself in soft sand through extensive movements of the ribs, allowing only the upper part of the head and the eyes to be seen, as well as the tip of the tail (it uses this to attract the attention of possible prey).

• It feeds on micromammals and small lizards.

• During winter, it is inactive in the northern zones of its area of distribution.

• It moves on the sand with characteristic undulatory movements that leave recognizable marks in its wake, marking its presence.

• It is not very aggressive; when it feels threatened, it emits a loud humming sound produced by the rubbing of its serrated flank scales against one another with undulatory body movements.

• The venom is neurotoxic and cytotoxic. It can be seriously dangerous for humans if the proper antiophidic serum is not received, but very few documented mortal accidents are known of from this species.

REPRODUCTION

Ovoviviparous.

The females give birth to three to five small snakes that are born surrounded by a casing that breaks shortly thereafter. When they are born, the babies measure from two to four inches.

STATUS

Unknown, though does not seem to be a rare species in the majority of its area of distribution.

The isolation in which it lives in the majority of the regions makes it difficult to evaluate its exact current status.

DISTRIBUTION

Israel, Egypt, Libya, Algeria, Tunisia, Morocco, Mauritania, Mali, Nigeria, and Sudan.

■ No subspecies have been described.

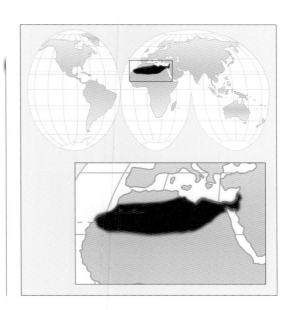

DABOIA LEBETINA

SUBFAMILY VIPERINAE

 (Linnaeus, 1758)

📄 Levantine Adder

Daboia lebetina
(Levantine Adder)
Adult specimen.

DESCRIPTION

This snake has an average length of 26 to 30 inches, but it can reach 36. This is a large and robust species of viper with a squat, heavy body.

It has 23 to 27 rows (the number varies according to the different subspecies) of keeled dorsal scales towards the middle of the body.

The head is triangular and round, well-differentiated from the body, with small, irregularly and mainly keeled cephalic scales. The supraocular scales are normally divided in various scales, usually three smaller ones. The rostral scale is high and narrow.

The adults' upper parts are a light gray or a greenish-gray, beige, yellow or reddish brownish-gray coloring.

Sometimes the subspecies, *D. l. schweizari*, may be a uniform brick red color. The back is covered with transversal blotches that are circular or oval, dark or lighter, and arranged in an alternating fashion; these may be joined forming a wavy line that is often diffused. The flanks have blotches that alternate with the dorsal ones. The upper part of the head lacks a pattern, but a light and dark line joins the eye to the commissure of the mouth. The lower parts tend to be whitish with darker blotches. The lower part of the tail's tip is generally yellowish.

HABITAT

It prefers mountainsides and sunny hills in steppe zones with abundant rocks and shrubs.

Close to fluvial valleys and sunny streams that, in summer, tend to become dry and form discontinuous puddles.

It also frequents cultivated zones like vineyards or fruit plantations.

In mountain zones up to an elevation of 4,921 feet.

BEHAVIOR

• It is mainly terrestrial and is diurnal in spring and fall, while in the middle of summer it is nocturnal or crepuscular.

• It appears between March and April after hibernation, which normally takes place in rodents' abandoned burrows on rocky hillsides oriented towards the south.

• It feeds mainly on rodents and birds.

• It is not considered an aggressive viper and, if bothered, prefers to flee or even threaten by puffing in a characteristic manner.

• If it actually bites, its bite is very dangerous for humans; its venom has cytotoxic and hemotoxic effects; is very efficient, and is considered one of the most powerful among the Euro-Asian vipers, after *Daboia russelli* and *Echis carinatus*.

REPRODUCTION

In part of its distribution it is oviparous and in another part ovoviviparous; the Cyclades Island's populations of *D. l. schweizeri* lay eggs, with embryos that are already well-developed, which can hatch in five to seven weeks, just like *D. l. obtusa* in central Asia; while the rest, such as the populations in Cyprus, give birth to completely developed babies.

The female has an annual cycle.

STATUS

They seem to be abundant locally.

The populations of *D. l. schweizeri* on the Cyclades islands, pursued for a long time and coveted by collectionists, are in serious danger and protected by law. This subspecies is included in the red book of endangered animals of the IUCN.

DISTRIBUTION

The Cyclades archipelago (Milos), Cyprus, from Israel to Lebanon and Syria, east and southeast of Turkey, the Caucasus, Iran, Afghanistan to Kazakstan and Pakistan.

In the past, populations in northern Africa were classified within this species, currently considered a separate species, *Daboia mauritanica*.

■ Four subspecies are recognized:

- *D. l. schweizeri*: on the Cyclades Archipelago.

- *D. l. lebetina*: Cyprus and nearby Turkish coasts.

- *D. l. obtusa*: from Israel to eastern Turkey, Afghanistan, and western Pakistan.

- *D. l. turanica*: Kazakstan, northern Iran, northeastern Pakistan, and Kashmir.

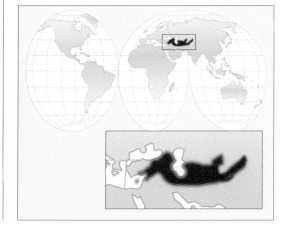

Side view.

Daboia lebetina
(Levantine Adder). Head.

Upper view.

(Shaw, 1802)

 Russell's Viper

DABOIA RUSSELLI
SUBFAMILY VIPERINAE

Daboia russelli
(Russell's Viper)
Adult specimen.

DESCRIPTION

It normally measures around four feet, although exceptional individuals can be found that are larger than five feet.

It has a voluminous cylindrical body that is narrower on both ends of the body.

The tail is short and obtuse with a length close to one-seventh of the entire size.

It has from 27 to 33 rows of keeled dorsal scales aside from the more lateral rows.

The head is flattened and triangular with a short snout and large nostrils, and covered by small overlapping scales.

The eyes are large, yellow, and have a vertical pupil.

The upper parts may have different brown or brownish-gray tones with a series of longitudinal large dark blotches bordered in white that go along the vertebral line of the trunk. Two more lines of similar blotches traverse each flank, from the nape of the neck to the tip of the tail. On the back part of the head there are two oblique dark converging bands. The stomach is white or yellowish with a few dark blotches in a crescent shape on the borders of the front ventral scales.

HABITAT

It is found mainly in flat open terrain along forest borders, prairies, and rocky zones with not very thick vegetation.

In southern India it has been found at elevations of up to 6,890 feet.

BEHAVIOR

• It is active mainly at twilight or at night.

• It is normally slow-moving and does not readily bite if not irritated. When bothered, it puffs hard, while remaining still and creates a louder sound than any other snake.

• It feeds mainly on rodents, although it does not scorn other prey.

• The young animals have a certain propensity to cannibalism, and are more prone to bite.

• When they attack they do so decisively and with notable effectiveness, even making spectacular jumps forwards, repeatedly trying to bite the aggressor.

• The fangs reach an average size of .6 inches. There is a reserve of five or six fangs behind each venomous fang. When they bite, they can inject up to 72 mg venom; 42 is the mortal dose for humans. The venom acts as a depressor of the vasomotor center; it destroys the blood and causes serious internal hemorrhages.

• Therefore, as it is cytotoxic and hemotoxic, death is caused by heart, respiratory failure, or septicemia.

• It is the ophidian that causes the most deaths in India, even more than the cobras or the bungarus.

REPRODUCTION

It is ovoviviparous.

There are pregnant females during every month of the year, and the gestation period exceeds six months.

It is a very prolific snake; has been cited to give birth to more than 79 babies at one time.

The newborns measure 8.5 to ten inches long.

STATUS

It is very common in some parts of its area of distribution, and very scarce in others.

It is common in Punjab, the west and south coast of India, rare in the Ganges Valley north of Bengal and Assam.

Abundant in Burma.

It is common in inhabited areas, attracted by a larger number of rodents.

DISTRIBUTION

Pakistan, India, Sri Lanka, Bangladesh, southern China, Taiwan, Malaysia, and Indonesia.

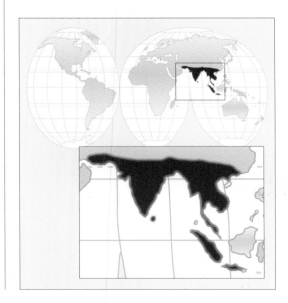

DABOIA XANTHINA

SUBFAMILY VIPERINAE

 (Gray, 1849)

 Ottoman Viper

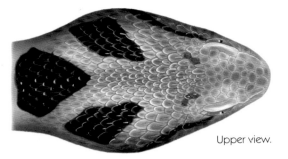

Upper view.

Side view.

DABOIA XANTHINA (Ottoman Viper). Details of head.

Daboia xanthina (Ottoman Viper). Adult specimen.

DESCRIPTION

Large, strong viper with a relatively slender body.

The dorsal scales are keeled, arranged in 23 rows (less frequently in 21 or 25). The upper part of the head is covered with small scales; only the supraocular scales are large and are raised in a way that is characteristic of this species.

The snout is fairly blunt, and somewhat round. The nasal orifice is in the center of a large nasal scale.

It has two rows of subocular scales between the eyes' lower border and the 10 supralabial scales.

The background color of the upper parts is generally a yellowish-white or brownish-gray. The dorsal pattern is usually comprised of an undulated band or a zigzag made up of 24 to 41 bright blotches that are black, dark brownish-gray, or brownish-gray with black borders.

It has a few dark barred vertical blotches on the flanks that alternate in a zigzag with the apexes of the dorsal border.

The upper part of the head has two dark blotches that converge towards the front part, sometimes joining the dorsal pattern. The head has a bright and colorful dark band from the eyes to the commissure of the mouth.

The lower parts are grayish with dark blotches generally in a crescent shape. The lower part of the tail is usually orangish or yellow.

HABITAT

It prefers sunny mountain and hillsides with somewhat random shrubs and rocky or stony zones where it can hide.

Often close to a water source.

Also in flat zones: in plains or in stony pasturelands.

It is also found in olive groves.

It lives from sea level to an elevation of 8,202 feet.

BEHAVIOR

• Predominantly diurnal.

• Various vipers are often found thermoregulating themselves by collectively basking in the sun on a rocky substrate.

• It is more nocturnal or crepuscular during the warmer periods of the year.

• Like the majority of vipers, it prefers to escape if bothered, but if required to defend itself, its actions are unforeseeable; this is why precaution should be taken in its presence.

• Before charging, it puffs and expands the body surface to look somewhat dangerous; it raises the fore part of the body and neck, moving its head back, keeping it parallel to the body's position. Then it can attack very quickly.

• It mainly hunts small mammals and birds.

• The young individuals mainly feed on lizards.

• The characteristics of its venom seem to vary

among southern and northern populations, but nonetheless, the venom is very dangerous and has a strong cytotoxic effect.

REPRODUCTION

It is ovoviviparous.

The gestation takes from three to four-and-one ha f months.

Two to 15 babies are born measuring from seven to eight inches long at birth; they are darker than the adults until the first time they molt.

STATUS

No information is known about the status of its populations.

DISTRIBUTION

European Turkey, the Mediterranean islands east of Greece.

Western and central Turkey.

The western border of its area of distribution is unclear.

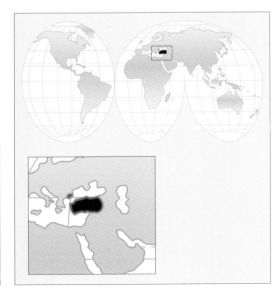

(Schneider, 1801)

Saw-scaled Viper

ECHIS CARINATUS

Echis carinatus
(Saw-scaled Viper).
Detail of the scales.

Side view.

Echis carinatus (Saw-scaled Viper). Adult specimen.

DESCRIPTION

It is a small species, usually less than 18 inches. It rarely reaches 24 inches.

Its body is cylindrical, short, and solid with a very rough looking appearance due to the serrated, very keeled scales.

The neck is considerably narrow in respect to the rest of the body.

The tail is short.

The head is wide and flat with a short round snout.

The eyes are large and have a vertical pupil and a yellow iris.

The cephalic scales are small and very keeled. The dorsal scales are very differentiated. The middle rows are straight and very keeled; the lateral ones are obliquely arranged, serrated, and also keeled.

The dorsal parts tend to be brownish-gray, yellowish, or a brownish-gray yellow, with a series of 25 to 31 rhomboidal or rounded blotches that are clear, often darker, and located above a vertebral line. These blotches may be joined. A series of blotches or white undulated lines can be distinguished on each side; these may be joined together, forming an undulated stria. The upper part of the head has a cruciform blotch or a blotch in a trident shape like a crown.

HABITAT

It mainly inhabits arid or semiarid regions. Deserts and savannahs with scarce vegetation.

Echis carinatus. Head. Adult specimen.

Upper view.

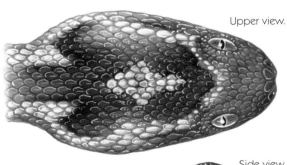

Side view.

BEHAVIOR

• It is mainly diurnal, and it is not unusual to see it basking in the sun in broad daylight.

• In spite of its appearance, it can move quickly if necessary.

• In the sandy zones, it advances on the sand with a special type of locomotion called sidewinds.

• It hibernates in winter in the northern area of its distribution.

• When threatened, it adopts very characteristic behavior, forming a double coil in the form of an eight with the head in the center.

• The coils rub against one another, creating a sound from the friction that is amplified by the inflated body of the alarmed snake.

• It feeds on large insects, scorpions, rats, lizards, geckos, and frogs.

• It readily bites at the slightest provocation and is extremely quick, making it a very dangerous snake. It may even raise itself completely from the floor when attacking.

• Its venom seems to be the most powerful of all vipers with the same dose. A dose of only five mg can be lethal for a human being. This venom varies according to the different subspecies which makes it difficult to treat with one specific serum.

• This species causes the most deaths in India along with the Russel Viper. The mortality of those bitten can reach almost 20 percent.

• The venom has hemotoxic and cytotoxic effects.

REPRODUCTION

It seems that some populations, like the African *E. c. laekeyi*, are oviparous, while others, such as the *E. c. sochureki*, in Pakistan, are ovoviviparous.

The females give birth to three to 15 babies.

The newborn babies measure from 4.5 to 6 inches.

STATUS

Probably the most abundant venomous snake.

In some regions they are collected during the monsoons and more than 5,000 specimens are caught in a three-month period.

DISTRIBUTION

It is very widely distributed in Africa north of the equator, the Middle East, Sri Lanka, Pakistan, and India.

■ Four subspecies are recognized, but some of them are cited by authors as separate species:

- *E. c. carinatus*: southern India and Sri Lanka.

- *E. c. leakeyi*: eastern Africa.

- *E. c. pyramidum*: Egypt and The Near East.

- *E. c. sochureki*: Pakistan.

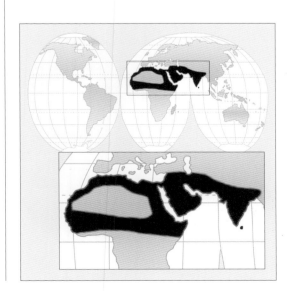

VIPERA AMMODYTES

SUBFAMILY **VIPERINAE**

 (Linnaeus, 1758)

 Nose-horned Viper

Vipera ammodytes (Nose-horned Viper). Adult specimen.

VIPERA AMMODYTES. Types of coloration. Side view.

DESCRIPTION

Robust, small snake that tends to reach between 24 and 32 inches in length, although some old specimens may exceed three feet.

The populations on Mediterranean islands tend to be smaller.

The females are somewhat larger than the males.

Like all vipers, the head is triangular, well-differentiated from the body, and the pupils vertical. However, this species is characterized by a horn covered with various scales on the tip of the snout.

The scales on the upper part of the head are small, except for the two large supraocular scales.

It has two rows of subocular scales between the eyes' lower border and the supralabial scales.

The body scales are keeled and are distributed in 21 to 23 rows on the middle of the body. It has between 150 and 163 ventral scales.

The dorsal coloration is extremely varied: gray, olive greenish, reddish, or brownish, sometimes even yellowish or pinkish. The melanic individuals are not rare. There is a very conspicuous zigzagged dark band all along the body on this background. The stomach is gray, reddish, or yellowish, many times with small dark random blotches. The lower tip of the tail may be red, green, or yellowish.

VIPERA AMMODYTES
Head.

Upper view.

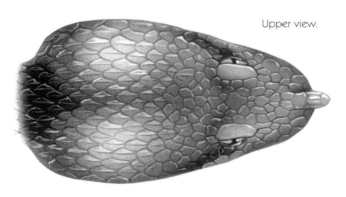

HABITAT

It prefers dry, very varied zones: low scrubland areas, sunny stony hillsides, forest margins and prairies, stone walls, abandoned gardens, rocky outcrops, surroundings of cultivated fields, etc.

It is sometimes also found along the borders of rivers, lakes, and swamps.

It lives from sea level to an elevation of 8,202 feet.

BEHAVIOR

• It is fundamentally active during the day and at twilight, although it often hunts its prey in the early hours of the night.

• It basically feeds on micromammals (rats, dormice, muskrats), lizards and birds' chicks, but may also occasionally capture rats and small snakes, sometimes even its own species.

• It hibernates for a period of two to six months depending on the bioclimatic conditions of its habitat, and tends to begin its active life during the month of March. A large number of individuals may meet in especially favorable places to spend the winter.

• It is timid and always tries to escape when faced with any threat.

• If it feels cornered, it threatens by emitting a loud whistle and raising the front of its body and arching its bach.

• It only tries to bite when someone attempts to trap it.

• Its venom is very powerful and has proteolytic and vasodepressive effects.

• It may be mortal for man, but there have been very few accidents with this species.

REPRODUCTION

Ovoviviparous.

The females give birth to four to 20 babies (generally five to 15) from the end of August to the beginning of September.

At birth, the babies measure between six and ten inches long.

During the first months of its life the babies feed on small lizards and somewhat large insects.

STATUS

The exact current status of its populations is unknown, but in many areas it is seriously affected by the destruction of its habitat.

DISTRIBUTION

Southeasternmost area of Europe and Anatolia.

■ Up to six subspecies are distinguished:

- *V. a. ammodytes*: Yugoslavia, Albania, Romania, and Bulgaria.

- *V. a. gregorwalineri*: Austria, Yugoslavia.

- *V. a. meridionalis*: Yugoslavia, Albania, Greece (including the Cyclades Islands), and western Turkey.

- *V. a. montandoni*: Romania, Bulgaria, European Turkey.

- *V. a. ruffoi*: Alpine region of northern Italy.

- *V. a. transcaucasiana*: northeastern Turkey, southwesternmost point of the former USSR and northern Iran.

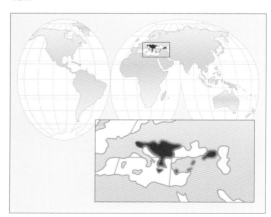

DESCRIPTION

Small, robust snake that tends to measure between 24 and 28 inches in length; the largest specimens reach no more than 35 inches.

The head is well differentiated from the body and the snout, though it does not have a real horn like *Vipera ammodytes*, it is raised slightly upwards.

The pupil is vertical and the upper half of the iris pale; the lower half is dark. The supraocular scales form a marked shield above the eyes.

The corporal scales are keeled and distributed in 21 to 23 rows on the middle part of the body.

It has between 133 and 169 ventral scales (normally 139 to 159), and between 27 and 50 pairs of subcaudal scales. The anal plate is not divided. It has two or three rows of subocular scales between the eye's lower border and the supralabial scales.

This species has a greater variability in coloration than all the species in the genera Vipera. The back may be yellowish, orangish, reddish, brownish-gray, olive greenish, gray, or black. There are always dark blotches on the head, but they can be of very different forms and sizes. There are also always dark blotches all along the length of the body; these may form transversal bars, a continuous longitudinal border, and may have a zigzag form or be in rhombus or circular forms.

The coloration of the males' stomach is dark, sometimes almost black, while the females' is a pale gray or pinkish color. On many specimens, the lower part of the tail is yellowish or orangish.

HABITAT

Lives in all types of environments: mountainous regions, dry sunny hillsides covered with rocks, shrublike zones, wooded areas, hills, stone walls, surroundings of cultivated areas, fluvial valleys, and in summer, even frequents rivers shores and humid zones.

It lives from sea level to an elevation of 9,514 feet in the Italian Alps.

BEHAVIOR

• A terrestrial snake with mainly diurnal activity, although in summer is also active at twilight.

• Feeds on micromammals (rats, topillos, muskrats, moles), lizards, (wall lizards) and occasionally on small birds (alaudidae, fringillidae, turdidae, motacillidae).

• Hibernates during the cold months of the year; its active life starts between the end of February and the beginning of March.

• It is a territorial species and each adult specimen occupies a space of between seven and 295 feet; males occupy almost double the amount of space as the females.

• If not expelled due to destruction of its habitat, it tends to occupy the same territory its entire life.

• The venom of some of its populations is stronger than the European viper, *Vipera berus*, and can be mortal for man.

 (Linnaeus, 1758)

 Asp Viper

Vipera aspis (Asp Viper). Adult specimen.

REPRODUCTION

Ovoviviparous.

At the end of summer it gives birth to between five and 15 babies, normally from six to eight.

The babies measure five to nine inches in length and weigh less than one-third ounce.

STATUS

It is not a very abundant species, but in general does not seem to be in danger. Only some populations are locally threatened, like those on Montecristo Island, Italy.

It is nationally protected in Switzerland.

DISTRIBUTION

Southern Europe.

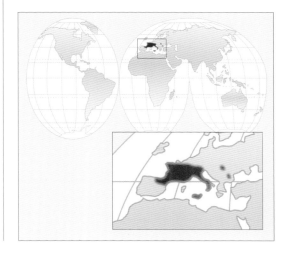

VIPERA ASPIS

SUBFAMILY **VIPERINAE**

■ Seven subspecies are distinguished:

- *V. a. aspis*: In the majority of its area of distribution.

- *V. a. atra*: Alps (southern France, Switzerland, northern Italy).

- *V. a. balcanica*: Southeastern Bosnia and southern Bulgaria.

- *V. a. francisciredi*: From southern Switzerland to central Italy, Slovenia, and northwestern Croatia.

- *V. a. hugyi*: Southern Italy and the island of Sicily.

- *V. a. montecristi*: The Island of Montecristo (Italy).

- *V. a. zinnikeri*: The Pyrenees, both on the Spanish and French side.

VIPERA ASPIS (Asp Viper).
Variation of coloration.
Side view.

VIPERA BERUS

SUBFAMILY VIPERINAE

 (Linnaeus, 1758)

Common Viper, Adder

Vipera berus
(Common Viper, Adder)
Adult specimen.

Vipera berus (Common Viper, Adder)
Chromatic variations. Side view.

DESCRIPTION

A small but robust snake that normally measures between 16 and 28 inches in length, although some older individuals reach a maximum of a little more than three feet.

The females are generally larger than the males.

The head is only slightly differentiated from the body, and the snout is round but not at all raised.

The eyes have a vertical pupil and a reddish iris.

The body's scales are keeled and arranged in 21 rows on the central part of the body (rarely 19, 20, 22 or 23). The scales on the head are small, but the frontal and parietal ones are large and quite developed. There is a series of nine subocular scales between the eyes' lower border and the supralabial scales. There are between 132 and 158 ventral scales and 23 to 46 pairs of subcaudal scales.

The dorsal coloration is very variable; it can be brownish–gray, gray, silver, yellowish, olive greenish, orangish, or reddish. Melanic (completely black) individuals frequent marshy and mountain regions. It has a marked dark zigzagged band all along the body that is sometimes undulated with a base of rhomboids which sometimes form isolated transversal bands. On the body's sides are a series of small irregular dark blotches.

A dark marking in the form of an X or a V is characteristic on the upper back part of the head; a dark band also extends from behind the eyes to the neck. The stomach is brownish–gray, gray, or black, often with lighter random blotches. The lower part of the tip of the tail is yellow, orangish, or reddish.

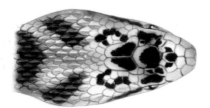

VIPERA BERUS
Head.
Upper view.

HABITAT

It lives in any type of environment and vegetation in European regions, except the typical Mediterranean and extremely dry zones.

It prefers biotopes with a great variation in temperature between day and night and with an elevated humidity: swamp shores, marshes, water currents, mountainous prairies close to the border of trees, quarries, margins of cultivated irrigated areas, caducous and perennial forest clearings, fluvial valleys.

From sea level to an elevation of 9,843 feet in the Alps and in some mountains in central Asia.

BEHAVIOR

• Mainly diurnal; it is only active at twilight when it is very hot.

• It is one of the species of ophidians that copes best with cold; it takes shelter by hiding in subterranean animals' abandoned burrows, under dense scrublands, among roots of trees, or mounds of stones.

• It hibernates for a fairly long period (between five and six months) depending on the environmental conditions in which it lives, although close to the poles it may spend eight to nine months inactive.

• Hundreds of individuals may concentrate themselves in the same winter refuge in especially favorable places.

• It is mainly terrestrial, but also swims very well, and has even been found swimming in the ocean close to the coast, most likely dragged in by the current.

• It feeds on micromammals, amphibians, small lizards, birds, and eggs.

• Its strong neurotoxic venom, which also has hemotoxic and cytotoxic effects, has some toxins that are among the most active and complex of the subfamily Viperinae, but human bites are rare and are not usually fatal if proper measures are taken.

REPRODUCTION

Ovoviviparous.

At the end of summer two to 20 small vipers are born (generally from six to 14) that measure between six and nine inches in length at birth.

STATUS

In days gone by it was abundant, but in recent decades it has become rare in many zones of its area of distribution, which is why it is protected in many European countries such as Switzerland, Austria, Germany, or England.

DISTRIBUTION

Central and northern Europe and central and easternmost sector of Asia.

This species of terrestrial snake has the widest area of distribution of all ophidians.

■ Three subspecies are distinguished:

- V. b. berus: In the majority of its area of distribution.

- V. b. bosniensis: Bosnia, Slovenia, Croatia, Serbia, Macedonia, Montenegro, western Bulgaria, and northern Albania.

- V. b. sachalinensis: Southeastern Siberia, northern Mongolia, and the Sahalin and Schantar Islands.

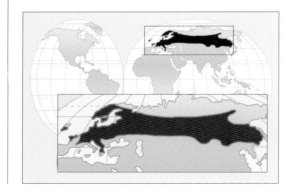

Guenther, 1863

 Cantil, Mexican Moccasin

AGKISTRODON BILINEATUS

SUBFAMILY CROTALINAE

Agkistrodon bilineatus
(Cantil).
Adult specimen.
Detail of the head.

DESCRIPTION

This snake has a robust body with a relatively long tail; it normally exceeds 32 inches, although some specimens may measure up to 54 inches.

The dorsal scales are keeled and the solid head clearly stands out from the neck. It has 23 rows of scales on the middle of the body. It generally has nine large symmetrical cephalic plates, but these may be irregular in some specimens.

The background color varies from a black indigo to a chocolate brown and it has bright and colorful transversal large and small white or cream marks on the lateral scales that stand out on a dark background. The color of the head is fairly uniform and is highlighted by two pale lines on each side; one of them goes above the eye and borders the upper part of the head; the lower one extends from the prenasal scale by the supralabial scales along the entire mandible. The tongue is orange or red with a yellow tip.

The stomach is brown with isolated cream or white dots.

The young individuals have a variety of colors with more reddish brown tones and the distal part of the tail is a bright yellow.

This species is characterized by having longer fangs than any other species in North America.

HABITAT

It inhabits dry topical forests, spiny scrubland areas, and savannahs.

It is also found in rainforests in the south of the Yucatan Peninsula, normally close to bodies of water with currents, like marshes, rivers, streams, or swamps.

BEHAVIOR

• Its customs are similar to *Agkistrodon piscivorus*.
• Lives next to bodies of water and their environs; often tends to bask in the sun, although it is predominantly nocturnal.
• When frightened, it takes refuge in the water.
• It feeds on a wide variety of prey, mainly small mammals but also on snakes, amphibians, and fish.
• The young specimens attract their prey, consisting of insects, lizards, and frogs, by moving and raising their brightly colored yellow tail, imitating a worm.
• When provoked, it can be fairly aggressive, repeatedly moving its tail backwards and forwards and constantly charging at the aggressor; it is also able to make incredible jumps.
• This species' bites can cause death–in some cases in a question of hours. It induces powerful necrotic effects that often require the amputation of the limb.

REPRODUCTION

An ovoviviparous species.
The females give birth to 8 to 20 babies.

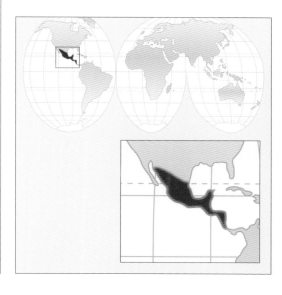

STATUS

There is no information regarding the state of its population, although in the Yucatan Peninsula at least, it is not an abundant species.

DISTRIBUTION

■ Four subspecies are currently recognized:

- *A. b. taylori*: Northeastern Mexico.

- *A. b. bilineatus*: All along the Pacific coast of Mexico, Guatemala, and El Salvador.

- *A. b. russeolus*: The Yucatan Peninsula.

- *A. b. howardgloydi*: All along the Pacific coast of Honduras, Nicaragua, and Costa Rica.

Agkistrodon bilineatus
(Cantil). Adult specimen.
Detail of the head.

AGKISTRODON CONTORTRIX

 (Linnaeus, 1766)

SUBFAMILY **CROTALINAE**

 Copperhead

Agkistrodon contortrix
(Copperhead).
Adult specimen.
Detail of the head.

DESCRIPTION

Its size varies between 22 and 53 inches; clearly dimorphic, the females reaching a larger size while the males are smaller, with thicker tails.

The body is robust with a slightly triangular section and the scales slightly keeled and arranged in 23 to 25 rows around the body.

The head is clearly triangular and spear-shaped. It has a thermoreceptive pit on each side of the head, located between the eye and the nostril, and is covered with somewhat regular large scales, which is characteristic of the entire genus.

The tail does not have a rattle.

It has only one anal plate.

The color on the head is uniform, without marks, generally an orange or copper, just like the rest of the body; color varies among subspecies. The vertical pupils are yellow. The body is a copper, orange, or pinkish color with a variable number of chestnut blotches that may or may not join dorsally in the form of saddles.

Also called a moccasin snake.

HABITAT

It prefers open forests, especially the hills with abundant rocky zones.

Often found close to streams.

Frequently lives close to human populations, but also on floodable flat coastal land.

It is found from sea level up to an elevation of 4,921 feet.

BEHAVIOR

• During winter it often remains in communal hibernation, even with other species, and each year tends to show up in the same place.

• In spring it disperses and remains hidden for a long time under the fallen trunks or among fallen leaves, camouflaged by its coloration.

• It is active at night during the hot months.

• Mainly feeds on rats but also on birds, lizards, small snakes, amphibians, and insects, especially on cicadas.

• When bothered, it repeatedly moves its tail against

the floor, creating a characteristic sound. It may also excrete a substance with a repulsive smell like cat's urine.

• Its venom is hemolytic and causes large hemorrhages in its prey. In humans, it produces pain, nausea, gangrene, hemorrhages, fever, and stupor.

• Because it tends to live close to human housing, it causes many accidents, but these accidents are rarely fatal.

REPRODUCTION

Copulation takes place in spring and is preceded by ritualistic combats between the males. Mating lasts a long time, from three to eight hours. The female is marked by a pheromone that makes her unattractive to the other males.

The females have a gestation period from three to nine months, producing two to ten babies that are identical to the adults except that the tip of their tails are usually yellow.

STATUS

Although abundant in most of its area of distribution, it is scarce in some places and protected or on the endangered animals' lists, such as in Massachusetts or in Iowa, where it is one of the rarer snakes.

DISTRIBUTION

From southwestern Massachusetts to Nebraska and southern Florida to western Texas.

■ Normally five subspecies are recognized: Southern Copperhead, *A. C. contortrix*; Northern Copperhead, *A. c. mokeson*; Broad-banded Copperhead, *A. c. laticinctus*; Osage Copperhead, *A. c. phaeogaster*; and Trans-Pecos Copperhead, *A. c. pictigaster*.

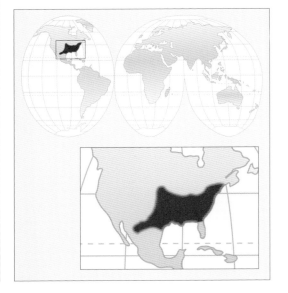

Agkistrodon contortrix
(Copperhead).
Adult specimen.

(Lacepede, 1789)

Water Moccasin
Cottonmouth

AGKISTRODON PISCIVORUS

SUBFAMILY CROTALINAE

Agkistrodon piscivorus
(Water Moccasin). Adult specimen.
Detail of the mouth open.

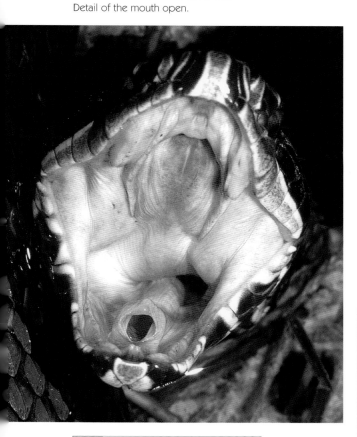

Agkistrodon piscivorus
(Water Moccasin).
Adult specimen.

DESCRIPTION

It can reach a length of six feet, although it is normally smaller.

The body is very heavy and robust with keeled scales arranged in 25 rows around the body.

The head is large, much wider than the nape of the neck and leveled on its upper part. The eyes have vertical pupils, which are not directly visible from above, unlike the harmless water snakes with whom it shares its habitat; the eyes are protected by large supraocular scales.

It has a thermoreceptive pit between the eyes and the nostrils.

The body is a light olive green, dark brown, or black with transversal irregular darker blotches that often have lighter marks on their interior. This pattern is generally lost on old individuals, while on the young ones it is much more bright and colorful. The head is of a uniform color, but a dark stripe stands out that goes from slightly in front of the eyes to the tip of the head, generally bordered by a thin yellow line. The nostrils tend to be covered by a dark vertical line.

HABITAT

Has semiaquatic habits; it is found close to water in marshes, lakes, rivers, irrigation dikes, rice fields, and in small mountain streams.

It lives from sea level to an elevation of 1,476 feet.

BEHAVIOR

• It mainly has nocturnal habits, although it is commonly observed basking in the sun on semisubmerged trunks, trying to recover its body temperature that has been lost from being immersed in water for long periods.

• When bothered in these conditions, it quickly submerges itself or swims to a safe area with the head elevated above the water in a characteristic way.

• This species tolerates cold better than other snakes, which is why it starts to hibernate later.

• It is not especially aggressive and normally does not attack if not bothered.

• As a response to the threat of a potential enemy, it adopts a very elaborate way of behaving that consists of remaining still and coiling up while opening its wide mouth, showing its spectacular white interior color (this is where its name comes from), as well as its venomous fangs.

• Its diet includes fish, salamanders, small mammals, lizards, baby alligators, and even other water snakes.

• Normally it bites its prey, envenoms them and lets them go; then it follows their trail and eats them when it is sure they are dead.

• Its bite may cause serious damage. Its venom is much more powerful than that of *Agkistrodon contortrix*, and can even lead to the death of its victim. However, there have been few accidents with this species. Its venom is hemotoxic.

REPRODUCTION

It is ovoviviparous.

Ovulation takes place every two years and gestation lasts for three to four months.

It gives birth to one to 15 babies that measure seven to 13 inches.

The young have bright and colorful colors and the tail is yellow.

STATUS

Its populations are not considered endangered. Possibly more common in certain especially favorable environments.

On many occasions, harmless water snakes are killed because they are confused with this species.

Its natural enemies are the Kingsnakes (*Lampropeltis*) and the large blue snakes.

DISTRIBUTION

From southeastern Virginia to the Florida Keys, and in the West, to Illinois, southern Missouri, Oklahoma, and central Texas.

There is an isolated population north of Missouri.

■ Three subspecies are known with wide overlapping zones:

Eastern Cottonmouth, *A. p. piscivorus*; Florida Cottonmouth, *A. p. conanti*; and Western Cottonmouth, *A. p. leucostoma*.

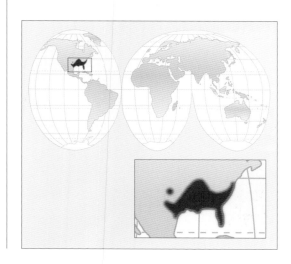

BOTHRIECHIS SCHLEGELI

SUBFAMILY **CROTALINAE**

 (Berthold, 1846)

 Eyelash Palm Pit Viper
Oropel

Bothriechis schlegeli (Eyelash Palm Pit Viper). Yellow phase.

BOTHRIECHIS SCHLEGELI (Eyelash Palm Pit Viper).
Adult specimen. Green phase.

DESCRIPTION

Small viper that does not exceed 24 inches.

Slender body with a prehensile pointed tail that makes up at least 15 percent of its total length.

It has a triangular head, a short snout, and a triangular rostral.

The eyes have vertical pupils.

The presence of two rows of four to five erect superciliary scales in the form of a saw, are very characteristic.

It has 21 to 25 (normally 23) rows of smaller keeled dorsal scales. The anal plate is not divided and the subcaudal scales mainly undivided.

The body coloration is extremely variable as far as the skin's color and pattern; members of the same population may have different body hues. The most common coloration is green, olive green, or gray–green spattered in black, with generally brownish–gray, brown, or reddish blotches on the head, in pairs on the parietal and occipital as well as on the postocular borders. The back may have zigzagged patterns or transversal bands, located somewhat randomly in the same color reaching the tail.

The bright yellow phase has been found in Honduras, Nicaragua, Costa Rica, and western Panama. They are a bright yellow gold both on the back and the ventral part; there are often some black or red blotches that vary in number and size and extend along the dorsal part. The iris has the same color as the body. One female's litter may include differently colored individuals.

HABITAT

Found mainly in the humid jungle, both in low zones and in the cloudy mountain forest.

From sea level to an elevation of 4,921 feet in Costa Rica and to 8,661 feet in Colombia.

BEHAVIOR

• This snake is arboreal with nocturnal habits; it spends the majority of its time resting, hiding among the foliage.

• Just like other arboreal pit vipers, it holds onto its prey to inject them with venom and when they are dead, it eats them.

• It is often found suspended from a branch by its prehensile tail during the entire process of deglutition.

• Although the venom is not as toxic as the majority of terrestrial vipers of the *Bothrops* genus, it is more so than other arboreal pit vipers.

• Because of this species' arboreal habits, it generally bites the upper part of the body.

• Three to six deaths from this species' bites are cited each year in Costa Rica.

• It feeds mainly on rats, small birds, lizards, and frogs.

REPRODUCTION

It generally gives birth to six to ten babies, although in captivity, litters have been cited of up to 20 babies.

STATUS

It is abundant in the majority of its area of distribution, but seems to be fairly rare in Guatemala and southern Mexico.

DISTRIBUTION

Southernmost point of Mexico, all countries in Central America, points in eastern Venezuela, Columbia, and northern Ecuador.

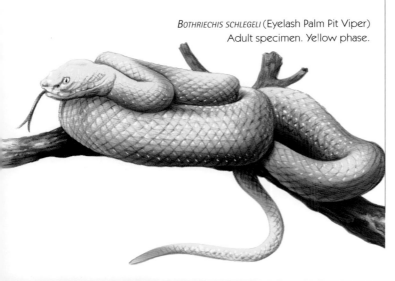

BOTHRIECHIS SCHLEGELI (Eyelash Palm Pit Viper)
Adult specimen. Yellow phase.

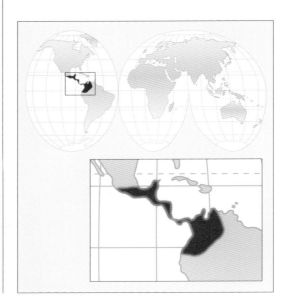

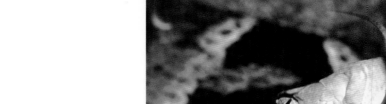
(Garman, 1883)

Terciopelo

BOTHROPS ASPER
SUBFAMILY CROTALINAE

DESCRIPTION

Fairly large snake that can exceed eight feet, but the majority of specimens vary between four and five feet.

The body is slender and laterally compressed, giving it a triangular cross section.

The head is flattened, clearly differentiated from the rest of the body, with a triangular profile.

The cephalic scales are a mix of small keeled scales and large scales, like the supraocular, preocular, and other more on the snout that form the canthus. It has supralabial scales. The dorsal scales are keeled, arranged around the body generally in odd numbered rows from 21 to 35.

The tail is short, the anal plate is undivided, and the subcaudal scales are generally divided into two rows.

The presence of thermoreceptive loreal pits is characteristic; they are found at points equidistant from the eye and the nostril.

Its pattern and color are highly variable. The dorsal color may vary from brown, olive green, gray, brown-gray, pink, to almost black. The upper part of the head is generally not marked, but the pale or yellow coloration of the lips and the canthus region is very characteristic. A dark band extends from behind the eye to the angle of the mouth.

The dorsal pattern habitually consists of a series of 18 to 25 triangular blotches on each side that are darker and bordered in white; they touch the dorsal line, forming a figure like a butterfly's wings. The stomach is yellow, green, or a whitish-gray with small dark blotches that increase in the posterior region.

BOTHROPS ASPER
Adult specimen. Head.

Side view.

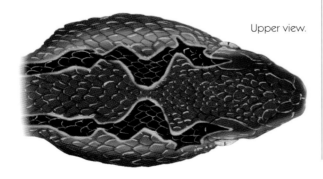

Upper view.

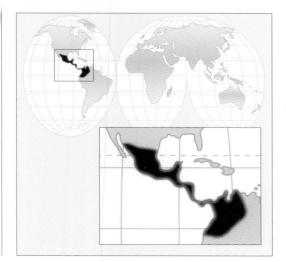

Bothrops asper (Terciopelo).
Adult specimen.

HABITAT

Can be found in a wide variety of habitats, but is mainly a species of the tropical humid jungle.

It is also found in dry tropical forests, pine savannahs, etc., although it is less common in these places.

BEHAVIOR

Although it is a predominantly terrestrial species, the young specimens can often be found in the shrubs.

It is active during twilight and at night, remaining almost inactive, if found, during the day.

It is very excitable and unpredictable when bothered; it can move quickly in any direction and defend itself very aggressively.

It may bite with the slightest provocation, and its venom is very toxic (although somewhat less than the similar species, Fer de Lance, *Bothrops atrox*).

It is more dangerous because it lives close to human settlements; that is why this species causes the majority of serious accidents in many zones in its area of distribution.

It actively hunts its prey, which consist of large quantities of small mammals, for the most part rodents.

The babies feed mainly on frogs and lizards.

REPRODUCTION

It is extremely prolific and can give birth to an average of 45 babies per labor (from five to 87).

STATUS

In some regions, it is the most frequently found snake.

It is the favorite prey of the Mussurana, *Clelia clelia*.

DISTRIBUTION

From Taumalipas (Mexico) to the northern part of Ecuador and Venezuela.

CALLOSELASMA RHODOSTOMA

SUBFAMILY CROTALINAE

 Cope, 1860

Malayan Pit Viper

Calloselasma rhodostoma
(Malayan Pit Viper).
Adult specimen.

DESCRIPTION

Medium viper that can reach three feet in length, although the most common size does not exceed two feet.

Its body has a triangular cross section with a large flat triangular head very differentiated from the rest of the body and a raised snout.

The eyes are small and yellowish-brown with vertical pupils.

As a distinguishing characteristic, it is worth pointing out that it is the only Asian pit viper with large cephalic scales; it has a total of nine and its body scales are smooth and keelless.

The upper part of the head is a rusty red or brown color with a characteristic yellow or pale line that goes from the nostrils by the eyes toward the back part of the head. Under this line, the upper and lower labial scales as well as the mental scales are a yellow or cream color. The zone behind the eyes tends to be the same color as the upper part of the head.

The body is a rosy-gray, ochre, or reddish color with a thin line from the nape of the neck to the tip of the tail. This line is flanked by 25 to 30 blotches in a semitriangular form that projects toward the sides. The ventral coloration tends to be white or cream.

It was previously classified within the genus *Agkistrodon*, although today it tends to be classified as a separate genus.

HABITAT

Often found in bamboo forests and on plantations (abandoned or inhabited) and in surrounding forest lands.

It is mainly terrestrial and likes to hide among the fallen leaves in clearings of dense wooded vegetation.

BEHAVIOR

• It tends to spend the hottest part of the day in the cool of the forests where the favorable conditions allow various individuals to meet.

• Mainly crepuscular; it may actively seek out its prey, above all, birds, amphibians, and small mammals.

• Sometimes it adopts the strategy of remaining still and lying in wait for its victim to come closer.

• To defend itself, it quickly and repeatedly strikes its tail against the floor, producing a sound similar to that of a rattlesnake.

• It normally has a very irascible character and may attack without the slightest provocation; this, together with the fact that it tends to inhabit farm areas, makes its envenomizations frequent, above all on farmers in the area. More than 600 bites have been registered per year, the largest percentage of them on legs, followed by hands.

• The venom is fairly potent and two percent of its bites are calculated to be mortal.

REPRODUCTION

This species is oviparous, which is unusual for pit vipers.

Each female lays 15 to 30 minute eggs in a small depression excavated in the soil and among the fallen leaves. Then it coils around them.

During the incubation, the female remains without feeding and does not leave the eggs; this protects them and also prevents them from dehydrating because the female occasionally drools on them.

STATUS

It seems to be very abundant in its entire area of distribution.

DISTRIBUTION

Thailand, Cambodia, Laos, Vietnam, Malaysia, and Indonesia (Java and Sumatra) and in the southernmost part of China.

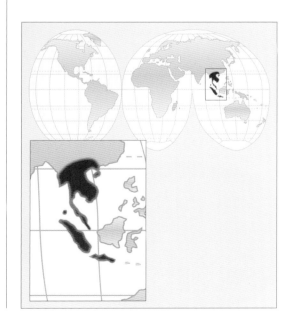

Beauvois, 1799

 Eastern Dimondback Rattlesnake

CROTALUS ADAMANTEUS
SUBFAMILY CROTALINAE

Crotalus adamanteus
(Eastern Dimondback Rattlesnake).
Adult specimen.

DESCRIPTION

It is the longest rattlesnake; can reach eight feet.
Its head is wide and well–differentiated from the neck with a mix of small and large scales. Its eyes are small with vertical pupils and prominent superciliary shields in relief.

It has two thermoreceptive pits on the snout that are extremely sensitive in distinguishing small variations in the surrounding temperature.

The body is solid and voluminous and its upper part is covered with keeled scales, distributed in 27 to 29 rows on the central part of the body.

The tail is fairly short and has an organ called a rattle that is constituted by a series of corneous rings from successive moltings. Each year two to four new layers are added.

The upper parts are a brownish blackish gray, olive green, or a muddy gray with a series of large dark rhomboidal blotches in the form of a diamond, bordered in a light tone all along the vertebral line.

It has two bright and colorful lines and pale oblique lines on each side of the face, the only rattlesnake in its area of distribution with such characteristics.

HABITAT

Pine or oak forests on plains that are generally clear and open to the light; also in low forests of dwarf palm trees.

BEHAVIOR

• It hides in gopher turtles' burrows, among large tree roots, and in similar places where it leaves in the early hours of morning and at sunset to bask in the sun for a little while; however, it is mainly nocturnal.

• It normally leads a discreet life, which is why many details about its biology are still little known.

• When surprised, it is generally less aggressive and nervous than other rattlesnakes, staying calmly coiled up. If the intruder keeps threatening it, it may try to escape by moving backwards and vigorously moving the rattle, while staring at its potential enemy. If it cannot escape, it adopts the typical defensive rattlesnake stance with the body coiled up, the head raised forming a ring, while the rattle sounds with increasing intensity. If the enemy keeps getting closer, it may then bite.

• Its venom is of average toxicity, less than *Crotalus atrox*, for example, but it injects it in large quantities, which is why its bites are always dangerous.

• The venom has hemotoxic and cytotoxic effects.

• It is a very active hunter that feeds on rodents and rabbits, although it also includes birds in its diet.

• Normally after biting and poisoning, it allows the prey to escape. Then it follows its trail, and once dead, swallows it.

REPRODUCTION

It is ovoviviparous.
It gives birth to more than 20 babies at the end of summer or at the beginning of fall.

STATUS

It is quickly disappearing from many areas of its distribution.

The growth of cities and suburban areas as well as the development of agriculture are destroying many of this species' habitats, especially in Florida.

Rattlesnake roundups, in which huge numbers of snakes are collected, are another reason behind this species' decline.

DISTRIBUTION

Florida (the Keys and the peninsula), northern and coastal areas of North Carolina, east of the Mississippi and Louisiana.

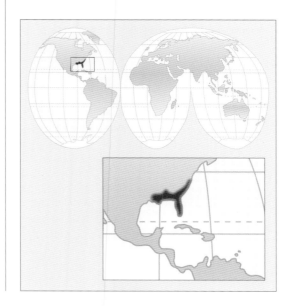

CROTALUS ATROX

SUBFAMILY CROTALINAE

 Baird and Girard, 1853

Western Diamondback Rattlesnake

Side view.

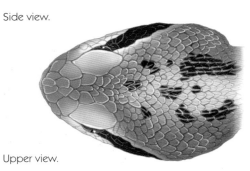

Upper view.

CROTALUS ATROX
Detail of the head.

Crotalus atrox (Western Diamondback Rattlesnake). Adult specimen.

DESCRIPTION

It is one of the largest rattlesnakes, only surpassed in size by the Eastern diamondback rattlesnake *Crotalus adamanteus*.

The largest specimens can reach seven feet in length. The body is heavy and the wide head is easily distinguishable from the neck because it is much thinner.

The rostral scale is wider than it is high. The dorsal scales are very keeled and are arranged in 23 to 29 rows on the middle of the body.

The most common body color is gray or brownish-gray with a tonality that gives it a dusty appearance; however, it can also be a pinkish-brown, reddish, yellowish, or whitish earth color. It is often the same hue as the floor in the place where it inhabits. The body's background color is normally marked with dark or black dots. It usually has 24 to 25 hexagonal, diamond-shaped darker dorsal blotches with lighter borders than on the back; these marks are often undefined because they are spattered by the already mentioned black dots. It may also have various series of smaller blotches on the flanks that are sometimes difficult to distinguish. The four to six black bands on the tail's white background are very characteristic of this species; they are ventrally incomplete. Due to this characteristic, it is sometimes called the *Coontail Snake*. There are two pale lines on each side of the face that join each corner of the eye with the supralabial scales; one of these lines joins the interior corner of the eye with the commissure of the mouth.

HABITAT

Arid or semiarid areas on plains, hills, and canyons with a wide variety of vegetation, from purely desert areas to prairies and open pine forests.

It is found in dry tropical forests in the southern part of its area of distribution (Mexico). It is often found close to ranches in small and large cities.

BEHAVIOR

• A large number of individuals may meet in appropriate places to hibernate along with other species of venomous or innocuous snakes. These large gatherings seem to be more common in the northern part of its area of distribution and in rocky regions.

• Although it mainly basks in the sun at the beginning of spring and at the end of fall, it is normally nocturnal and discreet; sometimes it is so discreet that it goes unnoticed, even though it lives very close to human dwellings.

• When bothered, it does not try to escape, rather it adopts the rattlesnakes' typical defensive posture; if the intruder continues approaching, the snake may bite during a quick charge.

• This species causes more medical problems in North America (it is guilty of more mortal poisonings) than any other snake in its area of distribution because it can inoculate more venom than the majority of other snakes.

• Its venom has hemotoxic and cytotoxic effects.

• It eats a large number of rodents and birds that it detects by the heat they give emit.

REPRODUCTION

The *Crotalus atrox* males participate in ritualized combat, which consists of a type of dance in which the two contenders raise the front part of their body, intertwine, and push one another with the body and head.

They are ovoviviparous and can give birth to more than two-dozen babies per labor at the end of summer.

The females breed biannually.

STATUS

Hunters decimate many specimens and snake collectors have extinguished some populations during the rattlesnake roundups.

In any case, it is considered to be the most abundant venomous snake extant in the southwest United States.

DISTRIBUTION

Western area of the United States and northern and eastern Mexico.

Isolated populations in southern Mexico.

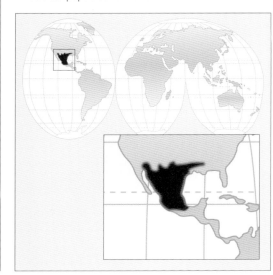

Hallowell, 1854

Sidewinder

CROTALUS CERASTES

SUBFAMILY CROTALINAE

Crotalus cerastes (Sidewinder). Adult specimen.

Crotalus cerastes (Sidewinder). Adult specimen.

DESCRIPTION

It is a small or medium rattlesnake whose length varies between 17 and 32 inches.

This snake is characterized by a few prominent triangular horns located above each eye; this is why it is also called Horned Rattlesnake.

It has a rough looking appearance with keeled scales arranged in 21 to 23 rows on the central part of the body.

The color of the body is generally similar to the environment in which it develops; this allows it to go unnoticed on the substratum. The back is cream, gray, or pinkish-gray, with small brown slightly defined dorsal blotches; the flanks may also be blotched brown. On the distal part that touches the rattle the dorsal blotches may be much darker. The head has two conspicuous dark stripes that join on the posterior part of each eye with the commissure of the mouth.

There are three subspecies:

- Mojave Desert Sidewinder, *C. c. cerastes*: The basal segment of the rattle is brown; it usually has 21 rows of dorsal scales.

- Sonoran Sidewinder, *C. c. cercobombus*: The rattle's basal segment is black on the adult animal; it normally has 21 rows of dorsal scales.

- Colorado Desert Sidewinder, *C. c. laterorepens*: The basal segment is black and the dorsal scales are normally distributed in 23 rows.

Once again, nature has presented a surprising case of adaptive convergence in which animals of different evolutive origin have a similar appearance and behavior because they live in similar habitats; therefore, this species is very similar to other snakes in desert places, such as the African Horned Viper, *Cerastes cerastes*.

HABITAT

Arid desert with dunes and sandy zones, especially in zones with mesquite, creosote, and paloverde shrubs, and different species of cactus.

It lives from below sea level to an elevation of 6,004 feet.

BEHAVIOR

• This snake has nocturnal habits and hides in rodents' burrows or stays buried in the sand, keeping its eyes on the surface with their conspicuous supra ocular horns.

• Its adaptation of moving on a sandy substrate is also notable; this is called sidewinding, typical of snakes adapted to loose sandy floors free of obstacles such as rocks or vegetation remains.

• This movement is made up of two different movements—one with the body moving forward and the other like a lateral jump; it leaves discontinuous J-shaped trails in the sand.

• It eats rats, kangaroos, and lizards found by the snake's sense of smell and vision, as well as by the heat they give off.

• The venom is considered moderately toxic, even though it may not inject much venom when it bites.

REPRODUCTION

After 150 to 160 days of gestation, the female gives birth to five to 18 babies at the end of summer or at the beginning of fall.

STATUS

It may be locally abundant and is valued in the Mojave Desert where its density is about one specimen per hectare; however, the exact current status of its populations and the possible repercussions from the progressive alteration of its desert habitat are unknown.

DISTRIBUTION

Southern Nevada and areas close to California, Utah, Arizona, and southern Mexico.

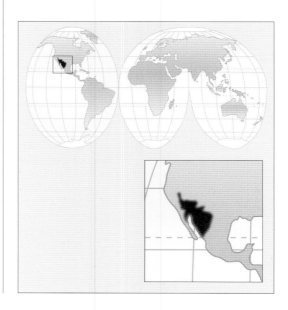

CROTALUS DURISSUS

SUBFAMILY CROTALINAE

 Linnaeus, 1758

Neotropical Rattlesnake

Crotalus durissus unicolor
(Neotropical Rattlesnake)
Adult specimen.
Detail of the head.

Crotalus durissus
(Neotropical Rattlesnake)
Adult specimen.

DESCRIPTION

The males of this species reach five feet while the females are generally smaller.

This snake has a triangular cross section that high-lights a conspicuous vertebral chain, much more marked on the front part of the body.

All the scales are very keeled, especially the vertebral ones, giving this species the roughest appearance of all rattlesnakes.

The head is solid with a short snout; it is well-sepa-rated from the body by a narrower neck.

The eyes are of moderate size with a vertical pupil.

The presence of a thermoreceptive pit is character-istic (it is also called a lacrimal or facial pit) that is located equidistantly from the eye and the nostrils.

The scales are distributed in 25 to 33 rows on the middle of the body. The number of rows varies according to the different geographic origins.

Body color is very variable throughout its very wide area of distribution; it is generally almost black, brown, gray-brown, reddish-brown, olive green, yellow-gray, or yellow, with 18 to 35 large diamond-shaped blotches on the back that turn into triangles on the flanks. The species in the most wooded zones are generally darker than those in arid climates. There is another series of secondary smaller lateral blotches that are often in contact with the ventral ones. A few parallel lines at the tip of the head and on the neck are characteristic of this species. The tail is normally dark brown or black.

HABITAT

It is found in semi-arid regions with dry or very dry tropical forests as well as in savannahs with palm trees and in open arid regions.

It is very rarely found in the rainforest.

BEHAVIOR

• It is diurnal or crepuscular depending on the season.

• During the day it often hides in abandoned burrows, cracks between rocks, under fallen trees, between large cacti, in termite nests, or in caves.

• The defensive posture is spectacular: the head and front third of the body are raised from the floor, the head is doubled over the neck and aimed towards the intruder, and the sound of the rattle increases in inten-sity if the situation becomes more threatening.

• This species causes serious envenomization in a large part of its area of distribution. The effects of its bite depend on the animal's origin, and vary between two extreme types represented by *C. d. durissus* in Mexico and Central America, that creates symptoms of tumefaction, hypofibrinogenemia, and local necrosis, and *C. d. terrificus*, in South America, with much more serious neurovegetative symptoms, paralysis of neck muscles and destruction of red corpuscles with acute kidney failure.

• It feeds almost completely on rodents, acting as a good natural control.

REPRODUCTION

It is ovoviviparous.

It can give birth to up to two-dozen babies, whose coloration is more vivid than that of the adults.

STATUS

Populations have been estimated as one individual per hectare in the area of Santa Rosa, in Guanacaste (Costa Rica).

DISTRIBUTION

Very wide but discontinuous, from southern Mexico to the center of Argentina.

Fourteen subspecies are recognized, although their taxonomy is somewhat confusing on occasions; *C. d. vegrandis* from Venezuela and *C. d. unicolor* from the island of Aruba are described as separate species by many authors.

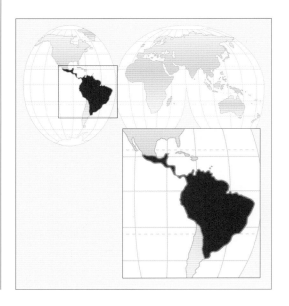

 (Kennicott, 1861)

Rock Rattlesnake

 CROTALUS LEPIDUS
SUBFAMILY CROTALINAE

Crotalus lepidus
(Rock Rattlesnake).
Adult specimen.
Detail of the head.

Crotalus lepidus (Rock Rattlesnake). Adult specimen.

DESCRIPTION

Small or medium rattlesnake, the largest specimens can reach 34 inches, but generally grow to 24 to 28 inches; the females are smaller than the males.

This snake has a small head with a rostral that is much wider than it is high, and it has a very character-istic feature of having the upper preocular scale verti-cally divided.

The body is slender with scales arranged in 23 rows.

The wide variable dark marks on the back in the form of blotches or regularly distributed bands, are a general characteristic of the species. The bands are generally bordered in a light color.

The body color greatly varies and is generally light or dark gray, green gray, or pinkish. It is abundantly dotted with earth tones, which sometimes gives it a mottled appearance.

This snake is also very sexually dimorphic; the males tend to display greenish tones, while the females tend to exhibit grayish tones. The distal tip of the tail is, particularly in males, a red or orange color.

This rattlesnake is one of the most variable in color and pattern; it has four subspecies that also have multiple variations.

HABITAT

Found mainly in mountainous zones with arid or semiarid climates.

Inhabits zones with rocky outcrops, on hills, canyons, and close to riverbanks.

Can also be found in pine or oak forests but also prefers zones with intense sunshine.

Can be found from 1,476 feet to an elevation of 9,514 feet.

BEHAVIOR

• This snake likes to bask in the sun on the rocks where its skin coloring allows it to go unnoticed.

• It is mainly diurnal, but is sometimes also active during hot nights.

• It hibernates in holes and cracks protected from winter freezing.

• It prefers to feed on reptiles, which it likes more than mammals and amphibians. It uses a different technique to hunt rodents: it bites the rat and then lets it go while following the dying rat's trail; it will swallow the rat once it is dead.

• The young individuals of the subspecies *C. l. klauberi* have a bright yellow tail that helps them to hunt lizards, which is their main prey.

• Their venom is not very strong; it has a toxicity that is similar to the Copperhead *Agkistrodom contor-trix*, although it is more powerful in causing hemor-rhaging.

REPRODUCTION

The males participate in ritualized mating combats like other species of the genus.

It gives birth to two to eight babies from July to August that measure an average of seven inches.

STATUS

It may be very common locally on hillsides with favorable conditions.

It is known in more than 40 towns in southeastern Arizona, and, although there are no quantitative esti-mates of its populations, it seems to be relatively common.

DISTRIBUTION

■ Four subspecies are recognized:

- *C. l. lepidus*: Inhabits southeastern New Mexico to southwestern Texas to the east, and the Mexican meseta to San Luis de Potosi.

- *C. l. klauberi*: From southeastern Arizona to south-western Texas, and to the west of the Mexican meseta to the north of Jalisco.

- *C. l. maculosus*: In Durango and Sinaloa.

- *C. l. morulus*: In the southeast of Tamaulipas.

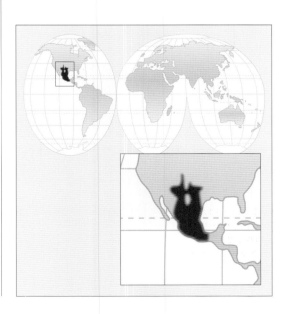

CROTALUS SCUTULATUS

SUBFAMILY **CROTALINAE**

📄 (Kennicott, 1861)

📄 Mojave Rattlesnake

CROTALUS SCUTULATUS
SCUTULATUS
(Mojave Rattlesnake)
Adult specimen.

powerful neurotoxic effects and no hemotoxic or proteolytic effects.

• However, human cases of envenomization are rare, although there are a high percentage of mortal cases.

• It feeds on rats, kangaroo rats, and other rodents, as well as other reptiles.

• This snake ambushes its prey or actively searches it out.

REPRODUCTION

After 170 days of gestation, it gives birth to two to 11 babies between July and September that measure nine to 11 inches.

STATUS

It seems to be locally abundant at least in some areas of Arizona where it is the most abundant species after *Crotalus atrox*.

Many specimens seem to be hit on highways because of their habit of coiling up on them.

It seems to hybridize naturally with *Crotalus viridis* in some regions in Texas.

DISTRIBUTION

- *C. s. scutulatus*: Southern Nevada, zones adjacent to California, Arizona, New Mexico, eastern Texas through central Mexico to Queretaro.

- *C. s. salvini*: South of its area of distribution in Puebla and west of Veracruz, Mexico.

DESCRIPTION

It generally does not exceed three feet in length, although its maximum cited length is .5 inches.

Because of its general appearance, it is often confused with the Western Diamoncback, *Crotalus atrox*, although its body is more slender.

The head is characterized by the large scales on the snout and between the suprocular scales. The rostral scale is generally wider than it is high. The scales are keeled and distributed in 25 rows.

Two subspecies are distinguished with different characteristics:

- The Mojave Rattlesnake, *C. s. scutulatus*: body has a greenish-brown, olive green, yellowish-greenish, or occasionally yellow or brown background color with a pattern formed by diamond or hexagonal-shaped blotches that are greenish-brown and bordered in white. The number of blotches may vary from 27 to 44. There are a series of black and white bands (generally two to eight black rings), with significantly wider white rings. The upper part of the head is a uniform color, except that the posterior margins of the supraocular scales may be dark. It has a white or yellowish line that extends from behind the eye to the commissure of the mouth.

- Salvin's Rattlesnake, *C. s. salvini*, varies in color from olive brown to a straw color, with 13 to 35 slightly irregular dorsal blotches, appearing as blotches or olive or black dots; they are fairly contrasted without being bordered in white. The upper part of the head may be irregularly marked with black pigment.

HABITAT

This species preferably inhabits deserts, and prairies with mesquite, creosote, or cacti, and in the southern part of its area of distribution, in pine and oak forests.

In the northern part of Mexico it inhabits flat land while in the south it prefers rocky zones like the lava outcrops.

BEHAVIOR

• It can be found basking in the sun in the early hours of the day, but when the temperature increases in the middle of the day, it takes refuge to protect itself from the sun's rays.

• It spends a lot of time taking shelter in burrows and cracks, often in the same holes that honey bees use.

• In the cooler months it may also be active in broad daylight, while during the hot months it is mainly nocturnal.

• It is often surprised crossing highways during hot nights.

• It is an extremely aggressive snake that bites if provoked.

• Its venom is very powerful, ten times more so than any other rattlesnake in North America, with a similar lethality to *Crotalus durissus*. The effects of this venom vary according to the geographic area; they particularly stand out in specimens that come from eastern Arizona and adjacent zones of New Mexico that have a special toxin called Mojave toxin; this venom has

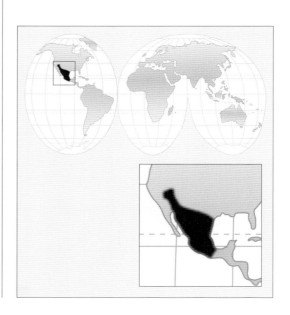

Linnaeus, 1766

Bushmaster

LACHESIS MUTA

SUBFAMILY CROTALINAE

Lachesis muta
(Bushmaster).
Adult specimen.

DESCRIPTION

Is the largest venomous snake in the New World and the largest Viperidae; it normally exceeds seven feet and occasionally reaches twelve feet.

The head is very round and clearly stands out from the body; it is covered with numerous small scales.

The presence of loreal pits (thermoreceptive) is characteristic; they are eye-size and are located at an equidistant point between the eye and the nostril.

The eye is relatively small with a vertical pupil.

The body is laterally compressed with a mid-dorsal crest that is more pronounced on the front region.

The scales are distributed in 31 to 39 rows on the middle of the body and are very keeled dorsally; they diminish laterally at the height of the crest until becoming flat. The anal plate is not divided.

The tail is short and is divided in four or five small spiny scales; it does not have a rattle.

The body is reddish-brown and yellowish brownish-gray with 20 to 37 diamond-shaped dark blotches along the back; these blotches form lateral triangles. The upper part of the head is often dark. It has a few powerful erectile fangs on the frontal part of the maxilla that can reach two inches in length and are perforated to conduct venom.

HABITAT

It is found in the rainforest it typically inhabits. Only inhabits dry tropical forest in Nicaragua and Colombia.

BEHAVIOR

• It often lives close to large trees with jungle buttresses, like ceibas, or close to fallen trunks.

• It is crepuscular and nocturnal and shows an impressive defensive conduct: when bothered, it raises its tail and makes it vibrate like a rattlesnake; then it raises the front part of the body in an S-form and inflates the neck. It may then attack the intruder with a quick jump and bite it.

• Although the venom is not particularly powerful, the large amount that it inoculates makes the bite more often mortal.

• Twenty-five envenomizations have been cited, of which 20 percent have been fatal even though the corresponding serums were administered to the patients. Although envenomizations are rare, this snake should be considered as potentially very dangerous.

• It mainly eats small mammals, particularly rodents that it hunts by taking advantage of its perfectly camouflage among the vegetation.

REPRODUCTION

It is the only American rattlesnake that lays eggs.

STATUS

It is a rare species that is fairly difficult to find; like all species linked to the rainforest, its felling often means the disappearance of this species.

DISTRIBUTION

■ Four subspecies have been described.

- *L. m. stenophrys*: On the Atlantic Coast of Costa Rica, and in Panama.

- *L. m. melanocephala*: On lowlands on the Pacific side of Costa Rica.

- *L. m. muta*: in the jungles of Colombia, Venezuela, Guianas, Brazil, Ecuador, Peru, Bolivia, and Trinidad.

- *L. m. rhombeata*: in the Atlantic forests of central-eastern Brazil.

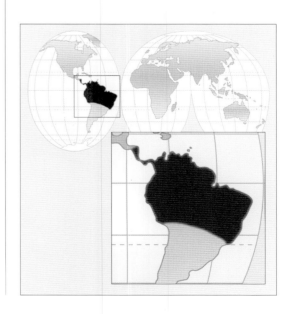

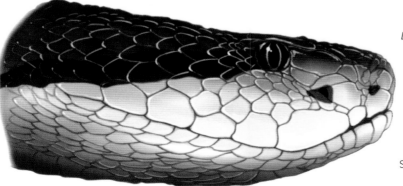

LACHESIS MUTA STENOPHRYS
Adult specimen.
Head.

Side view.

PORTHIDIUM NUMMIFER

SUBFAMILY CROTALINAE

 (Ruppel, 1845)

Jumping Pit Viper

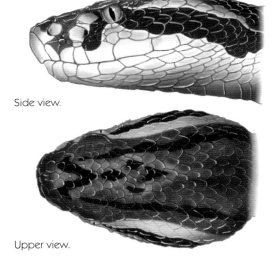

Side view.

Upper view.

Porthidium nummifer
(Jumping Pit Viper).
Adult specimen.

PORTHIDIUM NUMMIFER OCCIDUUM
Detail of the head.

DESCRIPTION

Small robust pit viper that is 16 to 24 inches long. It has an extremely rough appearance because its dorsal scales are profusely keeled.

There are 31 rows of scales on the middle of the body, 114 to 135 ventral scales, and 22 to 39 undivided subcaudal scales.

The body color varies from gray to beige with a pattern that consists of a series of 15 to 20 dark rhomboidal blotches that may or may not be joined on the vertebral part. Some of these blotches may be joined with the next and form a partial zigzag pattern. It also has other, smaller dark lateral blotches that may join the vertebral blotches in some populations.

The head is a uniform color that is unmarked except for an oblique band on the sides extending behind the eyes towards the end of the mandible.

HABITAT

Rainforests, wooded hills, and in the clearings and adjacent plantations.

Also in subtropical humid forests.

BEHAVIOR

• It is a predominantly terrestrial snake whose common name comes from its ability to jump large distances when it charges.

• When other specimens are provoked, they respond defensively like *Agkistrodon piscivorus*; they open the mouth wide and show the white palate.

• It has nocturnal habits, is slow–moving and not very aggressive.

• The individuals are generally found on the forest floor although specimens have occasionally been found climbing into hollows up to ten feet above ground.

• During the day it stays hidden under a fallen trunk and at twilight it is actively looking for small rodents, lizards, and frogs.

• Their venom does not seem to be as powerful as that of other pit vipers and their fangs are relatively small.

• Some people who were bitten in Guatemala and Honduras only experienced pain and swelling, but the symptoms disappeared in a few days.

REPRODUCTION

It is an ovoviviparous species.
At birth, the babies measure from four to five inches in length.

STATUS

Like all rainforest species, its destiny is closely linked to the survival of its habitat.

DISTRIBUTION

South of Mexico, Guatemala, El Salvador, Costa Rica, and Panama.

■ Three subspecies are currently recognized:

- *P. n. nummifer*: The Mexican Atlantic side of San Luis Potosi to Oaxaca.

- *P. n. mexicanum*: From Chiapas (Mexico) to the center of Panama.

- *P. n. occiduum*: Pacific side of Chiapas, Guatemala, and El Salvador.

*Porthidium
nummifer
mexicana*
Adult specimen.
Defensive behavior.

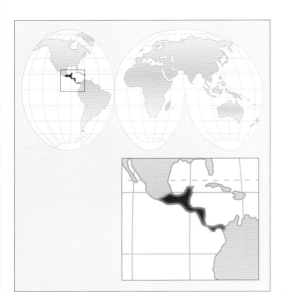

(Gray, 1830)

 Shore Pit Viper

TRIMERESURUS PURPUREOMACULATUS

SUBFAMILY **CROTALINAE**

Trimeresurus purpureomaculatus
(Shore Pit Viper).
Adult specimen.

DESCRIPTION

The adult specimens can reach 35 inches in length.
The snake's appearance is relatively robust and the scales are very keeled.

The head is solid-looking and clearly differentiated from the body, and the thermal pits are very visible.

All the head scales are small and irregularly arranged.

The tail is prehensile.

Variations in the coloration have been observed; the most common color is a yellowish-green with wide dark blotches on the back and other smaller ones on the sides. The ventral scales are white with black vertexes and the subcaudal scales are predominantly black. The second variety is uniformly blue or dark purple-brown. Some specimens have a white line on the lower part of each flank.

HABITAT

It mainly inhabits coastal mangrove swamp zones, where it is often found in the scrublands at a low elevation.

It is also common in marshes and on islands near the coast.

BEHAVIOR

• It has nocturnal and mainly arboreal habits, although it is not that unusual to find it on the floor.

• It spends a lot of time coiled in trees and shrubs, waiting for its possible prey; mainly lizards (geckos), birds, frogs, or small mammals.

• It is considered dangerous because it is very difficult to recognize among the vegetation, and is very irritable, biting fairly quickly at the slightest alarm.

• Its bites may have serious consequences.

REPRODUCTION

It is ovoviviparous and in Thailand in April and May it gives birth to 7 to 15 babies that are 10 inches long. The babies are already very aggressive at birth. When bothered, they make their tail vibrate.

STATUS

The state of its population is unknown although it does not seem to be endangered.

DISTRIBUTION

It inhabits southern Thailand, the Malaysian Peninsula, Singapore, Tenasserim, and Sumatra.

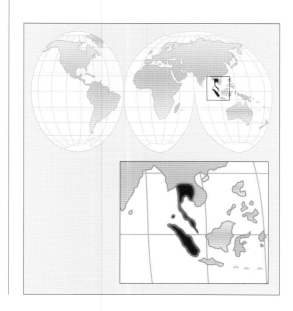

TRIMERESURUS WAGLERI

SUBFAMILY **CROTALINAE**

 (Boie, 1827)

 Wagler's Pit Viper
Temple Pit Viper

Trimeresurus wagleri
(Temple Pit Viper).
Adult specimen.

STATUS

A large number of this species are kept in the Snake Temple of Pennang, Malaysia, where they are incorporated into religious activities and freely handled by the priests.

It is also kept close to houses in some places in its area of distribution because it is believed that they bring good luck and keep away evil spirits.

DESCRIPTION

It can reach three feet in length.

It stands out for its disproportionately large head and solid body.

It has a bright and colorful coloration that can vary greatly from one population to another: it can be green or yellow with blotches or transversal bands that are white, red, dark green, or black. The upper part of the head is black with green blotches. The ventral part is white and the vertexes of the scales are black. The tail is black. The coloration of the young is different and consists mainly of a bright green with a red tail and two dorsal rows of dots or transversal bands, half red, half white.

Both eyes are yellow and are crossed by a wide bicolor line that is black and yellow or black and red, which joins them with the upper point of the snout and the back part of the head.

This species is also cited as *Tropidolaemus wagleri*.

BEHAVIOR

It is mainly active at night.

It lives almost exclusively in small trees and shrubs where it stays for a long time coiled up and hardly moving.

It diet is typical of arboreal pit vipers, consisting of small birds and mammals, which it surprises after quickly charging them. As arboreal snakes tend to do, it does not release its prey when bitten, instead, it swallows it in the same place, hanging by the strong prehensile tail. Although it is naturally venomous, its venom is not considered very active and its bite only causes apparently local effects.

It is not very aggressive and rarely bites, even when handled.

DISTRIBUTION

It inhabits southern Thailand, western Malaysia, Singapore, parts of Indonesia, and the Philippines.

HABITAT

It lives in mangrove swamps, in forests on plains and on hills that are at a fairly low elevation.

In trees and shrubs at a medium elevation, from sea level to 3,937 feet.

REPRODUCTION

It is ovoviviparous and can give birth to up to 41 babies per labor.

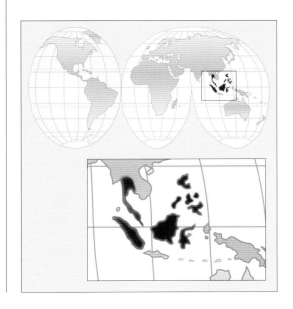

Boulenger, 1888

Fea's Viper

AZEMIOPS FEAE
SUBFAMILY AZEMIOPINAE

Azemiops feae (Fea's Viper).
Adult specimen. Detail of head.

Azemiops feae
(Fea's Viper).
Adult specimen.

DESCRIPTION

Reaches 32 inches in length and is considered one of the most primitive vipers.

The scales are flat and are arranged in 17 lines on the central part of the body.

This snake generally has a slender appearance, looking more like a typical Colubridae than a true viper.

The tail is short.

The head is covered with large scales and is more slightly round than it is triangular.

The snout is squared and rounded on both tips.

The body is a bluish–black color with a pattern that consists of 14 to 15 lateral orange bands that may or may not be joined on the vertebral zone.

The head is brown or a bright orange and vividly stands out from the rest of the body's coloration.

Some darker brown, symmetrical, elongated blotches are found on the upper part of the head.

It lacks thermoreceptive pits.

It has vertical pupils.

The stomach is gray with lighter edges.

HABITAT

Wooded mountainous areas at elevations from 1,969 to 4,921 feet.

It is found in bamboo forests with an abundance of rocky substratum and high humidity.

BEHAVIOR

• Hibernates during the coldest months of the year.
• When frightened, it vibrates its tail against the vegetation.
• It feeds on small mammals and lizards.
• Its venomous fangs as well as its venom sacks are relatively small.
• No envenomizations by this species have been reported.

REPRODUCTION

It is oviparous although many details about its reproductive behavior are unknown.

STATUS

The state of its populations is unknown.

Up until recently this was practically an unknown animal and specimens were rarely collected due to the remoteness of its area of distribution.

Today it can even be found in reptile markets with specimens that come from China; the effect this trade could have on its populations is unknown.

They barely survive in captivity.

DISTRIBUTION

Northern Vietnam, northern Burma, southern and central China and southeastern Tibet.

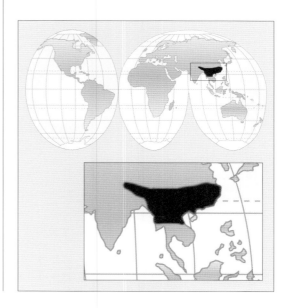

INDEX

BIBLIOGRAPHY

- AMUNDSEN By U. *Morelia s. Spilota.* Keeping and breeding the Diamond Python. Reptilia 8 (GB). M y A Lladó Hädinger. Barcelona 1999.

- BARBADILLO LUIS JAVIER. Anfibios y reptiles de la Península ibérica, Baleares y Canarias. Editorial Planeta SA. Barcelona , 1999.

- BARBADILLO LUIS JAVIER. Serpientes mitológicas,entre lo divino y lo satánico. La tierra que todos desearíamos, nº 46. Publicación medioambiental, S.L. Madrid, 2002.

- BAUCHOT ROLAND. Les serpents. Enciclopedie visualle. Paris, 1994.

- BEHLER JOHN L. The Audubon Society Field Guide to North American Reptiles and Amphibians. Alfred A.Knopf Inc. New York, 1979.

- BONS JACQUES. Amphibiens et Reptiles du Maroc (Sahara Occidental compris). Asociación Herpetológica Española. Barcelona, 1996.

- BRANCH BILL. Fied Guide to the Snakes and other Reptiles of Southern Africa. New Holland Publishers Ltd. London ,1988.

- BRUNO SILVIO. Guía de las serpientes de Europa. Ediciones Omega S.A. Barcelona, 1992.

- BURTON JOHN A. Snakes an illustrated guide. Blandfort. London, 1991.

- CAMPBELL JONATHAN A. The Venomous Reptiles of Latin America. Comstock Publishing Associates NY, 1989.

- CIMATI E. *Python anchietae.* La pitón enana de Anchieta. Reptilia nº 31. M y A . Lladó y Hädinger, C, B. Barcelona ,2001.

- CITES. IDENTIFICATION MANUAL. Volumen 3: Reptilia, amphibia, pisces. Editor Peter Dollinger. Secretariat of the Convention on international Trade in Endangered Species of wild Fauna and Flora. Lausanne, 1985.

- COBORN JOHN. The Atlas of Snakes of the World.T.F.H. Publications Inc NJ ,1991.

- CONANT ROGER. Peterson Field Guide Reptiles and Amphibians Eastern, Central North America. Houghton Mifflin Company. Boston, 1991.

- COX MEREL J. A photographic Guide to Snakes and other Reptiles of Malasia, Singapore and Thailand. New Holland Publishers (UK) Ltd. London 1998.

- DANIEL J.C. The book of Indian Reptiles.Bombay. Natural History Society. Oxford University Press. Bombay ,1983.

- DAS INDRANEIL. A photographic guide to Snakes and other reptiles of India. New Holland Publishers (UK) Ltd. London, 2002.

- DEORAS P.J . Snakes of India. National Book Trust India. New Delhi ,1965.

- DE SILVA ANSLEN. Colour Guide to the Snakes the Sri Lanka. R&A Publishing Limited. Avon ,1990.

- DONOVAN PAUL. *Calloselasma rhodostoma* la víbora de foseta de Malasia. Reptilia 37. M yA Lladó Hädinger, C. B . Barcelona ,2002.

- ERNST CARL H: Snakes in question. The Smithsonian answer book. Smithsonian Institution Press. Washington and London, 1996.

- ERNST CARL H. Venomous Reptiles of North America. Smithsonian Institution Press. Washington and London, 1992.

- FRUGIS SERGIO. Los Animales, gran enciclopedia ilustrada. Los Reptiles. Editorial Delta S.A. Barcelona 1981.

- GILLAM M. V. The *genus Psedonaja* (Serpentes: Elapidae) in the northern territory. Research bulletin number one. Terrirory Parks and Wildlife Comission. June ,1979.

- GLAW FRANK. A field guide to de Amphibians and Reptiles of Madagascar. Zoologisches Forschungsinstitut und Museum Alexander Koenig , Bonn ,1994.

- GONZÁLEZ HERBERT. La iconografía de la serpiente. Revista de Arqueología del siglo XXI, nº 255. M C Ediciones SA. Barcelona, 2002.

- GOW GRAEME F. Snakes of Australia. Angus &Robertson Publishers. Australia ,1976.

- GOYFFON M. La function venimeuse. Collection Biodiversité. Masson. Paris ,1995.

- GRASSÉ PIERRE-P. Traité de zoologie. Tome XIV. Masson et Cie, Éditeurs. Paris, 1970.

- JÜRGEN OBST FRITZ.The Completely illustrated Atlas of Reptiles and Amphibians for the Terrarium. T.F.H Publications Inc. NJ 1988.

- ISEMONGER. R.M. Snake of Africa. Cape & Transvaal Printers (PTY) Ltd. Cape Town, 1983.

- LANCINI V.ABDEM R. Serpientes de Venezuela. Ernesto Armitano Editor. Caracas, 1986.

- LEVITON ALAN E. Handbook to Middle East Amphibians and Reptiles. Society for the Study of Amphibians and Reptiles.1992.

- LIM LEONG KENG FRANCIS. Fascinating Snakes of Southeast Asia- An Introduction. Tropical Press Sdn.Bhd. Kuala Lumpur. Malaysia,1990.

- MARAIS JOHAN. Snakes. Grange Books. London, 1997.

- MARKEL RONALD G. Kingsnakes and Milk Snake. T. F. H Publication Inc. NJ, 1990.

- MATZ GILBERT. Guía del Terrario. Editorial Omega S.A. Barcelona , 1979.

- MEHRTENS JOHN M. Living Snake of the World in color. Sterling Publishing Co., Inc. New York, 1987.

- MERKER G. Rossi boas: Maravillosos animales para principiantes y experimentados. Reptilia nº 27. M y A Lladó Hädinger, C.B. Barcelona, 2001.

- PATTERSON ROD.Reptiles of Southern Africa. C.Struik (Pty) Ltd. Cape town,1987.

- PEREZ SANTOS CARLOS. Serpientes de Panamá. Biosfera. Publicaciones del comité español del programa Mab de la UNESCO. Sevilla, 1999.

- SALVADOR ALFREDO. Guía de Campo de los Anfibios y Reptiles, Islas Baleares y Canarias. Santiago Garcia Editor. León, 1985.

- SCHU.P.Chondropython viridis. Una joya en el terrario. Reptilia nº 20. M y A. Lladó Hädinger, C.B. Barcelona 1999.

- SWENNEY ROGER. Garter Snakes. Their Natural History and Care in Captivity.Blandford. London ,1992.

- STEBBINS ROBERT C. A field guide to Western Reptiles and Amphibians. The Peterson Field Guide Series. Houghton Mifflin Company. Boston, 1985.

- PARKER. H. W. Los Anfibios y los Reptiles .Ediciones Destino. Barcelona ,1975.

- PARKER. H.W. Los Reptiles. Ediciones Destino. Barcelona 1975.

- SCHULZ KLAUS - DIETER. A monograph of the Colubrid Snakes of the genus Elaphe Fitzinger. Koelts Scientific Books. Czech Republic, 1996.

- SPAWLS STEPHEN. The dangerous Snakes of the Africa. Blandford Press.London ,1995.

- ULRICH GRUBER. Guia de las serpientes de Europa, Norte de África y Próximo Oriente. Ediciones Omega,SA, Barcelona, 1993.

- WEBB J.E. Guide to living Reptiles. The Macmillan Press Ltd. London ,1978.

- WILSON STEPHEN.K. Australia's Reptiles. A photographic reference to the terrestrial Reptiles Of Australia. Collins Publishers Australia. Sidney, 1988.